BESTSELLING
BOOK SERIES
FROM IDG

Windows NT® Workstation 4 For Dummies®, 2nd

Network Hints

- Don't write down your password or share it with somebody else.
- Choose a password that's easy for you to remember but hard for someone else to guess: The name of your neighbor's dog, for example, or the color of your best friend's car.
- Use the password-protected screen saver when you leave your cubicle to gossip.
- Better yet, gossip using the Chat program, so you won't have to leave your seat.
- Double-click the Network Neighborhood icon to access files and folders on other computers.
- Always log off before turning off your computer. (Ask your Network Administrator if you're supposed to turn your computer off at all; some computers stay on 24 hours.)

Helpful Hints

- Don't turn off your computer without giving Windows NT fair warning. First, click on the Start button and then choose Shut Down from the menu. When Windows asks what you want the computer to do, click the Shut down button. Finally, when Windows NT says it's all right to turn off your computer, go ahead and turn it off.
- Don't know what a certain button does in a program? Rest your mouse pointer over the button for a few seconds; a helpful box often pops up to explain the button's purpose.
- If you're baffled, try pressing F1, that "function key" in the upper-left corner of your keyboard. A "help" window appears, bringing hints on your current program.
- To quickly organize the windows on the Desktop, click on the taskbar's clock with your right mouse button. When a menu appears, click on one of the tile options, and all your open windows will be neatly tiled across your screen.
- To keep icons organized in neat rows across your Desktop or in windows, click on the icon's background. When the menu pops up, choose Auto Arrange from the Arrange Icons menu.

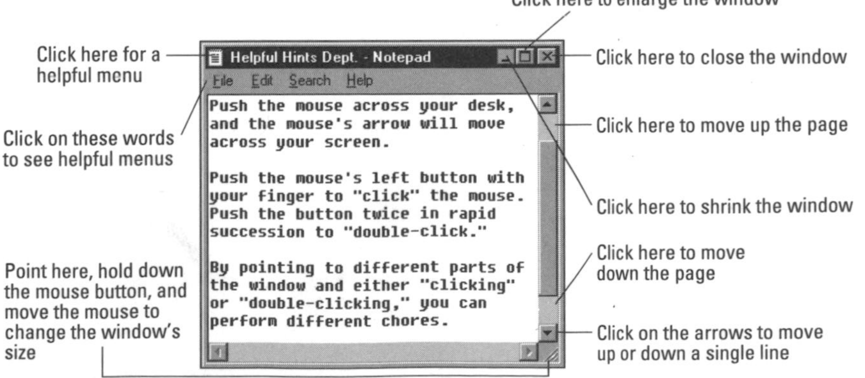

Click here to enlarge the window
Click here for a helpful menu
Helpful Hints Dept. - Notepad
File Edit Search Help
Click here to close the window
Click on these words to see helpful menus
Push the mouse across your desk, and the mouse's arrow will move across your screen.
Push the mouse's left button with your finger to "click" the mouse. Push the button twice in rapid succession to "double-click."
By pointing to different parts of the window and either "clicking" or "double-clicking," you can perform different chores.
Click here to move up the page
Click here to shrink the window
Click here to move down the page
Point here, hold down the mouse button, and move the mouse to change the window's size
Click on the arrows to move up or down a single line

...For Dummies: Bestselling Book Series for Beginners

Windows NT® Workstation 4 For Dummies®, 2nd Edition

Handling Files within a Program

To Do This . . .	Do This . . .
Start a new file	Press Alt, F, N.
Open an existing file	Press Alt, F, O.
Save a file	Press Alt, F, S.
Save a file under a new name	Press Alt, F, A.
Print a file	Press Alt, F, P.

Organizing a Pile of Windows

To Do This . . .	Do This . . .
See a list of all windows	Look at the names open on the taskbar.
Move from one window to another window	Press Alt+Tab+Tab or click on the window's name on the taskbar.
Tile the windows across the screen	Click on an empty part of the taskbar with the *right* mouse button and then click on Tile Horizontally or Tile Vertically.
Cascade the windows across the screen	Click on an empty part of the taskbar with the *right* mouse button and then click on Cascade.
Shrink a window into a taskbar button	Click on the window, press Alt+spacebar, and press N.
Make a window fill the screen	Click on the window, press Alt+spacebar, and press X.

DOS Window Stuff

To Do This . . .	Do This . . .
Toggle DOS program from a full-screen display to a window-sized display	Press Alt+Enter.
Change a DOS program froma taskbar button to a full screen	Click on the program's icon on the taskbar.
Close a DOS window	Use that program's normal exit command and then click on the X in the window's upper-right corner.

Explorer and My Computer

To Do This . . .	Do This . . .
Copy a file to another location on the *same* disk drive	Hold down Ctrl and drag it there.
Copy a file to a *different* disk drive	Drag it there.
Move a file to another location on the *same* disk drive	Drag it there.
Move a file to a *different* disk drive	Hold down Shift and drag it there.
Remember how to copy or move files	Hold down the *right* mouse button while dragging and then choose Copy or Move from the menu.
Select several files	Hold down Ctrl and click on the filenames.
Look at a different directory	Double-click on that directory's icon.

Cut and Paste Stuff

To Do This . . .	Press These Keys . . .
Copy highlighted stuff to the Clipboard	Ctrl+C or Ctrl+Insert.
Cut highlighted stuff to the Clipboard	Ctrl+X or Shift+Delete.
Paste stuff from the Clipboard to the current window	Ctrl+V or Shift+Insert.
Copy an entire screen to the Clipboard	PrintScreen (Shift+ PrintScreen on some keyboards).
Copy the current window to the Clipboard	Alt+PrintScreen.

Cheat Sheet $2.95 value. Item 0496-7.
For more information about IDG Books, call 1-800-762-2974.

...For Dummies: Bestselling Book Series for Beginners

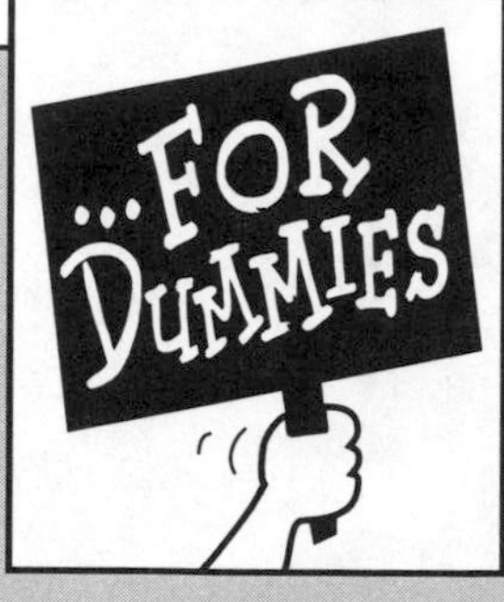

TM

References for the Rest of Us!®

BESTSELLING BOOK SERIES FROM IDG

Are you intimidated and confused by computers? Do you find that traditional manuals are overloaded with technical details you'll never use? Do your friends and family always call you to fix simple problems on their PCs? Then the *...For Dummies®* computer book series from IDG Books Worldwide is for you.

...For Dummies books are written for those frustrated computer users who know they aren't really dumb but find that PC hardware, software, and indeed the unique vocabulary of computing make them feel helpless. *...For Dummies* books use a lighthearted approach, a down-to-earth style, and even cartoons and humorous icons to diffuse computer novices' fears and build their confidence. Lighthearted but not lightweight, these books are a perfect survival guide for anyone forced to use a computer.

"I like my copy so much I told friends; now they bought copies."

— Irene C., Orwell, Ohio

"Quick, concise, nontechnical, and humorous."

— Jay A., Elburn, Illinois

"Thanks, I needed this book. Now I can sleep at night."

— Robin F., British Columbia, Canada

Already, millions of satisfied readers agree. They have made *...For Dummies* books the #1 introductory level computer book series and have written asking for more. So, if you're looking for the most fun and easy way to learn about computers, look to *...For Dummies* books to give you a helping hand.

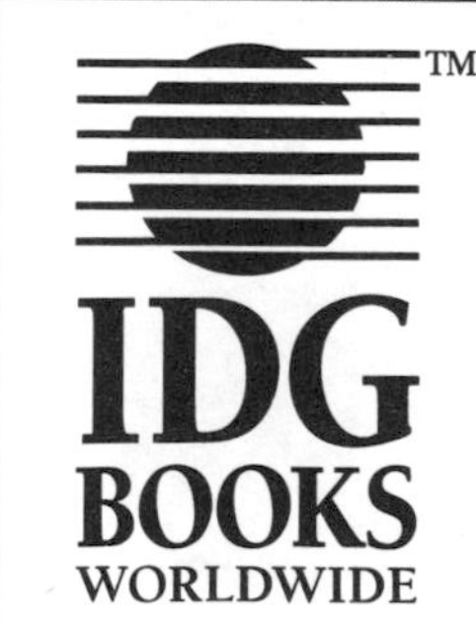

8/98

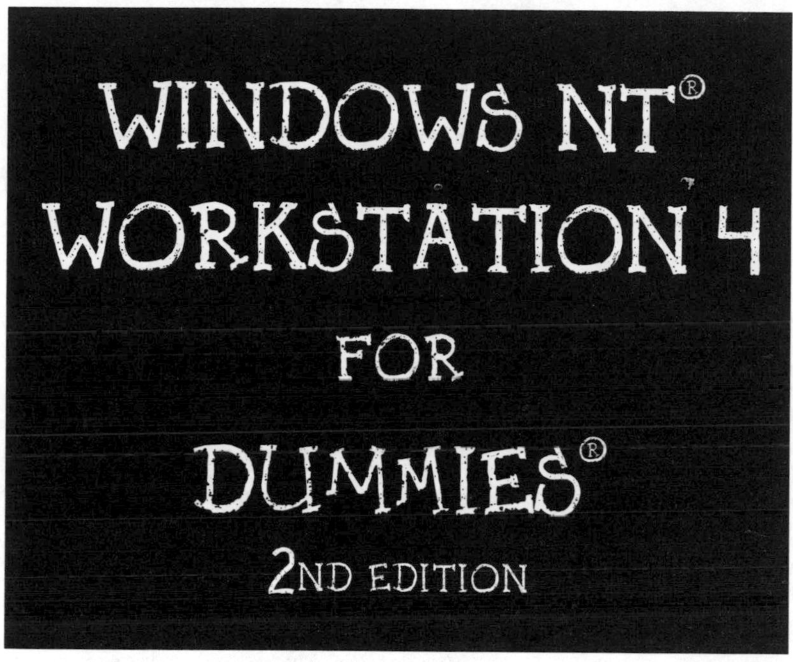

by Andy Rathbone & Sharon Crawford

IDG Books Worldwide, Inc.
An International Data Group Company

Foster City, CA ♦ Chicago, IL ♦ Indianapolis, IN ♦ New York, NY

Windows NT® Workstation 4 For Dummies®, 2nd Edition

Published by
IDG Books Worldwide, Inc.
An International Data Group Company
919 E. Hillsdale Blvd.
Suite 400
Foster City, CA 94404
www.idgbooks.com (IDG Books Worldwide Web site)
www.dummies.com (Dummies Press Web site)

Library of Congress Catalog Card No.: 98-89939

ISBN: 0-7645-0496-7

Printed in the United States of America

10 9 8 7 6 5 4 3 2 1

2B/RV/QR/ZZ/IN

Distributed in the United States by IDG Books Worldwide, Inc.

Distributed by Macmillan Canada for Canada; by Transworld Publishers Limited in the United Kingdom; by IDG Norge Books for Norway; by IDG Sweden Books for Sweden; by Woodslane Pty. Ltd. for Australia; by Woodslane (NZ) Ltd. for New Zealand; by Addison Wesley Longman Singapore Pte Ltd. for Singapore, Malaysia, Thailand, and Indonesia; by Norma Comunicaciones S.A. for Colombia; by Intersoft for South Africa; by International Thomson Publishing for Germany, Austria and Switzerland; by Distribuidora Cuspide for Argentina; by Livraria Cultura for Brazil; by Ediciencia S.A. for Ecuador; by Ediciones ZETA S.C.R. Ltda. for Peru; by WS Computer Publishing Corporation, Inc., for the Philippines; by Contemporanea de Ediciones for Venezuela; by Express Computer Distributors for the Caribbean and West Indies; by Micronesia Media Distributor, Inc. for Micronesia; by Grupo Editorial Norma S.A. for Guatemala; by Chips Computadoras S.A. de C.V. for Mexico; by Editorial Norma de Panama S.A. for Panama; by Wouters Import for Belgium; by American Bookshops for Finland. Authorized Sales Agent: Anthony Rudkin Associates for the Middle East and North Africa.

For general information on IDG Books Worldwide's books in the U.S., please call our Consumer Customer Service department at 800-762-2974. For reseller information, including discounts and premium sales, please call our Reseller Customer Service department at 800-434-3422.

For information on where to purchase IDG Books Worldwide's books outside the U.S., please contact our International Sales department at 317-596-5530 or fax 317-596-5692.

For information on foreign language translations, please contact our Foreign & Subsidiary Rights department at 650-655-3021 or fax 650-655-3281.

For sales inquiries and special prices for bulk quantities, please contact our Sales department at 650-655-3200 or write to the address above.

For information on using IDG Books Worldwide's books in the classroom or for ordering examination copies, please contact our Educational Sales department at 800-434-2086 or fax 317-596-5499.

For press review copies, author interviews, or other publicity information, please contact our Public Relations department at 650-655-3000 or fax 650-655-3299.

About the Authors

Andy Rathbone started geeking around with computers in 1985 when he bought a boxy CP/M Keypro 2X with lime-green letters. Like other budding nerds, he soon began playing with null-modem adapters, dialing up computer bulletin boards, and working part-time at Radio Shack.

Andy began combining his two interests, words and computers, by selling articles to a local computer magazine. During the next few years, Andy started ghostwriting computer books for more famous computer authors, as well as writing several hundred articles about computers for technoid publications like *Supercomputing Review, CompuServe Magazine, ID Systems, DataPro,* and *Shareware.*

In 1992, Andy and *DOS For Dummies* author/legend Dan Gookin teamed up to write *PCs For Dummies,* which was runner-up in the Computer Press Association's 1993 awards. Andy subsequently wrote the first edition of *Windows For Dummies* as well as *Windows 95 For Dummies* and *Windows 98 For Dummies.* He has also written *OS/2 For Dummies* and *Upgrading and Fixing PCs For Dummies.*

Andy lives with his most-excellent wife, Tina, and their cat in San Diego, California. When not writing, he fiddles with his MIDI synthesizer and tries to keep the cat off both keyboards.

Like Andy, **Sharon Crawford** came to computers in a roundabout way. In the early '80s, she was an electrician repairing subway cars in New York City. Though it seems astonishing that anyone would want to leave such a glamour job, she did.

After moving home to California, she went back to school to study the finer points of electronics and in 1988, armed with a degree and some ingenious lies, she landed her first technical writing job.

After a couple of years, Sharon was fortunate enough to get a job in the technical department of a computer book publishing house. After a few months, she convinced a gullible acquisitions editor to give her a shot at a book. Since then, Sharon and her husband Charlie Russel have collaborated on many books including *NT and UNIX Intranet Secrets* (IDG Books Worldwide, Inc.), *Running Windows NT Server 4.0* (Microsoft Press), and *Upgrading to Windows 98* (Sybex).

Sharon and Charlie live in a nice house on a hill with many cats and one dog. They have given up on trying to keep cats off any of the keyboards.

ABOUT IDG BOOKS WORLDWIDE

Welcome to the world of IDG Books Worldwide.

IDG Books Worldwide, Inc., is a subsidiary of International Data Group, the world's largest publisher of computer-related information and the leading global provider of information services on information technology. IDG was founded more than 30 years ago by Patrick J. McGovern and now employs more than 9,000 people worldwide. IDG publishes more than 290 computer publications in over 75 countries. More than 90 million people read one or more IDG publications each month.

Launched in 1990, IDG Books Worldwide is today the #1 publisher of best-selling computer books in the United States. We are proud to have received eight awards from the Computer Press Association in recognition of editorial excellence and three from Computer Currents' First Annual Readers' Choice Awards. Our best-selling *...For Dummies®* series has more than 50 million copies in print with translations in 31 languages. IDG Books Worldwide, through a joint venture with IDG's Hi-Tech Beijing, became the first U.S. publisher to publish a computer book in the People's Republic of China. In record time, IDG Books Worldwide has become the first choice for millions of readers around the world who want to learn how to better manage their businesses.

Our mission is simple: Every one of our books is designed to bring extra value and skill-building instructions to the reader. Our books are written by experts who understand and care about our readers. The knowledge base of our editorial staff comes from years of experience in publishing, education, and journalism — experience we use to produce books to carry us into the new millennium. In short, we care about books, so we attract the best people. We devote special attention to details such as audience, interior design, use of icons, and illustrations. And because we use an efficient process of authoring, editing, and desktop publishing our books electronically, we can spend more time ensuring superior content and less time on the technicalities of making books.

You can count on our commitment to deliver high-quality books at competitive prices on topics you want to read about. At IDG Books Worldwide, we continue in the IDG tradition of delivering quality for more than 30 years. You'll find no better book on a subject than one from IDG Books Worldwide.

John Kilcullen
Chairman and CEO
IDG Books Worldwide, Inc.

Steven Berkowitz
President and Publisher
IDG Books Worldwide, Inc.

Eighth Annual Computer Press Awards 1992

Ninth Annual Computer Press Awards 1993

Tenth Annual Computer Press Awards 1994

Eleventh Annual Computer Press Awards 1995

IDG is the world's leading IT media, research and exposition company. Founded, in 1964, IDG had 1997 revenues of $2.05 billion and has more than 9,000 employees worldwide. IDG offers the widest range of media options that reach IT buyers in 75 countries representing 95% of worldwide IT spending. IDG's diverse product and services portfolio spans six key areas including print publishing, online publishing, expositions and conferences, market research, education and training, and global marketing services. More than 90 million people read one or more of IDG's 290 magazines and newspapers, including IDG's leading global brands — Computerworld, PC World, Network World, Macworld and the Channel World family of publications. IDG Books Worldwide is one of the fastest-growing computer book publishers in the world, with more than 700 titles in 36 languages. The "...For Dummies®" series alone has more than 50 million copies in print. IDG offers online users the largest network of technology-specific Web sites around the world through IDG.net (http://www.idg.net), which comprises more than 225 targeted Web sites in 55 countries worldwide. International Data Corporation (IDC) is the world's largest provider of information technology data, analysis and consulting, with research centers in over 41 countries and more than 400 research analysts worldwide. IDG World Expo is a leading producer of more than 168 globally branded conferences and expositions in 35 countries including E3 (Electronic Entertainment Expo), Macworld Expo, ComNet, Windows World Expo, ICE (Internet Commerce Expo), Agenda, DEMO, and Spotlight. IDG's training subsidiary, ExecuTrain, is the world's largest computer training company, with more than 230 locations worldwide and 785 training courses. IDG Marketing Services helps industry-leading IT companies build international brand recognition by developing global integrated marketing programs via IDG's print, online and exposition products worldwide. Further information about the company can be found at www.idg.com. 10/8/98

Publisher's Acknowledgments

We're proud of this book; please register your comments through our IDG Books Worldwide Online Registration Form located at `http://my2cents.dummies.com`.

Some of the people who helped bring this book to market include the following:

Acquisitions, Editorial, and Media Development

Project Editor: Brian Kramer *(Previous Edition: Jennifer Ehrlich)*

Acquisitions Manager: Michael Kelly

Copy Editors: Donna Love *(Previous Edition: Tamara S. Castleman, Diane L. Giangrossi, Joe Jansen, Susan Diane Smith)*

Technical Editor: Jim McCarter

Editorial Manager: Leah P. Cameron

Editorial Assistant: Beth Parlon

Production

Associate Project Coordinator: Tom Missler

Layout and Graphics: Daniel P. Alexander, Angela F. Hunckler, Jane E. Martin, Brent Savage, Janet Seib, Brian Torwelle

Proofreaders: Kelli Botta, Nancy Price, Nancy Reinhart, Rebecca Senninger, Janet M. Withers

Indexer: Liz Cunningham

Special Help

David Mehring

General and Administrative

IDG Books Worldwide, Inc.: John Kilcullen, CEO; Steven Berkowitz, President and Publisher

IDG Books Technology Publishing: Brenda McLaughlin, Senior Vice President and Group Publisher

Dummies Technology Press and Dummies Editorial: Diane Graves Steele, Vice President and Associate Publisher; Mary Bednarek, Director of Acquisitions and Product Development; Kristin A. Cocks, Editorial Director

Dummies Trade Press: Kathleen A. Welton, Vice President and Publisher; Kevin Thornton, Acquisitions Manager

IDG Books Production for Dummies Press: Michael R. Britton, Vice President of Production and Creative Services; Cindy L. Phipps, Manager of Project Coordination, Production Proofreading, and Indexing; Kathie S. Schutte, Supervisor of Page Layout; Shelley Lea, Supervisor of Graphics and Design; Debbie J. Gates, Production Systems Specialist; Robert Springer, Supervisor of Proofreading; Debbie Stailey, Special Projects Coordinator; Tony Augsburger, Supervisor of Reprints and Bluelines

Dummies Packaging and Book Design: Patty Page, Manager, Promotions Marketing

♦

The publisher would like to give special thanks to Patrick J. McGovern, without whom this book would not have been possible.

♦

Contents at a Glance

Cartoons at a Glance

By Rich Tennant

"I told him we were looking for software that would give us greater productivity, so he sold me client software that came with these signs."

page 71

"I DON'T KNOW – SOME PARTS OF THE NETWORK SEEM JUST FINE, AND OTHER PARTS SEEM TO BE COMPLETELY OUT OF CONTROL."

page 323

"WHO'S GOT THE COMPUTER WITH THE SLOW RESPONSE TIME?"

page 7

"MY GOD, YOU'VE DONE IT! MILLIONS OF MICROSCOPIC SLINKY TOYS MOVING ACROSS CIRCUITS AT THE SPEED OF LIGHT FORMING THE FIRST SLINKY OPERATING SYSTEM!"

page 351

page 307

"OH YEAH, AND TRY NOT TO ENTER THE WRONG PASSWORD."

page 207

***Fax:* 978-546-7747 • *E-mail:* the5wave@tiac.net**

Table of Contents

Introduction

Welcome to *Windows NT Workstation 4 For Dummies,* 2nd Edition! Of course, you're no dummy. You're just one of the millions who *feel* like a dummy when sitting in front of a computer. This book looks similar to earlier *Windows For Dummies* books you may have seen through the years, but it's been completely revamped to describe Windows NT 4, the "business" version of Microsoft Windows. If you're moving up to Windows NT 4 from Windows NT 3.51, almost everything in this book will be new. If you're moving from Windows 95 or Windows 98, however, you'll find plenty of similarities, thank goodness.

Regardless of your Windows heritage, the basic premise of the book boils down to this: Some people want to be Windows wizards. They love interacting with dialog boxes. In their free moments, they randomly press keys on their keyboards, hoping to stumble onto a hidden, undocumented feature. They memorize long strings of computer commands while they're organizing their socks-and-underwear drawer.

And you? Well, you're light-years ahead of most computer nerds. You can make conversation with a neighbor without mumbling about the latest "Flash ROM Upgrades," for example. But when it comes to Windows and computers, the fascination just isn't there. You just want to get your work done, go home, feed the dog, walk the cat, and relax for a while. You have no intention of changing, and nothing's wrong with that.

That's where this book comes in handy. You'll pick up a few chunks of useful computing information while reading it. You certainly won't become a Windows NT wizard, but you'll know enough to get by quickly, cleanly, and with a minimum of pain so you can move on to the more pleasant things in life.

About This Book

Don't try to read this book in one sitting; you don't need to. Instead, treat this book like a dictionary or small encyclopedia. Turn to the page with the information you need, and say, "Ah, so that's what that's supposed to mean." Then put down the book and move on.

Don't bother trying to remember all the Windows NT buzzwords, like *NetBEUI* or *domain controller.* Leave that stuff for the computer geeks. In fact, if anything technical comes up in a chapter, a road sign warns you well in advance. That way, you can either slow down to read it or speed on around it.

You won't find any fancy computer jargon in this book. Instead, you find subjects like these, discussed in plain old English:

- Preparing yourself to brave the cold, corporate world of Windows NT
- Figuring out what to do when the network turns into a "not work"
- Starting programs by clicking on little buttons
- Making sure that your favorite old DOS- and Windows-based programs still run under the new version of Windows NT
- Finding common-language translations for those awfully technical networking terms

There's nothing to memorize and nothing to learn. Just turn to the right page, read the brief explanation, and get back to work. Unlike other books, this one enables you to bypass any technical hoopla and yet still get your work done.

How to Use This Book

Something in Windows NT will eventually leave you scratching your head. No other program brings so many buttons, bars, or babble to the screen. When something in Windows NT has you stumped, use this book as a reference. Look for the troublesome topic in this book's table of contents or index. The table of contents lists chapter and section titles and page numbers. The index lists topics and page numbers. Page through the table of contents or index to the spot that deals with that particular bit of computer obscurity, read only what you have to, close the book, and apply what you've read.

There's no learning involved. There's no remembering, either, unless you want to remember something so you don't have to grab the book the next time the same situation comes up.

If you're feeling spunky and want to learn something, read a little further. You'll find a few completely voluntary extra details or some cross-references to check out. There's no pressure, though. You won't be forced to learn anything that you don't want to or that you simply don't have time for.

If you have to type something into a little box on the computer screen, you see easy-to-follow text like this:

```
TYPE THESE LETTERS
```

In the preceding example, you type **TYPE THESE LETTERS** into the little box on-screen and then press the keyboard's Enter key. Typing words into a computer can be confusing, so a description of what you're supposed to type usually follows. That way, you can type the words exactly as they're supposed to be typed.

You won't, for example, accidentally type **"TYPE THESE LETTERS"** — complete with quotation marks. Computers are awfully picky about quotation marks and can do odd things when they see them.

Whenever we describe a message or information that you see on the screen, We present it like this:

```
This is a message on-screen.
```

Or if a relevant picture or message pops up onto the screen, you see the picture or message in the book.

This book doesn't wimp out by saying, "For further information, consult your manual." No need to pull on your wading boots. This book covers everything you need to know to use Windows NT Workstation. The only thing you don't find is technical information about using Windows NT Server.

See, Windows NT comes in two flavors: Workstation and Server. The administrator who runs the complicated network stuff uses the Server version of Windows NT. That software comes with bunches of extra parts that make the administrators chew on pencil erasers and look worried. Instead, you use the Workstation variety of NT. NT Workstation is designed for people who use computers to get their work done — not for technical people who have turned computers into their line of work.

And What about You?

Well, chances are that you have a computer. You have Windows NT — you use it at your office or perhaps in your home. You know what you want to the computer to do. The problem is making the computer do what you want it to do. You've gotten by one way or another, hopefully with the help of a computer guru — either a friend at the office or somebody down the street. Unfortunately, though, that computer guru isn't always around. This book can be a substitute for the computer guru during your times of need. Keep a fresh bag of Cheetos in your desk drawer, however, just in case you need a quick bribe.

How This Book Is Organized

The information in this book has been well sifted. The book contains six parts, and each part is divided into chapters related to the part's theme. Each chapter is divided into short sections to help you navigate Windows NT's stormy seas. Sometimes, you may find what you're looking for in a small, boxed tip. Other times, you may need to cruise through an entire section or chapter. It's up to you and the particular task at hand.

Here are the categories (the envelope, please).

Part I: Intro to Windows NT (Bare-Bones Stuff)

This book starts out with the basics. You find out how to turn on your computer and log onto the network. You examine all your computer's parts and what Windows NT does to them. This part explains all the Windows NT stuff that everybody thinks you already know; plus, it explains all that networking stuff the company's Network Administrator assumes you already know.

It explains the new features in the latest version of Windows NT (the one with the weird "Service Pack 4" installed), separating the wheat from the chaff while leaving out any thick, technical oatmeal. You discover whether your computer has enough oomph to run Windows NT, or whether its lack of horsepower would make decent water-cooler conversation. And you end this part (with great relief) by turning off your computer.

Part II: Making Windows NT Do Something

The biggest problem with using Windows NT isn't opening programs or moving windows around on-screen. It's making Windows NT do something useful. Here, you find ways to overcome the frustratingly playful tendencies that Windows NT displays so you can force it to shovel the walkway or blow leaves off the driveway.

Or if your computer is connected to everybody else's computer, you find out how to send and receive files from Jerry and Kathy's computer across the hall, all the while using the Chat program to decide where to eat lunch that day.

Part III: Using Windows NT Applications

Windows NT comes with a whole bunch of free programs. In this part, you find practical information about your new word processor, automatic phone dialer, Paint program, calculator, and bunches of other goodies. (If your computer has a CD-ROM drive, you even find out how to smuggle in some earphones and listen to your favorite jazz CDs while working.)

There's more. See, Windows NT can run not only Windows NT programs but programs from the older days. Here, you find out which buttons to poke in order to make Windows NT run your old Windows or DOS-based programs again.

Part IV: Been There, Done That: Quick References for Moving to Windows NT

Millions of people are using other versions of Windows, like Windows NT 3.51, Windows 3.1, Windows 95, and Windows 98. That means millions of people are muttering, "How do I make Windows NT work like my other version of Windows?" This part of the book offers quick tips, work-arounds, and quick-reference charts to help you get up and running with Windows NT 4.

Part V: Getting Help

Are your windows stuck? Broken? Do you need new screens? Although glass doesn't shatter when Windows NT crashes, those crashes can still hurt. In this part, you find some soothing salves for the most painful and irritating maladies.

Part VI: The Part of Tens

Everybody loves lists (unless they're published by the IRS and your name is on them). This part contains lists of Windows NT-related trivia: ten aggravating things about Windows NT (and how to fix them), ten things you shouldn't do under Windows NT, ten weird Windows NT icons and what they mean, ten ways to make Windows NT easier to use, ten mystifying acronyms, ten tranquil solutions to tense problems — things like that.

Icons Used in This Book

Already seen Windows NT, or any other version of Windows? Then you've probably noticed its icons, which are little pictures for starting various programs. The icons in this book fit right in. They're even a little easier to figure out:

Watch out! This signpost warns you that pointless technical information is coming around the bend. Swerve away from this icon, and you're safe from the nerdy technical drivel.

This icon alerts you to information that makes computing easier. For example, swinging your mouse overhead like a lasso is a great way to distract your coworkers when you don't want them to know you've forgotten your password for the third time that week.

Don't forget to remember these important points. (Or at least dog-ear the pages so you can look them up again a few days later.)

The computer itself won't explode while you're performing the delicate operations associated with this icon. Still, wearing gloves and proceeding with caution is a good idea when this icon is near.

Already familiar with another version of Windows? This icon marks information that can ease the cross-country move to Windows NT 4.

Face it: Some computer stuff definitely falls squarely into the realm of the pocket-protector crowd. Don't even bother attempting any of the maneuvers marked by this stuff. Just lean back in your chair, raise your hand, and slowly wave it back and forth until the office's Network Administrator comes over to fix the problem.

Where to Go from Here

Now you're ready for action. Give the pages a quick flip and maybe scan through a few sections that you know you'll need later. And remember: This is your book — your weapon against the computer criminals who've inflicted this whole complicated computer concept on you. So personalize your sword: Circle the paragraphs you find useful, highlight key concepts, cover up the technical drivel with sticky notes, and draw smiley faces in the margins. The more you mark up the book, the easier it will be for you to find the important stuff when you need it a few weeks later.

Part I
Intro to Windows NT (Bare-Bones Stuff)

"WHO'S GOT THE COMPUTER WITH THE SLOW RESPONSE TIME?"

In this part . . .

Windows NT is an exciting, modern way to use the computer. That means it's as confusing as a new car's dashboard. Even the most wizened old computer buffs will stumble in this strange new land of boxes, bars, and bizarre oddities like *peer to peer networking*.

Have you been thrust in front of a computer at work, where the Person in Charge told you that Windows NT is "easy-to-use"? Well, Windows NT can be intuitive, but that doesn't mean it's as easy to figure out as a feather duster.

In fact, most people are dragged into Windows NT without a choice. Maybe the gurus installed Windows NT at the office, where everyone had to learn it except for John, who cashed out his company's stock options and escaped the night before it was installed.

You can adjust to Windows NT, however, just like you eventually learned to live with the awful-tasting tap water when you visited your friends in San Diego.

Whatever your situation, this part keeps things safe and sane, with the water flowing smoothly. If you're new to computers, the first chapter answers the question you've been afraid to ask around the lunch room: "Just what is this Windows thing, anyway?"

Chapter 1

What Is Windows NT?

In This Chapter

- Understanding Windows and what it does
- Understanding Windows NT 4 and what it does
- Switching from Windows NT 3.51 to Windows NT 4
- Understanding the differences between Windows NT Workstation and Windows NT Server

Many years ago, a small company called Microsoft created a small piece of computer software called Windows. Nobody liked Windows, because it was awkward, looked weird, and barely worked.

Microsoft kept trying, however, and the now-flashy-and-popular Windows software comes preinstalled on millions of new computers around the world. In fact, Windows is more than just software — it has become a way of life. When Microsoft releases a new version, hordes of software junkies stay up all night just to be first in line when the computer stores open.

Many people will tell you that Microsoft Windows has grown into a computer paradise, filled with beautiful graphics and relaxing menus. But be prepared: Windows is no panacea, no matter how you want to pronounce that word. Whenever software becomes more friendly, computers become more complicated.

Besides, the simplest-looking things are often the most treacherous. Remember the first time you ate wontons with a pair of chopsticks?

This chapter looks at a version of Windows called Windows NT. The chapter explains what Windows NT is and what it's supposed to do. It explains how Windows NT differs from other versions of Windows you may have heard about.

Plus, you find out how Windows NT is really *two* programs — the relatively simple Windows NT Workstation and the horrendously complicated Windows NT Server. (Thank goodness you only have to mess with Windows NT Workstation in this book. . . .)

What Is This Windows Stuff, Anyway?

Windows is just another computer program, like zillions of other pieces of software lining the store shelves. But it's not a program in the normal sense — a letter-writing program, for example, or a game like *Flambé the Toupee.* Rather, Windows completely changes the way you work with your computer.

For years, computer programs made computers cling to a "typewriter" look. Just as on a typewriter, people typed letters and numbers into the computer. The computer listened and then responded by placing letters and numbers onto the screen. This time-tested system worked well. But it took a long time to learn, and it was as boring as an oral hygiene pamphlet.

These text-based systems were boring because computer geeks designed computers for other computer geeks. They thought that computers would be forever isolated in windowless rooms where somber young men with clipboards and white lab coats jotted down notes while the big reels whirled. Nobody expected normal people to use computers — especially not in their offices, their dens, or, heaven help us, their kitchens.

- Windows software dumps the old typewriter analogy and updates the *look* of computers. Windows replaces the words and numbers with pictures and buttons. It's splashy and modern, like an expensive new coffeemaker.
- Because Windows software looks and acts so differently from the old software, learning it can take a few days. After all, you probably couldn't make perfect coffee the first day you tried, either.
- Windows NT 4 is the latest version of Windows NT software. Windows NT 4 is the version that updates Windows NT 3.51, which updated Windows NT 3.50, which updated Windows NT 3.1, — you get the idea. Plus, you'll find a few Service Packs, also called "SPs" (pronounced *ess peas*), tossed in to fix the mistakes of previous versions.

What Does Windows NT 4 Do?

Like the mother with the whistle in the lunch court, Windows controls all the parts of your computer. You turn on your computer, start Windows NT, and start running Windows programs. Each program runs in its own little *window* on-screen. Yet Windows keeps things safe, even if the programs start throwing food at each other.

Windows NT is usually on a *network,* meaning it can let your computer talk to other computers, squirting information through little cables.

While it's keeping order, Windows makes computing a little easier. Windows purges an ugly computing custom called the *command line.* For years, people would have to type embarrassingly complicated code words to make their computers do things. To make a computer copy a file from one place to another, they might end up typing the following:

```
COPY C:\WORDS\REPORTS\CORP\BOON\JULY15.DOC A:\CORP
```

After the user typed that long string of garbage and pressed the Enter key on the keyboard, the computer would dutifully perform the easy part: copy a corporate report onto a floppy disk.

Those were tense, shoulder-tightening years for computer users. You had to memorize all the programs' names and remember where the programs lived on the computer. When it came to giving directions or offering tips, the computer was as useless as a Pittsburgh phone book in Paris.

Windows, by contrast, replaces most of the text with little pictures, or *icons,* as shown in Figure 1-1. To copy a file onto a floppy disk in Windows, for example, you look for the picture representing your file. It may look something like Figure 1-1.

Figure 1-1: Windows replaces the text-based commands with little push-button pictures.

Then you look for the picture of the floppy drive, as shown in Figure 1-2.

By pointing at the picture of the file with the mouse, holding down the mouse button, dragging the file to the floppy drive, and letting go of the mouse button, you can quickly and easily copy the file to the floppy disk. (Chapter 18 shows how to copy files — and do just about anything else — in less than four steps.)

- Windows fills the screen with lots of fun little boxes, pictures, and push-buttons; older-style computers were for no-nonsense minimalists who never put bumper stickers on their cars.

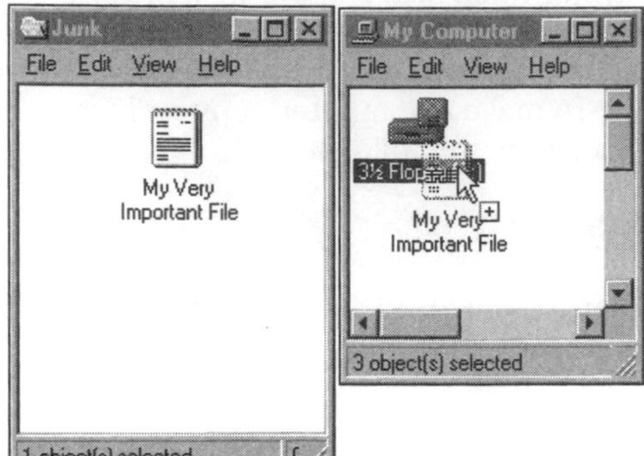

Figure 1-2: By manipulating the pictures, you can manipulate your files; here, a file is being copied to a floppy disk, for example.

- Some people say that colorful pictures make Windows easier to use; others say that Windows is a little too arty. To write a letter in Windows, for example, do you select the picture of the notepad, the notepad with the quill, or the clipboard? And what do you do with the icon of the lightbulb?

- A computer environment like Windows that uses little pictures and symbols is called a *graphical user interface,* or GUI. (It's pronounced *gooey,* believe it or not.) Pictures require more computing horsepower than letters and numbers, so Windows NT requires a relatively powerful computer. (You can find a list of its requirements in Chapter 2.)
- Windows gets its name from all the cute little windows on-screen. Each window shows some information: a picture, perhaps, or a program you're running. You can put several windows on-screen at the same time and jump from window to window, visiting different programs. (Actually, the windows look like little squares, but who would buy a program called Squares?)
- When the word *Windows* starts with a capital letter, it refers to the Windows program. When the word *windows* starts with a lowercase letter, it refers to windows you see on-screen. When the word Windows ends with the letters *NT,* it refers to Windows NT. This book covers the latest version of the Windows NT software, Windows NT 4 with the Service Pack 4 installed.

Because Windows uses graphics, it's much easier to use than to describe. To tell someone how to move through a document in a text-based program, you simply say, "Press the PgDn key." In Windows, you say, "Click in the vertical scroll bar beneath the scroll box." Those directions sound awfully weird, but after you've done it, you'll say, "Oh, is that all? Golly!" (Plus, you can still press the PgDn key in Windows if you don't want to.)

What's this "DOS" stuff all about?

An operating system controls a computer's innards at a bare-bones, blood-pumping level. It handles all the raw, messy mechanics of computing.

When you turn on a computer and electricity starts flowing through its electronic blood vessels, its operating system wakes up, takes control, and starts making things happen. It handles all the dreadful, background computing mechanics so you can concentrate on what's happening on-screen.

For years, IBM PCs used an operating system called *DOS* (Disk Operating System), and thousands of software companies wrote DOS-based programs. The text-based DOS protected users from that internal computer stuff, but DOS was pretty technical itself. So Microsoft invented Windows.

For years, Windows rode on top of DOS, insulating users from their computer's technical side. When you told Windows to do something, it would turn around and tell DOS to do something. Until recently, Windows was just a translator, converting languages and collecting cash for its services.

Best yet, Windows could still run DOS-based programs — which came in handy for long-time computer users who still had piles of DOS-based programs lying around.

Microsoft eventually created a new version of Windows called Windows 95, an operating system that mixed Windows technology with DOS. Windows 95 could still run DOS-based programs, yet it changed the way Windows looked and made Windows easier to use.

Windows NT 4 changes the look of Windows NT 3.51 in the same way Windows 95 changed the look of earlier versions of Windows. In fact, Windows NT and Windows 95 look almost identical on the surface.

Oh, and if you still have some old DOS-based programs lying around, take heart: Windows NT 4 still runs them. (It can also run older Windows-based programs, like the ones written for Windows 3.1, Windows 95, Windows 98, or Windows NT 3.51.)

Why Should I Bother Using Windows NT?

Most Windows NT users don't have a choice. They have to use Windows NT, or they don't get a paycheck. See, Windows NT is designed for large *networks* — huge groups of linked computers that live in large buildings decorated along the top with gargoyles and artichokes. Windows NT isn't particularly designed for home users or small offices with small networks — though it's certainly used in such places.

If you or your company isn't running a large network, then plain old Windows 95 or Windows 98 probably meets your needs better than Windows NT 4.

- Any version of Windows can be networked. In fact, Windows 95 and Windows 98 are used on networks even more than Windows NT Workstation. However, for networks where security is super-important, NT Workstation is best.

- While Windows 95 and Windows 98 can be networked, they're primarily used on freestanding desktop machines. Windows NT Workstation can also be used as a freestanding machine, but its main function in life is to be on a big network.
- Both Windows 95 and Windows 98 are easier to set up and configure than Windows NT. Modems, sound cards, and even software find Windows 95 and Windows 98 to be friendlier than Windows NT.
- Windows NT takes up lots more disk space than Windows 95 and about the same space as Windows 98. Even with a 2GB hard drive, who wants to give up 175MB just for Windows NT itself?
- Because it's designed for office folks, Windows NT is lousy at running the current breed of action games like Descent and Doom — unless those games come with a version that's written specifically for Windows NT. (And because corporations don't want games around the office, don't count on seeing many games written specifically for Windows NT.)
- Don't know what version of Windows NT you're running? Click on the My Computer icon with your right mouse button, then choose Properties from the menu that appears. You should spot the version number hidden in the screen that appears.

- If you have a Pentium Pro, you have an exception: You should use Windows NT 4, not Windows 95 or Windows 98. Due to a bit of technological weirdness, the Pentium Pro often runs Windows 95 or 98 programs more slowly than a plain old Pentium does. If you spent the extra money for a Pentium Pro, you may not get your money's worth unless you're running Windows NT 4.

Will I Like Windows NT 4 Better than Windows NT 3.51?

Windows NT 3.51 users are elbowing each other nervously by the watercooler and whispering the Big Question: Will Windows NT 4 be a big hassle, bringing the network down, clogging the e-mail, and making it impossible to print Kathy and Jeff's party fliers before 5 p.m.? Probably not. Windows NT 4 offers many improvements over Windows NT 3.51.

- First, Windows NT 4 is a little easier for beginners to figure out. A lot less pointing and clicking is involved when finding files and starting programs. For example, Windows NT 4 keeps track of the past 15 files or programs you've used and stores their names in a special spot. Want to load the file again? Just click on the file's name from the pop-up list.

- You'll see lots more little buttons with pictures on them — *icons* — used in Windows NT 4 programs. Don't know what the icon with the little policeman picture is supposed to do? Unlike earlier versions of Windows NT, Windows NT 4 lets you rest your mouse pointer over the icon: then, after a few seconds, a window pops up on-screen, explaining the icon's reason for living.

- Moving from Windows 3.1? Windows NT 4 finally allows for longer filenames. After 15 years of frustration, IBM-PC users can call their files something more descriptive than RPT45.TXT. In fact, you have 255 characters to describe your computer creations.
- Best of all, the computer shouldn't crash so darn often — if at all.
- Windows NT 4 automates many computing chores. To install a program, for example, just push the floppy disk (or compact disc) into the drive and click the Add/Remove Programs button. Windows searches all your drives for the installation program and runs it automatically.
- Dare I say the word *Macintosh*? Windows NT looks more and more like the age-old Mac every year. That means Windows NT makes Macintosh users feel more at home than ever.

What's the Difference between Windows NT Workstation and Windows NT Server?

Windows NT 4 software, like Windows NT 3.51, comes in two versions. One is called *Windows NT Server,* and the other is called *Windows NT Workstation*. They look quite similar but perform very different functions.

Think of them like this: Windows NT Workstation works sort of like a telephone. You use it to connect to other telephones and talk to other people. If you have a touch-tone phone, you can do fancy things, like call the water company and tell them to skip a delivery. Of course, Windows NT Workstation isn't a telephone; but, like a telephone that places calls, Windows NT Workstation links computers to a more centralized area in order to move information around.

That "centralized area" is where Windows NT Server lives, and it works much like the telephone's switchboard. It's the device that controls all the incoming and outgoing calls and decides which callers get busy signals when two people call at the same time. No, it's not a real switchboard. But Windows NT Server runs on the computer that all the workstations connect to when sending and receiving information from each other.

Windows NT Server is much more complicated than Windows NT Workstation. That's why you don't want to mess with it. (Plus, it costs a heck of a lot more.)

- If your boss *does* ask you to use Windows NT Server, it's only because your boss plans to turn you into that most feared of creatures, the dreaded Network Administrator. Ask for a big raise. Then ask for a bigger one. Then think about emigrating.
- You may have occasion to log onto a computer running NT Server, but unless your account on the network has administrator's rights, you won't be able to get at any of the truly dangerous stuff. In fact, whatever machine you use for logging onto the network, your Desktop will look just like it did the last time you logged off (anywhere on the network).
- Windows NT 4 Server requires a more powerful computer than Windows NT 4 Workstation. This is partially because of the software and partially because administrators lust after powerful computers the way teenage boys lust after Corvettes.

Bracing Yourself for Windows NT 4

When running Windows NT, notice that everything happens at the same time. Its many different parts run around like hamsters with an open cage door. Programs cover each other up on the screen. They overlap corners, hiding each other's important parts. Occasionally, they simply disappear.

Be prepared for a bit of frustration when things don't behave properly. You'll be tempted to stand up, bellow, and toss a nearby stapler across the room. After that, calmly pick up this book, find the trouble spot listed in the Index, and turn to the page with the answer.

- Windows software may be accommodating, but that can cause problems, too. For example, Windows NT often offers more than three ways for you to perform the same computing task. Don't bother memorizing each command. Just choose one method that works for you and stick with it.

- Windows NT runs best on a powerful computer with the key word *Pentium* (or maybe *testosterone*) somewhere in the description. It also runs on special types of computers called PowerPCs, Digital Alpha RISC, or MIPS RISC. You can find the finicky computer requirements for Windows NT in Chapter 2.

Chapter 2

Boring Information, Bothersome Computer Parts

In This Chapter

- Figuring out the names for the gizmos and gadgets on the computer
- Understanding what all those things do
- Finding out what stuff you need in order to use Windows NT
- Making a list of what computer equipment you have

This chapter describes computer gizmos and gadgets. Go ahead and ignore it. Who cares what all your computer gadgetry is called? Unless your computer is beeping like an off-the-hook telephone, don't bother messing with it. Just dog-ear the top of this page, say, "So that's where all that stuff is explained," and keep going.

In Windows NT, you just press the buttons. Windows NT scoots over to the right part of your computer and kick-starts the action. In case Windows NT stubs a toe, this chapter holds the Band-Aids. And as always, the foul-smelling technical chunks are clearly marked; just hold your nose while gingerly stepping over them.

The Computer

Most likely, your computer is that beige box with all the cables. That box is probably connected to a bunch of other beige boxes, and they all most likely answer to names like IBM (or IBM-compatible), DEC Alpha, PowerPC, Silicon Graphics Workstation, or something with the word MIPS on the case. Whereas earlier versions of Windows — like Windows 95 and Windows 3.1 — could run only on IBM or IBM-compatible computers (the computers currently found in most homes and small offices), Windows NT can run on much larger computers.

(Yawn. I told you this chapter would be boring.)

- Windows NT is an operating system. An *operating system* functions as the computer's consciousness, so to speak, making sure that your computer's internal organs stay alive and ready to perform your computing tasks.
- Like earlier versions of Windows, Windows NT can run on an IBM or IBM-compatible. But it can also run on larger, more powerful computers known as *workstations.* Costing megabucks, most workstations have testosterone-ridden names, like "FirePower Powerized ES4100" or "MIPS ArcSystem Magnum PC-50."

- Thinking of grabbing a copy of Windows NT from the DEC Alpha software shelf at work and running it on your Pentium at home? It won't work. See, Windows NT works on a DEC Alpha and an Intel-based Pentium, and it looks the same on both systems. But you need a Pentium version of Windows NT 4 for the Pentium, and a DEC Alpha version of Windows NT 4 for the DEC Alpha workstation. The same version of Windows NT 4 won't run on both a Pentium and a DEC Alpha computer.

- You can run Windows NT on particularly muscular laptops and notebook computers, with fast 486 or Pentium microprocessors. Some of these powerhouse computers can get pretty warm when running, though, so consider placing a thick magazine on your lap as a heat buffer.

  Laptop users, rejoice: Windows NT supports PC Cards (formerly known as PCMCIA cards) — a point in its favor — but it doesn't support advanced power management, meaning it will drain your batteries in a hurry.

Microprocessor

The computer's brain is a small chip of silicon buried deep inside the computer's case. Resembling a Girl Scout's Thin Mint with square corners, this flat little wafer is the *microprocessor,* but nerds tend to call it a *central processing unit,* or CPU. (You may have seen flashy microprocessor TV commercials that say, "Intel Inside," because Intel makes most CPUs for IBM-style computers.)

The most expensive part of a computer, the CPU determines the computer's breed, be it an IBM-compatible, RISC workstation, Macintosh, or something even more exotic.

Windows NT can run on a wide variety of microprocessors, as described in Table 2-1.

Table 2-1 Microprocessor Power Ratings

Computer Name	*More Technical Names*	*Micro-processor*	*Vintage*	*Comments*
IBM-compatible	PC, XT, AT, 386, 486SX 80486SX	8088, 80286, 80386,	1981–1986	These antique chips aren't powerful enough to run Windows NT. Donate these types of computers to the Red Cross.
IBM-compatible 486	Pentium, Pentium Pro, and Pentium II	X86 Architecture, 80486, Pentium, Pentium Pro	1989–present	The 486 computers can barely squeak by, but Windows NT runs much better on a Pentium, Pentium Pro, or Pentium II.
MIPS Technologies, Inc., RISC	Reduced Instruction Set Computer	MIPS R4000/ R4400	Early 1990s	Microprocessors designed for work-stations. Windows NT likes these.
Digital Equipment Corporation	Alpha Server	DEC Alpha AXP RISC DEC Alpha AXP RISC	Early 1990s	Microprocessors designed for work-stations. Windows NT likes these.
PowerPC	PowerPC RISC	PowerPC	Early 1990s	Microprocessors designed for work-stations. Windows NT likes these.
Any multi-processor	Multipro-cessor Architecture	Several micro-processors hooked together into a single computer	Mid-1990s	This design works like putting several engines into a single car to make it run faster; it's done by several chip manufacturers.

A microprocessor is the current evolution of the gadget that powered those little 1970s pocket calculators. It performs all the computer's background calculations, from juggling spreadsheets to putting a picture of Dilbert on-screen.

Windows NT works best with the Pentium, Pentium Pro, and workstation-style of computers. It's very slow on a 486, and it won't even run on a 386 that you may have lying around. In short, Windows NT is designed to run on the fast and powerful computers found at the corporate office — not on the less-powerful desktop PCs found in most homes.

Floppy Disks, Compact Discs (CDs), and Disk Drives

The computer's *disk drive,* that thin slot in its front side, is like the drawer at the bank's drive-up teller window. That disk drive enables you to send and retrieve information from the computer.

You can push anything that's flat into a disk drive, but the computer recognizes only two things: floppy disks and compact discs. Things get a little weird here, so hang on tight. See, by some bizarre bit of mechanical wizardry, computers store information as a stream of impulses that constantly switch in two directions: on or off. Floppy disks and compact discs (also known as CDs) use different types of switches, as described in the next couple of sections.

You might also find things like ZIP drives or Syquest drives — these act like large floppy disks that hold oodles more information. For more answers on those drives, check out Dan Gookin's *PCs For Dummies,* 6th Edition (IDG Books Worldwide, Inc.). It's stocked with other information about your computer and how to use it with a wide variety of gadgetry.

Floppy disk flipping

A floppy disk's disk drive spits little magnetic impulses onto a floppy disk to store information safely. The disk drive can slurp the information back off the floppy disk by reading the magnetic impulses. You simply push the disk into the disk drive and tell Windows whether to slurp or spit. That's known as copy to or copy from in computer parlance.

By copying information to or from floppies, you can transport snippets of information to and from computers.

Windows NT runs primarily on networks — and it's much easier to copy information from one computer to another on a network (that is, via network cables instead of disks), a process described in Chapters 9 and 13. These days, floppies primarily come in handy for storing a backup copy of a few important files, installing new software, or moving files between a laptop and desktop computer.

Floppy disks come in two main sizes: a sturdy $3\frac{1}{2}$-inch disk and a rather flimsy (and obsolete) $5\frac{1}{4}$-inch disk. Both are called floppy disks, but only the $5\frac{1}{4}$-inch disks flop around when you dangle them by one corner.

- For security reasons, some networked computers don't come with floppy drives. That keeps people from making copies of information and taking it home. (It also keeps them from putting naughty stuff onto the network.) All the valuable data stays lodged in the computers and moves back and forth through the networking cables.
- The 3½-inch disk drives automatically grab the disk when you push it in far enough. You hear it clunk, and the disk sinks down into the drive. If it doesn't, you're putting it in the wrong way. (The disk's silver edge goes in first, with the little round silver thing in the middle facing down.) To retrieve the disk, push the button protruding from around the drive's slot and then grab the disk when the drive kicks it out.
- The much rarer 5¼-inch disks require an extra step. Push the disk into the drive until the disk doesn't go in any farther and flip down the drive's little lever. (The disk's oval-shaped hole edge goes in first; the disk's smooth side faces up, with the rough-edged side facing down.) To retrieve the disk, flip the little lever back up and grab the disk as the drive kicks it out.
- A disk you can carry around the house is a floppy disk. A hidden disk that lurks deep in the bowels of the computer is a *hard disk* or *hard drive.*

  Hard disks are thick little Frisbees inside the computer that can hold hundreds of times more information than floppy disks. They're also much quicker at reading and writing information. (They're a great deal quieter, too, thank goodness.) Windows NT insists on using a hard disk because it's such a huge program. The programs that run under Windows NT can be pretty huge, too.
- Computer stores sell blank floppy disks so that you can copy your work onto them and put them in a safe place. Unless your new box of blank disks features the word *preformatted,* you can't use them straight out of the box. They must be formatted first. This merry little chore is covered in Chapter 13.

Floppy disks come in many flavors, each holding different amounts of information. Different disks are designed for different sizes and types of disk drives. The disk's box describes what sort of disks are inside, but the bare disks rarely offer a clue as to their capacity. Table 2-2 provides a handy identification chart for that disk you found behind the bookcase. If you're in a hurry, just look at the fourth disk in the table; it's the one nearly everybody uses.

Table 2-2 True-to-Life Disk Facts

Size	*Name*	*Storage Capacity*	*Label Jargon*	*Looks Like This*
5¹/₄-inch	Low-density	360K	DS/DD 40 tpi	Square, bendable, and usually black; has a large hole in the center that's lined with a little plastic reinforcing ring. (Totally obsolete.)
5¹/₄-inch	High-density	1.2MB	HD DS/HD 96 tpi	Most common. Square, bendable, and usually black; has a large hole in the center without a little plastic reinforcing ring, but that's not always a good indicator. (Mostly obsolete.)
3¹/₂-inch	Low-density	720K	DS/DD DD 135 tpi	Square and rigid; has a little arrow in one corner. The arrow points away from a single, small square hole in another corner. (Rapidly vanishing.)
3¹/₂-inch	High-density	1.44MB	DS/HD HD	Most common. Square and rigid; has a little arrow in one corner and two small square holes in corners opposite the arrow. The letters HD are often stamped on the disk. (Definitely the most common.)
3¹/₂-inch	Extended density	2.8MB	DS/ED ED	Square and rigid; very rare and you are not likely to ever see one. (If you think you may have one, though, look for little ED letters stamped on the disk.)

What disk drives does Windows NT like?

Face it: Windows NT Workstation 4.0 is no cute little Vietnamese pot-bellied pig — it's a hairy hog with big ears. First, it needs a minimum of 120MB of hard disk space and can easily take up 175MB. To be comfortable, your computer had better have a 1GB or larger hard disk to accommodate Windows NT and all your programs.

If you've never installed Windows NT, you need a 3½-inch disk drive to run a few "start up" floppies, and you need a CD-ROM drive. If you're upgrading from an earlier version of NT, all you need is a CD-ROM drive. The key word here is CD-ROM — Windows NT comes on a CD because it's simply too humongous to fit on floppy disks.

Be forewarned, however, that Windows NT comes with high-density disks. If your 3½-inch disk drive isn't high capacity, your Windows NT disks won't work.

Finally, be aware that the terms *capacity* and *density* are often used interchangeably. The important part is the first part — high or low.

Disk do's and doughnuts

- Do label your disks so you know what's on them.
- Do at least make a valiant effort to peel off a disk's old label before sticking on a new one. (After a while, those stacks of old labels make the disk too fat to fit into the drive.)
- Do copy important files from your hard disk to floppy disks on a regular basis. (This routine is called *backing up* in computer lingo. You can buy special backup packages to make this chore a little easier. Not much easier, but a little. Or make the leap and buy a system that automates much of the backup process.)
- Do not try to use high-density disks in a low-capacity drive. They don't work right.
- Do not use low-density disks in a high-capacity drive unless you absolutely must. They weren't designed for high-capacity drives, and they can cause problems.
- Do not listen to silver-tongued people who say you can *notch* a low-density disk to turn it into a high-density disk. This method just doesn't work consistently and reliably.
- Do not leave disks lying in the sun.
- Do not place disks next to magnets. Don't place them next to magnets disguised as paper clip holders, either, or next to other common magnetized desktop items, such as older telephones.

What does "write-protected" mean?

Write-protection is supposed to be a helpful safety feature, but most people discover it through an abrupt bit of computer rudeness: Windows NT stops them short with the threatening message shown in Figure 2-1 while they're trying to copy a file to a floppy disk.

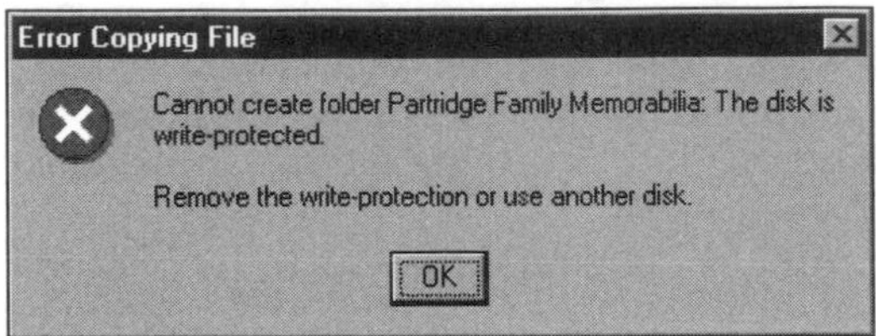

Error Copying File
Cannot create folder Partridge Family Memorabilia: The disk is write-protected.
Remove the write-protection or use another disk.
OK

Figure 2-1: Windows NT won't write to a disk that's been write-protected.

A write-protected disk has simply been tweaked so that nobody can copy to it or delete the files it contains. Write-protection is a simple procedure, surprisingly enough, requiring no government registration. You can write-protect and unwrite-protect disks in the privacy of your own office cubicle.

- To write-protect a 3 1/2-inch disk, look for a tiny, black sliding tab in a square hole in the disk's corner. Slide the tab with a pencil or your thumbnail so that the hole is uncovered. The disk is now write-protected.
- To remove the write-protection on a 3 1/2-inch disk, slide the little black plastic thingy so that the hole is covered up.
- If you encounter the write-protect error shown in Figure 2-1, wait until the drive stops making noise and the little light on the front of the drive goes out. Then click on the OK button to remove the Error message window. Remove the disk, unwrite-protect the disk, and put the disk back in the drive. Finally, repeat what you were doing before you were so rudely interrupted.

Driving with compact discs

Compact discs look like the things you've been sliding into your stereo's CD player for the past decade. And in fact, if you slide an Allman Brothers CD into your computer's CD-ROM drive, you can whistle along to Dickey Betts' slide guitar while you work. (Hopefully your computer has a sound card and speakers.)

Instead of storing information in the form of magnetic impulses, CDs store information as little blips for a little focused beam of light to read. Because light-beam blips can be more precise than a floppy disk's magnetic impulses, CDs can hold a lot more information — about 680MB of information, in fact.

- Because CD-ROM drives can hold so much information, they're the premier way of installing Windows NT and just about every other software package for sale these days.
- You can't write to a CD-ROM drive; you can only read information from it. That means a CD is always write-protected.
- I lied. You can write information to CDs with special CD-ROM drives called CD Recordable drives. You don't find those attached to Windows NT workstations very often. Some Recordable CD-ROM drives (also called *CD-R drives*) can not only write stuff to a disc, they let you erase your old stuff and write new stuff. (They're called Read/Write, or *CD-RW drives.*)
- Compact disc is spelled with a c to confuse people accustomed to seeing disk spelled with a k.

The Mouse and That Double-Click Stuff

The *mouse* is that rounded plastic thing that looks like a bar of electronic soap. Marketing people thought that the word mouse sounded like fun, so the name stuck. Actually, think of your mouse as your electronic finger because you use it in Windows NT to point at stuff on-screen.

A mouse has a little roller, or mouse ball, embedded in its belly. (Where were the animal-rights people?) When you move the mouse across your desk, the ball rubs against electronic sensor gizmos. The gizmos record the mouse's movements and send the information down the mouse's tail, which connects to the back of the computer.

As you move the mouse, you see an arrow, or pointer, move simultaneously across the computer screen. Here's where your electronic finger comes in: When the arrow points at a picture of a button on-screen, you press, or click, the left button on the mouse. The button is selected, just as if you'd pressed it with your finger. It's a cool bit of 3-D computer graphics that makes you want to click buttons again and again.

- You control just about everything in Windows NT by pointing at it with the mouse and pressing and releasing the mouse button, or clicking. (The mouse pitches in with a helpful clicking noise when you press its button.)
- The plural of mouse is mice, just like the ones cats chew on. It's not mouses.

- Fold-down airline trays don't have enough room for a laptop, a mouse, and a beverage, so laptoppers often substitute trackballs for mice. A trackball is a small, upside-down mouse that clips to the keyboard. You roll the mouse's ball with your thumb to move the on-screen arrow. You use your other fingers to inadvertently spill your beverage.
- Most mice run in two modes: Microsoft-compatible mode or some funky third-party way. Microsoft created Windows, so you have fewer problems if you run the mouse in the Microsoft-compatible mode. Also, mice come in three breeds: bus, PS/2, and serial. Windows NT works with all three breeds, so it doesn't care which you have, and neither should you.
- A mouse won't work by itself; it needs software called a *driver*. A driver listens to the mouse location information coming down the tail and puts the mouse's location in a special spot in the computer's memory. All your other programs can glance at that spot to see where you've pushed the mouse this time. For still more information on drivers, scurry to the section on mouse manipulations in Chapter 11.
- If your mouse doesn't work with Windows NT (it gets the shivers, it scurries around at random, or the arrow doesn't move), the driver (the software — not your hand) is probably to blame. Visit Chapter 11 for help.

The mouse arrow changes shape, depending on what it's pointing at in Windows. When it changes shape, you know that it's ready to perform a new task. Table 2-3 is a handy reference for the different uniforms the mouse pointer wears for different jobs. (Beware, however, that you can customize your mouse pointers; your pointers may not look exactly like the ones in the table. Head to Chapter 11 for mouse-pointer customization tips.)

Table 2-3 The Various Shapes of the Mouse Pointer

Shape	*What It Points At*	*What to Do When You See It*
(arrow)	Just about anything on-screen	Use this pointer for moving from place to place on-screen.
(four-headed arrow)	A single window	Uh-oh. You've somehow selected the annoying size or move option from the Control menu. Moving the mouse or pressing the cursor-control keys now makes the current window bigger or smaller. Press Enter when you're done or press Esc if you want to get away from this uncomfortable bit of weirdness.

Shape	*What It Points At*	*What to Do When You See It*
↕	The top or bottom edge of a window	Hold down the mouse button and move the mouse back and forth to make the window grow taller or shorter. Let go when you like the window's new size.
↔	The left or right edge of a window	Hold down the mouse button and move the mouse back and forth to make the window fatter or skinnier. Let go when you like the window's new size.
↘	The corner of a window	Hold down the mouse button and move the mouse anywhere to make the window fat, skinny, tall, or short. Let go when you're through playing.
I	A program or box that accepts text	Put the pointer where you want words to appear; then click on the button and start typing the letters or numbers. (This pointer is called an *I-beam,* in techno terms.)
☝	A word with a hidden meaning in the Windows help system	Click the mouse, and Windows trots out some more helpful information about that particular subject.
⌛	Nothing (Windows is busy ignoring you.)	Move the mouse in wild circles and watch the hourglass spin around until Windows NT catches up with you. This usually happens when you are loading large files or copying stuff to a floppy disk.

Don't worry about memorizing all the various shapes that the pointer takes on. The pointer changes shape automatically at the appropriate times. I've described the shapes here just so you won't think that your pointer's goofing off when it changes shape.

The breeds of mice

A serial mouse, a bus mouse, and a port mouse all look the same: They're all little plastic things with tails stretching toward the computer's rear. When the tails reach the back of the computer, the mice's tails differ subtly. A serial mouse plugs into an oblong doodad called a *serial port.* Almost all computers come with a preinstalled serial port that nerds call *COM1.*

The tails from bus and port mice don't head for the serial port. Instead, each of those tails has a little round end that plugs into a little round hole in the computer's rear. If your mouse says "PS/2" or "PS/2 compatible" on its belly, you have a port mouse. If your mouse plugs into a hole mounted on a silver card, you have the rarer bus mouse design.

Windows NT can usually guess which mouse you have, and it installs itself correctly. But if you accidentally yank your mouse cord from the back of your computer, now you know which hole to plug it back into.

Finally, some cordless mice don't have tails at all. But they have a receiving unit — a little box that plugs into one of the three areas discussed above.

Cards and Monitors

The monitor is the thing you stare at all day until you go home to watch TV. The front of the monitor, called its *screen* or *display,* is where all the Windows NT action takes place. The screen is where you can watch the windows as they bump around, occasionally cover each other up, and generally behave like nine people eyeing a recently delivered eight-slice pizza.

Monitors have two cords so they won't be mistaken for a mouse. One cord plugs into the electrical outlet; the other cord heads for the video card, a special piece of electronics poking out from behind the computer. The computer tells the video card what it's doing; the card translates the events into graphics information and shoots it up the cable into the monitor, where it appears on-screen.

- Like herbivores and cellulose-digesting gut microorganisms, monitors and video cards come in symbiotic pairs. Neither can function without the other, and it's best to buy them in matched sets so that they get along.
- Unlike other parts of the computer, the video card and monitor don't require any special care and feeding. Just wipe the dust off the screen every once in a while.

Spray plain old glass cleaner on a rag and then wipe off the dust with the newly dampened rag. If you spray glass cleaner directly on the screen, the fluid drips down into the monitor's casing, annoying the trolls who sleep under the bridge.

- Some glass cleaners contain alcohol, which can cloud the antiglare screens found on some fancy new monitors. When in doubt, check your monitor's manual to see whether glass cleaner is allowed.
- When you first install Windows NT, it interrogates the video card and monitor until they reveal their brand name and orientation. Windows NT usually gets the right answer from them and sets itself up automatically so that everything works the first time. (A little tweaking later on may help, though, as described in Chapter 11.)
- For such simple gadgets, monitors and cards command a dazzling array of nerdy terms. Ignore them all. Windows picks the appropriate video settings automatically and moves on to the hard stuff, like mouse drivers.

Ignore these awful graphics terms

Some people describe their monitors as *boxy* or *covered with cat hair;* others use the following strange scientific terms:

- **Pixel:** A *pixel* is a fancy name for an individual dot on-screen. Everything on-screen is made up of bunches of graphic dots, or pixels. Each pixel is a different shade or color, which creates the image. (Squint up close to the screen, and you may be able to make out an individual pixel.) Monochrome monitors are often called *gray-scale monitors* because their pixels can show only shades of gray.
- **Resolution:** The *resolution* is the number of pixels on a screen — specifically, the number of pixels across (horizontal) and down (vertical). More pixels means greater resolution: smaller letters and more information packed onto the same-sized screen. People with small monitors usually use 640x480 resolution. People with larger monitors often switch to 1024x768 resolution so that they can fit more windows on-screen and impress their coworkers.
- **Color:** The term *color* describes the number of colors that the card and monitor display on-screen. The number of colors can change, however, depending on the current resolution. When the card runs at a low resolution, for example, it can use its leftover memory to display more colors. At a 1024x768 resolution, you may see only 256 colors on-screen. With a lower resolution of 640x480, you may be able to see 16.7 million colors. Windows NT usually runs fastest with 256 colors, and unless you're using a high-resolution color photo of your first-born child for your monitor's background, you won't need more colors than that.
- **Mode:** A predetermined combination of pixels, resolution, and colors is described as a *graphics mode.* Right out of the box, Windows NT can handle the mode needs of most people. If the video card hails from a weird mode planet, you need a *driver* from the folks who made the card.

You don't need to know any of this stuff. If you're feeling particularly modular, however, you can change the Windows graphics modes after reading Chapter 11.

Keyboards

Computer keyboards look pretty much like typewriter keyboards with a few dark growths around the perimeter. In the center lie the familiar white typewriter keys. The grayish keys with obtuse code words live along the outside edges. They're described next.

Groups of keys

Obtuse code-word sorters divvy those outside-edge keys into key groups:

- **Function keys:** These F keys either sit along the top of the keyboard in one long row or clump together in two short rows along the keyboard's left side. Function keys boss around programs. For example, you can press F1 to demand help whenever you're stumped in Windows NT.
- **Numeric keypad:** Zippy-fingered bankers like this thingy: a square, calculator-like pad of numbers along the right edge of most keyboards. (You have to press a key called Num Lock above those numbers, though, before they work. Otherwise, they're cursor-control keys, described next.)
- **Cursor-control keys:** If you haven't pressed the magical Num Lock key, the keys on that square, calculator-like pad of numbers are the cursor-control keys. These keys have little arrows that show which direction the cursor will be moved on-screen. (The arrowless 5 key doesn't do anything except try to overcome its low self-esteem.) Some keyboards have a second set of cursor-control keys next to the numeric keypad. Both sets do the same thing. Additional cursor-control keys are Home, End, PgUp, and PgDn (or Page Up and Page Down). To move down a page in a word-processing program, for example, you press the PgDn key.
- **Windows keys:** A new breed of keyboard, the 104-key Windows keyboard, has a few extra keys. (But they're real yawners.) One key simply brings up the Start menu — just as if you'd clicked on the Start button. (You'll find two of those keys, next to the Alt key on each side of the Spacebar.) The other key brings up the menu for the currently open window.

More key principles

Other keyboard keys you need to be familiar with follow:

- **Shift:** Just as on a typewriter, this key creates uppercase letters or the symbols %#@$, which make great G-rated swear words.
- **Alt:** Watch out for this one! When you press Alt (which stands for Alternate), Windows NT moves the cursor to the little menus at the top of the current window. If you're trapped up there and can't get out, you probably pressed Alt by mistake. Press Alt again to free yourself.

- **Ctrl:** This key (which stands for Control) works like the Shift key, but it's for weird computer combinations. For example, holding down the Ctrl key while pressing Esc (described next) brings up the Windows NT Start button menu, in case your mouse has died or isn't handy.
- **Esc:** This key, which stands for Escape, was a pipe dream of the computer's creators. They added Esc as an escape hatch from malfunctioning computers. By pressing Esc, the user was supposed to be able to escape whatever inner turmoil the computer was currently going through. Esc doesn't always work that way, but give it a try. It sometimes enables you to escape when you're trapped in a menu or a dastardly dialog box. (Those traps are described in Chapter 6.)
- **Scroll Lock:** This one's too weird to bother with. Ignore it. (It's no relation to a scroll bar, either.) If a little keyboard light glows next to your Scroll Lock key, press the Scroll Lock key to turn it off. (The key is often labeled Scrl Lk or something equally obnoxious.)
- **Delete:** Press the Delete key (sometimes labeled Del), and the unlucky character sitting to the right of the cursor disappears. Any highlighted information disappears as well. Poof.
- **Backspace:** Press the Backspace key, and the unlucky character to the left of the cursor disappears. The Backspace key is on the top row, near the right side of the keyboard; it has a left-pointing arrow on it. Oh, and the Backspace key deletes any highlighted information, too.
- **Insert:** Pressing Insert (sometimes labeled Ins) puts you in Insert mode. As you type, any existing words are scooted to the right, letting you add stuff. The opposite of Insert mode is Overwrite mode, where everything you type replaces any text in its way. Press Insert to toggle between these two modes.

  Ugly disclaimer: Some Windows-based programs, such as Notepad, are always in Insert mode. You simply cannot move to Overwrite mode, no matter how hard you pound the Insert key.
- **Enter:** This key works pretty much like a typewriter's Return key but with a big exception: Don't press Enter at the end of each line. A word processor can sense when you're about to type off the edge of the screen. It herds your words down to the next line automatically. So just press Enter at the end of each paragraph.

  You also want to press Enter when Windows NT asks you to type something — the name of a file, for example, or the number of pages you want to print — into a special box.
- **Caps Lock:** If you've mastered the Caps Lock key on a typewriter, you'll be pleased to find no surprises here. (Okay, there's one surprise. Caps Lock affects only your letters. It has no effect on punctuation symbols or the numbers along the top row.)

- **Tab:** You won't find any surprises here, either, except that Tab is equal to five spaces in some word processors and eight spaces in others. Still other word processors enable you to set Tab to whatever number you want. Plus, a startling Tab Tip follows.

  Press Tab to move from one box to the next when filling out a form in Windows NT. (Sometimes, these forms are called dialog boxes.)

A mouse works best for most Windows NT tasks, like starting programs or choosing among various options. Sometimes the keyboard comes in handy, however. Windows comes with shortcut keys to replace just about anything you can do with a mouse. Pressing a few keys can be quicker than wading through heaps of menus with a mouse. (The shortcut keys are described in Chapter 5, in the section on when to use the keyboard.)

If you don't own a mouse or a trackball, you can control Windows exclusively with a keyboard. But it's awkward, like watching Barney try to floss his back molars.

Those little bumps on your f and j keys are there so you can put your fingers on the right keys when you're typing in the dark.

Print Screen: The one fun, weird code key

Windows NT fixed something dreadfully confusing about an IBM computer's keyboard: the Print Screen key (sometimes called PrtScr, Print Scrn, or something similar). In the old days of computing, pressing the Print Screen key sent a snapshot of the screen directly to the printer. Imagine the convenience!

Unfortunately, nobody bothered to update the Print Screen key to handle graphics. If a screen shows anything other than straight text, pressing the Print Screen key sends a wild jumble of garbled symbols to the printer. And if the printer isn't connected, turned on, and waiting, the computer stops cold.

Windows NT fixes the Print Screen woes. Pressing the Print Screen key now sends a picture of the screen to a special place in Windows that is known as the *Clipbook*. When the image is in the Clipbook, you can call up the Clipbook's Clipboard and paste that image into your programs or save it to disk. You can even print the screen's picture if you paste the image from the Clipboard into Paint, the Windows NT drawing program.

- With some older computers, you have to hold down Shift while you press Print Screen, or you get just an asterisk on-screen. Not nearly as much fun.
- The Clipbook and Clipboard are described in Chapter 10.

Modems

Modems are little mechanical gadgets that translate a computer's information into squealing sounds that can be sent and received over plain, ordinary phone lines.

Because computers can store sound, text, numbers, pretty pictures, and video, they can send and receive all that information over a modem as well. In fact, computers use this sophisticated technology when connected to the Internet's World Wide Web: Their owners use a modem to watch a live video of somebody's ant farm (`www.atomicweb.com/antfarm.html`), or connect to the Federal Bureau of Investigation's Ten Most Wanted Fugitives list (`www.fbi.gov/mostwanted.htm`) to see whether they recognize any relatives.

- The computers on both ends of the phone lines need modems in order to talk to each other. That's why people who want to talk on the Internet's World Wide Web need to pay money to an Internet Server. The Internet Server provides a way for your modem to talk to other computers on the Internet, and the Internet Server charges money for that privilege. (This confusing stuff is made much more clear in Chapter 16, thank goodness.)
- Modems need special communications software to make them work. Windows NT comes with a communications program called Internet Explorer for probing the World Wide Web. This software, known as a Web browser, lets people "surf the Net." (Chapter 16 covers Internet Explorer.)
- Windows NT also comes with a program called HyperTerminal for calling other computers directly, without going through a provider. (See Chapter 14 for more information on HyperTerminal.)
- Another program that comes with Windows NT is called Exchange, which can transport mail not only through modems but through the network. (Exchange gets its due in Chapter 16.)
- People also use modems to call America Online, CompuServe, and other online services. Online services are huge computers stuffed with information like stock prices, weather updates, news, and message areas, where people can swap talk about flatware, UFOs, and how much the online service is costing them. (Online services cost anywhere from about $10 a month to more than $20 an hour, all charged to the user's credit card.)

Printers

Realizing that the paperless office still lies several years down the road, Microsoft made sure that Windows NT can shake hands and make enthusiastic gestures with more than 200 types of printers.

If you're lucky, you have in your office a printer that you can use. If you're not lucky, you have a printer connected to the network, meaning you have to walk down the hall to grab your printed items.

- Even the fanciest printers must be turned on before Windows NT can print to them. (You'd be surprised how easily you can forget this little fact in the heat of the moment.)
- Windows NT prints in a WYSIWYG (what you see is what you get) format, which means that what you see on-screen is reasonably close to what you see on the printed page.

- When you click on the Print button in a Windows NT program or use the menu to send something to the printer, a little picture of a printer appears in the bar that runs along the edge of your screen. Double-click on the picture of the printer, and you can see a list (known as a queue) of all the files waiting to be printed. (The longer the list, the longer you have to wait for your own file.)

Networks

Networks connect PCs so that employees can share information. Coworkers can send stuff to a single printer, for example, or send messages to each other asking whether Marilyn has passed out the paychecks yet.

You're probably on a network if you can answer "yes" to any of these questions:

- Can your coworkers and you share a printer, data, or messages without standing up and yelling across the room?
- When your computer stops working, do you hear simultaneous batches of moans and groans from coworkers down the hall?
- Are you using Windows NT?
- Do you have a *Network Administrator?*
  - Most networks require a paid human attendant known as a Network Administrator. This person controls everything that happens on the network and can pass out additional privileges, like letting your files have priority in reaching the office printer.

- It pays to be nice to your Network Administrator.
- For what it's worth: You don't have to be running Windows NT Workstation as your operating system to participate on an NT network. NT Server can link Apple computers, UNIX computers, and PCs running Windows 98, Windows 95, Windows 3.1*x*, OS/2, or DOS.
- For more information about networks, start with Chapter 4.

Sound Cards (Disgusting Bioactive Noises)

For years, PC owners looked enviously at Macintosh owners — especially when the Macs ejected a disk. The Macintosh could make a cute barfing sound when ejecting a disk. Macs come with sound built in; they can barf, giggle, and make really disgusting noises that won't be mentioned here. (Any Mac owner will be happy to play them back for you.)

But the tight shirts at IBM decided there was no place for sound on a Serious Business Machine. Early versions of Windows finally fixed that mistake, so now the accounting department's computers can barf as loudly as the ones in the art department down the hall.

- Windows NT can still barf, but it needs a computer with two things: a sound card and a speaker. And unfortunately, many computers around the office lack these amenities.
- Nevertheless, Windows NT comes with some pleasant sounds already included, but it doesn't have any barf noises. Most computer gurus can either find a copy for you or personally record one.
- Just like the Macintosh, Windows NT enables you to assign cool sounds to various Windows functions. For example, you can make your computer scream louder than you do when it crashes. For more information, refer to the section in Chapter 11 on making cool sounds with multimedia.

Parts Required by Windows NT

Table 2-4 compares what Windows NT asks for on the side of the box with what you really need before it works well.

Table 2-4 What Windows Requires

Listed, Ethereal Requirements	*Normal, Human Requirements*
Intel 486/25, Pentium, Pentium Pro, or RISC-based microprocessor (like the MIPS R4x), DEC Alpha AXP, or PowerPC	Fast Pentium or workstation
12MB of RAM for Intel-based computers; 16MB of RAM for other types of computers	32MB of RAM for Intel-based computers; 64MB of RAM for other computers
VGA card and monitor	Fast SuperVGA card and 17-inch monitor
Hard disk with 118MB free for Intel; 149MB free for workstations	1GB hard disk
CD-ROM drive (unless Windows NT is being installed over a network)	Quad-speed or faster CD-ROM drive
Options: Mouse	*Required:* Mouse, preferably Microsoft-compatible
Options: Network card and cables	*Required:* Network card and cables

Chapter 3

Windows NT Stuff Everybody Thinks You Already Know

In This Chapter

- Understanding Windows NT buzzwords
- Nailing down the Windows NT basics

When the first version of Windows hit the market in 1985, it failed miserably. The weakling computers of the day could barely add numbers, yet Windows forced them to paint the screen with heavy-duty graphics. Windows was slow and ugly, and most people didn't think it would last a year.

Today's powerhouse computers can not only calculate the trendiest financial forecast algorithms but create feature-length motion pictures as well. And Windows, with its fashionable color schemes — like Lilac, Maple, and Slate — has turned into a trendy worldwide best-seller.

Because Windows has been around for so long, a lot of computer geeks have had a head start in learning its special language. To help you catch up; this chapter is a tourist's alphabetized guidebook to those Windows words that the nerds have been batting around for ten years.

Backing Up Your Work

A computer can store bunches of files on its hard disk. And that multitude of files can be a problem. When the hard disk eventually dies, it takes all its stored files down with it. Pffffft.

Computer users who don't like anguished pffffft sounds back up their hard disks religiously by making a second copy of it for safekeeping. They do so in four main ways:

- **Floppies:** Some people copy all their files from the hard disk to a bunch of floppy disks. Although custom-written backup programs make this task easier, it's still a time-consuming chore. Who wants to spend an extra hour backing up computer files after finishing a day's work?

  Using an older backup program that didn't come with Windows NT? If your backup program doesn't claim to be "Windows NT compatible," don't use it. These old backup programs probably won't know how to back up files using Windows NT's special ways of storing files. If you try to use an old backup program with Windows NT, the backup won't be reliable.

- **Tape backup unit:** This special computerized tape recorder either lives inside the computer like a disk drive or plugs into the computer's rear. Either way, the gizmo tape-records all the information on your hard disk. Then when your hard disk dies, you still have all your files on tape. The faithful tape backup unit plays back all your information onto the new hard disk. No scrounging for floppy disks.

  Windows NT comes with Backup, a program that automatically copies files from your hard disk to a tape backup drive. You can't use the Windows NT backup program except with a tape drive.

  The tape backup unit can cost from $150 to $1,000, depending on the size of your computer's hard disk. Some people back up their work every day, using a new tape for each day of the week. If they discover on Thursday that last Monday's report had important information, they can pop Monday's tape into the backup unit and grab the report.

- **Removable disks:** These guys work like floppy disks, but are usually a little larger. And although they're just a little larger, they can hold more than a hundred times as much information. (Look for the Ditto Zip and Jaz units.)

- **Automatic network backup:** The luckiest people don't need to worry about backing up their hard disks at all. They work on a network that handles all the backup chores automatically. Because Windows NT is primarily used on networks, you probably don't need to worry about backing up your hard disk.

  But a lot depends on how much you trust your Network Administrator to do a complete daily backup. Take this little test:

  1) Do you spot your Network Administrator playing "House of Cards" with floppy disks and tapes?

  2) Does your Network Administrator keep a packed suitcase in his or her office at all times?

  If your answer to either of these questions is "yes," you should at least consider copying your most valuable files to floppies.

Clicking

Computers make plenty of clicking sounds, but only one click counts: the one that occurs when you press a button on a mouse. You'll find yourself clicking the mouse hundreds of times in Windows NT. For example, to push an on-screen button marked Push Me, you move the mouse until the mouse pointer rests over the Push Me button, and then you click the mouse button.

- When you hear people say, "Press the button on the mouse," they leave out an important detail: *Release* the button after you press it. Press the button with your index finger and release it, just as you press a button on a touch-tone phone. (See the "Dragging and Dropping" section for an important exception.)
- Most mice have two buttons; some have three, and some esoteric models for traffic engineers have more than 32. Windows NT listens mostly to clicks coming from the button on the left side of your mouse. It's the one under your index finger. Refer to Chapter 11 for more mouse button tricks (including how to turn your mouse into a left-handed mouse).

Hey, when do I use the left mouse button, and when do I use the right mouse button?

When somebody tells you to "click" something in Windows NT, he almost always means that you should "click with your left mouse button." That's because most Windows NT users are right-handed, and their index fingers hover over the mouse's left button, making that button an easy target.

Windows NT, however, also lets you click your *right* mouse button, and it regards the two actions as completely different.

Pointing at something and clicking the right button often brings up a secret hidden menu with some extra options. Right-click on a blank portion of your Desktop, for example, and a menu pops up, allowing you to organize your Desktop's icons or change the way your display looks. Right-clicking on an icon often brings up a hidden menu as well.

The right mouse button is designed for users who like to feel that they're doing something sneaky. That's why clicking the right mouse button often brings up a hidden menu of extra options.

You'll rarely, if ever, have to use the right mouse button. Just about every option it offers can be accomplished in other ways. But once you experience the joys of being sneaky, you may find yourself using the right mouse button as often as the left.

Windows NT 3.51 only listened to clicks coming from the left side of your mouse. Windows NT 4 listens to clicks coming from both buttons. (See the "Hey, when do I use the left mouse button, and when do I use the right mouse button?" sidebar.)

- Most Windows NT applications also listen to clicks coming from the right button as well as from the left button.
- Don't confuse a click with a double-click. For more rodent details, see "The Mouse," "Double-Clicking," and "Pointers/Arrows," later in this chapter. The insatiably curious can find even more mouse stuff in Chapter 2.

The Command Line

Some people don't like clicking on little pictures to get things done, which is how Windows is set up. They prefer to type stern code words to boss their computers around. Windows NT accommodates both crowds by including a *command line,* as shown in Figure 3-1.

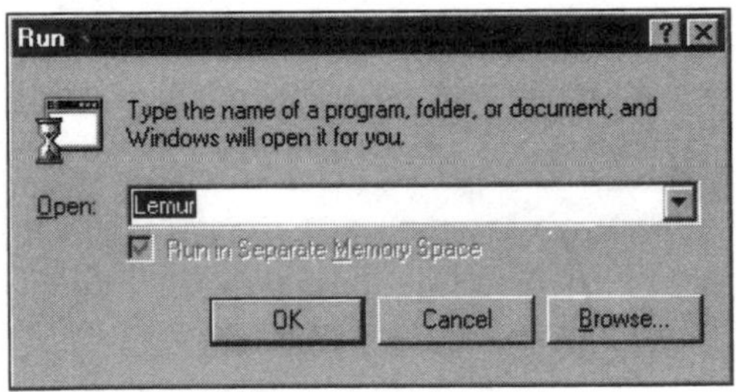

Figure 3-1: Type a command line in the Run box and press Enter, and Windows NT attempts to carry out the command.

After you type a program's name at the command line and press Enter, Windows NT rummages around, looking for that program. If Windows NT succeeds, it loads the program and brings it to the screen for your working pleasure. If it doesn't find it, it burps back with the bit of ugliness shown in Figure 3-2.

- The most common reason Windows NT burps back is because you spelled the file's name wrong. Windows NT is more critical than an English teacher in a bad mood. You must be exact.

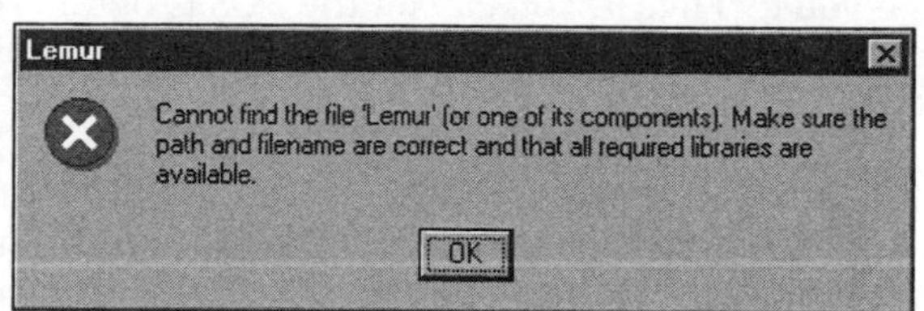

Figure 3-2: If Windows NT can't carry out your command, it responds with a message like this.

- Don't confuse the command line with the command prompt, although the two usually go hand in hand. The *command line* is the information you type next to the command prompt. *The command prompt* is the thing you find described if you move your eyes to the section "The Command Prompt."
- For the most part, Windows NT replaces typing stuff at the command line with a more pleasant way of computing: pressing buttons or clicking on pictures. You find a command line hidden in the Start button's menu, however, if you want to boss your computer around that way. Just click on Run from the Start button. Command lines can pop up unexpectedly in a few other programs as well. For information about the command line's alternative, see "Graphical User Interfaces."

The Command Prompt

Some people haven't switched to the newer, Windows breed of programs. They're still using the programs they bought several years ago, back when using a DOS program was trendy. Luckily, Windows NT not only can run DOS programs but can provide a DOS prompt (also called a command prompt) for the needy. Click on the Start button, click on the word Programs, and click on Command Prompt from the menu. (It's next to an icon that says MS-DOS.)

The DOS prompt rhymes with the boss chomped, and it's a symbol that looks somewhat like the following:

```
C:\>
```

Type the name of your program at the command prompt and press Enter, and the program begins. Windows NT waits in the background while you run a DOS session, or, if you feel like it, you can let the DOS program run in the background while you run some Windows NT programs. (See "Multitasking and Task Switching.")

You don't even need to head for a DOS window to run a DOS program. Just double-click on the DOS program's name from My Computer or Windows Explorer, and the program merrily begins humming along, just as if you'd started it from the command prompt.

If you've been rudely dumped at the DOS command prompt, you can scoot quickly to Windows NT by typing the following no-nonsense word:

```
C:\> EXIT
```

That is, you type EXIT and follow it with a press of the Enter key.

Windows NT's command prompt is quite versatile. You type in the name of a DOS program — or program using any version of Windows — and Windows NT searches for the program and runs it.

The Cursor

A typewriter has a little mechanical arm that strikes the page, creating the desired letter. Computers don't have little mechanical arms (except in science fiction movies), so they have *cursors:* little blinking lines that show where that next letter will appear in the text.

Cursors appear only when Windows NT is ready for you to type text, numbers, or symbols — usually when you write letters or reports.

- The cursor and the mouse pointer are different things that perform different tasks. When you start typing, text appears at the cursor's location, not at the pointer's location.

  You can distinguish between the cursor and the mouse pointer with one look: Cursors always blink steadily; mouse pointers never do. For more information, check out "Pointers/Arrows" in this chapter or Table 2-3 in Chapter 2.

- You can move the cursor to a new place in the document by using the keyboard's cursor-control keys (the keys with little arrows). Or you can point to a spot with the mouse pointer and click the button. The cursor leaps to that new spot.

Defaults (And the "Any Key")

Finally, a computer term that can be safely ignored. Clap your hands and square-dance with a neighbor! Here's the lowdown on the, er, hoedown: Some programs present a terse list of inexplicable choices and casually suggest that you choose the only option that's not listed: the default option.

Don't chew your tongue in despair. Just press Enter.

Those wily programmers have predetermined what option works best for 99 percent of the people using the program. So if people just press Enter, the program automatically makes the right choice and moves on to the next complicated question.

- The default option is similar to the oft-mentioned any key because neither of them appears on your keyboard (or on anybody else's, either — no matter how much money the person paid).
- When a program says to press any key, simply press the spacebar. (The Shift keys don't do the trick, by the way.)
- Default can also be taken to mean standard option or what to select when you're completely stumped. For example, "People riding in elevators often stare at their shoes by default."

Desktop (And Wallpapering It)

To keep from reverting to revolting computer terms, Windows NT uses familiar office lingo. For example, all the action in Windows NT takes place on the Windows NT Desktop. The *Desktop* is the background area of the screen, where all the programs pile up.

Windows NT comes with a drab green Desktop. To jazz things up, you can cover the Desktop with pictures, or *wallpaper.* Windows NT comes with several pictures you can use for wallpaper (and Chapter 11 can help you hang one of them up).

You can customize the wallpaper to fit your own personality: pictures of dogs playing poker, for example, or giant cantaloupe slugs. You can even draw your own wallpaper with the built-in Windows NT Paint program. Paint saves your work in the required wallpaper format: a special bitmap file ending in the letters BMP.

Double-Clicking

Windows NT places a great significance on something pretty simple: pressing a button on the mouse and releasing it. Pressing and releasing the button once is known as a *click*. Pressing and releasing the button twice in rapid succession is a *double-click*.

Windows NT watches carefully to see whether you've clicked or double-clicked on its more sensitive parts. The two actions are completely different: Clicking usually just selects something; double-clicking not only selects something, but it kick starts it into action, like launching a program.

- A double-click can take some practice to master, even if you have fingers. If you click too slowly, Windows NT thinks you're clicking twice — not double-clicking. Try clicking a little faster next time, and Windows NT will probably catch on.
- Can't click fast enough for Windows NT to tell the difference between a mere click and a rapid-fire double-click? Then grab the office computer guru and say that you need to have your Control Panel called up and your clicks fixed. If the guru looks too disgruntled to approach, tiptoe to the section on tinkering with the Control Panel in Chapter 11; you can find mouse adjustment instructions there.

Dragging and Dropping

Although the term drag and drop sounds as if it's straight out of a hitman's handbook, it's really a nonviolent mouse trick in Windows NT. Dragging and dropping is a way of moving something — say, a picture of an emu egg — from one part of your screen to another.

To drag, put the mouse pointer over the egg and hold down the mouse button. As you move the mouse across your desk, the pointer drags the egg across the screen. Put the pointer/egg where you want it, and then release the mouse button. The egg drops, uncracked. (If you hold down the right mouse button while dragging, Windows NT tosses a little menu in your face, asking whether you're *sure* that you want to move that egg across the screen.)

For more mouse fun, see "Clicking," "Double-Clicking," "The Mouse," and "Pointers/Arrows," in this chapter and, if you're not yet weak at the knees, the information on the parts of your computer in Chapter 2.

Drivers

Although Windows NT does plenty of work, it hires help when necessary. When Windows NT needs to talk to unfamiliar parts of your computer, it lets special drivers do the translation. A *driver* is a piece of software that enables Windows NT to communicate with parts of your computer.

Hundreds of computer companies sell computer attachables, from printers to sound cards to sprinkler systems. Microsoft requires these companies to write drivers for their products so that Windows NT knows the polite way to address them.

- Sometimes computer nerds say that your mouse driver is all messed up. They're not talking about your hand, even though your hand is what steers the mouse. They're talking about the piece of software that helps Windows NT talk and listen to the mouse.

- New versions of Windows NT often require new drivers. If you send a begging letter to the company that made your mouse, the company may mail you a new, updated driver on a floppy disk. Occasionally, you can get these new drivers directly from Microsoft, or if you're lucky, your children can help you find the driver on the company's "Web page" on the Internet. Check with the Network Administrator before doing any driver activities, though.

Files

A *file* is a collection of information in a form that the computer can play with. A *program file* contains instructions telling the computer to do something useful; like add up the money you spent on take-out food last month. A *data file* contains information you've created, like a picture of a golf ball you drew in the Windows NT Paint program.

- Files can't be touched or handled; they're invisible, unearthly things. Somebody figured out how to store files as little impulses on a round piece of specially coated plastic, or disk.

- A file is referred to by its filename. Early versions of Windows made people call files by a single word containing no more than eight characters. For example, FILENAME could be the name of a file, as could REPORT, SPONGE, or X. Yes, thinking up descriptive filenames back in those days was difficult.

  It was so difficult that Windows NT 4 and Windows 95 finally broke the barrier: Now you can call files by bunches of words, as long as the words (and spaces) don't total more than 255 characters.

- Filenames have optional extensions of up to three letters that usually refer to the program that created them. For example, the Windows NT Notepad program automatically saves files with the extension TXT. Microsoft realized that most people don't care about file extensions, so Windows NT no longer lists a file's extension when it's displaying filenames.

  You'll still see a file extension when Windows NT is confused about what program created a particular file — then Windows NT displays that confusing file's file extension on the screen, and asks you to choose which program created it. Once you tell Windows NT which programs create which files, it usually remembers which extensions come from which programs.

- Filenames still have more rules and regulations than the Department of Motor Vehicles, so for more information than you'll ever want to know about filenames, flip to Chapter 13.

Folders and Directories

In your everyday paper world, files are stored in folders in a cabinet. In the computer world, files are stored in a *directory* on a disk. Dusty old file cabinets are boring, but directories are even more dreadfully boring: They'll never hold any long-lost baseball cards.

So Windows NT swapped metaphors. Instead of holding files in directories, Windows NT holds files in folders. You can see the little pictures of the folders on your monitor.

The folders in Windows NT are really just directories, if you've already grown used to that term.

Maintaining files and working with folders can be painful experiences, so they're explained in Chapter 13. In the meantime, just think of folders and directories as separate work areas to keep files organized. Different directories and folders hold different projects; you move from directory to directory as you work on different things with your computer.

Windows NT 3.51 stored files in directories. Windows NT 4 stores files in folders. The two terms mean the same thing.

- A file cabinet's Vegetables folder can have an Asparagus folder nested inside for organizing material further.

- Technically, a folder in a folder is a nested subfolder that keeps related files from getting lost. For example, you can have subfolders for Steamed Asparagus and Raw Asparagus in the Asparagus subfolder, which lives in the Vegetable folder.

Graphical User Interfaces

The way people communicate with computers is called an interface. For example, the Enterprise's computer used a verbal interface — Captain Kirk just spoke to it.

Windows NT uses a *graphical user interface.* People talk to the computer through graphical symbols, or pictures. A graphical user interface works kind of like informational travel kiosks at airports — you select some little button symbols right on the screen to find out which hotels offer free airport shuttles.

- A graphical user interface is called a *GUI,* pronounced gooey, as in Huey, Dewey, Louie, and GUI.
- Despite what you read in the Microsoft full-page ads, Windows NT isn't the only GUI for a personal computer. Lesser-known systems like OS/2 Warp, UNIX, and Linux are also GUIs (pronounced gooeys, as in those are Huey's GUIs).
- The little graphical symbols or buttons in a graphical user interface are called icons.

Hardware and Software

Alert! Alert! Fasten your seat belt so you don't slump forward when reading about these two particularly boring terms: *hardware* and *software*.

Your CD player is hardware; so are the stereo amplifier, speakers, and batteries in the boombox. By itself, the CD player doesn't do anything but hum. It needs music to disturb the neighbors. The music is the software, or the information processed by the CD player.

- Now you can unfasten your seat belt and relax for a bit. Computer hardware refers to anything you can touch, including hard things like a printer, a monitor, disks, and disk drives.
- Software is the ethereal stuff that makes the hardware do something fun. A piece of software is called a *program*. Programs come on disks (or CDs, if you've anted up for the latest computer gear).
- Software has very little to do with lingerie.
- When somber technical nerds (STNs) say, "It must be a hardware problem," they mean that something must be wrong with your computer itself: its disk drive, keyboard, or central processing unit (CPU). When they say, "It must be a software problem," they mean that something is wrong with the program you're trying to run from the disk.

Icons

An icon is a little picture. Windows NT fills the screen with icons. You choose among them to make Windows NT do different things. For example, you choose the Printer icon, the little picture of the printer, to make your computer print something. Icons are just fancy names for cute buttons.

You'll find icons in just about every Windows NT-based program.

- Windows NT relies on icons for nearly everything, from opening files to releasing the winged monkeys.
- Some icons have explanatory titles, like Open File or Terrorize Dorothy. Others make you guess (for example, the Little Lightbulb icon, which brings up a little tip for using the program).
- For more icon stuff, see "Graphical User Interfaces" earlier in this chapter.

- Can't figure out an icon's function in life? Rest your mouse pointer over it for a few moments; in many Windows NT-based programs, a box pops up to give you helpful material explaining what the icon is supposed to do.

Kilobytes, Megabytes, and So On

Figuring out the size of a real file folder is easy: Just look at the thickness of the papers stuffed in and around it. But computer files are invisible, so their size is measured in *bytes* (which is pronounced like what Dracula does).

A byte is pretty much like a character or letter in a word. For example, the word *sodium-free* contains 11 bytes. (The hyphen counts as a byte.) Computer nerds picked up the metric system a lot more quickly than the rest of us, so bytes are measured in kilos (1,000), megas (1,000,000), and gigas (way huge).

A page of double-spaced text is about 1,000 bytes, known as 1 kilobyte, which is often abbreviated as 1K. One thousand of those kilobytes is a megabyte, or 1MB. Your computer's hard disk is full of bytes; most hard disks today contain between 200MB and 1GB (a gigabyte).

Big Warning Department: Today's software sticks a bunch of special coding and graphics into documents these days: A single page of text can easily consume 40K of space.

If you're working on a large network, your own computer may not have a large hard disk. Instead, the hard disk (or hard disks — some computers have a whole bunch of them) may be attached to a big computer — the computer running Windows NT Server. Everybody in the office then accesses the information on the server through the network cables, like four people sharing one milkshake with a handful of straws.

- Unlike hard disks, which come in a wide variety of sizes to meet different needs, almost all floppy disks hold 1.4MB of information. (A few older varieties hold less.)
- All files are measured in bytes, regardless of whether they contain text. For example, that Windows NT logo some people use as background art for their Windows NT Desktop takes up 78,736 bytes. (For information on using that Windows NT logo, see Chapter 11. Chapter 11 shows how to use your own files for wallpaper.)
- The Windows NT Explorer or My Computer window can tell you how many bytes each of your files consumes. (Or click on the file's name with your right mouse button and choose Properties from the menu that pops up.) To find out more, check out the information on Explorer in Chapter 13.

One kilobyte doesn't really equal 1,000 bytes. That would be too easy. Instead, this byte stuff is based on the number two. One kilobyte is really 1,024 bytes, which is 2 raised to the 10th power, or 2^{10}. (Computers love mathematical details, especially when a 2 is involved.) For more byte-size information, see Table 3-1.

Table 3-1 Ultra-Precise Details from the Slide-Rule Crowd

Term	*Abbreviation*	*Rough Size*	*Ultra-Precise Size*
Byte	1 byte	1 byte	
Kilobyte	K or KB	1,000 bytes	1,024 bytes
Megabyte	M or MB	1,000,000 bytes	1,048,576 bytes
Gigabyte	G or GB	1,000,000,000 bytes	1,073,741,824 bytes

Loading, Running, Executing, and Launching

Paper files are yanked from a file cabinet and placed onto a desk for easy reference. On a computer, files are loaded from a disk and placed into the computer's memory so you can do important stuff with them. You can't work with a file or program until it has been loaded into the computer's memory.

When you run, execute, or launch a program, you're merely starting it up so you can use it. Load means pretty much the same thing, but some people fine-tune its meaning to describe when a program file brings in a data file.

- The Windows NT Start button enables picture lovers to start programs by using icons. The Windows NT Explorer enables text-and-word lovers to start programs by clicking on names in a list (although Explorer lets you click on icons, too, if you prefer).
- If you're feeling particularly bold, you can load programs by using the command line hidden in the Start button. For the full dirt, check out the information on the Start button in Chapter 12 and the information on Explorer in Chapter 13.

Memory

Whoa! How did this ugly memory stuff creep in here? Luckily, it all boils down to one key sentence:

The more memory a computer has, the more pleasantly Windows NT behaves.

- Memory is measured in bytes, just like a file. All computers sold today have at least 640 kilobytes, or 640K, of memory; most come with much, much more memory.
- Windows NT requires Intel computers (fast 486 and Pentiums) to have at least 12 megabytes, or 12MB, of memory, or it won't even bother to come out of the box. And it won't play nicely with others unless you provide 16MB or more of memory.

Memory and hard disk space are both measured in bytes, but they're two different things: Memory is what the computer uses for quick, on-the-fly calculations when programs are up and running on-screen. Hard disk space is what the computer uses to store unused files and programs.

Everybody's computer contains more hard disk space than memory because hard disks — also known as hard drives — are a great deal cheaper. Also, a hard disk remembers things even when the computer is turned off. A computer's memory, on the other hand, is washed completely clean whenever someone turns it off or pokes its reset button.

The Mouse

A mouse is a smooth little plastic thing that looks like Soap on a Rope. It rests on a little roller, or ball, and its tail plugs into the back of the PC. When you push the mouse across your desk, the mouse sends its current location through its tail to the PC. By moving the mouse around on the desk, you move a corresponding arrow across the screen.

You can wiggle the mouse in circles and watch the arrow make spirals. Or to be practical, you can maneuver the on-screen arrow over an on-screen button and click the mouse button to boss Windows NT around. (Refer to "Clicking," "Double-Clicking," and "Pointers/Arrows" in this chapter and, if you haven't run out of steam, turn to Chapter 2 for information on the parts of your computer.)

Multitasking and Task Switching

Windows NT can run two or more programs at the same time, but computer nerds take overly tedious steps to describe the process. So skip this section because you'll never need to know it.

Even though the words task switching and multitasking often have an exclamation point in computer ads, there's nothing really exciting about them.

When you run two programs and switch back and forth between them, you're task switching. For example, if Terry calls while you're reading a book, you put down the book and talk to Terry. You are task switching: stopping one task and starting another. The process is similar to running your word processor and then stopping to look up a phone number in the Exchange program.

But when you run two programs simultaneously, you're multitasking. For example, if you continue reading your book while listening to Terry talk about the fabulous special on string beans at the grocery store, you're multitasking: performing two tasks at the same time. In Windows NT, multitasking can be as simple as playing a Solitaire game while printing something in the background.

These two concepts differ only subtly, and yet computer nerds make a big deal out of the difference. Everybody else shrugs and says, "So what?"

Networks

Networks connect PCs with cables so that employees can share equipment and information. Employees can all send stuff to one printer, for example, or they can send messages back and forth talking about Jane's weird new hairstyle.

Windows NT, which was built for networks, does something a little strange: It makes networks almost invisible to their users. When you open a file on your computer, the network automatically fetches that file from another computer way down the hall — yet the file pops onto your screen quickly and easily, just as if it were stored inside your own computer.

Of course, this explanation assumes that the network is working correctly and that somebody else in the office hasn't already grabbed that file onto his or her own computer. It also assumes that you've been granted access to that file, that you haven't forgotten your logon password, and that your computer's network cable hasn't fallen out.

Just be glad that you, as a Windows NT beginner, are safely absolved from knowing anything about networks. Leave network stuff to that poor person in charge known as the Network Administrator.

Plug and Play

Historically, installing new hardware devices has required substantial technical expertise to configure and load hardware and software. Basically, that means only geeks could figure out how to fix their computers and add new gadgets to them.

So a bunch of computer vendors hunched together around a table and came up with Plug and Play — a way for Windows to set up new gadgets for your computer automatically, with little or no human intervention. You plug in your latest gadget, and Windows "interviews" it, checking to see what special settings it needs. Then Windows automatically flips the right switches.

Because Windows keeps track of which switches are flipped, none of the parts argue over who got the best settings. Better yet, users don't have to do anything but plug the darn thing into their computers and flip the On switch.

At least, that's the way it was supposed to work. But Windows NT doesn't support Plug and Play. Unlike Windows 95 or Windows 98, Windows NT can't recognize newly installed gadgets automatically.

- Gadgets that say "Plug and Play" on their boxes aren't any easier to install under Windows NT than gadgets that don't feature those words. Sure, they probably still work. You just have to flip all the switches yourself to install the thing.
- Some people refer to Plug and Play as PnP.
- Other, more skeptical people refer to Plug and Play as Plug and Pray. (The technology is still rather new.)

Pointers/Arrows

This one sounds easy at first: When you roll the mouse around on your desk, you see a little arrow move around on-screen. That arrow is your pointer, and it is also called an arrow. (Almost everything in Windows NT has two names.)

The pointer serves as your electronic index finger. Instead of pushing an on-screen button with your finger, you move the pointer over that button and click the left button on the mouse.

So what's the hard part? Well, that pointer doesn't always stay an arrow. Depending on where the pointer is located on the Windows NT screen, it can turn into a straight line, a two-headed arrow, a four-headed arrow, a little pillar, or a zillion other things. Each of the symbols makes the mouse do something slightly different. Luckily, you'll find these and other arrowheads covered in Chapter 2.

Programs/Applications

Most people call a computer program a program. In Windows NT, programs are called applications.

- We dunno why.
- Those free programs that came with Windows NT (HyperTerminal, WordPad, Phone Dialer, and so on) aren't called programs or applications. They're called Windows NT applets.
- This book uses the terms program and application interchangeably, because they're pretty much the same thing. But it hardly uses the name applet at all because it sounds so funny.

Quitting or Exiting Programs

Done working with a program? Then feel free to "turn it off" by quitting or exiting the program.

Exiting Windows NT programs is fairly easy because all the programs are supposed to use the same special exit command. You simply click on the little X in the upper-right corner of the program's window. Or if you prefer using the keyboard, you hold down the Alt key (either one of them, if you have two) and press the key labeled F4. (The F4 key is a function key; function keys are either in one row along the top of your keyboard or in two rows along its leftmost edge. Check out Chapter 2 for more function key fun.)

If you're done with a program but think you may need to use it again really soon, just minimize the program: Find the three little squares in the program's topmost, right corner, and click in the square with the little bar. The window shrinks itself down into a little icon along your computer's taskbar — that bar running along an edge of your screen. (Click on that minimized program's icon when you're ready to use the program again.)

Don't quit a program by just flicking off your computer's power switch. Doing so can foul up your computer's innards. Instead, you must leave the program responsibly so that it has time to perform its housekeeping chores before it shuts down.

- When you press Alt+F4 or click on the little X in the upper-right corner, the program asks whether you want to save any changes you've made to the file. Normally, you click on the button that says something like "Yes, by all means, save the work I've spent the last three hours trying to create." (If you've muffed things up horribly, click on the No button. Windows NT disregards any work you've done and lets you start over from scratch.)
- If by some broad stretch of your fingers you press Alt+F4 by accident, click on the button that says Cancel, and the program pretends that you never tried to leave it. You can continue as if nothing happened.
- The Alt+F4 trick doesn't work for any of those old DOS-based programs you may have lying around — even if they're running in their own window. You must exit the DOS program by using that program's own special exit keys, which differ from program to program. Complicated? Well, yes. That's why people are switching to Windows.

  How can you tell the difference between DOS-based programs and Windows-based programs? DOS programs don't have the same "look and feel" as Windows programs, nor do they have the same familiar menu bar across their top, with words like "File" and "Edit."

- Windows NT 3.51-and Windows 3.1-based programs have a square button, located in the uppermost left corner, that looks like an aerial view of a single-slot toaster. Double-clicking on that toaster exits the program. Windows NT still lets you close most Windows programs by either double-clicking in the uppermost left corner (although the programs don't have that toaster anymore). However, single-clicking on the X in the program's uppermost right corner is usually easier. But either action tells the program that you want to close it down.

- Save your work before exiting a program or turning off your computer. Computers aren't smart enough to save it automatically (although they're usually polite enough to ask if you'd like them to save it for you).

Quitting or Exiting Windows NT 4

When you're ready to throw in the computing towel and head for greener pastures, you need to stop, or quit, any programs you've been using. The terms quit and exit mean pretty much the same thing: make the current program on-screen stop running so you can go away and do something a little more rewarding.

To quit Windows NT, click on the Start button and choose the Shut Down command. A box pops up, as shown in Figure 3-3.

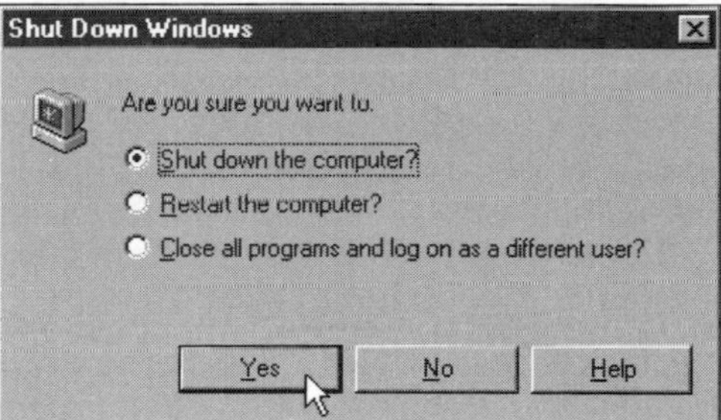

Figure 3-3: Choosing the Shut Down command brings up a variety of options.

Each option does something slightly different:

- **Shut down the computer?:** This option "logs you off" the computer and prepares the animal for being turned off. The computer shuts down all your currently running Windows NT-based programs (politely asking whether you'd like to save any unsaved work) and then leaves a message on the screen saying that turning off the computer is safe. (If you choose this option by mistake, just click the Restart button in the middle of the message to rev the thing up again.)

  Although you should always turn off your monitor when you're through computing for the day, ask your Network Administrator whether or not you should turn off your computer. Network Administrators treat matters like that very seriously.

- **Restart the computer?:** Choose this option if the computer seems to be acting weird. Windows NT basically saves all your work, shuts down your programs, and restarts the computer from scratch. Something akin to shaking a pillowcase, this option can sometimes knock out the pebble that was causing so much grief.

- **Close all programs and log on as a different user?:** Choose this option if you're unsure of what else to choose. It "logs you off" the computer, essentially locking up your own account. Other people can use the computer — in fact, the computer tells passersby that they can press Ctrl+Alt+Delete to log on if they'd like to use the computer. But they have to log on with their own passwords and use their own accounts.

Save Command

Save means to send the work you just created on your computer to a disk for safekeeping. Unless you specifically save your work, your computer thinks you've just been fiddling around for the past four hours. You need to specifically tell the computer to save your work before it will safely store the work on a disk.

Thanks to Microsoft's snapping leather whips, all Windows NT-based programs use the same Save command, no matter what company wrote them. Press and release the Alt, F, and S keys in any Windows NT program, in that order, and the computer saves your work.

If you're saving something for the first time, Windows NT asks you to think up a filename for the work and pick a folder (the thing that earlier versions of Windows referred to as a directory) to stuff the new file into. Luckily, this stuff is covered in Chapter 5.

- You can save files to a hard disk or a floppy disk.
- If you prefer using the mouse to save files, click on the word File from the row of words along the top of the program. When a menu drops down, choose Save.
- Choose descriptive filenames for your work. Windows NT gives you 255 characters to work with, so a file named "June Report on Squeegee Sales" is easier to relocate than one named "Stuff."
- Some programs, like Microsoft Word for Windows, have an autosave feature that automatically saves your work every five minutes or so.

Save As Command

Huh? Save as what? A chemical compound? Naw, the Save As command just gives you a chance to save your work with a different name and in a different location.

Suppose that you open the July 1998 Financial Report file in your Stuff folder and change a few sentences around. You want to save the changes, but you don't want to lose the original stuff. So you choose Save As and type in the new name, **July 1998 Financial Report Number 2**.

- The Save As command is identical to the Save command when you're first trying to save something new: You can choose a fresh name and location for your work.
- 'Tis better to have loved and lost than to have choked on a meatball and coughed.

Shortcuts

The shortcut concept has appealed to most people since childhood: Why bother walking around the block to get to school when a shortcut through Mr. McGurdy's backyard can get you there twice as fast?

The same goes for Windows NT. Instead of wading through a bunch of menus to get somewhere, you can create a shortcut and assign it to an icon. Then when you double-click on the shortcut icon, Windows NT immediately takes you there and loads the file.

You can create a shortcut to your word processor, for example, and leave the shortcut icon sitting on your Desktop within easy reach. A shortcut is simply a push button that loads a file or program. You can even make shortcuts for accessing your printer, disk drive, or a popular folder. In fact, shortcuts are so much fun, we cover them again in Chapter 12.

- The ever-helpful Start button automatically makes a shortcut to the last 15 documents you've opened. Click on the Start button, choose Documents, and you see shortcuts waiting for you to discover them.
- Unfortunately, the Start button keeps track of only the last 15 documents you've opened. If you're looking for the sixteenth one, you won't find a shortcut waiting. Also, not all programs tell the Start button about recently opened documents; the shortcuts then don't appear on the list. (It's not your fault, if that makes you feel better.)

- A shortcut in Windows NT is very similar to an icon in Windows NT 3.51 Program Manager: a push button that starts a program. If you delete a shortcut, you haven't deleted a program; you've just removed a button that started that program. You'll find much more information about shortcuts in Chapter 12.

Temp Files

Like children who don't put away the peanut butter jar, Windows NT-based programs leave things lying around. These things are called *temp files* — secret files that the program creates to store stuff in while the program's running. The program normally deletes those temp files automatically when you exit it. It occasionally forgets, however, and leaves them cluttering up your hard disk. Stern lectures leave very little impression.

- Temp files usually (but not always) end with the letters TMP. Common temp filenames include `~DOCOD37.TMP`, `~WRI3FOE.TMP`, the occasional stray `~$DIBLCA.ASD`, and similar-looking files that start with the wavy ~ thing. (Some people call it a tilde.)

- If you exit Windows NT the naughty way — by just flicking the computer's Off switch — Windows NT doesn't have a chance to clean up its temp file mess, nor to shut down its network properly. If you keep exiting this way, you'll eventually see hundreds of TMP files lying around your hard disk, and the Network Administrator hanging around your desk with ax in hand. Be sure to exit Windows NT the Good Bear way: by clicking on the Start button and choosing Shut down from the menu that pops up.
- You don't really need to worry about temp files. Just remember that if you exit your programs the way you're supposed to, you reduce the likelihood of the Network Administrator visiting your workstation bearing an unfriendly look.

The Windows

Windows NT lets you run several programs at the same time by placing them in windows. A window is just a little box.

You can move the boxes around. You can make them bigger or smaller. You can make them fill your entire screen. You can make them turn into little icons at the bottom of your screen. You can spend hours playing with windows. In fact, most frustrated new Windows NT users do.

- You can put as many windows on-screen as you want, peeping at all of them at the same time or just looking into each one individually. This activity appeals to the voyeur in all of us. (Window peeking, moving, and resizing information appears in Chapter 7.)
- For instructions on how to retrieve a lost window from the pile, head immediately to Chapter 8.

- When you shrunk a window in Windows NT 3.51, the window would turn itself into a little icon and sit along the bottom of your screen, waiting for further action. In Windows NT 4, however, shrunken windows turn into little buttons on a bar known as a taskbar. You can find much more information about the taskbar in Chapter 12.

Chapter 4

Network Things Administrators Think You Already Know

In This Chapter

- Understanding the network terms used in connection with Windows NT
- Cross-referencing chapters where topics introduced are talked about in detail

People who run networks are distracted, sometimes distraught, and generally bursting at the seams with jolly jargon and acronyms. They love this alien language so much, they've even got an acronym for acronyms — TLA — which stands for Three-Letter Acronym!

However, you don't have to adopt a foreign tongue. Just practice a look of alert intelligence and always be prepared to demonstrate the look. After you have that look down, whip it out when you hear a term that is totally meaningless to you. Nod — alertly and intelligently — and scoot back to your cubicle and this chapter.

For quick translations of those pesky TLAs — pardon, three-letter acronyms — check out Chapter 24.

Account or User Account

In most corporate settings, security is a big issue. Like everybody else, businesses have secrets, including financial records, personnel files, and even real-live trade secrets — all things that some people should see and others shouldn't.

All these things have to be on the network somewhere. Not only do the corporate bigwigs need to keep spies from finding out the secret recipe for the company's Super Salsa, but they also need to keep you from finding out that Roger (the weasel!) is making more money than anyone else in the department.

The primary way to control who can access different things on the network is the *account* (also called user account), which is what the Network Administrator sets up for you on your first day of work. You're given a username (like RathboneA or SharonC) and a password.

- Your first password is given to you by the Network Administrator, but you're required to provide your own, secret password as soon as you log on for the first time.
- Without an account, you can't use any machine on the network. The computers all ignore you. Your user account is defined by the administrator and pretty much says what you can and can't do on the network.
- The Network Administrator, being all-powerful, can change just about any of the settings in your account, so appeal to that person when you want to check out the new color printer or play with the CD-ROM tower, because you won't be able to play with these toys without permission.

Client/Server

Client/server is the term for the kind of network Windows NT sets up. Here's how it works: The *server* is the big machine or machines that store great big files, applications, or other types of information. Your own computer is the *client*. The network is the medium by which you get at these big files. After you've done what you need to do, the files are saved back on the server.

Think of it as going into a restaurant to eat. That makes you the client. Your server (who in California is probably named Brad or Ronni) hands over your soup. There's a fly in it, so you send it back. The server takes it into the kitchen, fishes out the fly, and brings the same soup back. This is the basic client/server relationship — in the end, the server has the last word, whether you know it or not.

Servers are the machines on a network that provide services to other computers so that these other computers can spend their time doing their regular business. For example

- *File servers* mean that workstations don't have to have humongous hard disks. You can fetch files from servers and return the files when you're done.
- *Print servers* handle directing printing traffic to the right printers and determining what prints first and what can wait. This means not only that printers can be shared but also that your computer doesn't have to wait for a printer to be free before getting rid of the print job and moving on to other tasks.

Controller, backup controller

On a network with *domains* (described later in this chapter), each domain has at least one controller and one backup controller. The *domain controller* is the computer that stores all the information about the domain — details about users, computers, security settings, and so forth.

The controller is where all the NT Workstations check in at logon, logoff, and many times in between. (Don't worry — this "logon, logoff" stuff gets its own explanation later in this chapter.) That's why at least one backup controller must have the same information that the controller has. That way when (not if) the primary controller is busy (or overworked, or just plain too tired to function at the moment), the backup controller can jump in and keep everything operational.

The point? If a computer freaks out, all the company's important information won't freak out with it. At least, that's what Microsoft means when it says Windows NT is a very "stable environment."

On an NT network, the server always runs Windows NT Server. Because you're reading this book, you're probably running Windows NT Workstation — the client portion of Windows NT.

Computer Name

Just like people, pets, and some beloved automobiles, every networked computer has its own name. With all the information flowing back and forth on the network, the names let Windows NT keep track of where everything is coming from and where it's going to. Also, names are much nicer than numbers. For example, RECEPTIONIST is easier to recognize than AC432SUB5695. Computer names are usually pretty short but can be as long as 15 characters.

To see the names of computers on your network, double-click on your Desktop's Network Neighborhood icon, described later in this chapter.

Domain

A *domain* is a collection of computers on a network. It's usually set up to group together all the people in one department or all the people doing the same kind of work. Many networks have only one domain; a really big network can have many domains.

- Knowing what domain you're in is important only if you want to play Hearts with your friend in another domain. In that case, the administrator has to give you permission to talk to the other domain (try to come up with a reason that doesn't include recreational topics).
- To qualify as a domain, the group of computers must designate one of its number to be a controller — the computer that bosses around everyone else in the domain.

Computers in a domain need to have only a couple of things in common: They all use the same servers, and they all have the same rules about security.

Exchange

Exchange is the part of Windows NT that handles messaging — in other words, all your internal and external electronic mail goes through Exchange (your faxes, too, eventually).

Have a look at Chapter 16 for advice on using Exchange.

File systems (FAT, NTFS)

Windows NT can use one of two methods for storing files on hard disks. One is FAT (File Allocation Table), the method used by DOS and Windows 3.*x*. The other is NTFS (New Technology File System), which stores information much more efficiently and is more secure. NTFS is a formatting method created by Windows NT.

The biggest disadvantage to NTFS is that computers running any operating system other than Windows NT can't read an NTFS-formatted hard disk unless it's through a network. But NTFS can read hard disks formatted as FAT or VFAT.

The original Windows 95 uses VFAT — a version of FAT modified to allow long filenames. Windows 98 and the updated version of Windows 95 have another system available — FAT32, which is better than FAT but can't be used by NT (for dreary technical reasons too boring to discuss). Except for the long filenames, VFAT looks like FAT, acts like FAT and is indistinguishable from FAT. (And, contrary to popular belief, VFAT does not stand for Very FAT.)

If a computer is using NTFS, you can't boot the machine from a floppy disk. That means someone can't get access to a computer without going through logon. Network Administrators love being able to foil snoops. (That's because they started their careers as snoops themselves.)

Finally, if you don't understand this whole FAT, VFAT, NTFS stuff, don't worry. It's something for Network Administrators to chew their lower lips over, not you.

Home Directory

A *home directory* is where you store all your computer files; everyone on the network has one. The home directory can be on your own machine, but more often it's on one of the servers. Under most conditions, where it is doesn't make any difference to you.

If you can log on from more than one computer, your home directory is on a server somewhere. Very handy. Not so handy when the server in question is out of action, because then you can be out of action, too.

Logoff

When your computer is on, you are known to be on the network because you used your account to sign on. So if you go away and leave your computer on, some nefarious person (or the three-year-old child of a nice person) can come along and mess things up. And if your user account is the one that's active, guess who gets blamed?

That's why it's important to log off when leaving your computer in any area where other people can get to it. Logging off is simply telling the operating system that you're leaving and that it should break the network connections in an orderly fashion. (Very important to networks — order.)

Just going to the lunchroom for a caffeine fix? See the logging off section in Chapter 5 for a way to protect your computer without having to log off completely.

Quick answer department: For a quick way to log off your computer, click the Start button in the bottom-left corner of your screen and choose Shut Down from the menu. Then click on the button that says Close all programs and log on as a different user. That quickly logs you off the network and lets you head for the deli.

Logon

As with a military base, you can't just wander onto a network. A network has a sentry here, too, only it's called the *domain controller*. You identify yourself (your username) and supply your password. If everything's okay, you're allowed to pass. If it's not, you're shot dead. No, wait, that's not done on networks anymore. Instead, you just get a rude sort of message that says something's wrong, and you're denied entry.

Maybe you typed in your password incorrectly (remember, the password is *case sensitive,* meaning it considers Bullfrog and bullfrog to be two different passwords). Or perhaps you misspelled your username. Try again.

If repeated tries don't get you on, it's time to wave your hand for help. (The administrator probably did something dumb but unintentional, so don't be hard on the poor schlub.)

Mapped Drive

A *mapped drive* is a hard drive (hard disk) on another computer that shows up in Explorer (or My Computer) as if it were on your own machine. For instance, Nancy's C drive could show up on your computer as your own F drive. When you copy things to your F drive, it automatically is mapped to Nancy's C drive. The drive has to be shared for you to map it. (See "Sharing" later in this section.)

If you have a powerful urge to map a hard disk that's on another computer so that it looks just like one of your hard drives, saunter over to Chapter 9 for the step-by-step on how to do it.

With Version 4.0, mapped drives are a lot less necessary than they used to be, because of the addition of Network Neighborhood. You can access any of the shared drives, files, and folders by just clicking your way through the computers, drives, and folders listed in Network Neighborhood. If you find yourself constantly using a particular drive or folder on another person's computer, however, you may want to map that drive so it appears as a letter on your own computer. Mapped drives are sort of a cumbersome, network version of shortcuts.

Member Server

A member server is a computer running Windows NT Server that's not a controller. A machine like that probably holds big databases or other files that a lot of people have to be able to get at — and get at quickly. A member server is good for that because it doesn't have to do any of the controller work and can dedicate itself to serving up files (or whatever its main role in life is).

- For the most part, whether a computer is a plain member server or a controller server makes no difference to you. Breathe a sigh of relief.
- "Member server" is really a Microsoft term. Most people just say, "server," or "file server," either of which works just as well.

Network Administrator

Every network needs an administrator to keep the network going. This is the haggard-looking person you see scuttling down the corridor to fix a non-working printer or the accounting department's e-mail.

Sometimes the administrator is Ken in the next cubicle, who spends an hour a day maintaining the network. More likely, it's stressed-out Stella, who's there when you arrive for work and is the last one to leave at night.

The administrator (though a network may have more than one) is the person you go to when you can't log on or log off, when you can't find other computers on the network, or when your system has collapsed in some undignified way.

Network Administrators, being very much like real people, respond differently to different stimuli. Until you know whether your administrator is a charming fellow or a real pickle-puss, it's important to tread carefully. And regardless of the administrator's personality, always provide the occasional small offering, such as Doritos or Jolt cola (which is mother's milk to them).

Network

A *network* is no more than a bunch of computers connected together to share information of some sort. The connection can be permanent, in the form of cables, or it can be temporary, using phone lines or even wireless links. Networks can include all sorts of bells and whistles — huge masses of technology so Barbara can send you e-mail asking whether you wanna have lunch on Tuesday.

You can find more info on Networks in Chapters 9 and 16.

Network Neighborhood

The Network Neighborhood is right on your Desktop.

Double-click on the icon, and you see all the computers on your domain (at least the ones you're allowed to see), including your own. By clicking your way through the folders, you can get at any document, file, folder, or program that's being shared.

Network Neighborhood has an icon for your computer, and you can use it to get at things on your own machine. Yes, it is a very roundabout way to open a file. Using Network Neighborhood to get what you want is covered in Chapter 9.

Password

A password, along with your username, is what you need whenever you want to fire up your computer and log onto the network. Your first password is probably given to you, but then you're required to make up one of your very own almost immediately.

Everything you'd ever care to know about passwords is at the very beginning of Chapter 5.

Find out early what your network's policy is about passwords. In some cases, you can be required to change yours every 60 days or so. You don't want to be caught unaware one morning when you're in a desperate hurry and the logon procedure cheerily announces that you have to provide a new password before proceeding. Yikes.

Peer-to-Peer

Peer-to-peer is a type of network that doesn't have controllers. Every machine in the network is equal. It seems very democratic, but someone still has to administer the network, even if it's not a very big job. Otherwise, people give different names to printers and hard disks, and soon your office starts looking like the floor of the New York Stock Exchange, with people standing around yelling at each other.

- Peer-to-peer is a perfectly good way to set up any computer network with ten or fewer computers, even if they're not running Windows NT. Each computer acts as both a client and a server.
- Peer-to-peer networks are sometimes called workgroups.

Permissions

Permissions are bestowed by the Network Administrator (and a few other honchos) and basically say who gets to use what things in what way. For example, you need permission to use either a printer on the network or the cool Games folder on Nick's computer. Nick can't do it himself.

Permissions are also graciously granted for you to open particular folders, use a network fax, or get an Internet connection. Permissions can be so specific that they're assigned down to the individual file level (but only on a hard disk that's using that complicated NTFS stuff discussed earlier).

- The usual kind of permission is called full control, which means that you can do whatever you like with the object: Read it, change it, save it, and even delete it.
- Other levels of permission, commonly found with files and folders, let you read the files but not change them, or both read and change but not delete. Yep, those Network Administrators are attending to some pretty bothersome details. (And those details get a good shake-down in Chapter 9.)

- Permissions are talked about interchangeably with rights, but they're not the same thing. Permissions apply to particular things; rights apply to the system as a whole. This only matters in the administrator's alternate universe. In the real world, you can use whichever word pops into your head first.

Remote Access

If you've ever called up CompuServe or America Online, you've already done remote access. It just means that you can use a computer to connect to another computer (or network of computers) even if you're not directly connected by a network cable.

Windows NT has remote access built in. If your company uses remote access, you (or somebody) can phone in from Beijing or Biloxi, connect to the network, and do whatever business you need to do, just as if you were in the next cubicle.

Remote access business is sometimes handled by a Remote Access server, which is a computer that receives the phone calls, handles the verification process (keeping strangers out), and directs traffic. Any old computer can be a Remote Access server because even the pokiest computer can handle data a zillion times faster than a phone line.

Resource

Resource is just a generic name to cover anything that's shared over the network — a file, a folder, a printer. If you can see it on your screen, it's a resource. Just because it's a resource doesn't necessarily mean you have permission to use it. See the section, "Permissions," in this chapter.

Server

Server is an annoying term because it's used to mean different things. Most of the time, it means a controller on the network. But you can also have computers called file servers, print servers, fax servers — on and on.

Even so, you're safe in assuming that every server on a Windows NT network does the following things:

- Uses Windows NT Server as its operating system
- Provides something to the workstation (that's you) that the workstation doesn't have

The second item sums up the strength of a network with servers: Expensive hardware can be shared, and processor work can be farmed out to computers that have little else to do.

- If you're speaking of the big kahuna on the network, the controller, always say The Server. (A reverent or bitter tone can be added, depending on the circumstance, but always speak in Capital Letters.)
- The "Client/Server" entry earlier in this chapter has more on the relationship between you and The Server.

Sharing

Unless you're a member of the Network Administrator's inner circle, you have nothing to say about what's shared. The administrator and a few other cronies with some of the administrator's powers are the only ones who can determine that.

But once something's shared, you can make use of shared folders (directories) on other computers. And you can use any of the shared printers or other resources on the network — providing you also have permission to use them.

TCP/IP

TCP/IP is a term that the technically tiresome throw around with great abandon. Simply put, TCP/IP is the protocol that the Internet works on — and probably your network, too. A protocol is a set of rules about how data is transmitted back and forth. Computers using different protocols can't talk to each other.

Okay, here it comes. TCP/IP stands for Transmission Control Protocol/ Internet Protocol.

Username

Two pieces of information are needed to log onto the network: your password and your username. Your username is not exactly the same as your real name, because most networks have a standard way of assigning usernames.

For example, every username on one network may be a person's last name plus a first initial, or each one may be a first name plus some number of letters from the last name. The standard was determined when the network was set up so that there could be some consistency. So Cathy O'Dea may end up being CathyO, or Wayne Wong's username could be WongWay, depending on the network.

- You may be able to change a truly unfortunate username if you appeal at once to the administrator's good graces. But don't wait — the longer you have it, the harder it is to change.
- You're assigned a username at the same time you get your starting password.
- Passwords will (and should) change, but your username goes on forever.

Workgroup

A workgroup is a collection of Windows computers that are grouped together because they're all doing the same kind of work or they're all in the same department. Within the workgroup, all the computers are peers, and the users themselves decide what is shared with other members of the group. Workgroups can be part of an actual client/server network.

If you're assigned to a workgroup, you log on to the workgroup or you log onto the domain you're part of. You can't be in two places at once, as Lt. Columbo loved to point out.

Workstation

In general, when people talk about a workstation, they mean some big, powerful hotshot computer that can calculate rocket trajectories in real time. True, some workstations can do all that and more. But in the world of Windows NT, a workstation is any computer that's running Windows NT Workstation as its operating system.

That the two types of computers may coincide is irrelevant.

Part II

Making Windows NT Do Something

"I told him we were looking for software that would give us greater productivity, so he sold me client software that came with these signs."

In this part . . .

After you get used to its rough edges, Windows NT can be more fun than a plastic snap-together stegosaurus from the bottom of a Cracker Jack box. It's especially fun to show neighboring coworkers the built-in screen savers, like the one that straps you into a starship and cruises toward the Fifth Quadrant's snack shop at warp speed. You can even adjust the ship's speed through the Windows NT Control Panel.

Unfortunately, some spoil-sport will eventually mutter the words that brings everything back to Earth: "Let's see Windows NT do something useful, like send e-mail, or teach Bill not to leave his old sandwiches in the lunch room's refrigerator for longer than two months."

Toss this eminently practical part at them to quiet 'em down.

Chapter 5

Getting to Work with Windows NT

In This Chapter

- Logging onto Windows NT
- Starting a program
- Finding the secret pull-down menus
- Loading a file
- Putting two programs on-screen
- Using the keyboard
- Printing your work
- Saving your work
- Quitting Windows NT

Welcome to the world of Windows NT, where your computer lives in social contact with bunches of other computers. Here, networking no longer refers to people trying to find better jobs at cocktail parties. No, in the Windows NT world, networking refers to how the computers interact, hopefully coexisting in peace and harmony.

Consider this chapter a guide toward Social Etiquette in Windows NT. Here, you discover how to make Windows NT not only recognize you but treat you politely when you sit in front of your computer. You find out where the programs live and how to address them properly. You see where some of the other computers live and how to find the right ones.

The chapter explains how to coax Windows NT into running two or more programs simultaneously without complaining. It also shows how to send your work to the printer so you can convince doubting coworkers that you are, indeed, capable of making Windows NT do something useful.

Finally, you find out how to log off Windows NT — a required method of bidding your computer adieu until you meet again.

Logging Onto Windows NT

When a Windows NT Workstation starts its day, the computer goes through its usual ritual of checking to see that all of its parts are still present and working. That's nothing unusual. What is unusual is the first real screen that you see. In front of the Windows NT logo is a box (complete with a creepy animated hand) that instructs you to "press Ctrl+Alt+Delete to log on."

Go ahead and hold down all three keys simultaneously. (Most people use both hands for this.) This key combination opens the Logon Information box, where you're asked to type in your username and password. Enter them into the appropriate boxes and click on OK.

- Pressing Ctrl+Alt+Delete while running some earlier versions of Windows or DOS causes the computer to die violently, taking all your unsaved work down with it. Windows NT is much more mild-mannered about the magical Ctrl+Alt+Delete sequence, so don't be scared if the computer tells you to press those keys — it's okay now.
- The User Name box already contains the name of the last person to use the computer. If that isn't you, double-click on the name in the User Name box to highlight it, and type your username instead.
- Remember that passwords are case-sensitive. If your password is WormHead and you type in Wormhead, the network, already disgusted, refuses to let you in.

- If you can't log on the first time, try again. After several tries, if you still can't get access, it's time to raise your hand and play Ask the Network Administrator.

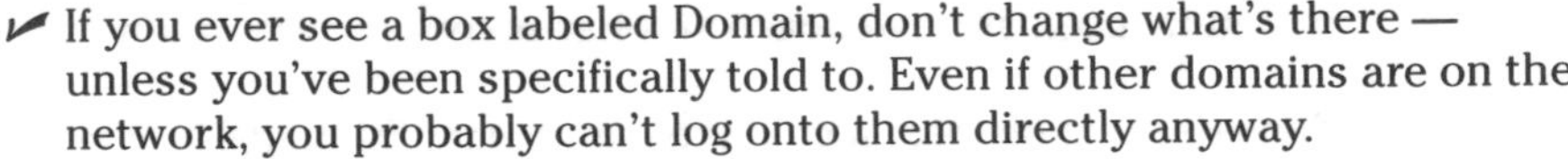

- If you ever see a box labeled Domain, don't change what's there — unless you've been specifically told to. Even if other domains are on the network, you probably can't log onto them directly anyway.

Changing your password

Even if it's not required, changing your password every few months is a good idea. To do so, log in using your old password, and then press Ctrl+Alt+Del to open the Windows NT Security box. Click on Change Password and type in your old password, then your new one (twice). The next time you logon, you start using the new password.

Oh, NO! I can't remember my password

If you suddenly can't remember your password, don't panic. Just stop for a minute and don't think. Get a drink of water. Call your mom like you promised. Write down your choices for the football pool.

Still can't remember? *Now* you can try thinking. Did you write it down somewhere safe? So safe, you don't know where? What kinds of passwords do you usually choose? What were you doing when you changed it the last time?

If in the end, you can't come up with your password, you will have to go to the Network Administrator. The administrator can change your password to a new one, tell you what the new one is so you can logon, and require you to change the new password into a private one that only you know. (Again!)

- The administrator can't find out what your password is and tell you.
- The administrator can only delete private passwords and assign new ones.
- It's true that this is a pretty easy administrative task, but if you require it too often, your reputation as a Responsible Person is bound to suffer.

Starting Your Favorite Program

When Windows NT first takes over your computer, it turns your screen into a Desktop. However, "Desktop" is merely a fancy name for a plate of buttons with labels underneath them. Click on a button, and a program hops to the screen in its own little window.

Click on the Start button in the bottom-left corner of the screen, move the mouse over the menus, and you'll see even more buttons to choose from, as seen in Figure 5-1.

Because the buttons have little pictures on them, they're called icons. An icon offers clues to the program it represents. For example, the icon on the desktop with the computers and cables stands for Network Neighborhood, a program that lets people talk to other computers on their network.

See the dark bar shading the Windows NT Explorer icon's title in Figure 5-1? The bar means that the Windows NT Explorer program is *highlighted:* It's queued up and ready to go. If you press the Enter key while the Windows NT Explorer is highlighted, Explorer hops to the forefront. (Don't press Enter, though, because Explorer is too boring to play with right now.)

Now, it's time to try some of this stuff yourself. Roll your mouse around until its arrow hovers over the button that says Start.

Click your mouse button, and the Start menu pops up on the screen, as shown in Figure 5-2. Next, click on Programs, and another menu full of buttons shoots out, as shown in Figure 5-3. Click on Accessories to see yet another menu, shown in Figure 5-4. Click on Games to see the last menu on the chain. And if you're not too exhausted, click on Freecell (shown in Figure 5-5) and play a few rounds of the Windows NT card game.

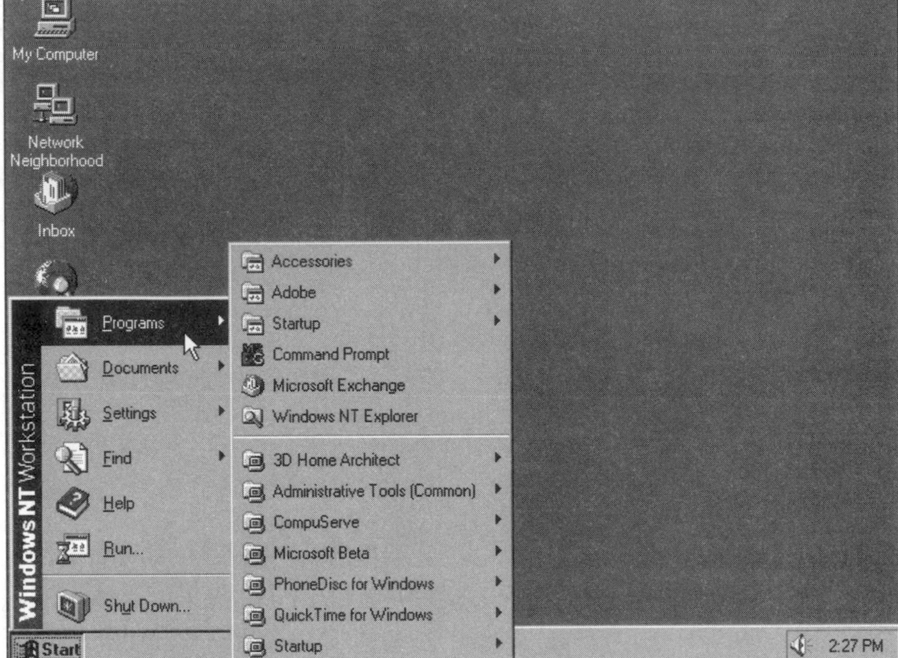

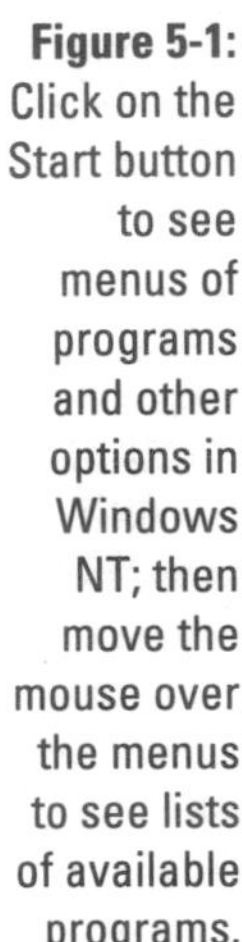

Figure 5-1: Click on the Start button to see menus of programs and other options in Windows NT; then move the mouse over the menus to see lists of available programs.

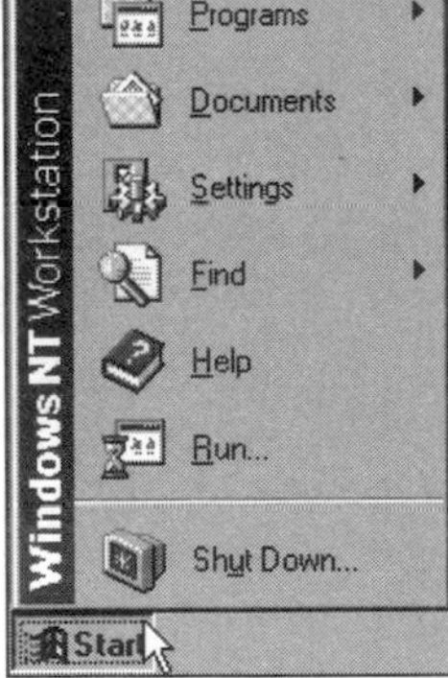

Figure 5-2: To start a program in Windows NT, click on the Start button.

- The Start button is just a big panel of buttons. When you press one of the buttons by pointing at it and clicking with the mouse, the program assigned to that button heads for the top of the screen and appears in a little window.
- You don't have to click your way through all those buttons hiding beneath the Start button. Click on the Start button and then just hover your mouse pointer over the other menu areas that you'd like to open. Windows NT opens them without even waiting for your clicks.

Bond . . . James Bond — to the white courtesy telephone, please!

Passwords are the cloak-and-dagger part of the network business because keeping out unauthorized folk is a security focus for most institutions. Passwords are also the bane of both network users and administrators, and here's why.

The administrator wants you, the user, to change your password frequently in case other people discover it and use it, to refrain from writing it down, and to choose something that's hard for other people to guess. On the other hand, you, the user, want an easy-to-remember password that never has to be changed. Those two different goals can create a slight conflict, but not one that's impossible to deal with.

Passwords can be as long as 14 characters, but unless you're a speed typist, you'll be happier in the 6 to 8 character range.

A good password is

- At least six characters long
- A mix of lowercase and uppercase characters, with at least one non-alphabetic character

Bad passwords are

- Your name or initials
- Names or initials of family members
- Your dog's name or initials
- Your birth date or the birth date of a family member
- A variation on your username
- Your phone number or phone numbers of friends or family
- Popular obscenities — even when spelled backwards.

One good method is to turn a catch phrase or family joke into an acronym. For example, I've used the password *Wk?Wc?,* which is just a shortened version of "Who knows? Who cares?" Or do the same with a song or a book title. (Don't use the title of the book that's on your desk next to the computer.)

Passwords, unlike usernames and filenames, are *always* case-sensitive. If your password is *Wk?Wc?* and you type in **WK?WC?**, the password won't be recognized.

Overall password policy is set by the administrator. So passwords may be required to have a minimum length, and you may have to change your password at regular intervals.

- Icons can stand for files as well as for programs. Clicking on Documents in the Start menu usually brings up shortcut buttons that take you to 15 of your most recently used documents.
- Microsoft has already set up the Start button to include icons for the most popular programs and files that Windows NT found as it installed itself on your computer — stuff like 1-2-3 and WordPerfect. If you want to add some other programs and files, however, check out the section in Chapter 12 on customizing your Start button.

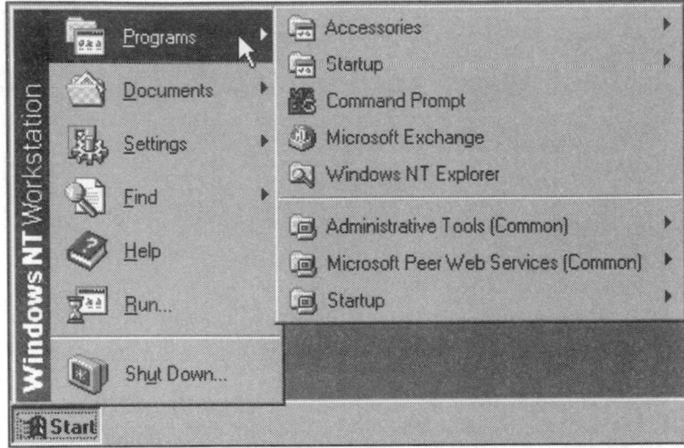

Figure 5-3: Click on Programs and follow the menu as it grows.

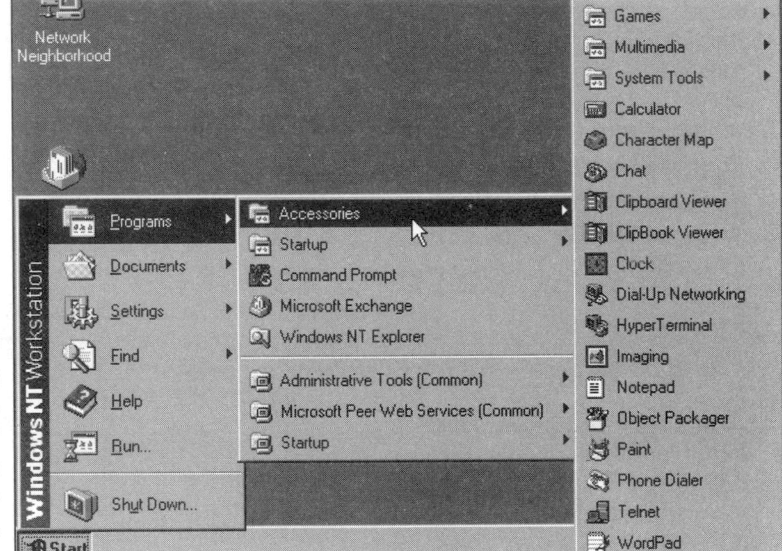

Figure 5-4: Click on the type of program you'd like to load.

- If you're kind of sketchy about all this double-click stuff, head to the mouse section in Chapter 2.
- Despise mice? You don't need a mouse for the Start button. Hold down the Ctrl key and press the Esc key to make the Start menu appear. Then press the arrow keys to navigate the various menus. Highlighted the program you want? Press Enter, and the program begins to run.
- If the icon you're after in the Start menu has a little black bar around its name, it's highlighted. If you just press the Enter key, the highlighted program loads itself into a little window. Or you can still double-click on it to load it. Windows NT lets you do things in a bunch of different ways.
- This chapter gives you just a quick tour of Windows NT. You can find glowing descriptions of the Start button in Chapter 12.

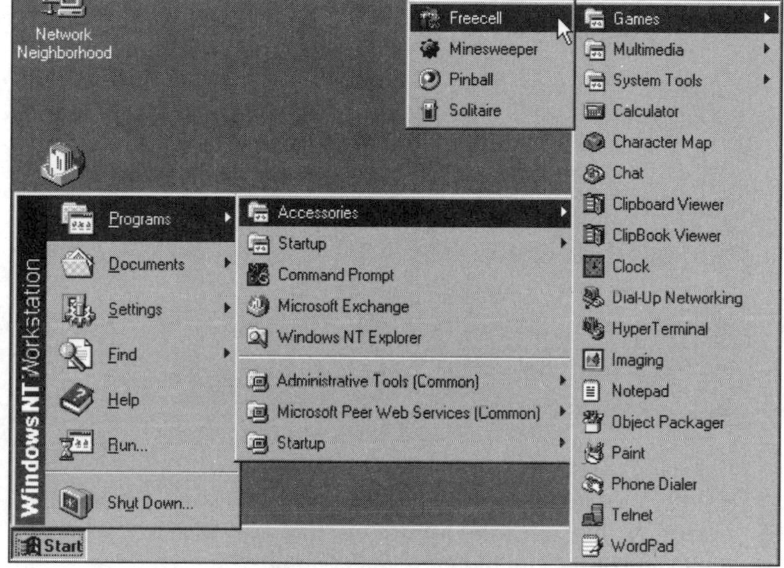

Figure 5-5: Click on your program's name or icon to load it.

Using pull-down menus

Windows NT, bless its heart, makes an honest effort toward making computing easier. For example, the Start button puts a bunch of options on the screen in front of you. You just choose the one you want, and Windows NT takes it from there.

But if Windows NT put all its options on the screen at the same time, it would look more crowded than the 14-page menu at the House of Hui restaurant. To avoid resorting to fine print, Windows NT hides some menus in special locations on the screen. When you click the mouse in the right place, more options leap toward you, like whether you'd prefer your Dim Sum chicken feet to be spicy or tepid.

For example, load the Windows NT word-processing program, WordPad, by clicking on the Start button, choosing Programs, clicking on the Accessories area, and choosing WordPad.

See the row of words beginning with File that rests along the top edge of WordPad? You'll find a row of words—called a *menu bar* — across the top of just about every Windows NT-based program. Move your mouse pointer over the word File and click once.

A menu opens from beneath File. This menu is called a *pull-down menu,* if you're interested, and it looks like what you see in Figure 5-6.

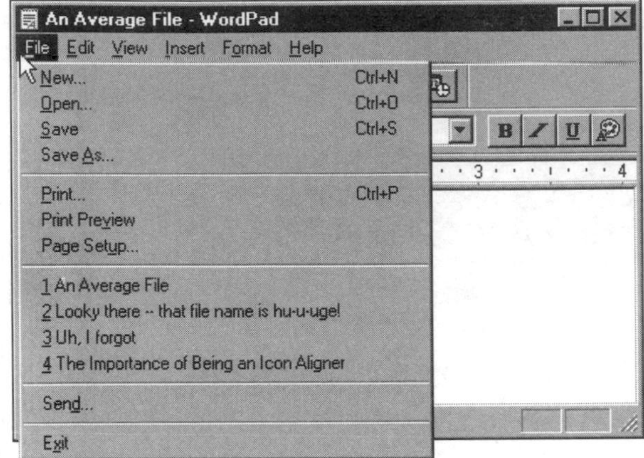

Figure 5-6: Click on a word along the top of any window to reveal a secret pull-down menu.

- Pull-down menus open from any of those key words along the top of a window. Just click the mouse on the word and the menu tumbles down like shoeboxes falling off a closet shelf.
- To close the menu, click the mouse someplace away from the menu. (Or press the Esc key on the keyboard.)
- Different Windows NT-based programs have different words across the menu bar, but almost all the bars begin with the word File. The File pull-down menu contains file-related options, like Open, Save, Print, and Push Back Cuticles.
- You'll find pull-down menus sprinkled liberally throughout Windows NT.

- Oh yeah — to close that WordPad program, click on the box with the little X in the program's upper-right corner.

Loading a file

First, here's the bad news: Loading a file into a Windows NT-based program can be a mite complicated sometimes. Second, loading a file means the same thing as opening a file.

Now that those trifles have been dispensed with, here's the good news: All Windows NT-based programs load files in the exact same way. So once you know the proper etiquette for one program, you're prepared for all the others!

Here's the scoop: The problem with loading a file is that you have to find the file first. So to open a file in any Windows NT-based program, do the following:

1. **Look for the program's menu bar, that row of important-looking words along its top. Because you're after a file, click on File.**

   A most-welcome pull-down menu descends from the word File. The menu has a list of important-looking words.

2. **Because you want to open a file, move the mouse to the word Open and click once again.**

   Yet another box hops onto the screen, as shown in Figure 5-7 — you'll see this box named Open appear over and over again in Windows NT.

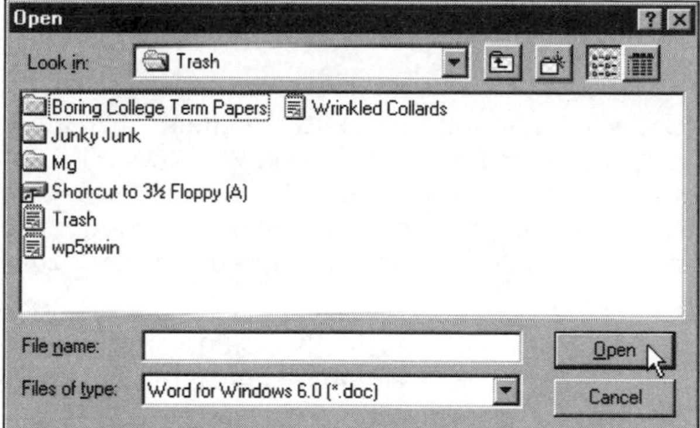

Figure 5-7: Almost every Windows NT-based program tosses this box at you when you open or save a file.

3. **See the list of filenames inside the box? Point at one of them with the mouse and click the button.**

   That file's name shows up in the box called File name.

4. **Click on the Open button.**

   WordPad opens the file and displays it on-screen.

If you don't have a mouse, press the Tab key until a little square appears around one of the file's names. Then press the arrow keys until the file you want is highlighted, and press Enter.

You've done it! You've loaded a file into a program! Those are the same stone steps you'll walk across in any Windows NT-based program, whether it was written by Microsoft or by the teenager down the street. All the programs work in the same way.

- You can speed things up by simply double-clicking on a file's name; that does the same thing as single-clicking on the filename and then clicking on Open. Or you can click on the name once to highlight it (it turns blue), and then press the Enter key. Windows NT is full of multiple options like that. (Different strokes for different folks and all.)

- If you've changed an open file, even by an accidental press of the spacebar, WordPad takes it for granted that you've changed the file for the better. When you try to load another file, WordPad cautiously asks whether you want to save the changes you've made to the current file. Click on the No button unless you do, indeed, want to save that version you've haphazardly changed.
- The Open box has a bunch of options in it. You can open files that are stored in different folders or on other disk drives. You can also call up files that were created by certain programs, filtering out the ones you won't be needing. All this more complicated Open box stuff is explained in Chapter 6.
- If you're still a little murky on the concepts of files, folders, directories, and drives, flip to Chapter 13 for an explanation of Explorer.

- Trying to load a file that you've recently opened? Then click on Documents from the Start button menu. There, Windows NT lists the last 15 documents you opened. Click on your document's name, and Windows NT loads that document into the program that created it and brings both the program and document to the screen. Modern convenience at its best.
- Or go at it from the other direction: Click on the Start button, choose Find, and then choose Files or Folders. Type in the file's name or what little part of the name you know. Click on Find Now. A whole bunch of files will probably show up in the process of the search. Just double-click on the one you want to open. All the uses for the Find program are covered in Chapter 8.

Putting two programs on-screen simultaneously

After seeing the lavish amount of money somebody spent for Windows NT and the computer systems powerful enough to cart it around, you're not going to be content with only one program on your screen. You want to fill the screen with programs, all running in their own little windows.

How do you put a second program on the screen? Well, if you've opened WordPad by double-clicking on its icon in the Start button's menu, then you're probably already itching to load Freecell, the solitaire game. Simply click on the Start button and start moving through the menus, as described in the "Starting Your Favorite Program" section earlier in this chapter. When you spot Freecell in the Games area, click on it, and it hops to the screen.

- This section is intentionally short. When working in Windows NT, you almost always have two or more programs on the screen at the same time. It's nothing really special, so belaboring the point here is unnecessary.

- The special part comes when you move information between the two programs, which we explain in Chapter 10.
- If you want to move multiple windows around on the screen, move yourself to Chapter 7.
- If you've started up Freecell, you may be wondering where the WordPad window disappeared to. The Freecell window is now covering up the WordPad window. To get WordPad back, check out the information on retrieving lost windows in Chapter 8. (Or if you see a button called WordPad along the bottom of your screen, click on it — WordPad is immediately resurrected from the bottom of the Desktop.)
- To switch between windows, just click on the one you want. When you click on a window, it immediately becomes the active window — the window where all the activity takes place. For more information on switching between windows, switch to Chapter 7.
- Can't find Freecell? Unfortunately, Freecell isn't automatically installed on all computers running Windows NT. To correct this oversight, use the Control Panel's Add/Remove Programs icon. (And while you're there, look for the cool Pinball game, too.) Chapter 11 dishes out more information on how to add or remove programs.
- Still can't find Freecell? Then it quite likely wasn't installed and can't be installed because those folks in management decided, for their own bizarre reasons, that you shouldn't be playing games on what they call "company time."

Using the Keyboard

It's a good thing Microsoft doesn't design automobiles. Each car would have a steering wheel, a joystick, a remote control, and handles on the back for people who prefer to push. Windows NT offers almost a dozen ways for you to perform the simplest tasks.

For example, check out the top of any window where that important-looking row of words hides above secret pull-down menus. Some of the words have certain letters underlined. What gives? Well, it's a secret way for you to open their menus without using the mouse. This sleight of hand depends on the Alt key, that key resting next to your keyboard's spacebar.

Press (and release) the Alt key and keep an eye on the row of words in the WordPad menu bar. The first word, File, darkens immediately after you release the Alt key. You haven't damaged it; you've selected it, just as if you'd clicked on it with the mouse. The different color means that it's highlighted.

Now, look a few steps to the right on the menu bar — see how the letter V in View is underlined? Press V on the keyboard, and the pull-down menu hidden below View falls down, like a mushroom off a pizza.

That's the secret underlined-letter trick! And pressing Alt and V is often faster than plowing through a truckload of mouse menus — especially if you think that the whole mouse concept is rather frivolous anyway.

- You can access almost every command in Windows NT by using the Alt key rather than a mouse. Press the Alt key and then press the key for the underlined letter. That option, or command, then begins to work.
- If you've accidentally pressed the Alt key and find yourself trapped in Menu Land, press the Alt key again to return to normal. If that doesn't work, try pressing the Esc key.
- As pull-down menus continue to appear, you can keep plowing through them by selecting underlined letters until you accomplish your ultimate goal. For example, pressing Alt and then V brings down the View pull-down menu. Pressing R subsequently activates the Ruler option from the View menu and immediately turns off the Ruler from the top of the word processor's screen. (If you liked the Ruler, press Alt, V, and R again to toggle the Ruler back on.)

When you see a word with an underlined letter in a menu, press and release your Alt key. Then press that underlined letter to choose that menu item.

Printing Your Work

Eventually, you'll want to transfer a copy of your finely honed work to the printed page so you can pass it around. Printing something from any Windows NT-based program (or application, or applet, whatever you want to call it) takes only three keystrokes. Press and release the Alt key and then press the letters F and P. Click the Enter button, and what you see on your screen is whisked to a printer.

Pressing the Alt key activates the words along the top, known as the menu bar. The letter F wakes up the File menu, and the letter P tells the program to send its stuff to the printer — pronto. (See the preceding section for more menu-oriented details.)

- Alternatively, you can use the mouse to click on the word File and then click on the word Print from the pull-down menu. Depending on the RPM of your mouse ball and the elasticity of your wrist, the mouse and keyboard methods can be equally quick.
- If nothing comes out of the printer after a few minutes, try putting in paper and making sure the printer's turned on.

- Some programs, like WordPad, have a little picture of a printer along their top. Clicking on that printer icon is a quick way of telling the program to shuffle your work to the printer. Because your work shoots directly to the printer, however, it bypasses all the menus that let you add fancy printing features: Printing more than one copy, for example, or only printing page 3.

Saving Your Work

Any time you create something in a Windows NT-based program, be it a picture of a spoon or a letter to *The New York Times* begging for a decent comics page, you want to save it to disk.

Saving your work means placing a copy of it onto a disk, be it the mysterious hard disk inside your computer or a floppy disk, one of those things you're always tempted to use as beverage coasters. (They make lousy coasters, so don't try it.)

Luckily, Windows NT makes it easy for you to save your work. You need only press three keys, just as if you were printing your work or opening a file. To save your work, press and release the Alt key, press F, and then press S.

If you prefer to push the mouse around, click on File from the Windows NT menu bar. When the secret pull-down menu appears, click on Save. Your mouse pointer turns into an hourglass, asking you to hold your horses while Windows NT shuffles your work from the program to your hard disk or a floppy disk for safekeeping.

That's it!

- If you're saving your work for the first time, you see a familiar-looking box: It's the same box you see when opening a file. See how the letters in the File name box are highlighted? The computer is always paying attention to the highlighted areas, so anything you type appears in that box. Type in a name for the file and press Enter.
- If Windows NT throws a box in your face saying something like `This filename is not valid`, you haven't adhered to the ridiculously strict filename guidelines discussed in Chapter 13.
- Just as files can be loaded from different directories and disk drives, they can be saved to them as well. You can choose among different directories and drives by clicking on various parts of the Save As box. All this stuff is explained in Chapter 13.

But I don't have a printer attached to my computer!

Printing is a breeze in Windows NT whether you have a printer attached to your computer or you use a printer that's all the way down the hall. Depending on your position in the food chain, you may be able to print to one or to many printers.

To find out what printers are available to you, double-click on your desktop's My Computer icon and then double-click on the Printers folder. If you see a bunch of printers, right-click on each one until you find one that has a check mark next to Set As Default. That's the printer your computer uses if you're printing something from Notepad or another program that doesn't let you pick a particular printer.

It's also the automatic choice of your programs. When you choose Print from the File menu, though, you can choose any other printer that's been made available to you. That means you can print to the nearest ordinary printer for most things, specify the fancy color printer for your charts, and choose the special high-speed printer for those 1,000-page printing jobs.

To use printers other than the default one, choose Print from your program's File menu. In the window that opens, the default printer is shown in the box labeled Name. But just click on the little downward arrow next to the text box, and a list of the available printers opens. Pick the one you want and then click on the OK button.

Now here's the hard part: Usually, the name that the Network Administrator chooses for the printer is good enough to tell you the type of printer involved. But nothing in any of these boxes is likely to tell you where the printer is actually *located.* A smart and caring administrator may name a printer Tektronix Color Printer in Editorial Department, but much more commonly, the printer is called Unity 1200XL v.47.0. Most helpful, yes?

In these cases, you have no choice but to ask. Start, as usual, with the person in the next cubicle and work your way up. Sure, it takes a little more effort, but then again, you're trying to do something a little fancier than print to the *normal* printer.

For more on network printing, see Chapter 9.

Logging Off Windows NT

Ah! The most pleasant thing you'll do with Windows NT all day could very well be to stop using it. And you do that the same way you started: by using the Start button, the friendly little helper that popped up the first time you started Windows NT.

Other Windows NT-based programs come and go, but the Start button is always on your screen somewhere. (And if it's currently playing hide-and-go-seek, press Ctrl+Esc to make it reveal itself.)

To log off Windows NT, click on the Start button and click on the Shut Down command from the Start button's menu. Windows NT, tearful that you're leaving, sends out one last plea, as shown in Figure 5-8.

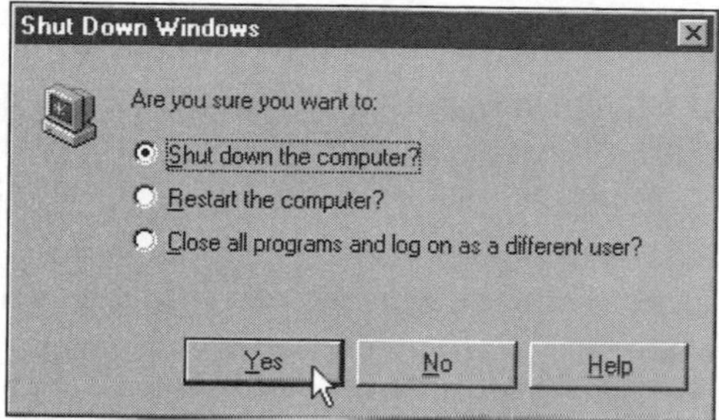

Figure 5-8: Be sure to shut down your computer before leaving it for the day.

If you mean business, click on the Yes button or press Enter. Windows NT starts to put all its parts away, preparing to leave the screen of your computer. If, by some odd mistake, you've clicked on the Shut Down button in error, click on the No button, and Windows NT ignores your faux pas. (Keyboard users must press Tab to highlight the No button, and then press Enter.)

- Be sure to shut down Windows NT through its official Shut Down program before turning off your computer. Otherwise, Windows NT can't properly prepare your computer for the event, which leads to future troubles.
- Holding down Alt and pressing F4 tells Windows NT that you want to stop working in your current program and close it down. If you press Alt+F4 while no programs are running, Windows NT figures you've had enough for one day, and it acts as if you chose its Shut Down command.
- When you tell Windows NT you want to quit, it searches through all your open windows to see whether you've saved all your work. If it finds any work you've forgotten to save, it tosses a box your way, letting you click on the OK button to save the work. Whew!
- If you happen to have any of those old DOS-based programs running, Windows NT stops and tells you to quit your DOS programs first. See, Windows NT knows how to shut down Windows NT-based programs because they all use the same command. But all DOS programs are different. You have to shut the program down manually, using whatever exit sequence you normally use in that program.
- If your computer has a sound card, you hear a pleasant wind-chimes sound telling you that it's time to go home and relax. (Or time to buy a sound card if you haven't yet succumbed to the urge.)
- You don't always have to log off completely. If you're just going down to hall to find out whether Linda has any jujubes, use a password-protected screen saver. When you come back with your teeth all stuck together, you only have to type in your password, and you're ready to go again.

- Or if you want to stay logged in but don't want anyone messing with your machine, press Ctrl+Alt+Del to open the Windows NT Security box, and then click the Lock Workstation button. When you come back, you'll need to press Ctrl+Alt+Del again and type in your password, and when you do, your computer screen will look the same as it did when you left.
- Chapter 11 has all the stuff about choosing and setting up screen savers with or without a password.

Do I *have* to log off and turn off my computer?

You don't *have* to turn off your computer when you're done computing. In fact, because some people share computers at the office, you'll annoy your coworkers if you *do* shut down the computer.

But you must log off when you're done using the computer — before leaving the keyboard and going to lunch, for example — be sure to follow these steps:

1. **Click on the Start button's Shut Down command.**
2. **Click on the Close all programs and log on as a different user command.**

   Doing so tells Windows NT that you're through using the computer.
3. **Press Enter.**

Windows NT then "logs you off" the computer and leaves the computer sitting there with a blank look on its face, waiting for somebody else to log on.

Why bother? Because by making people log on with passwords, the Network Administrator can keep evil people off the network. And when you log off, you effectively lock the computer back up, keeping other people from doing naughty things to the computer when you're the one who's currently logged on.

Chapter 6

Examining All Those Buttons, Bars, and Boxes

In This Chapter

- Looking at a typical window
- Getting into bars
- Changing borders
- Getting to know the button family
- Disregarding the dopey Control-menu button
- Dialog box stuff: text boxes, drop-down list boxes, list boxes, and other gibberish
- Just tell me how to open a file!
- Hey! When do I click, and when do I double-click?

As children, just about all of us played with elevator buttons until our parents told us to knock it off. An elevator gave such an awesome feeling of power: Push a little button, watch the mammoth doors slide shut, and feel the responsive push as the spaceship floor begins to surge upward. What fun!

Part of an elevator's attraction still comes from its simplicity. To stop at the third floor, you merely press the button marked 3. No problems there. The push-and-stand-back-while-the-door-closes concept is classic in its simplicity.

Windows NT takes the elevator-button concept to an extreme, unfortunately, and it loses something in the process. First, some of the Windows NT buttons don't even look like buttons. Most of them have ambiguous little pictures rather than clearly marked labels. And the worst of it comes with their terminology: The phrase "push the button" becomes "click the scroll bar above or below the scroll box on vertical scroll bars." Yuck!

When braving your way through Windows NT, don't bother learning all these dorky terms. Instead, treat this chapter as a field guide, something you can grab when you stumble across a confusing new button or box that you've never encountered before. Just page through until you find its picture. Read the description to find out whether that particular object is deadly or just mildly poisonous. Then read to find out where you're supposed to poke it with the mouse pointer.

You get used to the critter after you click on it a few times. Just don't bother remembering the scientific name *vertical scroll bar,* and you'll be fine.

A Typical Window

Nobody wants a field guide without pictures, so Figure 6-1 shows a typical window with its parts labeled.

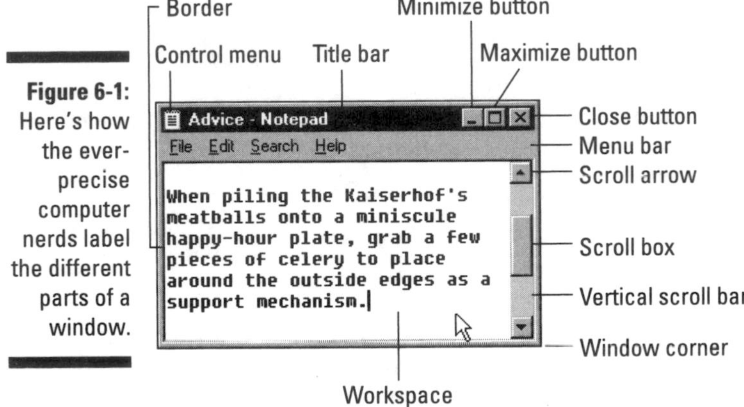

Figure 6-1: Here's how the ever-precise computer nerds label the different parts of a window.

Just as boxers grimace differently depending on where they've been punched, windows behave differently depending on where they've been clicked. The following sections describe the correct places to click and, if that doesn't work, the best places to punch.

- Windows NT is full of little weird-shaped buttons, borders, and boxes. You don't have to remember their Latin or Greek etymologies. The important part is just knowing what part you're supposed to click on. Then you can start worrying about whether you're supposed to single-click or double-click. (And that little dilemma is explained near the end of this chapter.)
- After you click on a few windows a few times, you realize how easy bossing them around really is. The hard part is learning everything for the first time, just like when you stalled the car while learning how to use the stick shift.

Bars

Windows NT is filled with bars; perhaps that's why some of its programs seem a bit groggy and hung over. *Bars* simply are thick stripes along the edges of a window. You find several different types of bars in Windows NT.

The title bar

The *title bar* is that topmost strip in any window (see Figure 6-2). It lists the name of the program as well as the name of any open file. For example, the title bar in Figure 6-2 comes from Windows NT Notepad.

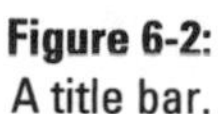

Figure 6-2: A title bar.

If you just open Notepad and don't bother choosing a filename, Windows NT uses the name Untitled until you save the file and can think of a little more descriptive name. (For example, an untitled file may be full of notes you've jotted down from an energetic phone conversation with Ed McMahon.) Then when you type in the new name for the file, your newly created filename replaces the admittedly vague Untitled in the title bar.

- The title bar shows the name of the current program and file. If you've just started to create a file, the title bar refers to that file's name as Untitled.
- The title bar can serve as a handle for moving a window around on-screen. Point at the title bar, hold down the mouse button, and move the mouse around. An outline of the window moves as you move the mouse. After you place the outline in a new spot, let go of the mouse button. The window leaps to that new spot and sets up camp.
- When you're working on a window, its title bar is *highlighted,* meaning that it's a different color from the title bar of any other open window. By glancing at all the title bars on-screen, you can quickly tell which window you're currently using.

The menu bar

Windows NT has menus everywhere. But if menus appeared all at once, everybody would think about deep-fried appetizers rather than computer commands. So Windows NT hides its menus in something called a *menu bar* (see Figure 6-3).

Figure 6-3: A menu bar.

Lying below the title bar, the menu bar keeps those little menus hidden behind little words. To reveal secret options associated with those words, click on one of the words.

If you think mice are for milksops, then use the brawny Alt key instead. A quick tap of the Alt key activates the menu words across the top of the window. Press the arrow keys to the right or left until you've selected the word you're after; then press the down-arrow key to expose the hidden menu. (You can also press a word's underlined letter to bring it to life, but that tip is explained later in more detail.)

For example, to see the entrees under the word Edit, click your mouse button on Edit (or press Alt and then E). A secret menu tumbles down from a trap door, as shown in Figure 6-4, presenting all sorts of edit-related options.

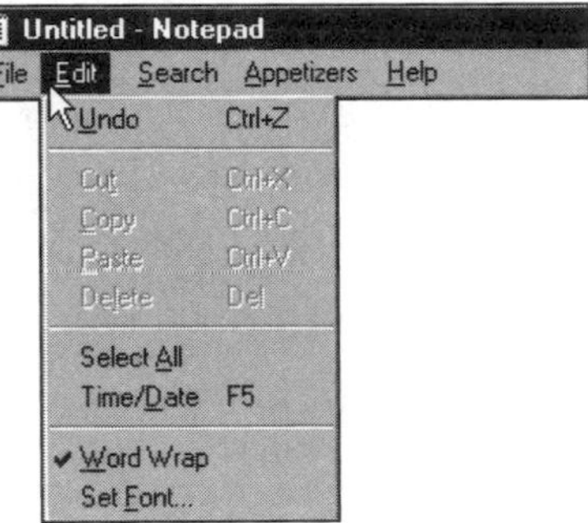

Figure 6-4: Select any word in the menu bar to reveal its secret hidden menu.

- When you select a key word in a menu bar, a menu comes tumbling down. The menu contains options related to that particular key word.
- Just as restaurants sometimes run out of specials, a window sometimes isn't capable of offering all its menu items. Any unavailable options are grayed out, as the Cut, Copy, Paste, and Delete options are in Figure 6-4.
- If you've accidentally selected the wrong word, causing the wrong menu to jump down, just sigh resignedly. (S-i-i-i-igh.) Then select the word you really want. The first menu disappears, and the new one appears below the new word.

- If you want out of Menu Land completely, click the mouse pointer back down on your work in the window's workspace — usually the area where you've been typing stuff. (Or press the Alt key, whichever method comes to mind sooner.)
- Some menu items have shortcut keys listed next to them, such as the Ctrl+Z key combination next to the Undo option in Figure 6-4. Just hold down the Ctrl key and press the letter Z to undo your last effort. The Undo option takes place immediately, and you don't have to wait for the menu to tumble down.

If you find yourself performing the same task on a menu over and over, check to see whether the task has a shortcut key next to it. By pressing the shortcut key, you can bypass the menu altogether, performing that task instantly.

The scroll bar

The *scroll bar,* which looks like an elevator shaft, is along the edge of a window (see Figure 6-5). Inside the shaft, a little freight elevator (the scroll box) travels up and down as you page through your work. In fact, by glancing at the little elevator, you can tell whether you're near the top of a document, the middle, or the bottom.

Figure 6-5: Scroll bars enable you to page through everything that's in a window.

For example, if you're looking at stuff near the top of a document, the elevator box is near the top of its little shaft. If you're working on the bottom portion of your work, the elevator box dangles near the bottom. You can watch the little box travel up or down as you press the PgUp or PgDn key. (Yes, distractions are easy to come by in Windows NT.)

Here's where the little box in the scroll bar comes into play: By clicking in various places on that scroll bar, you can quickly move around in a document without pressing the PgUp or PgDn key.

- Instead of pressing the PgUp key, click in the elevator shaft above the little elevator (the scroll box). The box jumps up the shaft a little bit, and the document moves up one page, too. Click below the scroll box, and your view moves down, just as with the PgDn key.
- To move your view up line by line, click on the boxed-in arrow (scroll arrow) at the top of the scroll bar. If you hold down the mouse button while the mouse pointer is over that arrow, more and more of your document appears, line by line.
- Scroll bars that run along the bottom of a window move your view from side to side rather than up and down. They're handy for viewing spreadsheets that extend off the right side of your screen.
- Some scroll bars don't have a little scroll box inside them, and then you have to use the little arrows to move around. There's no little elevator to play with. Sniff. Sniff.
- Want to move around in a hurry? Then put the mouse pointer on the little elevator box, hold down the mouse button, and drag the little elevator box up or down inside the shaft. For example, if you drag the box up toward the top of its shaft and release it, you can view the top of the document. Dragging it and releasing it down low takes you near the end.
- Windows NT 4 adds another dimension to some scroll bars: the little elevator's size. If the elevator is swollen up so big that it's practically filling the scroll bar, then the window is currently displaying practically all the information the file has to offer. But if the elevator is a tiny box in a huge scroll bar, then you're viewing only a tiny amount of the information contained in the file.
- If you don't have a mouse, you can't play with the elevator. To view the top of your document, hold down Ctrl and press Home. To see the bottom, hold down Ctrl and press End. Or press the PgUp or PgDn key to move one page at a time.

The taskbar

Windows NT converts your computer monitor's screen into a desktop. But because your newly computerized desktop is probably only 14 inches wide, all your programs and windows cover each other up like memos tossed onto a spike.

To keep track of the action, Windows NT introduces the *taskbar,* which lies along the bottom of your screen and simply lists what windows are currently open. If you've found the Start button, you've found the taskbar — the Start button lives on the taskbar's left end.

Undoing what you've just done

Windows NT offers a zillion different ways for you to do the same thing. Here are three ways to access the Undo option, which unspills the milk you've just spilled:

- Click on the word Edit and then click on the word Undo from the menu that falls down. (This approach is known as wading through the menus.) The last command you gave is undone, saving you from any damage.
- Press and release the Alt key, then press the letter E (for Edit), and then press the letter U (for Undo). (This Alt key method is handy when you don't have a mouse.) Your last bungle is unbungled, reversing any grievous penalties.
- Hold down the Ctrl key and press the Z key. (This little quickie is known as the shortcut-key method.) The last mistake you made is reversed, sparing you from further shame.

Don't feel like you have to learn all three methods. For example, if you can remember the Ctrl+Z key combination, you can forget about the menu method and the Alt key method.

Or if you don't want to remember anything, stick with the menu method. Just pluck the Undo command as it appears on the menu.

Finally, if you don't have a mouse, you have to remember the Alt key or Ctrl key business until you remember to buy a mouse.

- Whenever you open a window, Windows NT tosses that window's name onto a button on the taskbar.
- To switch from one window to another, just click on the desired window's name from its button on the taskbar. Wham! That window shoots to the top of the pile.
- All those open windows looking too crowded? Then click on the taskbar with your right mouse button and choose the Minimize All Windows option. All your currently open windows turn into buttons on the taskbar.

- In Windows NT 3.51, pressing Ctrl+Esc opened a dialog box called the Task List that listed all the currently running programs. In Windows NT 4, clicking on the taskbar with the right mouse button brings up a menu that includes Task Manager. The Applications tab in Task Manager lists all the programs you have running.
- You can find more information about the taskbar in Chapter 12.

Borders

A *border* is that thin edge enclosing a window. Compared with a bar, it's really tiny.

- You use borders to change a window's size. You can find out how to do that in Chapter 7.
- You can't use a mouse to change a window's size if the window doesn't have a border.
- If you like to trifle in details, you can make a border thicker or thinner through the Windows NT Control Panel, which is discussed in Chapter 11. In fact, laptop owners often thicken their windows' borders to make them a little easier to grab with those awkward trackballs.

Other than that, you won't be using borders much.

The Button Family

Three basic species of buttons flourish throughout the Windows NT environment: command buttons, option buttons, and minimize/maximize buttons. The three species are closely related, and yet they look and act quite differently.

Command buttons

Command buttons may be the simplest buttons to figure out — Microsoft labeled them! Command buttons are most commonly found in *dialog boxes,* which are little pop-up forms that Windows NT makes you fill out before it will work for you.

For example, when you ask Windows NT to open a file, it often sends out a form in a dialog box. You have to fill out the form, telling Windows NT what file you're after, where it's located, and other equally cumbersome details.

Table 6-1 identifies some of the more common command buttons that you encounter in Windows NT.

Table 6-1	Common Windows NT Command Buttons	
Command Button	***Habitat***	***Description***
OK	Found in nearly every pop-up dialog box	A click on this button says, "I'm done filling out the form, and I'm ready to move on." Windows NT then reads what you've typed into the form and processes your request. (Pressing the Enter key does the same thing as clicking on the OK button.)
Cancel	Found in nearly every pop-up dialog box	If you've somehow loused things up when filling out a form, click on this Cancel button. The pop-up box disappears, and everything returns to normal. Whew! (The Esc key does the same thing.)
Help	Found in nearly every pop-up dialog box	Stumped? Click on this button. Yet another box pops up, this time offering help on your current situation. (The F1 function key does the same thing.) **Extremely Cool Tip:** If you see a question mark in the top-right corner of the window, click on it and then click on the part of the window that says something confusing. If you're lucky, Windows NT tosses out an extra bit of helpful information.
Setup... Settings... Pizza...	Found less often in pop-up dialog boxes	If you encounter a button with ellipsis dots (...) after the word, brace yourself: Selecting that button brings yet another box to the screen. From there, you must choose even more settings, options, or toppings.

- By clicking on a command button, you're telling Windows NT to carry out the command that's written on the button. (Luckily, no command buttons are labeled Explode.)
- See how the OK button in Table 6-1 has a slightly darker border than the others? That darker border means that the button is highlighted.

Anything in Windows NT that's highlighted takes effect as soon as you press the Enter key; you don't have to select it.

- Some command buttons have underlined letters that you don't really notice until you stare at them. An underlined letter tells you that you can press that command button by holding down the Alt key while pressing the underlined letter. (That way, you don't have to click or double-click if your mouse is goofing up.)
- Instead of scooting your mouse to the Cancel button when you've goofed in a dialog box, just press your Esc key. It does the same thing.

If you've clicked on the wrong command button but haven't yet lifted your finger from the mouse button, stop! There's still hope. Command buttons take effect only after you've lifted your finger from the mouse button. So keep your finger pressed on the button and scoot the mouse pointer away from the button. When the pointer no longer rests on the button, gently lift your finger. Whew! Just try that trick on an elevator.

Option buttons

Sometimes Windows NT gets ornery and forces you to choose just a single option. For example, you can elect to finish the report that's due Monday, or you can spend your time using the office network to play with the World Wide Web. You can't choose both, so Windows NT won't let you select both of the options.

Windows NT handles this situation with an option button. When you choose one option, the little dot hops over to it. If you choose the other option, the little dot hops over to it instead. You find option buttons in many dialog boxes. Figure 6-6 shows an example.

- Although Windows NT tempts you with several choices in an option box, it lets you select only one of them. It moves the dot (and little dotted borderline) back and forth between the options as your decision wavers. Click on the OK button when you've reached a decision. The dotted option then takes effect.
- If you can choose more than one option, Windows NT won't present you with option buttons. Instead, it offers the more liberal *check boxes,* which are described in a separate section later in this chapter.
- Option buttons are round. Command buttons, described in the previous section, are rectangular.

Some old-time computer engineers refer to option buttons as *radio buttons,* after those push-buttons on car radios that switch from station to station, one station at a time.

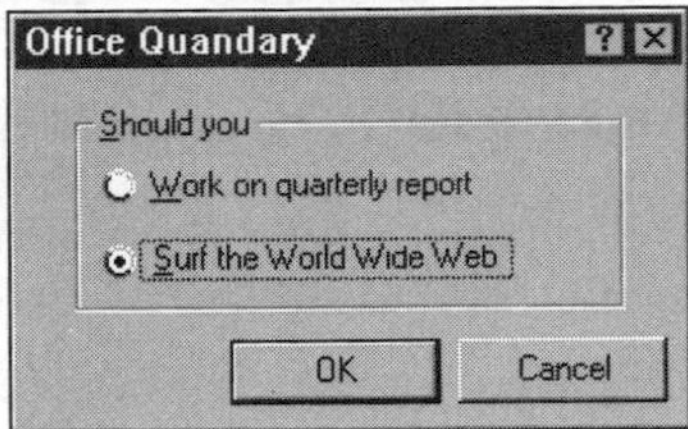

Figure 6-6: When you choose an option, the black dot hops to it.

Minimize/maximize buttons

All the little windows in Windows NT often cover each other up like teenage fans in the front row of a Spice Girls concert. To restore order, you need to separate the windows by using their minimize/maximize buttons.

These buttons enable you to enlarge the window you want to play with or shrink all the others so they're out of the way.

The *minimize button* (shown in the margin) is one of three buttons in the upper-right corner of every window.

A single click on the minimize button makes its window disappear and then reappear as a tiny button on the taskbar along the bottom of your screen. (Click on that taskbar button to return the window to its normal size.) Keyboard users can press Alt, the spacebar, and then N to minimize their current window.

- Minimizing a window doesn't destroy its contents; it just transforms the window into a little button on the bar that runs along the bottom of the screen (the taskbar).
- To make the button on the taskbar turn back into an on-screen window, click on it. The button reverts to a window in the same size and location as before you shrank it. (Keyboard users can hold down Alt while pressing Tab — a little box will start showing the currently running programs. Let go of the Alt key when the box chooses your program.)
- *Closing a window* and *minimizing a window* are two different things. Closing a window purges it from the computer's memory. In order to reopen it, you need to load it from your hard drive again. Turning a window into an icon keeps it handy, loaded into memory and ready to be used at an instant's notice.

The *maximize button* (shown in the margin) is in the upper-right corner of every window, too.

Don't bother with this Control-menu button stuff

The Control-menu button provides a quick exit from any window: Just give the little ornament a quick double-click. Other than that feature, however, the Control-menu button is pretty useless, redundant, and repetitive.

By clicking once on the Control-menu button, you get a pull-down menu with a bunch of options. Choose the Move option, and you can move around the window with the keyboard's arrow keys. (But using the mouse is a much easier way to move a window, as you find out in Chapter 7.)

Choosing the Size option lets you change a window's size. (But that's much easier with a mouse, too, as you find out in Chapter 7.)

Don't bother with the menu's Minimize and Maximize options, either. Those two options have their own dedicated buttons, right in the window's other top corner. Click on the minimize button (the button with the little line on it) to minimize the window; click on the maximize button (the button with the big square on it) to maximize the window. Simple. No need for you to bumble through a menu for the Minimize and Maximize options when minimize and maximize buttons are already staring you in the face.

Forget about Restore. Just double-click on the window's title bar to restore it to its former, less-than-full-screen size.

The Close option is redundant. You could have closed the window by double-clicking on the Control-menu button in the first place and avoided the hassle of going through a menu. Or you can click once on the dedicated close button — the button with the X on it in the window's far-upper-right corner.

So don't bother messing with the Control-menu button — it's just a waste of time.

(You may need to play with it if you're using a laptop and don't have a mouse, however. But even then, you should invest in a trackball, as described in Chapter 2. Until then, press Alt and the spacebar to bring up the Control menu and then press any of the underlined letters to access the function.)

A single click on the maximize button makes the window swell up something fierce, taking up as much space on-screen as possible. Keyboard users can press Alt, the spacebar, and then X to maximize their windows.

- If you're frustrated with all those windows that are overlapping each other, click on your current window's maximize button. The window muscles its way to the top, filling the screen like a real program.
- Immediately after you maximize a window, its little maximize button turns into a restore button (described momentarily). The restore button lets you shrink the window back down when you're through giving it the whole playing field.

You don't have to click on the maximize button to maximize a window. Just double-click on its *title bar,* the thick strip bearing the window's name along the window's top. That double-click does the same thing as clicking on the maximize button, and the title bar is a lot easier to aim for.

In the upper-right corner of every maximized window is the *restore button* (shown in the margin).

When a window is maximized, a click on this button returns the window to the size it was before you maximized it. (Keyboard users can press Alt, the spacebar, and then R.)

- Restore buttons appear only in windows that fill the entire screen (which is no great loss because you need a restore button only when the window is maximized).
- DOS-based programs can run in a window. But when they're in a window, they can't fill the entire screen, even if you click on the maximize button. DOS windows just can't grow as large as normal windows. Perhaps they smoked cigarettes in their youth. (Or maybe they didn't read the trick about changing fonts in a DOS window, described in Chapter 15.)
- When DOS-based programs aren't running in a window, they can fill the entire screen. Windows NT hides in the background, tapping its toe until the programs finish and it can grab the screen again. For more information on this confusing DOS stuff, troop to Chapter 15.

The Dopey Control-Menu Button

Just as all houses have circuit breakers or fuse boxes, all windows have Control-menu buttons. This button hides in the top-left corner of almost every window, where it looks like an inconspicuous hood ornament. (Sharp-eyed readers will notice that the button is actually a miniature icon representing the program.)

That little hood ornament hides a menu full of functions, but they're all pretty dopey, so ignore them all except for this one here: Double-click on the Control-menu button whenever you want to leave a window.

Dialog Box Stuff (Lots of Gibberish)

Sooner or later, you'll have to sit down and tell Windows NT something personal. You'll want to tell Windows NT the name of a file to open, for example, or the name of a file to print. To handle this personal chatter, Windows NT sends out a dialog box.

A dialog box is merely another little window. But instead of containing a program, it contains a little form or checklist for you to fill out. These forms can have bunches of different parts, which are discussed in the following sections. Don't bother trying to remember the names of the parts, however — *how* they work is more important.

Text boxes

A text box works just like a fill-in-the-blanks test in history class. You can type anything you want into a text box — even numbers. For example, Figure 6-7 shows a dialog box that pops up when you want to search for some words or characters in WordPad.

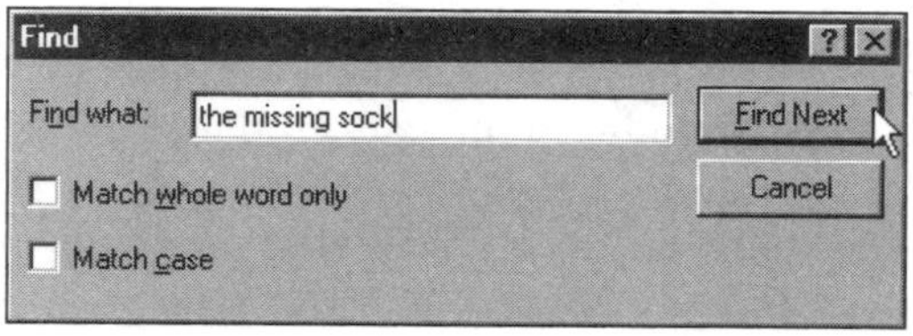

Figure 6-7: This dialog box from WordPad contains a text box.

When you type words or characters into this box and press the Enter key, WordPad searches for them. If it finds them, it shows them to you on the page. If it doesn't find them, it sends out a robotic message saying it's finished searching.

- Two clues let you know whether a text box is *active* (that is, ready for you to start typing stuff into it): The box's current information is highlighted, or a cursor is blinking inside the box. In either case, just start typing the new stuff. (The older highlighted information disappears as the new stuff replaces it.)
- If the text box isn't highlighted, or no blinking cursor is inside it, then it's not ready for you to start typing. To announce your presence, click inside it. Then start typing. Or press Tab until the box becomes highlighted or has a cursor.
- If you click inside a text box that already contains words, you must delete the information with the Delete or Backspace key before you can start typing in new information. (Or you can double-click on the old information; that way, the incoming text automatically replaces the old text.)

When one just isn't enough

Because Windows NT can display only one pattern on your Desktop at a time, you can select only one pattern from the Desktop's list box. Other list boxes, like those in Explorer, let you choose a bunch of things simultaneously. Here's how:

- To select more than one item, hold down the Ctrl key and click on each item you want. Each item stays highlighted.
- To select a bunch of adjacent items from a list box, click on the first item you want. Then hold down Shift and click on the last item you want. Windows NT immediately highlights the first item, last item, and every item in between. Pretty sneaky, huh?

Regular list boxes

Some boxes don't let you type stuff into them — they already contain information. Boxes containing lists of information are called, appropriately enough, *list boxes*. For example, WordPad brings up a list box if you're bored enough to want to change its font (see Figure 6-8).

Figure 6-8: By selecting a font from the list box, you change the way letters look in WordPad.

- See how the Times New Roman font is highlighted? It's the currently selected font. Press Enter (or click on the OK command button), and WordPad uses that font in your current paragraph.
- See the scroll bars along the side of the list box? They work just as they do anywhere else: Click on the little scroll arrows (or press the up or down arrow on your keyboard) to move the list up or down, and you can see any names that don't fit in the box.

- Many list boxes have a text box above them. When you click on a name in the list box, that name hops into the text box. Sure, you can type the name into the text box yourself, but that's not nearly as much fun.
- When confronted with a bunch of names in a list box, type the first letter of the name you're after. Windows NT immediately scrolls down the list to the first name beginning with that letter.

Drop-down list boxes

List boxes are convenient, but they take up a lot of room. So Windows NT sometimes hides list boxes, just as it hides pull-down menus. Then if you click in the right place, the list box appears, ready for your perusal.

So where's the right place? It's that downward-pointing arrow button, just like the one shown next to the box beside the Font option in Figure 6-9. Figure 6-10 shows the drop-down list that appears when you click on the downward-pointing arrow button.

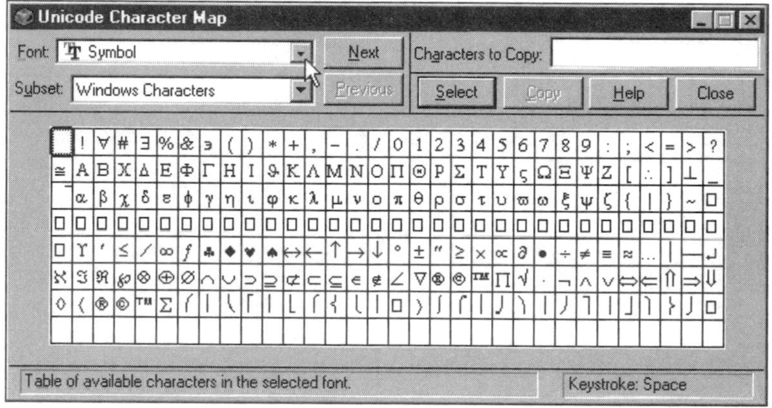

Figure 6-9: Click on the downward-pointing arrow next to the Font box to see a drop-down list box.

To make a drop-down list box drop down without using a mouse, press the Tab key until you highlight the box next to the little arrow. Hold down the Alt key and press the down-arrow key, and the drop-down list starts to dangle.

- Unlike regular list boxes, drop-down list boxes don't have a text box above them. That thing that looks like a text box just shows the currently selected item from the list; you can't type anything in there.
- To scoot around quickly in a drop-down list box, press the first letter of the item you're after. The first item beginning with that letter is instantly highlighted. You can press the up- or down-arrow key to see the ones nearby.

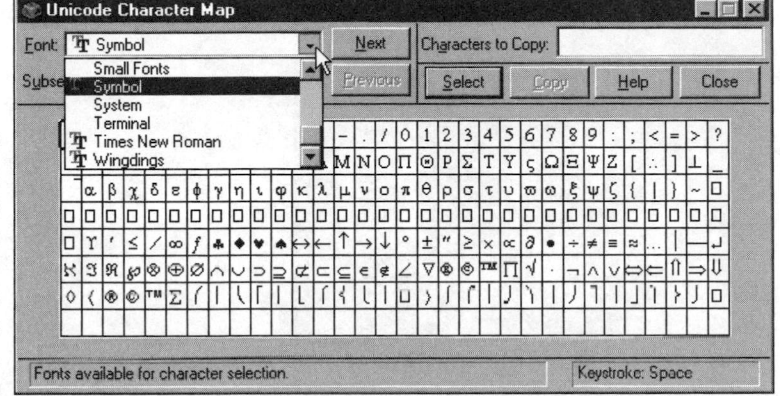

Figure 6-10: A list box drops down to display all the fonts that are available.

- Another way to scoot around quickly in a drop-down list box is to click on the scroll bar to its right. (We discuss scroll bars earlier in this chapter, if you need a refresher.)
- You can choose only one item from the list of a drop-down list box.

Check boxes

Sometimes you can choose from a whopping number of options in a dialog box. A check box is next to each option, and if you want that option, you click in the box. If you don't want it, you leave the box blank. (Keyboard users can press the up- or down-arrow key until a check box is highlighted and then press the spacebar.) For example, with the check boxes in the dialog box shown in Figure 6-11, you pick and choose how the Windows NT taskbar behaves.

- By clicking in a check box, you change its setting. A click in an empty square turns on that option. If the square already has a check mark in it, a click turns off that option, removing the check mark.
- You can click next to as many check boxes as you want. With option buttons, those things that look the same but are round, you can select only one option.

Sliding controls

Rich Microsoft programmers, impressed by track lights and sliding light switches in luxurious model homes, have started to add sliding controls to Windows NT. These "virtual" light switches are easy to use and don't wear out nearly as quickly as the real ones do. To slide a control in Windows NT — to adjust the volume level, for example — just drag and drop the sliding lever, like the one shown in Figure 6-12.

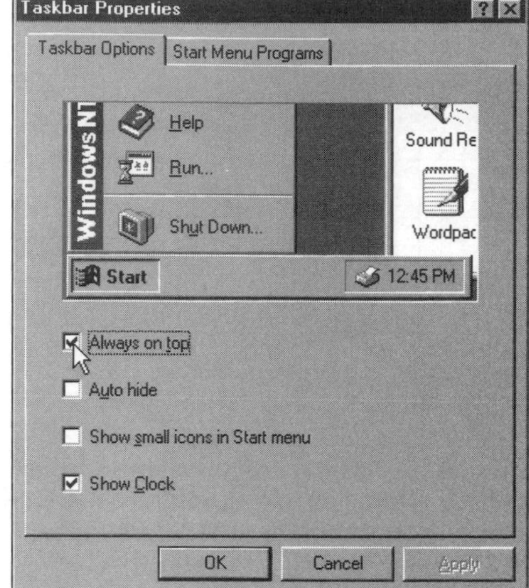

Figure 6-11: A check mark appears in each check box you've chosen.

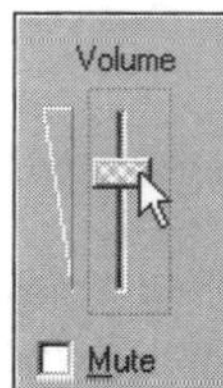

Figure 6-12: To slide a lever, drag it until the lever moves to where you want it.

Point at the lever with the mouse and, while holding down the mouse button, move the mouse in the direction you want the sliding lever to move. As you move the mouse, the lever moves, too. When you move the lever to a comfortable spot, let go of the mouse button, and Windows NT leaves the lever at its new position. That's it.

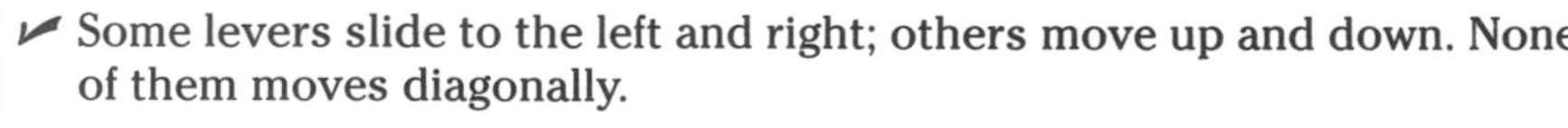

- Some levers slide to the left and right; others move up and down. None of them moves diagonally.
- To change the volume in Windows NT, click on the little speaker near the clock in the bottom-right corner. A sliding volume control appears, ready to be dragged up or down.
- No mouse? Then go buy one. In the meantime, whenever you encounter a sliding control, press Tab until a little box appears over the sliding lever; then press your arrow keys in the direction you'd like the lever to slide.

Just Tell Me How to Open a File!

Enough with the labels and terms. Forget the buttons and bars. How do you load a file into a program? This section gives you the scoop. You follow these same steps every time you load a file into a program.

Opening a file is a file-related activity, so start by finding the word File in the window's menu bar (see Figure 6-13).

Figure 6-13: To open a file, you first select the word File in the window's menu bar.

Then simply do the following:

1. **Click on the word File (or press Alt and then F) to knock down that word's hidden little menu.**

   Figure 6-14 shows the File pull-down menu.

Figure 6-14: When you select File, the File pull-down menu appears.

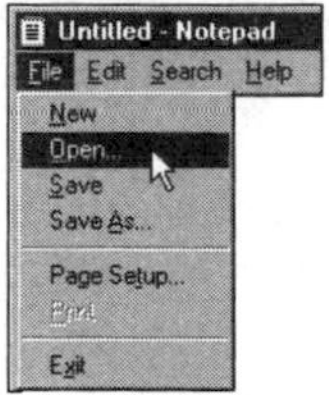

2. **Click on the word Open (or press O) to bring up the Open dialog box.**

   You can predict that the word Open will call up a dialog box because of the trailing ... things beside the word Open on-screen. (Those ... things are called an *ellipsis* or *three dots,* depending on the tightness of your English teacher's hair bun.)

Figure 6-15 shows the Open dialog box that leaps to the front of the screen. In fact, a similar dialog box appears almost any time you mess with the File pull-down menu in any program.

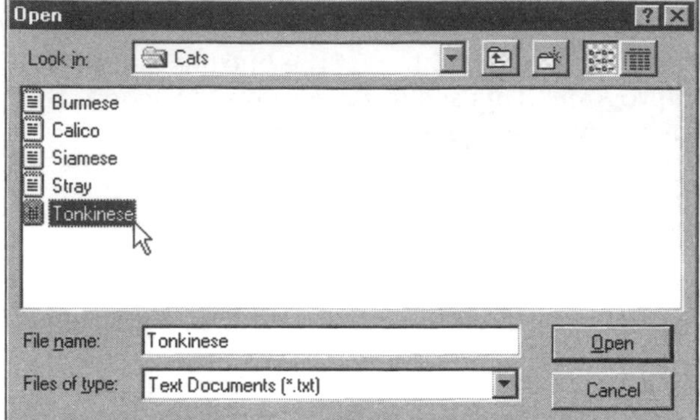

Figure 6-15: This type of Open dialog box appears whenever you open a file in any Windows NT- or Windows 95/98-based program.

- If you find your filename listed in the list box that appears the first time you click Open, you're in luck. Double-click on the file's name, and it automatically jumps into the program. Or hold down Alt and press N, type in the file's name, and press Enter. Or click on the file's name once and press Enter. Or curse Windows NT for giving you so many options for such a simple procedure.
- If you don't find the file's name, it's probably in a different *folder* (also known as a directory). Click on the little Look in box along the top, and Windows NT displays a bunch of other folders to rummage through. Each time you click on a different folder, that folder's contents appear in the first list box.
- Can't find the right folder? Then perhaps that file is on a different drive. Click on one of the other Drive icons listed in the Look in box to search in a different drive. *Drive icons* are those little gray box things; folder icons look like, well, folders.
- Could the file be named something strange? Then click on the Files of type drop-down list box (or hold down Alt and press T) to choose a different file type. To see all the files in a directory, choose the All Files (*.*) option. Then all the files in that directory show up.

- Don't know what those little icons along the top are supposed to do? Then rest your mouse pointer over the one that has you stumped. After a second or so, the increasingly polite Windows NT brings a box of explanatory information to the screen.
- This stuff is incredibly mind-numbing, of course, if you've never been exposed to directories, drives, folders, wildcards, or other equally carnivorous carryovers from the Windows NT DOS days. For a more rigorous explanation of this scary file-management stuff, troop to Chapter 13.

- Still using older programs from Windows 3.1 or Windows NT 3.51? Then you'll still come across the older-style boxes for opening files.

Hey! When Do I Click, and When Do I Double-Click?

When do you just click and when do you double-click is certainly a legitimate question, but Microsoft only coughs up a vague answer. Microsoft says that you should click when you're selecting something in Windows NT and you should double-click when you're carrying out an action.

Huh?

Well, you're *selecting* something when you're highlighting it. For example, you may select a check box, an option button, an icon, or a file's name. You click on it to select it, and then you look at it to make sure that it looks OK. If you're satisfied with your selection, you click on the OK button to complete the job.

To select something is to set it up for later use.

When you *choose* something, however, the response is more immediate. For example, if you double-click on a filename, that file immediately loads itself into your program. The double-click says, "I'm choosing this file, and I want it now, buster." The double-click alleviates the need to confirm your selection by clicking on the OK button.

You choose something you want to have carried out immediately.

- All right, this is still vague. So always start off by trying a single-click. If that doesn't do the job, then try a double-click. This strategy is usually a lot safer than double-clicking first and asking questions later.
- If you accidentally double-click rather than single-click, it usually doesn't matter. But if something terrible happens, hold down the Ctrl key and press Z. You can usually undo any damage.
- If Windows NT keeps mistaking your purposeful double-click for two disjointed single-clicks, then head for the section in Chapter 11 on tinkering with the Control Panel. Adjusting Windows NT so that it recognizes a double-click when you make one is pretty easy.
- Don't know when you're supposed to use your left mouse button and when you're supposed to use your right mouse button? Everybody assumes you already know this important tidbit of information, so it's covered in Chapter 3.

But clicking doesn't work that way in Windows Explorer!

Okay, time to confess — Windows Explorer doesn't work exactly as you'd expect. Here's how it works.

In the left pane of Explorer, you see that some icons have little plus signs next to them. That means more folders live inside of them, like those nested Russian dolls. To see what's inside a folder, click on its plus sign. (Or to package the folders back inside, click on the minus sign.)

Whether you single-click or double-click doesn't matter — the folders spread out below their "parent" folder on the left side of Explorer.

The moral? If a single doesn't work, try a double, and vice versa. For more on the Explorer and its mysterious ways, stroll over to Chapter 13.

Chapter 7

Moving the Windows Around

In This Chapter

- Moving a window to the top of the pile
- Moving a window from here to there
- Making windows bigger or smaller
- Shrinking windows onto the taskbar
- Turning taskbar icons back into windows
- Switching from window to window
- Fiddling with the taskbar

Ah, the power of Windows NT. Using separate windows, you can put a spreadsheet, a drawing program, and a word processor on-screen at the same time.

You can copy a hot-looking graphic from your drawing program and toss it into your memo. Stick a chunk of your spreadsheet into your memo, too. And why not? All three windows can be on-screen at the same time.

You have only one problem: With so many windows on-screen at the same time, you can't see anything but a confusing jumble of programs.

This chapter shows how to move those darn windows around on-screen so you can see at least one of them.

Moving a Window to the Top of the Pile

Take a good look at the mixture of windows on-screen. Sometimes you can recognize a tiny portion of the window you're after. If so, you're in luck. Move the mouse pointer until it hovers over that tiny portion of the window and then click the mouse button. Shazam! Windows NT immediately brings the clicked-on window to the front of the screen.

That newly enlarged window probably covers up strategic parts of other windows. But at least you can get some work done, one window at a time.

Can't see any part of your misplaced window? Then look for its name along the buttons that usually live along the bottom of your screen. (That's called the taskbar, and it's discussed later in this chapter.) Click on the name, and the window magically appears.

Windows NT places a lot of windows on-screen simultaneously. But unless you have two heads, you'll probably use just one window at a time, leaving the remaining programs to wait patiently in the background. The window that's on top, ready to be used, is called the *active window*.

- Although many windows may be on-screen, you can enter information into only one of them: the active window. To make a window active, click on any part of it. The window rises to the top, ready to do your bidding.
- The active window is the one with the most lively title bar along its top — this title bar is a brighter color than all the others.
- The last window you've clicked on is the active window. All your subsequent keystrokes and mouse movements affect that window.
- Some programs can run in the background, even if they're not in the currently active window. Some communications programs can keep talking to other computers in the background, for example, and some spreadsheets can merrily crunch numbers, unconcerned with whether they're the currently active window. Imagine!

Another way to move to a window is by clicking on its name in the Windows NT taskbar. See "The Window-Manipulating Taskbar and Its Cohorts" section later in this chapter.

Moving a Window from Here to There

Sometimes you want to move a window to a different place on-screen (the screen is known in Windows NT parlance as the Desktop). Maybe part of the window hangs off the edge of the Desktop, and you want it centered. Or maybe you want to put two windows on-screen side by side so you can compare their contents.

In either case, you can move a window by grabbing its title bar, that thick bar along its top. Put the mouse pointer over the window's title bar and hold down the mouse button. Now use the title bar as the window's handle. When you move the mouse around, you tug the window along with it.

When you've moved the window to where you want it to stay, release the mouse button to release the window. The window stays put and on top of the pile.

- The process of holding down the mouse button while moving the mouse is called dragging. When you let go of the mouse button, you're dropping what you've dragged.
- When placing two windows next to each other on-screen, you usually need to change their size as well as their location. The very next section tells how to change a window's size, but don't forget to read "The Window-Manipulating Taskbar and Its Cohorts" section later in this chapter. It's full of tips and tricks for resizing windows as well as moving them around.
- Stuck with a keyboard and no mouse? Press Alt, the spacebar, and M. Then use the arrow keys to move the window around. Press Enter when the window is in the right place.

Making a Window Bigger or Smaller

Moving the windows around isn't enough sometimes — they still cover each other up. Luckily, you don't need any special hardware to make them bigger or smaller. See that thin little border running around the edge of the window? Use the mouse to yank on a window's corner border, and you can change its size.

First, point at the corner with the mouse arrow. When the mouse arrow is positioned over the corner, the arrow becomes two-headed. Now hold down the mouse button and drag the corner in or out to make the window smaller or bigger. The window's border expands or contracts as you tug on it with the mouse, so you can see what you're doing.

When you're done yanking and the window's border looks about the right size, let go of the mouse button. The window immediately redraws itself, taking the new position.

Here's the procedure, step by step:

1. **Point the mouse pointer at the edge of the corner.**

   It turns into a two-headed arrow, as shown in Figure 7-1.

Figure 7-1: When the mouse points at the window's bottom corner, the arrow grows a second head.

2. **Hold down the mouse button and move the two-headed arrow in or out to make the window bigger or smaller.**

   Figure 7-2 shows how the new outline takes shape when you pull the corner inward to make the window smaller.

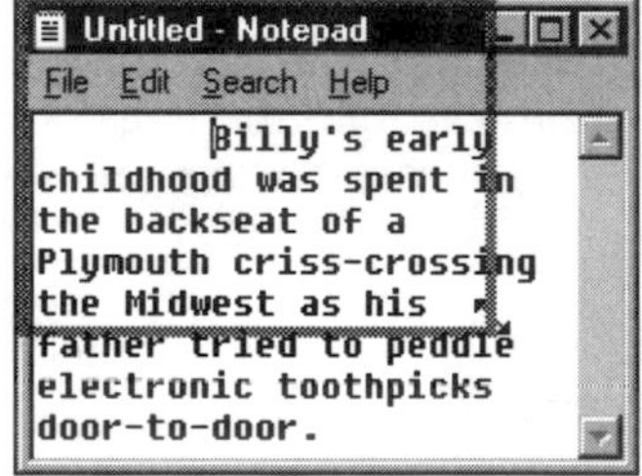

Figure 7-2: As you move the mouse, the window's border changes to reflect its new shape.

3. **Release the mouse button.**

   The window shapes itself to fit into the border you just created. That's it! (See Figure 7-3.)

Figure 7-3: Release the mouse button, and the window fills its newly adjusted border.

If a window is hanging off the edge of the screen and you can't seem to position it so that all of it fits on-screen, try shrinking it first. Grab a visible corner and drag it toward the window's center. Release the mouse button, and the window shrinks itself to fit in its now smaller border. Then grab the window's title bar and hold down the mouse button. When you drag the title bar back toward the center of the screen, you can see the whole window once again.

Making a Window Fill the Whole Screen

Sooner or later, you get tired of all this New Age, multiwindow mumbo jumbo. Why can't you just put one huge window on-screen? Well, you can.

To make any window grow as big as it gets, double-click on its title bar, that topmost bar along the top of the window. The window leaps up to fill the screen, covering up all the other windows.

To bring the pumped-up window back to normal size, double-click on its title bar once again. The window shrinks to its former size, and you can see everything that it was covering up.

- When a window fills the entire screen, it loses its borders. That means you can no longer change its size by tugging on its title bar or dragging its borders. Those borders just aren't there anymore.
- If you're morally opposed to double-clicking on a window's title bar to expand it, you can expand it another way: Click on the window's maximize button, the middlemost of the three little boxes in its top-right corner. The window hastily fills the entire screen. At the same time, the maximize button turns into a restore button; click on the restore button when you want the window to return to its previous size.

  See Chapter 6 for more information on the maximize, minimize, and restore buttons.
- DOS-based programs running in on-screen windows don't usually fill the screen. When you double-click on their title bars, they get bigger, but Windows NT still keeps 'em relatively small. If you take them out of the window, however, they fill the screen completely and shove Windows NT completely into the background. To take a DOS-based program out of a window, click on the DOS window to make it active and then hold down the Alt key and press Enter. The DOS program suddenly lunges for the entire screen, and Windows NT disappears. To bring it back, hold down the Alt key and press Enter again. (For more of this DOS stuff, see Chapter 15.)

Shrinking Windows to the Taskbar

Windows spawn windows. You start with one window to write a letter to Mother. You open another window to check her address, for example, and then yet another to see whether you've forgotten any recent birthdays. Before you know it, four more windows are crowded across the Desktop.

To combat the clutter, Windows NT provides a simple means of window control: You can stuff a screen-cluttering window into a tiny button at the bottom of the screen.

See the three buttons lurking in just about every window's top-right corner? Click on the minimize button — the button with the little line in it. Whoosh! The window disappears — but a little button listing that window's name still lives on the bar running along the bottom of your screen (the taskbar). Click on that window's button on the taskbar, and your window hops back onto the screen, ready for action.

Or if you have a whole lot of windows making a mess of your screen, you can shrink them all to the taskbar. Just click the little desktop icon on the taskbar:

The difference can be dramatic. Figure 7-4 shows a Desktop with a bunch of open windows.

Figure 7-5 shows that same Desktop after all windows have been packed into their buttons along the taskbar.

The windows are still readily available, mind you. Just click on a window's button from the taskbar along the bottom of the screen, and that window instantly leaps back to its former place on-screen (see Figure 7-6).

- To shrink an open window so that it's out of the way, click on the leftmost of the three buttons in the window's top-right corner. The window minimizes itself into a button and lines itself up on the taskbar.
- Each button on the taskbar has a label so that you can tell which program the button represents.
- When you minimize a window, you neither destroy its contents nor close it. You merely change its shape. It is still loaded into memory, waiting for you to play with it again.
- To put the window back where it was, click on its button on the taskbar. It hops back up to the same place it was before.

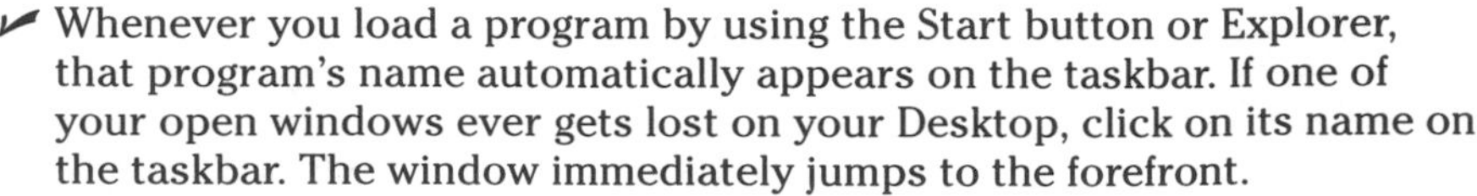

- Whenever you load a program by using the Start button or Explorer, that program's name automatically appears on the taskbar. If one of your open windows ever gets lost on your Desktop, click on its name on the taskbar. The window immediately jumps to the forefront.

Figure 7-4: A Desktop can be distracting if too many windows are open simultaneously.

Figure 7-5: Here's the same Desktop that's shown in Figure 7-4. Seeing what's going on is easier when the open windows are turned into icons.

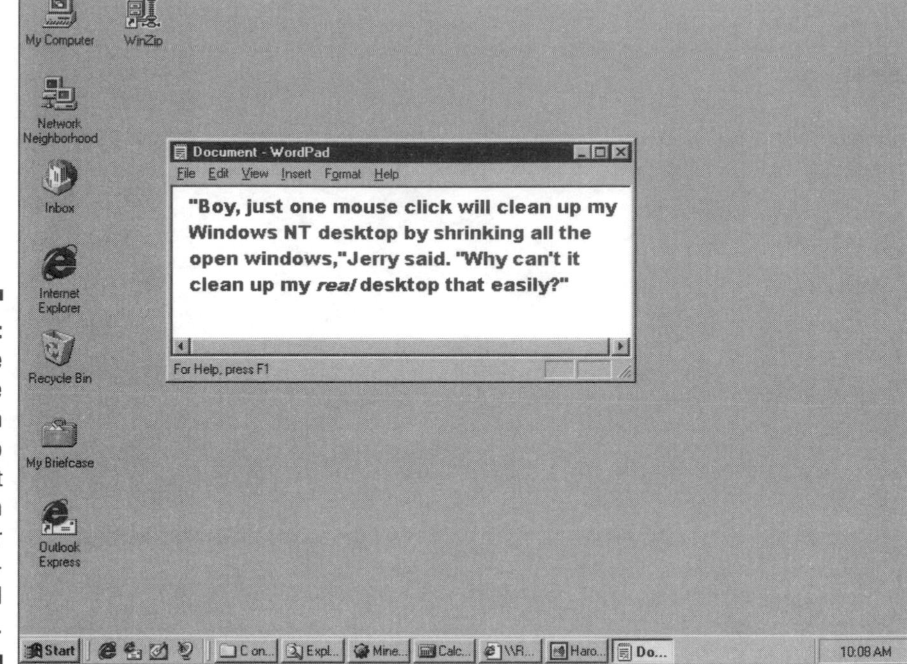

Figure 7-6: Click on the icon for the program you want to see, and it pops open on your newly-tidied Desktop.

- Want to shrink just one window? Click the window's icon on the taskbar and zoom! It's minimized.
- Keyboard users can press Alt, the spacebar, and N to minimize a window. Holding down Alt and pressing the Tab key restores the window to its former glory. (That fun little tip gets its own section, "The Alt+Tab trick," later in this chapter.)

Turning Taskbar Buttons Back into Windows

To turn a minimized window at the bottom of the screen back into a useful program in the middle of the screen, just click on its name on the taskbar. Pretty simple, huh?

Keeping your icons straight

Don't be confused by a program's icon on your Desktop and a program's button on the taskbar along the bottom of your screen. They're two different things. The button at the bottom of the screen stands for a program that has already been loaded into the computer's memory; it's ready for immediate action. The icon on your Desktop or in Windows NT Explorer stands for a program that is sitting on the computer's hard disk, waiting to be loaded.

If you mistakenly click on the icon in Explorer or on the Desktop rather than the button on the taskbar at the bottom of the screen, you load a *second* copy of that program. That means two versions of the program are loaded: one running as a window and the other running as a taskbar button waiting to be turned back into a window.

You'll see two buttons on the taskbar with the same name. Running two versions can cause confusion — especially if you start entering stuff into both versions of the same program. You won't know which window has the *right* version!

If two buttons on the taskbar say the same thing, you probably opened two copies of the same program. Click on each button to compare the windows, and close the one that you don't need so you don't get confused as to which is which!

- If you prefer wading through menus, just click on the shrunken window's button with your right mouse button. A Control menu shoots out the top of the button's head. Choose the menu's Restore option, and the program leaps back to its former window position.
- In addition to using a click, you can use a few other methods to turn icons back into program windows. The very next section describes one way, and "The Window-Manipulating Taskbar and Its Cohorts" section later in this chapter describes another.

Switching from Window to Window

Sometimes switching from window to window is easy. If you can see any part of the window you want — a corner, a bar, or a piece of dust — just click on it. That's all it takes to bring that window to the front of the screen, ready for action.

You can also just click on that window's button on the taskbar along the bottom of your screen. The following sections give a few extra tricks for switching from window to window to window.

The Alt+Tab trick

This trick is so fun that Microsoft should have plastered it across the front of the Windows NT box instead of hiding it in the middle of the manual.

Hold down the Alt key and press the Tab key. A most welcome box pops up in the center of the screen, naming all the programs currently loaded into your computer's memory.

If the program you're after has a little box around it, like the Cabbage Recipes icon in Figure 7-7, rejoice! And remove your finger from the Alt key. The window named in that box leaps to the screen.

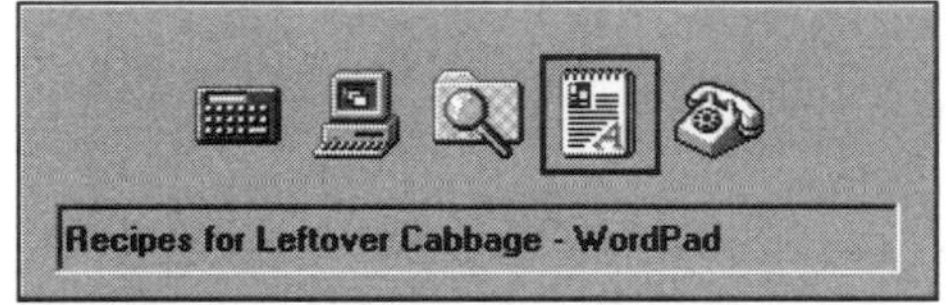

Figure 7-7: Hold down Alt and keep pressing Tab until a box appears around your desired program; then release Alt to make that program come to the top of the screen.

If you're looking for a different program, keep your finger on the Alt key and press the Tab key once again. At each press of Tab, Windows NT moves its little box around the name of another open program. When the box reaches the program that you want, release the Alt key and then hoot and holler. The program leaps to the screen, ready for your working pleasure.

- The Alt+Tab trick works even if you're running a DOS-based program full-screen with Windows NT lurking in the background. The DOS program disappears while the pop-up box has its moment in the sun. (And the DOS program returns when you're done playing around, too.)
- The Alt+Tab trick cycles through all the currently open programs, whether the programs are running in on-screen windows or living their lives as buttons on the taskbar. When you release the Alt key, the program currently listed in the pop-up window leaps to life.

The Alt+Esc trick

The concept is getting kind of stale with this one, but here goes: If you hold down the Alt key and press the Esc key, Windows NT cycles through all the open programs but in a slightly less efficient way.

Instead of bringing the program's name to a big box in the middle of the screen, Windows NT simply highlights the program, whether it's in a window or sitting as a button on the taskbar. Sometimes this method can be handy, but usually it's a little slower.

If Windows NT highlights a program resting on the taskbar, the Alt+Esc trick simply highlights that program's button at the bottom of the screen. That's not much of a visual indicator, and most of the time it won't even catch your eye.

When the window you want is highlighted, release the Alt key. If it's an open window, it becomes the active window. But if you release the Alt key while a button's name is highlighted, you need to take one more step: You need to click on the button to get the window on-screen.

The Window-Manipulating Taskbar and Its Cohorts

This section introduces one of the handiest tricks in Windows NT, so pull your chair in a little closer. Windows NT comes with a special program that keeps track of all the open programs. Called the taskbar, it always knows what programs are running and where they are. Shown in Figure 7-8, the taskbar normally lives along the bottom of your screen, although Chapter 11 shows how to move it to any edge you want.

From the taskbar, you can perform powerful magic on your open windows, as shown in the next few sections.

- See how the button for Calculator looks "pushed in" in Figure 7-8? That's because Calculator is the currently active window on the Desktop. One of your taskbar's buttons always looks "pushed in" unless you close or minimize all the windows on your Desktop.

- Don't see the taskbar? Then hold down Ctrl and press Esc. Windows NT instantly brings the taskbar to the surface, ready to do your bidding.
- If you have a Desktop folder open, that folder also shows as a button on the taskbar.

Figure 7-8: Always handy, the taskbar lists your currently running programs and lets you bring them to the forefront by clicking on their names.

Switching to another window

See a window you'd like to play with listed on the taskbar? Just click on its name, and it rises to the surface. Simple (especially if you've ever labored under Windows NT 3.51). If the taskbar isn't showing for some reason, pressing Ctrl+Esc calls it to the forefront.

Closing a window from the taskbar

Mad at a program? Then kill it. Click on the program's name on the taskbar with your right mouse button and then click on the word Close from the menu that pops up (or press C). The highlighted program quits, just as if you'd chosen its Exit command from within its own window.

The departing program gives you a chance to save any work before it quits and disappears from the screen.

Cascading and tiling windows

Sometimes those windows are scattered everywhere. How can you clean up in a hurry? By using the taskbar's Cascade and Tile commands. Right-click (use the right mouse button) on a blank spot on the taskbar — the spot on or near the clock is usually good — and the Cascade and Tile commands appear.

The commands organize your open windows in drastically different ways. Figure 7-9 shows what your screen looks like when you choose the Cascade command.

Talk about neat and orderly! The taskbar grabs all the windows and deals them out like cards across the Desktop. When you choose the taskbar's Cascade command, all the open windows are lined up neatly on-screen with their title bars showing.

The Tile Horizontally and Tile Vertically commands rearrange the windows, too, but in a slightly different way (see Figure 7-10).

The Tile commands arrange all the currently open windows across the screen, giving each one the same amount of space. This arrangement helps you find a window that has been missing for a few hours.

Note: Both the Tile and Cascade commands arrange only open windows. They don't open up any windows currently shrunken into buttons on the taskbar.

Arranging icons on the Desktop

The taskbar can be considered a housekeeper of sorts, but it only does windows. It arranges the open windows neatly across the screen, but it doesn't touch any icons living on your Desktop.

If the open windows look fine but the Desktop's icons look a little shabby, click on a blank area of your Desktop with your right mouse button. When the menu pops up from nowhere, click the Arrange Icons command and choose the way you'd like Windows NT to line up your icons: by Name, Type, Size, or Date.

Or simply choose the Auto Arrange option from the same menu. Then your Desktop's icons will always stay in neat, orderly rows.

Finding the taskbar

Taskbar not along the bottom of your screen? Then hold down Ctrl and press Esc, and the taskbar instantly appears. If you'd prefer that the taskbar not disappear sometimes, head for Chapter 12, where we explain how to customize your taskbar so it doesn't bail on you.

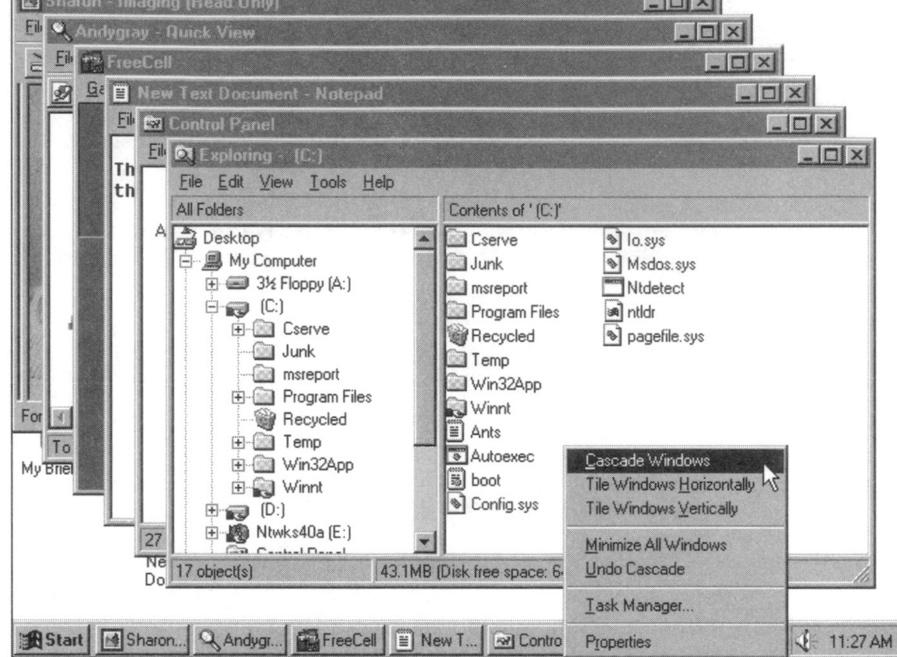

Figure 7-9: The taskbar's Cascade command piles all the open windows neatly across the screen. It's a favorite command of blackjack players.

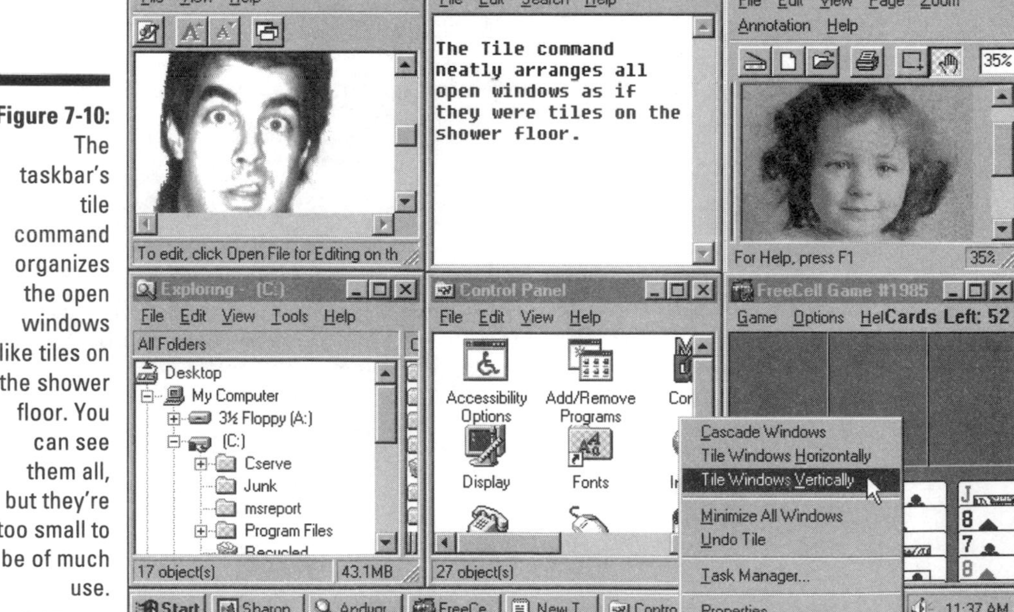

Figure 7-10: The taskbar's tile command organizes the open windows like tiles on the shower floor. You can see them all, but they're too small to be of much use.

Chapter 8

I Can't Find It!

In This Chapter

- Finding lost windows
- Finding lost files
- Finding your way back to Windows NT from DOS
- Finding misplaced snippets of information
- Finding the right icon with Quick View

Sooner or later, Windows NT gives you that head-scratching feeling. "Golly," you say, as you frantically tug on your mouse cord, "that window was right there a second ago. Where did it go?"

When Windows NT starts playing hide-and-seek with your programs, files, windows, or other information, this chapter tells you where to search and how to make it stop playing foolish games. Then when you find your Solitaire window, you can get back to work.

Plucking a Lost Window from the Taskbar

Forget about that huge, 1940s rolltop mahogany desk in the resale shop window. The Windows NT peewee desktop can't be any bigger than the size of your monitor.

In a way, Windows NT works more like those spike memo holders than like an actual desktop. Every time you open a new window, you're tossing another piece of information onto the spike. The window on top is relatively easy to see, but what's lying directly underneath it?

If you can see a window's ragged edge protruding from any part of the pile, click on it. The window magically rushes to the top of the pile. But what if you can't see any part of the window at all? How do you know it's even on the Desktop?

You can solve this mystery by calling up your helpful Windows NT detective: the taskbar. The taskbar keeps a master list of everything that's happening on your screen (even the invisible stuff).

If the taskbar isn't squatting along one edge of your screen, hold down your Ctrl key and press the Esc key. The taskbar pops into action (see Figure 8-1).

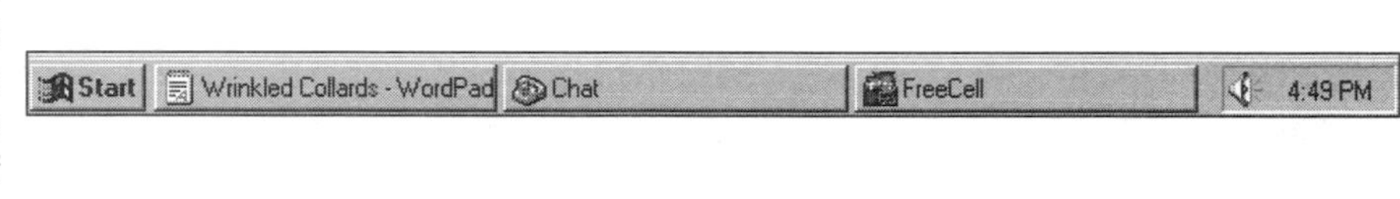

Figure 8-1: The mighty taskbar always contains an up-to-date list of all open windows.

See the list of programs stamped onto buttons on the taskbar? Your missing window is somewhere on the list. When you spot it, click on its name, and the taskbar instantly tosses your newfound window to the top of the pile.

- Most of the time, the taskbar performs admirably in tracking down lost windows. If your window isn't on the list, then you probably closed it. Closing a window, also known as exiting a window, takes it off your Desktop and out of your computer's memory. To get that window back, you need to open it again, using the services of the Start button (see Chapter 12), the Explorer (see Chapter 13), or the My Computer program (also in Chapter 13).
- I lied. Sometimes a window can be running and yet not listed on the taskbar. Some utility programmers figure that people don't need to see their programs or their icons. Berkeley Systems' After Dark screen saver, for example, can be running on your screen and yet not show up on the taskbar. It simply runs in the background. (***Hint:*** Sometimes pressing Alt+Tab brings up the program's icon, as explained in Chapter 7.)
- Sometimes you see your missing program listed on the taskbar, and you click on its name to dredge it from the depths. But even though the taskbar brings the missing program to the top, you still can't find it on your Desktop. The program may be hanging off the edge of your Desktop, so check out the very next section.

Finding a Window That's off the Edge of the Screen

Even a window at the top of the pile can be nearly invisible. A window can be moved anywhere on the Windows NT Desktop, including off the screen. In fact, you can inadvertently move 99 percent of a window off the screen, leaving just a tiny corner showing (see Figure 8-2). Clicking on the window's name in the taskbar won't be much help in this case, unfortunately. The window's already on top, but it's still too far off the screen to be of any use.

- If you can see any part of the rogue window's title bar, that thick strip along the window's top, hold the mouse button down and drag the traveler back to the center of the screen.
- Sometimes a window's title bar can be completely off the top of the screen. How can you drag it back into view? Start by clicking on any part of the window that shows. Then hold down your Alt key and press the spacebar. A menu appears from nowhere. Select the word Move, and a mysterious four-headed arrow appears. Press your arrow keys until the window's border moves to a more manageable location and then press Enter. Whew! Don't let it stray that far again!

Figure 8-2: WordPad is almost completely off the bottom-right corner of the screen, making it difficult to locate.

- For an easier way to make Windows NT not only track down all your criminally hidden windows but also line them up on the screen in mug-shot fashion, check out the next two sections.

Cascading Windows (The Deal-All-the-Windows in-Front-of-Me Approach)

Are you ready to turn Windows NT into a personal card dealer who gathers up all your haphazardly tossed windows and deals them out neatly on the Desktop in front of you?

To turn the taskbar into a card dealer, click on a blank area of your taskbar — near the clock is good — with your right mouse button, and a menu pops up. Click on the Cascade option, and the taskbar gathers all your open windows and deals them out in front of you, just like in a game of blackjack.

Each window's title bar is neatly exposed, ready to be grabbed and reprimanded with a quick click of the mouse.

- If the missing window doesn't appear in the stack of neatly dealt windows, perhaps it's been minimized. The Cascade command gathers and deals only the open windows; it leaves the minimized windows resting as buttons along the taskbar. The solution? Click on the missing window's button on the taskbar before cascading the windows across the screen.
- For more about the Cascade command, check out Chapter 7.

Tiling Windows (The Stick-Everything-on-the Screen-at-Once Approach)

Windows NT can stick all your open windows onto the screen at the same time. You can finally see all of them — no overlapping corners, edges, or menu flaps. Sound too good to be true? It is. Windows NT shrinks all the windows so they fit on the screen. And some of the weird-shaped windows still overlap. But, hey, at least you can see most of them.

Click on a blank area of the taskbar with your right mouse button and choose Tile Vertically or Tile Horizontally from the pop-up menu.

- The Tile command pulls all the open windows onto the screen at the same time. If you have two open windows, each of them takes up half the screen. With three windows, each window gets a third of the screen. If you have 12 windows, each window takes up one-twelfth of the available space. (They're very small.)
- The Tile Vertically command arranges the windows vertically, like socks hanging from a clothesline. Tile Horizontally arranges the windows horizontally, like a stack of folded sweatshirts. The difference is the most pronounced if you're tiling only a few windows, however.
- You can find more information about the Tile command in Chapter 7. The minimize button is covered in Chapter 6.

DOS without Getting Lost

Windows NT gets tricky if you start running DOS programs. Unlike Windows programs, hoggy DOS programs expect to have the entire computer to themselves. Windows NT has to trick them into thinking everything is normal.

As part of one trick, Windows NT enables you to run a DOS program so that it takes up the whole screen, just as if you weren't using Windows NT at all. All you see on the screen is the DOS program. Windows NT gives no clue that it is lurking somewhere in the background.

This trick makes the DOS program happier, but it can cause headaches for you. You can have a hard time remembering exactly what's happening. Are you running a DOS program under Windows NT? Did some nasty person boot up an old version of DOS on your computer? Sometimes Windows NT waits in the background while a weird command prompt sits on the screen with no program showing at all. With all these options, getting lost is easy.

- If you think that you may be lost at a command prompt, type the word EXIT (lowercase works, too) and then press Enter:

  ```
  C:\> EXIT
  ```

  That is, type exit and then press the Enter key. If Windows NT is waiting in the background, it lurches back to life, banishing the command prompt in the process. If you want to return to that command prompt for some unlikely reason, click on the Start button and then click on Command Prompt from the Programs menu.
- If you're stuck in a DOS program and want to get back to another window, hold down the Alt key and press Esc. If Windows NT is lurking in the background, it leaps back to the screen, turning your DOS program into a button along the taskbar. Then, because you're back to Windows NT, you can grab the window you really want.

- For more soothing salves to treat DOS-program confusion, check out Chapter 15.

Finding Lost Files, Folders, or Computers (But Not Misplaced Laptops)

Windows NT has gotten much better at finding lost files and folders. And it should; after all, it's the one who's hiding the darn things. If one of your files, folders, or programs (or computers, if you're on a network) runs off into the electronic mists, make Windows NT do the work in getting the darn thing back by doing the following:

1. **Click on the Start button.**
2. **Choose the Find option.**
3. **Depending on what you're searching for, choose either Computer or Files or Folders from the pop-up menu, as shown in Figure 8-3.**

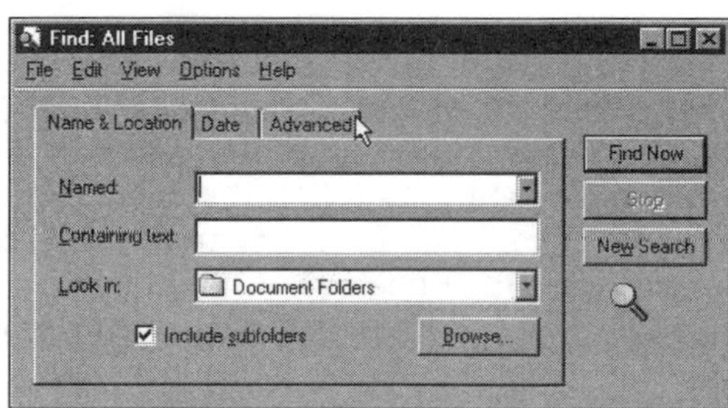

Figure 8-3: Windows NT can search your computer for lost files, folders, and, if you're on a network, lost computers.

An incredibly detailed program pops up, letting you search for files meeting the most minute criteria. Best yet, it can simply search for missing files by their names. For example, suppose that your file called HYDRATOR INSPECTION disappeared over the weekend. To make matters worse, you're not even sure you spelled Hydrator correctly when saving the file.

The solution? Choose the Find program's Files or Folders command and type in any part of the filename you can remember. In this case, type **drat** into the Named box and click on the Find Now button. The Find program lists any file or folder with a name that contains drat, as shown in Figure 8-4. Quick and simple.

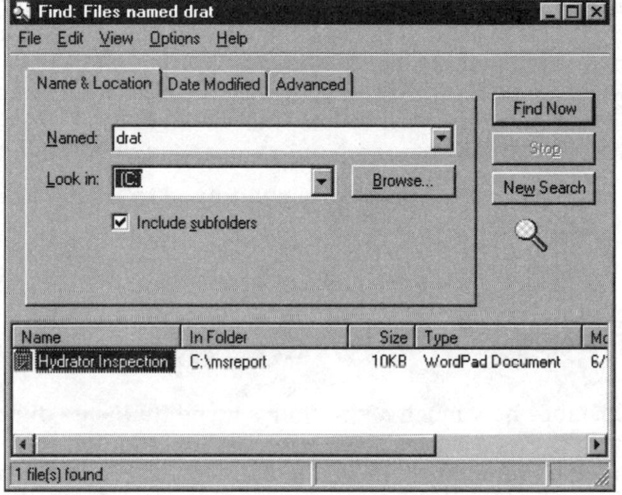

Figure 8-4: Here, the Windows NT Find program sniffed out a file with drat as part of its name.

- Of course, you don't have to keep things quick and simple. For example, the Find program normally searches drive C — your computer's hard disk. If you prefer that it search every nook and cranny — all your hard disks and even any floppy disks or CD-ROM drives — click on the little downward-pointing arrow near the Look in box. After a menu drops down, click on the My Computer setting. That tells the Find program to look everywhere on your computer.
- Make sure that a check mark appears in the Include subfolders box, shown in Figure 8-4. If that option's not checked, the Find program searches through only your first layer of folders — it doesn't look inside any folders living inside of other folders.
- Can't remember what you called a file but know the time and date you created it? Then click on the Date Modified tab along the program's top. That lets you narrow down the search to files created only during certain times. (This feature is especially handy for finding files you know you created yesterday.)
- For a quick peek inside some of the files the Find program turned up, click on the file's name with your right mouse button and choose Quick View from the menu that pops up. Windows NT shows you the file's contents without making you load the program that created the file.
- The Advanced option lets people search for specific types of files: Bitmap files, Faxes, Configuration settings, and other more complicated options. To be on the safe side, leave it set for All Files and Folders, so that you know the Find command is searching through everything.

- The Find Computers command lets you locate any other computer on your network, providing you know the exact name of the computer — which may be something like ADMIN_B52_K2. Is that likely? A far, far easier way is to double-click on your Desktop's Network Neighborhood icon and look for your missing computer listed in there. You still must know the name of the computer, but at least you don't have to spell it.
- For the scoop on using Network Neighborhood to search for computers, see Chapter 9.

Finding Snippets of Stored Information

Help! You remember how much Mr. Jennings loved that wine during lunch, so you stealthily typed the wine's name into your computer. Now, at Christmas time, you don't remember the name of the file where you saved the wine's name. You don't remember the date you created the file, either, or even the folder where you stashed the file. In fact, the only thing you remember is how you described the wine's hard-hitting bouquet when typing it into your computer: "Like an alligator snap from behind a barge."

Luckily, that's all Windows NT needs to find your file. All you have to do is the following:

1. **Click on the Start button.**
2. **Choose Find and then choose Files or Folders.**

   The result is shown in Figure 8-3.
3. **After the Find program pops up, click on the tab marked Advanced.**
4. **Next, click on the box marked Containing text, and type the word you want to search for.**

   In this example, you'd type **barge**, as shown in Figure 8-5.

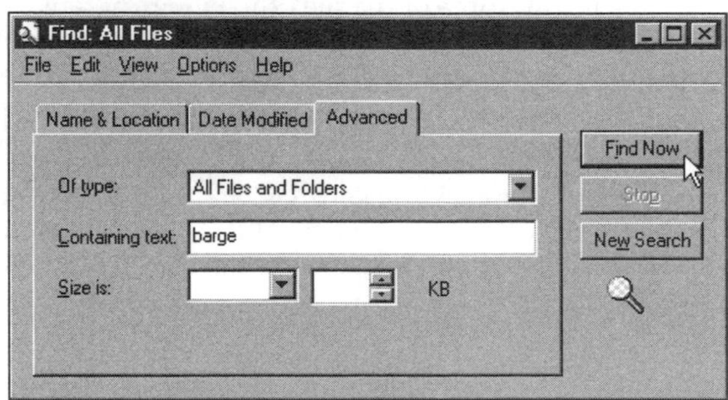

Figure 8-5: The Windows NT Find program can search the entire computer for a file containing the word barge.

Finding a file you created in the past 24 hours

With all its folders, files, and menus piled onto a little desktop, Windows NT is as good at losing files as it is at creating them. Ever lost a file that you *know* you created within the past 24 hours? Or maybe you created it within the past week?

This little trick helps you track down all the files you created in the past 24 hours. (Or within any other interval of time, too.)

1. **Choose Find from the Start button.**
2. **Choose Files or Folders.**
3. **Click on the Date Modified tab.**
4. **Click on the Find all files created or modified button.**

   Windows NT gives you three options, as shown in the accompanying figure.

   - Clicking on the *bottom* button makes Windows NT list all the files created on your computer in the past 24 hours. This feature comes in handy if you can't find a file you created a few hours ago.
   - Clicking on the *middle* button makes Windows NT list all the files created on your computer in the past month. The least handy of the trio, this button usually brings up many files — too many to sort through easily.
   - Clicking on the *top* button lets you tell Windows NT to list all the files created between two dates. If you remember the date you created a file — give or take a few days — this option can be your best shot.

5. **Click on the Find Now button.**

   Windows NT dutifully collects the files you told it to find in Step 4 and lists them in its bottom window.

   The Quick View command, described in an upcoming section in this chapter, works on the files listed in the Find program's window. Click on the filename with your right mouse button, and choose Quick View from the pop-up menu to see what's inside that file.

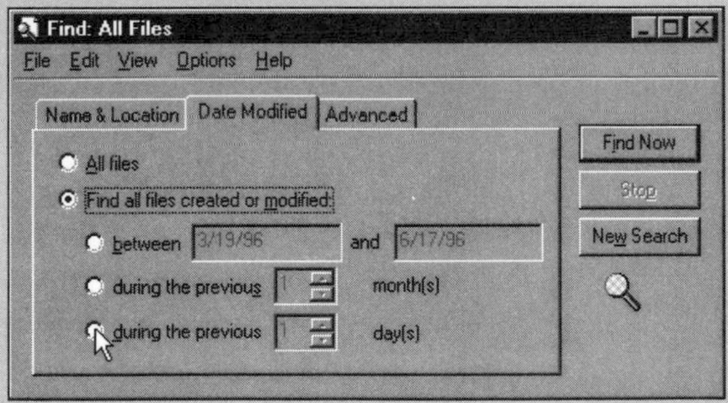

Just like in the previous section, the Find program searches the computer, looking for files meeting your specifications. This time, however, it searches inside the files themselves, looking for the information you're after.

- Feel free to limit your search, using any of the tips and examples discussed in the previous section; they apply here as well.
- CD-ROM discs take a long time to search. You can speed things up by telling the Find program to limit its search to hard disks. (Just popping the CD out of the drive is one way to keep the Find program from searching it.)

- When searching for files containing certain words, type in the words least likely to turn up in other files. For example, the word barge is more unique than like, an, snap, or behind; therefore, it's more likely to bring up the file you need. And if barge doesn't work, try alligator.

Peeking into Icons with Quick View

When you open a real manila folder, separating the food coupons from the letters to a congressperson is easy; the pieces of paper look completely different. But although Windows NT sticks titles beneath all the icons in its folders, the icons often look like one big blur, as shown in Figure 8-6. Which icon stands for what? And where is that letter to the congressperson, anyway?

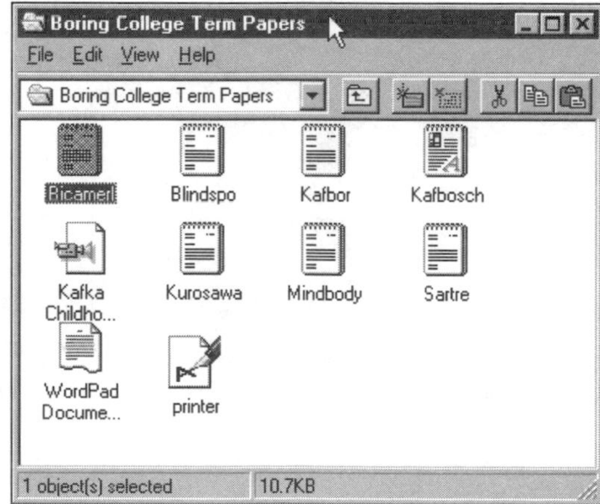

Figure 8-6: Even with their labels, the icons in Windows NT are sometimes hard to tell apart from each other.

You can double-click on an icon to see what file it stands for — a double-click tells Windows NT to load the file into the program that created it and bring them both to the screen. But a faster way exists to get a sneak peek of what's inside many Windows NT icons. Here's how the Quick View feature works:

1. **While pointing at an icon, click your right mouse button.**

   A menu pops up, as shown in Figure 8-7. If Windows NT recognizes the type of file, you see the option Quick View on the menu.

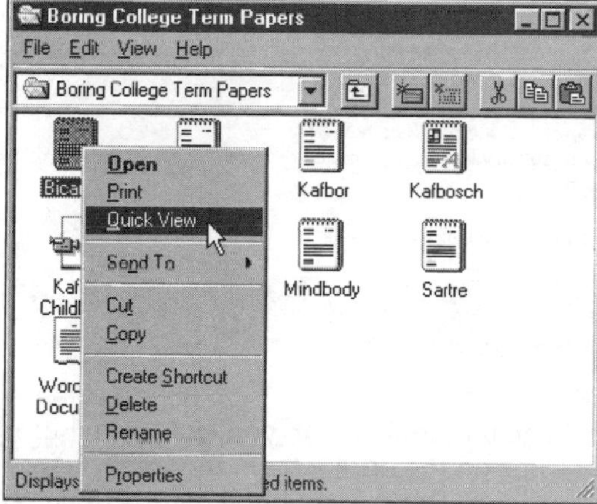

Figure 8-7: Click on an icon with your right mouse button to see if Windows NT offers the Quick View option.

2. **Choose Quick View from the menu.**

   As shown in Figure 8-8, the Quick View option shows you what's inside the file without taking the time to load the program that created it. This option is a quick way to sort through files with similar-looking icons.

- Windows NT 4 lets you use up to 255 characters when naming files. Some of your older files may still have their older, 8-character file names. By using Quick View, you can peek into your old files and give them better names. First, peek into the file to see what's in there. After you decide on a longer, more descriptive name, choose the Rename command. (It's on the same menu as the Quick View command.)
- The Quick View command works with a few dozen of the most popular formats, including Lotus 1-2-3, Bitmap, WordPad, Microsoft Word for Windows, and WordPerfect. A company called Inso sells a special "add-on" Quick View utility called Quick View Plus that lets you peek inside more than 200 types of files. You can reach them at `www.inso.com` on the Web.

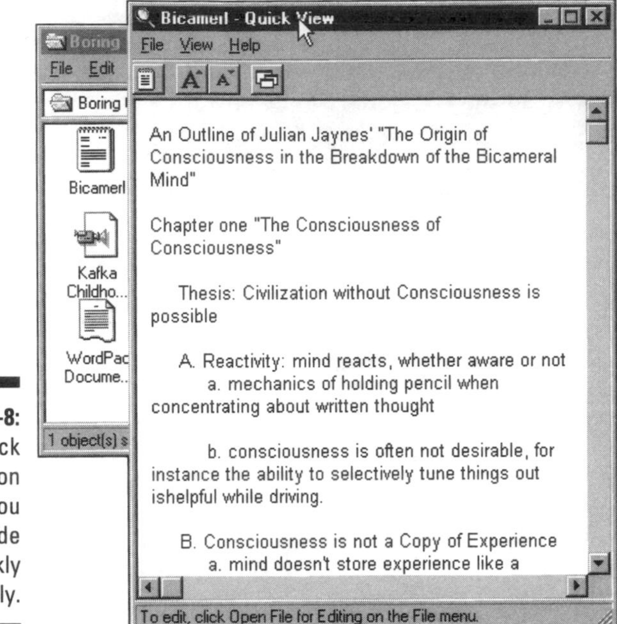

Figure 8-8: The Quick View option lets you peek inside files quickly and easily.

- After you find the file you're looking for, you can open it easily from within Quick View: Click on the little icon in the upper-left corner — the icon beneath the word File. Quick View immediately opens the file for editing.

Chapter 9

Sharing It All on the Network

In This Chapter

- Defining a network
- Finding other computers on the network
- Finding files and folders on other computers
- Making visiting easy
- Giving permission to others to look at your files
- Adding and using network printers

A *network* is simply a bunch of computers and a few printers connected by cables or phone connections. When the network works right, everybody shares information quickly and easily, tossing computerized data back and forth like Frisbee-slingers in the park.

You use a network whenever you visit a bank's Automated Teller Machine (ATM). The key-pad-bearing ATM is a very simple computer that sends your account number, password, and request for money to the bank's Big Computer downtown. The Big Computer knows all about you and tells the ATM that giving you the cash is okay (or not) — even if you've never visited that particular ATM before.

Networks of personal computers work much like the ATMs — except the software is more complicated than an ATM's keypad, the computers are more complicated than ATM terminals, and, unfortunately, the computers never slip you any cash.

If you connect two machines at home so they can both use the same printer, you've made a network. Or, networks can connect thousands of computers in hundreds of locations on multiple continents. But size rarely matters from the network user's point of view: Your work is likely to take you to just a few places on the network, over and over. It's like driving a car: The car can take you anywhere, but most of your driving is from home to work to Bronco Billy's Pizza Palace.

This chapter explains how to share information on a network. It shows how to grab information from other computers, as well as how to let other people grab files off your own computer. It explains how to send stuff to the printer, even if the printer doesn't plug directly into your own computer. Plus the chapter tosses in a few tips on how to muddle your way through things if the Network Administrator *still* hasn't returned from the deli down the street.

What's an Intranet?

An *intranet* — though it sounds complicated — is actually easier to use than the usual, run-of-the-mill computer network. An intranet is simply a company's network that includes *Web pages* — those funky World Wide Web things all the trendy people murmur about at coffee shops. (If you've never seen an intranet Web page, check out Figure 9-1.)

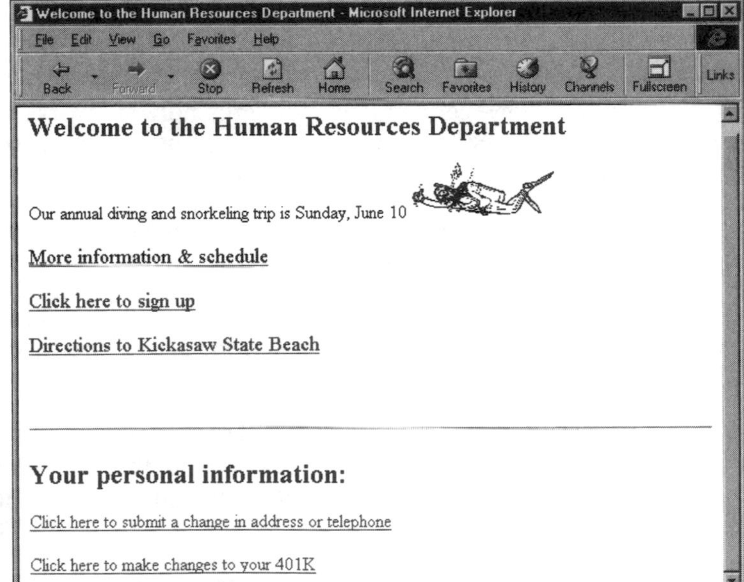

Figure 9-1: An intranet Web page is just like the ones shown on the Internet.

Like magazine pages, Web pages display pictures, charts, text, and other fancy visual doodads that make them easier to see and use. However, Web pages also contain secret entries: special *links* to other Web pages. Move your mouse pointer over the Web page until the arrow turns into a hand, like the one shown in the left margin.

Click the mouse, and a new page leaps to the screen, bringing up a new Web page that relates to whatever subject you clicked on.

Internet Web pages are designed for the whole world to access. When you see the cryptic words `http://www.vw.com` in a magazine's glossy Volkswagen ad, you're looking at the company's Internet address. By heading there, you can see the Volkswagen Internet page and peruse the history of VW vans.

Intranet Web pages, by contrast, are designed for internal use inside a corporation. They're more like corporate newsletters, set up on the network to give information on company picnics, holidays, and impending layoffs.

- Yes, it's easy to click on those little Web links, over and over again, moving from Web page to Web page, just like pushing the remote control on the TV set. (Does the term *Web surfing* come to mind?)
- On a Windows NT network, you navigate both intranet and Internet Web pages by opening Internet Explorer.
- Trek over to Chapter 16 for more on Internet Explorer, Web pages, and Web surfing.

How Do I Know What Computers I Can Access on a Network?

Some kind soul may *tell* you where to find things on your network. It's much more likely you'll have to grab a torch and go spelunking on your own with the Network Neighborhood, described in the next section.

If you're worried about getting into trouble, the rule is simple: Windows NT rarely lets you peer into networked areas where you're not supposed to. In fact, it's so security conscious that you probably won't be able to see things that you should!

- If you accidentally double-click on a "restricted" folder or file that's not open to you, you just see an "access denied" message. No harm done.
- If you're supposed to be able to read a folder on someone else's computer and you can't, just casually tell the Network Administrator, "Pardon me bloke, but I don't seem to have permission to access folder X on computer Y. Could you check into that? There's a good chap." If you have a lorgnette handy, it may help to wave it around.

- If you do accidentally find yourself in a folder where you obviously don't belong — for example, the folder of employee evaluations on your supervisor's computer — that should also be brought to the Network Administrator's attention.

Checking Out the Network Neighborhood

The absolute fastest way to see what's connected to your computer is to head for the Desktop and double-click on the Network Neighborhood icon shown in the accompanying figure.

A window pops open — see Figure 9-2— showing a bunch of computers (including yours).

Double-click on the Entire Network icon shows a list of all the little "subnet-works" of computers on the network, as shown in Figure 9-3.

- The computers listed in the Network Neighborhood window are the ones you're allowed to peek inside. Double-click on one of them, and you can see whatever folders are available for browsing.
- Networks being what they are, it's hard to predict what you'll see in your particular Network Neighborhood. Just about everybody's net-work is set up differently. But there's absolutely no rule against looking around.

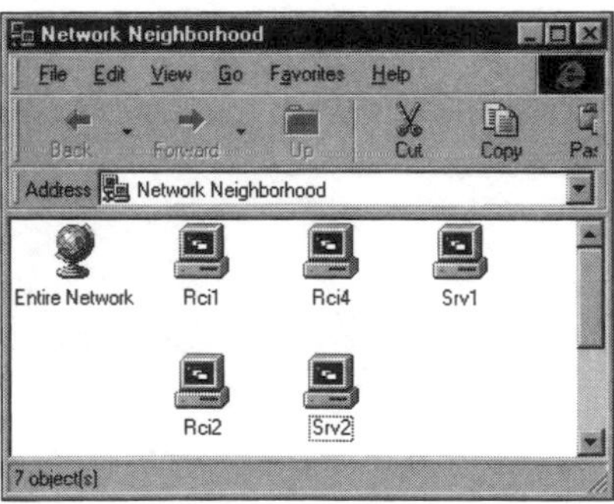

Figure 9-2: After you've double-clicked on the Network Neighborhood icon, you see the computers accessible to your own computer.

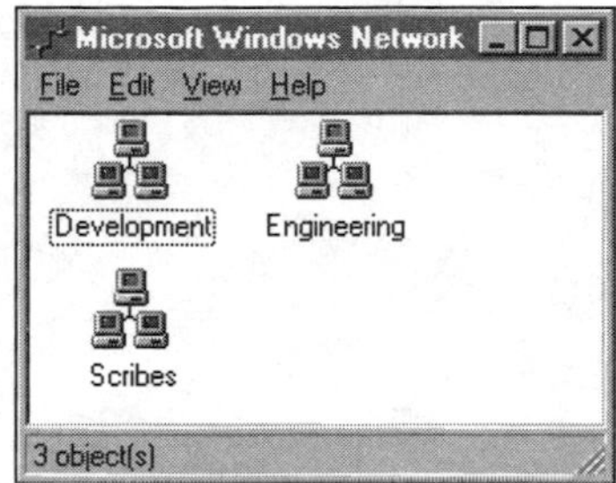

Figure 9-3: A network can contain collections of smaller networks to keep things organized.

After I get on the network, what am I looking at?

When you double-click on a computer in Network Neighborhood, you only see what your Network Administrator has set up to be *shared*. Sometimes only folders are shared, sometimes it's the whole hard disk.

The disk (or a folder or even a single file) can be shared with everybody or with some people and not with others. When an entire disk is shared, for example, it just means that other people have permission to come into that computer and stroll around that particular hard disk, pinching peaches and thumping melons.

The level of security all depends on how your network is set up. Some networks are quite open, with only a few folders that are not public. Other networks, where security is a big issue, have strict limits on what you can see.

Figure 9-4 shows a good-natured computer that's sharing all its hard disks and a printer. Figure 9-5 shows a much more paranoid model with basically nothing shared.

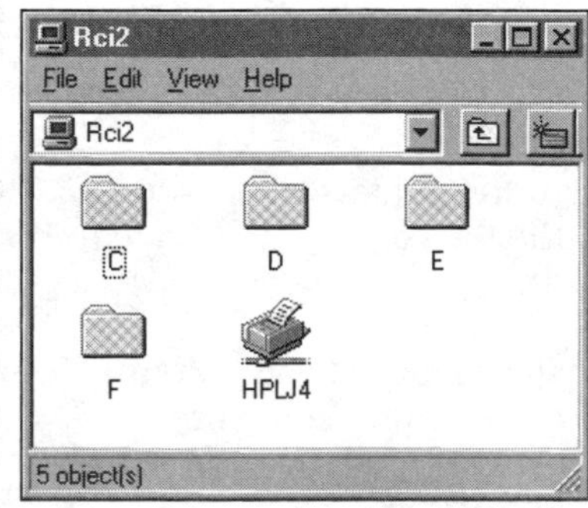

Figure 9-4: This computer has nothing to hide (although the labels on the drives could be a little more informative).

- Figure 9-5's NETLOGON folder is part of Network Administration and is either empty or without interest to normal people like yourself.

Figure 9-5: This computer has basically nothing to offer a visitor.

- Likewise, that computer's Printers folder won't have anything in it that you don't see in your own Printers folder.

Opening files on other computers

To open a file (or folder) on another computer, just double-click on Network Neighborhood, double-click on the name of the computer you want, and just keep clicking through the folders until you find the file you want.

- You find many more file-and-folder opening tips in Chapter 13, by the way. That's why this section is so short.
- Still, all this double-click can be a pain, especially if you need to grab the same file several times a day, or even several times a week. So, the next section shows an easier way to get that file where you want it — and quickly.

Grabbing network files the quick way (with shortcuts)

After you find a file — maybe four or five folders deep — on another computer, you can make a shortcut to the file so you don't have to do all that spelunking the next time you want it.

Here's an example showing a file called 1996 Sales By Month. Say this file is on another computer but you like to peek at it frequently.

1. **Double-click on Network Neighborhood.**

   A window opens, showing the computers you can access.

2. **Double-click on the computer where the file is located.**

   A window shows you the folders available on that computer.

3. **Keep double-clicking on the folders until you locate the file you want to send.**

4. **Right-click on that file's icon and, while holding that right mouse button down, drag the file out of the window and onto your Desktop.**

5. **Release the right mouse button and click on Create Shortcut(s) Here from the little menu that pops open.**

Presto, you created a shortcut that can access the 1996 Sales By Month file immediately: Simply by double-clicking on the file, you make your computer shoot its skinny arms through the network cables, grab the 1996 Sales By Month file, and bring it up on your computer screen.

- Unfortunately, this neat trick doesn't always work. That's because this process assumes you actually have *permission* to use the file. If you have not been given permission to play with that file — as described later in this chapter — you'll just see an ugly "access denied" message.
- Second, you need to have the right program on your computer. If you're trying to open a file that was made in Excel, as in the previous example, you must be able to run Excel for the file to open. That goes for all the files you see. You need whatever program goes with the file to open the file.
- To save changes to the file, just select Save from the program's File menu. It doesn't matter whether you're working from a shortcut or directly on the file, the savvy program knows where the file came from and saves it back to its original spot.
- Much more on opening and saving files is coming up in Chapter 13. Go take a look if you just can't wait.

How do I save a new file to another computer?

If you make up a brand new file or folder and you want to save it to another computer on your network, the steps are just the reverse of the long version of opening a file on another computer.

1. **Choose Save As from the program's File menu and begin clicking through the Network Neighborhood (see Figure 9-6) until you find the computer, drive, and folder where you want to save your file.**

2. **After you get to the folder where the file is to be saved, type a name for the file in the File name box and click once on the Save button.**

   That's all there is to it.

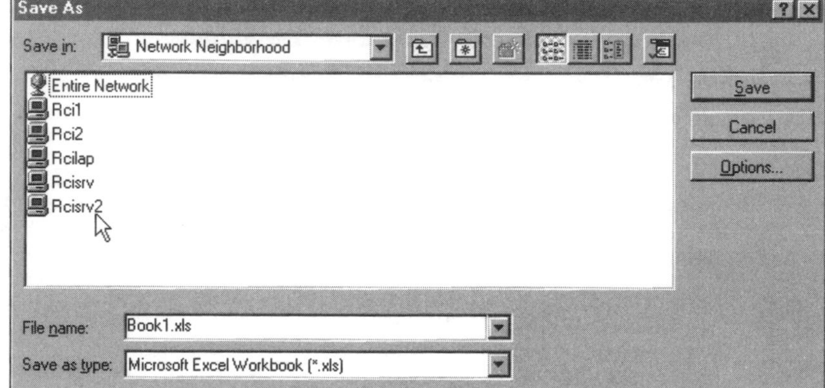

Figure 9-6: Starting the trek to another computer to save a new file.

This method is best only if you don't have to do it too often. If you need frequent access to another computer, try one of the methods in the next section.

Making Frequent Visits to a Friendly Computer Much Easier

If you often visit other particular computers (or parts of them) on your network, there's no sense wasting time with extra pointing and clicking through the menus. Instead, try some of the tips in the following sections to make your visits easier and faster.

Make a shortcut to the computer

Once again, shortcuts can save the day.

1. **Double-click on Network Neighborhood and find the oft-used computer.**
2. **Right-click on the computer and, while holding down the mouse button, drag the computer's icon out of the window and onto the Desktop.**

3. **Release the mouse button and select Create Shortcut(s) Here from the menu that pops up (see Figure 9-7).**

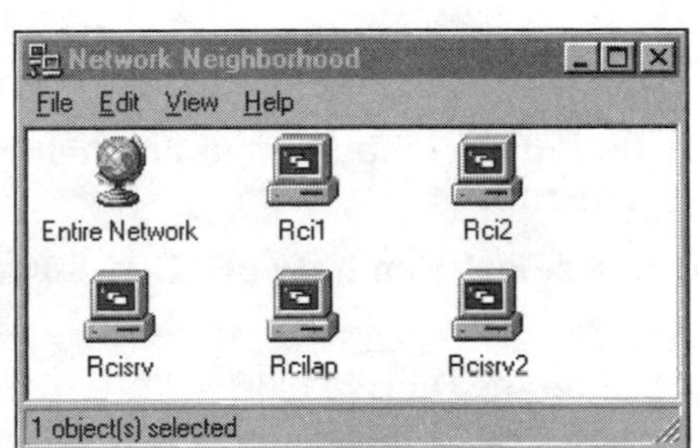

Figure 9-7: After making a shortcut to a frequently used computer on a network, you can double-click on the shortcut to access the networked computer's contents quickly.

- Keep the shortcut on your Desktop or drag it into a folder somewhere — whatever's convenient.
- Shortcuts to folders and hard disks and practically anything else can be made the same way. They're as handy as Handiwipes at a barbecue.

Mapping a network drive

When you open the Explorer icon or the My Computer icon, you see a list of the hard disks on your computer (as well as a few other goodies, depending on what's installed). If you want, Windows NT can make any other computer's shared drives or folders act as if they were drives on *your* computer.

For example, if Windows NT takes Gerald's C drive and displays that drive as your own computer's G drive, it has *mapped* Gerald's drive onto your computer.

A mapped drive is even better than a shortcut in one important respect: Many older programs don't recognize newfangled stuff like Network Neighborhood; they flat out refuse to open or save files to anywhere other than your own computer.

Mapping the drive tricks those programs into cooperating because they think they're working exclusively with your own computer — even though it's *really* Gerald's.

Here's how it works:

1. **Double-click on Network Neighborhood and find the other computer's folder or drive that you want to show as one of your own computer's drives.**

   For example, double-click on Judy's computer and find her D drive, where she keeps her golf statistics.

2. **Right-click on the object and select Map Network Drive from the menu.**

   In this case, you'd right-click on the D drive icon.

   Your options are shown in Figure 9-8.

   The computer automatically chooses your best option for Drive, so ignore that one. Leave the Reconnect at Logon box checked so you can have access to Judy's drive whenever you log on to your computer.

Figure 9-8: Most of the necessary information is already filled in.

Drive: This is the letter that the new drive will be assigned on your computer. It's usually the next one in the alphabet after your current ones.

Connect As: Use this only if you need to have the drive connect in another name other than your logon name. This sometimes happens in a multi-domain environment, or other special circumstances. When it's necessary, you enter the other user name and are then prompted for that user's password. After you provide it, the drive is mapped. Generally, however, this box is left blank.

Reconnect at Logon: Check this box and every time you log onto your computer, the connection is made to the computer where this drive physically resides. If you don't check the box, the connection isn't made until you actually go to use the drive.

3. **Click on OK after you're done.**

   Open Explorer or My Computer and take a look after you're through. See the "E" drive in Figure 9-9? That's how Judy's D drive in Figure 9-8 ended up looking after being mapped onto your computer.

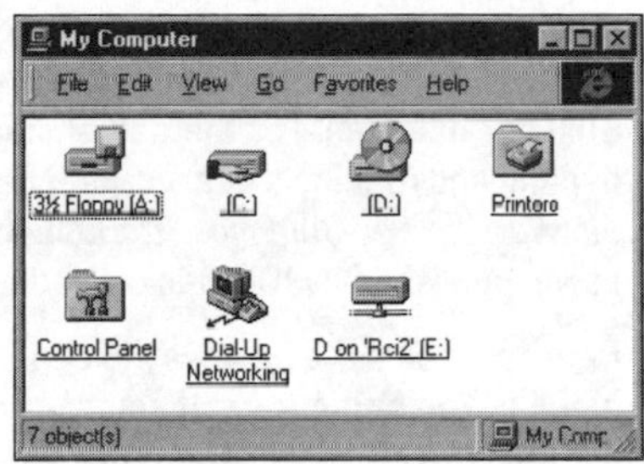

Figure 9-9: After being mapped, the drive on the other computer is listed as if it were your own computer's disk drive.

- It didn't work? Maybe you're trying to map something that hasn't been shared — and you'll have to ask the Network Administrator to do that.
- Folders can be harder to map than drives, because they take a little more effort to share. That means you must tap the Network Administrator on the shoulder.
- The key word is "Network Administrator," discussed in the next section.

- Actually, don't bother to raise your hand. A *hard disk,* a *hard drive,* and a *disk drive* are three different words that describe the same thing: A computer device for storing files. The terms can be used interchangeably, although the term "networked drives" usually appears more often than "networked disks."

Make the Administrator Do It

The administrator of the network can share another computer's folder or files *for* you. In fact, that may have already happened. Figure 9-10 shows a computer with one folder shared: The LapDesk folder.

Do-it-yourself networking

Do you brazenly rip off those "Do Not Remove" tags from your pillows? Don't always shake well before using? Then you're a good candidate to make your own network. It's not for the totally risk-averse but it's not a big deal either.

Two or more computers running Windows NT, Windows 98, Windows 95, or Windows for Workgroups 3.11 can be connected in a peer-to-peer network. With a peer-to-peer connection, all the computers can share printers and use each other's files. What fun! This is the easiest kind of network to set up and should be used whenever you have fewer than ten computers to connect.

You'll need what's called a Network Interface Card — one for each machine. You'll also need enough wire ("cabling" to the cognoscenti) to reach from one computer to the next. You can buy network cards and cabling for less than $100 per machine. For the actual steps of connecting and running a peer-to-peer network, get *Networking For Dummies,* 3rd Edition, by Doug Lowe, published by IDG Books Worldwide.

Peer-to-peer is the best way to connect maybe half a dozen computers. If you have more than six that have to communicate, you probably need a client/server network. This is a much bigger deal, though *Networking For Dummies* can talk you through that as well.

The Network Administrator can map drives for you, too. This isn't a bad approach, providing the administrator is actually approachable. And, best of all, if something goes wrong, you don't take the rap for it.

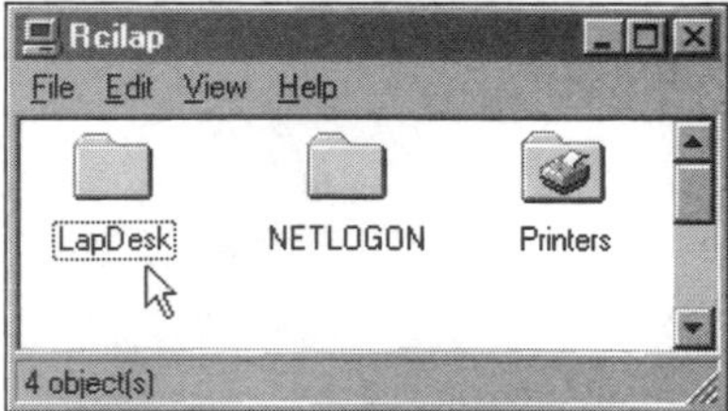

Figure 9-10: The administrator has made one folder available.

Running a Program That Lives on Someone Else's Computer

Two main ways exist to run a program that doesn't live on your own computer's hard disk.

If you're lucky, the administrator put the program's icon on your computer, and then set up a big server computer to run that program over the network. When you double-click on the program's icon, the program leaps to the screen, ready for some quick, rough-and-tumble action.

Administrators usually do this with things like the e-mail program or a company-wide database. Sometimes they're big programs like Microsoft Access or CorelDRAW!. Either way, if the program doesn't work, you need to ask for help; that stuff's not in your job description.

The second way to run a distant program is to head for Network Neighborhood or a mapped drive, find the program's icon, and double-click on it. Sometimes the program runs, and, unfortunately, sometimes it doesn't. See, Windows NT is security conscious; it's full of bars and windows that keep out evil-minded intruders as well as cat-loving people who simply want to get their work done.

If your pointing and clicking doesn't bring your program into action, you may need to bring a Network Administrator into the fray.

There's no disgrace in asking for help on a network. No need to think "I should know this by now!" Maybe you should, just as we all should be feasting on organic sprouts, thinking only pure thoughts, and running five miles every day. But the fact is, as mere humans, we forget and do dumb things. (So do Network Administrators, though it's best to pretend that this isn't so.)

How Do I Share Stuff on My Computer?

Sharing on a network is not much different than it was when you were a kid. You could share voluntarily or Mom would *persuade* you to share.

Sad to say, your mom is probably not running your network. So the persuasion has turned into administrator fiat.

But the rules for sharing differ depending on whether *you* made the file (or folder) or whether somebody else created it.

Generally, if you *didn't* create the file or folder, you can still read it and change it. However, you can't delete that file or folder, or change the rules about who *else* can play with it.

But, if you *did* create it, you can make all sorts of interesting rules about who gets to poke and prod it.

- When you make a new folder or a file, you are designated — as far as the network's concerned — as the owner of the new object.
- As the owner, you have full control over the object. You can make it available to everyone or keep it completely private. By default, the administrator has permission to use the object, but, as the owner, you can remove that permission.
- An administrator *can* force the issue by "taking ownership" of the file or folder in question. But it can't be done without your knowledge. If the administrator takes ownership, he or she can't give it back. So if your files no longer show you as the owner, you know what happened.
- Yes, the network can be like a giant chess game, although it usually moves a little faster.
- Setting permissions for your files is covered in the next sections.

Make your own workgroup — astound your friends!

Suppose you're working with several people on a Big Important Project. You want to store all the project's files on your own computer, but stuffed inside a networked folder accessible to everyone on the project team.

Here's the catch, though: Your computer is part of a big network, and you don't want *everybody* on the network to be able to peek inside your Big Important Project's folder.

How can you let the normal network people access your computer in their normal, network way, but keep them out of your new, Big Important Project folder?

Of course, the Network Administrator can take care of this for you, but if these things come up too often, the administrator can surely turn surly. Or, if you're working on something really cool, the project may be so hush-hush that even the administrator shouldn't be in on it.

The answer is to make a workgroup consisting of your project's cohorts, and grant everyone in the group permission to access the project's folder and files.

The upcoming steps show how to do the deed.

Making your own workgroup not only borders on TechnoLand, it takes a firm footstep into the country. Be sure to read these steps carefully. Your best bet is to find a helper who's already familiar with the process before proceeding.

1. **Click on the taskbar's Start button, click on Programs, and choose User Manager from the Administrative Tools (Common) option.**

   A complicated-looking window appears.

2. **Choose New Local Group from the User menu.**

   A much simpler-looking window appears.

3. **Think up and type a name for your group in the Group Name box.**
4. **Click on the Add button to add members to the group.**
5. **In the Add Users and Groups window, shown in Figure 9-11, click on the names of people or global groups and then the Add button.**

   The selected people or groups appear in the window labeled Add Names.

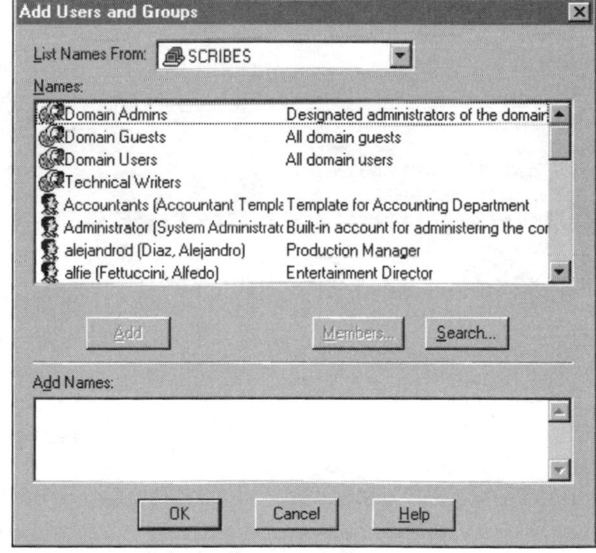

Figure 9-11: Click on the names of people to add to a new local group.

6. **After you have everyone you want, click on the OK button and return to the New Local Group (see Figure 9-12).**

As you can see in Figure 9-12, the New Local Group consists of Alice Wong, the Production Manager, all members of the Technical Writing group, and the administrator.

If you just want *some* members of the Technical Writing group, you must select them individually because no other way exists to select only part of a group. To pick out the lucky ones, highlight the group in the Add Users and Groups window (refer to Figure 9-11) and click on the Members button. The new window that opens shows you everybody who's a member of the group. You can highlight certain members and click on the Add button.

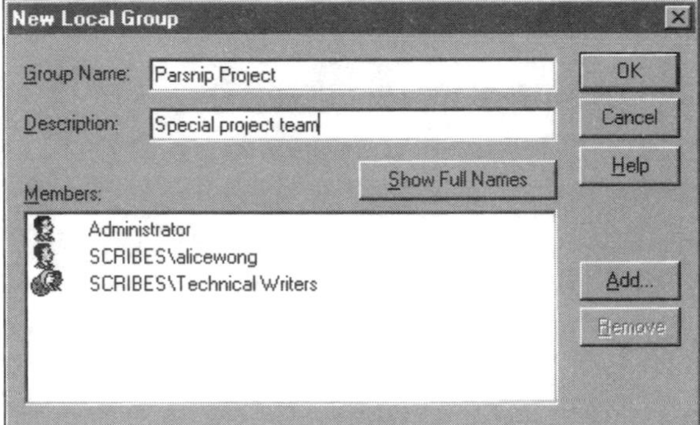

Figure 9-12: The members of the new Parsnip Project group.

To remove an individual or group from a group you made, just highlight the name and click on the Remove button.

Graciously Granting Permissions

Now you have a group, but you still have to give the members of the group some purpose in life. In this example, the Parsnip Project team members are all using a folder on your computer. The folder contains files and probably other folders. In the following steps, you can see how to give access permission to the project team.

1. **Open Windows Explorer.**

   We're not talking about Internet Explorer here; instead, click on My Computer with your right mouse button and click on Explore from the menu. Then, find the folder you want to let the team use. (Or create the folder now, as explained in Chapter 13.)

2. **Right-click on the folder and choose Properties from the menu to open the Properties box (see Figure 9-13).**

3. **Click on the Security tab and then the Permissions button.**

Now you're at a window that looks similar to Figure 9-14. You can see that a whole bunch of people have access to the Parsnip Files. The idea is that you don't want anyone except the Parsnip Team (and you, of course) to be able to use the folder. So you need to add the people you want and remove the ones you don't want.

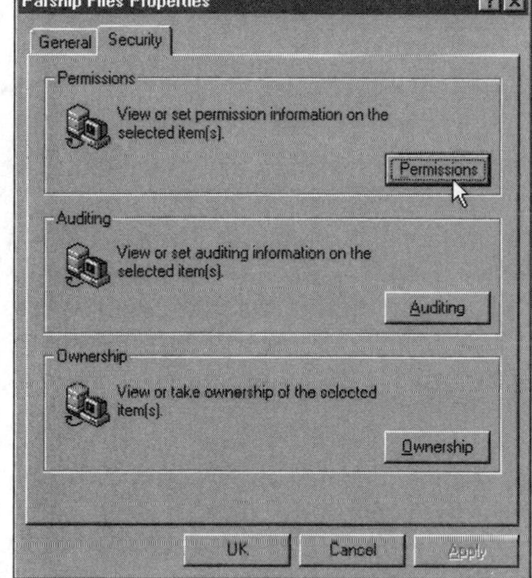

Figure 9-13: The Properties box lets you set permissions for others to access files and folders.

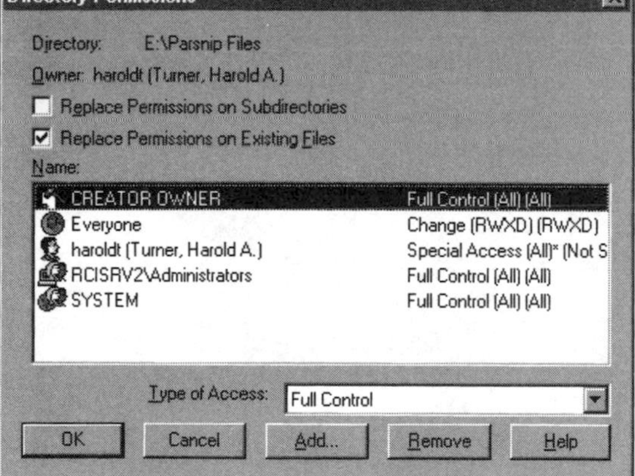

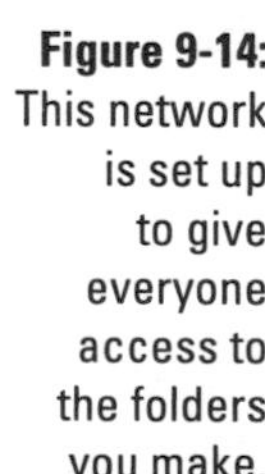

Figure 9-14: This network is set up to give everyone access to the folders you make.

- In this example, you're haroldt (Turner, Harold A.), so you obviously have access to the folder because you made it. Not so obvious is that you're also the CREATOR OWNER. Both permissions are shown because you can let someone else own the folder if you want to.
- Although several people and groups are listed in the Permissions box, not everyone is equal. Click on each group and see what changes in the Type of Access box at the bottom of the window.

4. **Highlight Everyone and click on the Remove button. Then do the same for any others you want to exclude.**
5. **Click on the Add button and select your group from the list shown in Figure 9-15.**

   Because local groups — the kind you just made — are shown only on the computer where they're made, you may have to select your own computer's name from the List Names From box.

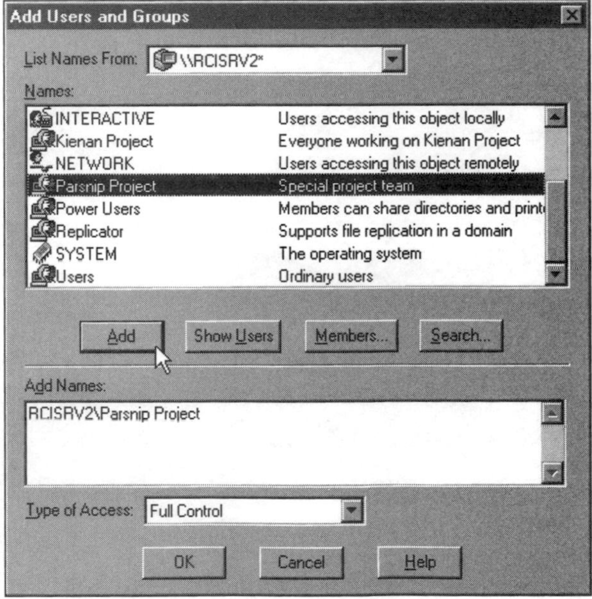

Figure 9-15: Add your project team to the list of those who have permission to get at the folder.

6. **Click on Add again and then click on OK. (Be sure that the Type of Access box is set correctly.)**

   You have many types of access, but *Full Control* is the one you should give to everybody. This means everyone can read, write, change, and add files. If you can't trust someone in your group to have Full Control, you have a problem that can't be solved by setting access rules. Under *very special and limited* circumstances, you can specify access as *Read* (the person or group can read the files but not change them in any way).

7. **Back in the Directory Permissions window (refer to Figure 9-14), consider the two check boxes:**

   - Replace Permissions on Subdirectories. Check this box if you want everyone in the Directory Permissions to be able to access folders inside the Parsnip Project folder.
   - Replace Permissions on Existing Files. Check this box if files inside the Parsnip Project folder may already have different permissions set.

8. **Highlight each person/group on the list and check that the selection in the Type of Access box is correct for each one. Then click on OK.**

- You don't have to make your own workgroup to grant permissions. Right-click on the file or folder in Explorer and choose Properties from the menu.
- You can add or remove existing groups or members of groups to the list of people who have access, and you can pick out the kind of access granted to each person or group.
- Feel free to experiment with permissions, but don't forget to always leave full access for yourself. And it's wise not to experiment with permissions on folders that other people actually have to use. You can drive the person in the next cubicle to the point of neighborly cubicide.

File Manager still sets your permissions

Yes, the old stalwart from Windows 3.*x* is still around but staying modestly in the background. To find File Manager, open Explorer and look for your WINNT folder. Inside that is a folder called SYSTEM32. And inside that you find a program called WINFILE.EXE. (It may show up without the .EXE extension.) The icon next to it looks like a little two-drawer file cabinet.

You can double-click on the file to open File Manager. To change permissions on a file or folder, highlight it, and choose the Security menu and then Permissions. Everything then works the same way as from the Properties page.

If you just can't break that File Manager habit, make a shortcut for it. Right-click on WINFILE.EXE and drag it to your Desktop. Release the mouse button and select Create Shortcut. You can later move the shortcut to a folder or to your Start menu or just leave it on the Desktop.

The Printers Are on the Network!

If you see your new computer and observe that no printer is attached, you may (being a reasonable person) assume that using a network printer is going to complicate your life. But even reasonable people are wrong now and again.

Generally speaking, only one difference exists between using a network printer and a printer that's directly attached to your own computer: With a network printer, you usually have to get up off your chair to pick up your printed pages. Admittedly, this situation isn't as nice as having those pages slip directly into your hands, but it's not much more complicated.

Looking for printers on the network

If no printer is directly plugged into your computer, you can easily find out what printers you can use.

1. **Click on the taskbar's Start button.**
2. **Choose Printers from the Settings menu.**

   A window appears listing one or more printers, plus the Add Printer icon.

That's it. The printers listed in the window are the ones your computer can send information to.

If the printers all have dumb incomprehensible names, right-click on them in turn, choosing Properties from the menu each time. As shown in Figure 9-16, this brings up a box with a little information about the type of printer and its location.

Picking a favorite printer for everyday use

If you're lucky enough to have a whole bunch of printers you can use, you need to set one of them as the default printer. That designation just means that all your Windows print jobs go to that printer unless you intervene.

Right-click on the printer you want to use most of the time and then click on Set As Default (see Figure 9-17). A check mark in front of Set As Default means the printer has already been made the default printer.

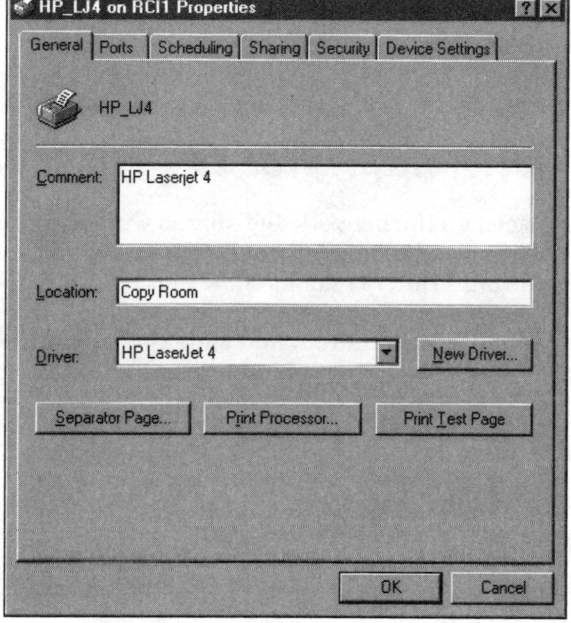

Figure 9-16: Right-click on a printer icon and choose Properties from the menu to see information about it.

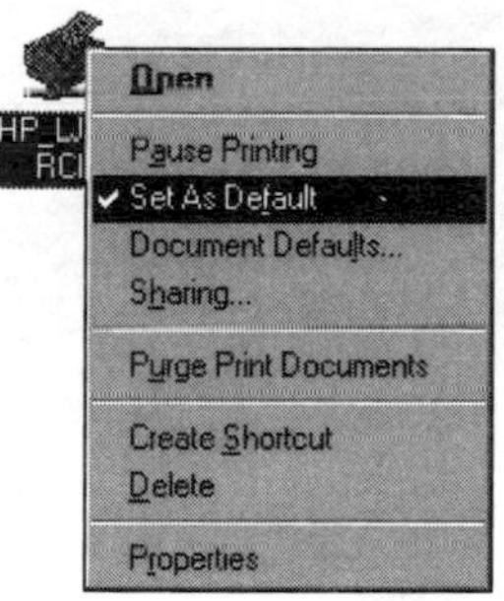

Figure 9-17: The check mark means that this printer is the one your Windows programs use unless you make a change.

- Only one printer at a time can be the default printer for your computer. To change which printer is the one used by default, just right-click on the one you want and then click on Set As Default.
- Wanna use a different printer for just one print job? Look at the File menu in the program you're using. Select the Printer Setup item if one exists. Otherwise, just select Print. In the window that opens, look for a drop-down list of printers and select the one you want.

- Next time you use that program, check the Printer Setup to see what printer is chosen. Some applications are smart enough to go back to the default printer, and others are not. Sigh.

Adding a network printer to your machine

If a new printer is placed on the network and shared with everyone, you'll be able to use it — but only after you tell your computer about it. To add a networked printer to your Printers folder, follow these steps.

1. **Click on the taskbar's Start button, and slide the mouse up to Settings and over to Printers. Click on Printers.**
2. **In the Printers folder, double-click on Add Printer.**
3. **A helpful wizard program opens, as shown in Figure 9-18.**

   Check the Network printer server box to tell the wizard that the printer you want to use is on the network.

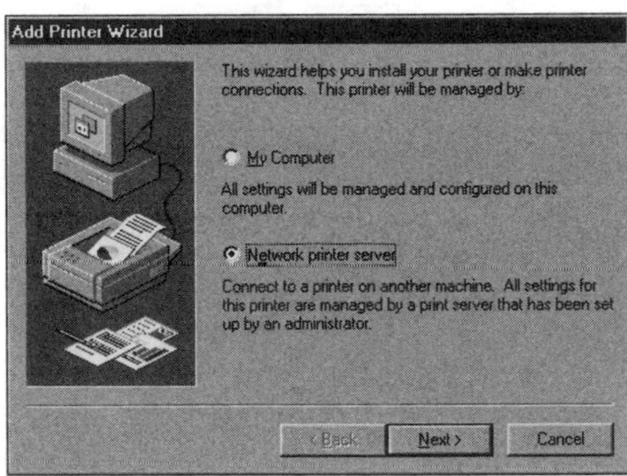

Figure 9-18: The Add Printer Wizard does all the work of installing a new networked printer. (And about time too.)

4. **On the wizard's next page, select the printer you want to add and then click on the OK button.**

Even if a printer actually exists, you may not be able to see it on the network because you haven't been granted access to it. The administrator is the only one who can fix that for you. But if you can see it, you probably have the right to use it, so go ahead and try.

Chapter 10

Shuffling Words, Pictures, and Sounds from One Place to Another

In This Chapter

- Understanding cutting, copying, and pasting
- Highlighting what you need
- Cutting, copying, deleting, and pasting what you highlighted
- Making the best use of the Clipboard and Clipbook Viewer
- Putting scraps on the Desktop
- Discovering Object Linking and Embedding
- Controlling Print Manager

Until Windows came along, IBM-compatible computers lived in a dismal DOS world where they had a terrible time sharing anything. The DOS programs were rigid, egotistical things, with no sense of community. Information created by one DOS program couldn't always be shared with another program. Older versions of these programs passed down this selfish system to newer versions, enforcing the segregation with proprietary file formats and compatibility tests.

To counter this bad trip, the Windows programmers created a communal Windows workplace where all the programs could groove together peacefully. In the harmonious tribal village of Windows, programs share their information openly to make a more beautiful environment for all.

In the Windows co-op, all the windows can beam their vibes to each other freely, without fear of rejection. Work created by one Windows program is accepted totally and lovingly by any other Windows program. Windows programs treat each other equally, even if one program is wearing some pretty freaky threads or, in some gatherings, no threads at all.

How does it work? When two programs are on the screen, you can simply copy or move information from one window to another without fear of rejection, humiliation, or, worst of all, corporate attorneys.

This chapter shows you how easily you can move those good vibes from one window to another.

Examining the Cut-and-Paste Concept (And Copy, Too)

Windows NT took a tip from the kindergartners and made cut and paste an integral part of all its programs. Information can be electronically cut from one window and pasted into another window with little fuss and even less mess.

Just about any part of a window is up for grabs. You can highlight an exceptionally well-written paragraph in your word processor, for example, or a spreadsheet chart that tracks the value of your Indian-head pennies. After highlighting the desired information, you press a button to copy or cut it from its window.

At the press of the button, the information heads for a special place in Windows NT called the Clipboard. From there, you can paste it into any other open window.

The beauty of Windows NT is that with all those windows on-screen at the same time, you can easily grab bits and pieces from any of them and paste all the parts into a new window.

- Unlike DOS programs, Windows programs are designed to work together, so taking information from one window and putting it into another window is easy. Sticking a map onto your party fliers, for example, is really easy.
- Cutting and pasting works well for the big stuff, like sticking big charts into memos. But don't overlook it for the small stuff, too. For example, copying someone's name and address from your address book program is quicker than typing it by hand at the top of your letter. Or, to avoid typographical errors, you can copy an answer from the Windows NT Calculator and paste it into another program.
- Cutting and pasting is different from that weird Object Linking and Embedding stuff (OLE) you may have heard people raving about. That more powerful (and, naturally, more confusing) OLE stuff gets its own section later in this chapter.

- When you cut or copy some information, it immediately transfers to a special Windows program called Clipboard Viewer. From the Clipboard, it can be pasted into other windows. The Clipboard has its own bag of tricks, so it gets its own section later in this chapter.

Highlighting the Important Stuff

Before you can grab information from a window, you have to tell the window exactly what parts you want to grab. The easiest way to tell it is to highlight the information with a mouse.

You can highlight a single letter, an entire novel, or anything in between. You can highlight pictures of water lilies. You can even highlight sounds so that you can paste sneezes into other files (see the "Looking at Cool Object Linking and Embedding Stuff" section later in this chapter).

In most cases, highlighting involves one swift trick with the mouse: Put the mouse arrow or cursor at the beginning of the information you want and hold down the mouse button. Then move the mouse to the end of the information and release the button. That's it! All the stuff lying between your mouse moves is highlighted. The information usually turns a different color so that you can see what you grabbed. An example of highlighted text is shown in Figure 10-1.

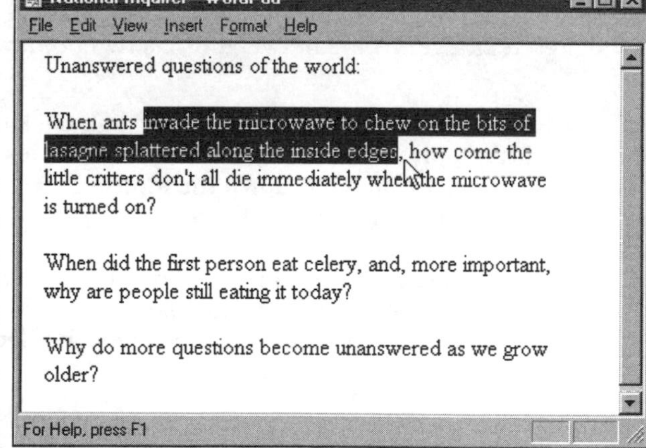

Figure 10-1: Highlighted text turns a different color for easy visibility.

If you're mouseless, use the arrow keys to put the cursor at the beginning of the stuff you want to grab. Then hold down the Shift key and press the arrow keys until the cursor is at the end of what you want to grab. You see the stuff on-screen become highlighted as you move the arrow keys. This trick works with almost every Windows NT program. (If you're after text, hold down the Ctrl key and the text is highlighted word by word.)

Some programs have a few shortcuts for highlighting parts of their information:

- To highlight a single word in Notepad, WordPad, or most text boxes, point at it with the mouse and double-click. The word turns black, meaning that it's highlighted. (In WordPad, you can hold down the button on its second click and then, by moving the mouse around, you can quickly highlight additional text word by word.)
- To highlight a single line in WordPad, click next to it in the left margin. Keep holding down the mouse button and move the mouse up or down to highlight additional text line by line.
- To highlight a paragraph in WordPad, double-click next to it in the left margin. Keep holding down the mouse button on the second click and move the mouse to highlight additional text paragraph by paragraph.
- To highlight an entire document in WordPad, hold down the Ctrl key and click anywhere in the left margin. (To highlight the entire document in Notepad, press and release the Alt key and then press E and then A. So much for consistency between Windows NT programs. . . .)
- To highlight a portion of text in just about any Windows NT program, click on the text's beginning, hold down the Shift key, and click on the end of the desired text. Everything between those two points becomes highlighted.
- To highlight part of a picture or drawing while in Paint, click on the Select tool — the little tool button with the dotted lines in a square. After clicking on the Select tool, hold down the mouse button and slide the mouse over the desired part of the picture.

After you highlight text, you must either cut it or copy it immediately. If you do anything else, like absentmindedly click the mouse someplace else in your document, all your highlighted text reverts to normal, just like Cinderella after midnight.

Be careful after you highlight a bunch of text. If you press any key — the spacebar, for example — Windows NT immediately replaces your highlighted text with the character that you type — in this case, a space. To reverse that calamity and bring your highlighted text back to life, hold down Alt and press the Backspace key.

Those cranky old DOS windows have their own methods of highlighting information. Check out the section "Using Copy and Paste with a DOS Program," later in this chapter, for the real dirt.

Deleting, Cutting, or Copying What You Highlighted

After you highlight some information (which is described in the preceding section, in case you just entered the classroom), you're ready to start playing with it. You can delete it, cut it, or copy it. All three options differ drastically.

Deleting the information

Deleting the information just wipes it out. Zap! It just disappears from the window. To delete highlighted information, press the Delete or Backspace key.

- If you accidentally delete the wrong thing, panic. Then hold down the Ctrl key and press the letter Z. Your deletion is graciously undone. Any deleted information pops back up on-screen. Whew!
- Holding down the Alt key and pressing the Backspace key also undoes your last mistake. (Unless you've just said something dumb at a party. Then use Ctrl+Z.)

Cutting the information

Cutting the highlighted information wipes it off the screen, just as the Delete command does, but with a big difference: When the information is removed from the window, it is copied to a special Windows NT storage tank called the Clipboard.

When you're looking at the screen, cutting and deleting look identical. In fact, the first few times you try to cut something, you feel panicky, thinking that you may have accidentally deleted it instead. (This feeling never really goes away, either.)

To cut highlighted stuff, hold down the Ctrl key and press the X key. (Get it? That's an X, as in you're crossing, or X-ing, something out.) Whoosh! The highlighted text disappears from the window, scoots through the underground tubes of Windows NT, and waits on the Clipboard for further action.

- One way to tell whether your Cut command actually worked is to paste the information back into your document. If it appears, you know that the command worked, and you can cut it out again right away. If it doesn't appear, you know that something has gone dreadfully wrong. (For the Paste command, discussed a little later, hold down the Ctrl key and press the V key.)

- **Little known fact department:** You can also cut highlighted stuff by highlighting it, holding down Shift, and pressing the Del key. To Paste stuff, you can hold down Shift and press Insert. Some people find this "Delete" and "Insert" metaphor a little easier to remember.

Copying the information

Compared with cutting or deleting, copying information is quite anticlimactic. When you cut or delete, the information disappears from the screen. But, when you copy information to the Clipboard, the highlighted information just sits there in the window. In fact, it looks as if nothing has happened, so you repeat the Copy command a few times before giving up and hope it worked.

To copy highlighted information, hold down the Ctrl key and press the C key. Although nothing seems to happen, that information really does head for the Clipboard.

- To copy an image of the entire Windows NT Desktop (the whole screen) to the Clipboard, press the Print Screen key, which is sometimes labeled PrtSc or something similar. (Some older keyboards make you hold down the Shift key simultaneously.) A snapshot of your screen heads for the Clipboard, ready to be pasted someplace else. Computer nerds call this snapshot a *screen shot.* All the pictures of windows in this book are screen shots. (And, no, the information doesn't also head for your printer.)
- To copy an image of your currently active window (just one window — nothing surrounding it), hold down the Alt key while you press your Print Screen key. The window's picture appears on the Clipboard. (You usually don't have to hold down the Shift key with this one, even for wacky keyboards. But if Alt+Print Screen doesn't work, hey, try holding down the Shift key anyway.)

Finding out more about cutting, copying, and deleting

Want to know more about cutting, copying, and deleting? Read on (you really should read this stuff):

- Windows NT often puts toolbars across the tops of its programs. Figure 10-2 shows the toolbar buttons that stand for cutting, copying, and pasting things.
- The cut, copy, and paste process works differently in DOS windows. See "Using Copy and Paste with a DOS Program" in this chapter for a dose of DOS details.
- If you prefer to use menus, the Cut, Copy, and Paste commands tumble down after you choose the word Edit on any menu bar.
- If you're using the Print Screen key trick to copy a window or the entire screen to the Clipboard (see the preceding section), one important component is left out: The mouse arrow is not included in the picture, even if it was in plain sight when you took the picture. (Are you asking yourself how all the little arrows got in this book's pictures? Well, we drew a lot of 'em in by hand!)
- Sometimes figuring out whether the Cut or Copy commands are really working is difficult. To know for sure, keep the Windows Clipboard Viewer showing at the bottom of the screen. Then you can watch the images appear on it when you press the buttons. (Clipboard Viewer is listed on the Start menu under Accessories, which is listed in the Programs section. Not listed? Head for Chapter 11; you must tell Windows NT to install the Clipboard Viewer program.)
- Don't be confused when you open Clipboard Viewer and see the local Clipbook window plus another window labeled ClipBook Viewer. First, take a deep breath and read the section a little later in this chapter called "ClipBook Viewer — Enemy or Foe?"

- Don't keep screen shots or large graphics on the Clipboard any longer than necessary. They consume a great deal of memory that your other programs could be using. To clear off any memory-hogging detritus, copy a single word to the Clipboard or call up Clipboard Viewer and press Delete.

Figure 10-2: From left to right, clicking on these toolbar buttons cuts, copies, or pastes information.

Pasting Information into Another Window

After you cut or copy information to the special Windows NT Clipboard storage tank, it's ready for travel. You can paste that information into just about any other window.

Pasting is relatively straightforward compared with highlighting, copying, or cutting: Click the mouse anywhere in the destination window and click on the spot where you want the stuff to appear. Then hold down the Ctrl key and press the V key. Presto! Anything that's sitting on the Clipboard immediately leaps into that window.

- Another way to paste stuff is to hold down the Shift key and press Insert. That combination does the same thing as Ctrl+V. (It also is the command those funny-looking Macintosh computers use to paste stuff.)
- You also can choose the Paste command from a window's menu bar. Choose the word Edit and then choose the word Paste. But don't choose the words Paste Special. That command is for more advanced pasting like the Object Linking and Embedding stuff, which gets its own section later in this chapter.
- Some programs have toolbars along their top. Clicking on the Paste button, shown in Figure 10-2, pastes the Clipboard's current contents into your document.
- The Paste command inserts a copy of the information that's sitting on the Clipboard. The information stays on the Clipboard, so you can keep pasting it into other windows if you want. In fact, the Clipboard's contents stay the same until a new Cut or Copy command replaces them with new information.

Using Copy and Paste with a DOS Program

DOS programs all behave a little strangely under Windows NT. Likewise, the Copy and Paste commands work a little differently. It gets kind of complicated, so you should really think about ditching your DOS programs and switching to Windows programs if you're serious about copying and pasting.

You must remember certain rules when you use the Copy and Paste commands with DOS programs:

- **Rule 1:** You can't cut text or anything else from a DOS program in Windows NT. You can only copy stuff. The original information always remains in your DOS program.
- **Rule 2:** You can't paste anything but text into most DOS programs.
- **Rule 3:** You can't paste text into a DOS program if it's running in full-screen mode, meaning that it's taking up the entire screen.
- **Rule 4:** If you copy information from a DOS program, you need to decide beforehand whether you want to copy a picture from the DOS window or copy text — actual words. You can't copy a picture out of a DOS program unless the DOS program is running in a window. The upcoming two sections explain the procedures for copying pictures and text from a DOS program.
- **Rule 5:** Copying and pasting from DOS programs is decidedly complicated and tedious, as evidenced by Rules 1 through 4.

Copying a picture from a DOS program

To copy a picture from a DOS program, run the program in its own window on-screen. Then hold down the Alt key while pressing the Print Screen key.

The Alt+Print Screen key trick copies a graphic image of the DOS window to the Windows NT Clipboard. From there, you can paste the picture into the Windows NT graphics program, Paint, and clean it up a little before copying it to its final destination.

- This method gives you a snapshot of the DOS program that is running in the window. It is surrounded by typical window dressing, like menu bars, title bars, scroll bars, and the like. You can erase these extraneous elements in Paint to make the picture look better.
- If you use this trick to copy a DOS program that's showing only text, you get just a picture of that text. You can't copy the text into a word processor or arrange it into paragraphs. It's just a picture, like a Polaroid snapshot of an open book.

Copying text from a DOS program

If the DOS program is running full-screen, press your Print Screen key. (Some keyboards make you hold down the Shift key simultaneously.) Even though Windows NT is running invisibly in the background, it dredges all the text showing in the DOS program and copies it onto the Clipboard. (Not to the printer, though. Print Screen doesn't do that in Windows NT.)

If the DOS program is running in a window on-screen, here's how to grab that text using a mouse:

1. **Click on the tiny icon in the program's upper-left corner and choose Edit from the menu that drops down.**
2. **Choose Mark from the menu that shoots out from the word Edit.**

   A tiny flashing square appears in the upper-left corner of the screen, as barely visible in Figure 10-3.

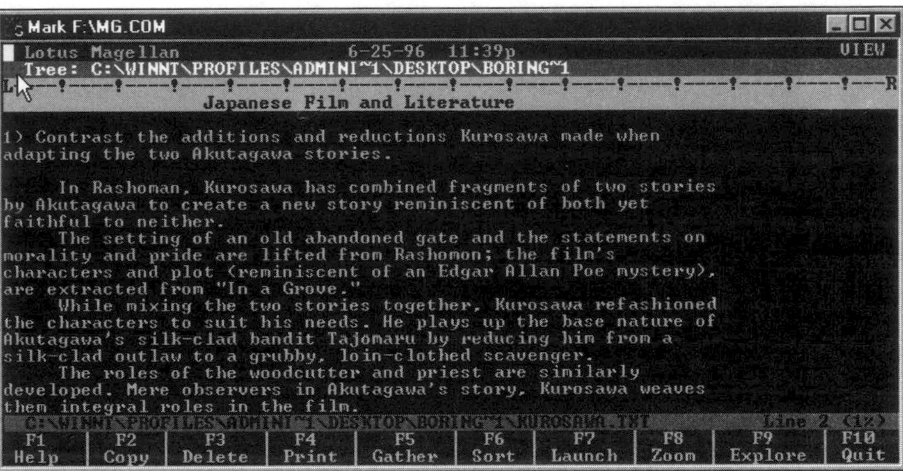

Figure 10-3: Click on the tiny icon in the upper-left corner and then choose Mark from the Edit menu; a tiny flashing square appears in the window's upper-left corner.

3. **Hold down the mouse button when you're at the beginning of what you want to grab, move the mouse to the end of the text, and then release the mouse button.**

   Your screen looks similar to the one shown in Figure 10-4.

4. **After the information you're after changes color, press Enter.**

   Wham! Windows NT copies that highlighted text to the Clipboard.

- If you grab text from a DOS application in a window, you can grab it only in square- or rectangular-shaped chunks. That limitation is not as bad as it seems, though, because Windows NT tosses out any extraneous spaces at the ends of lines.

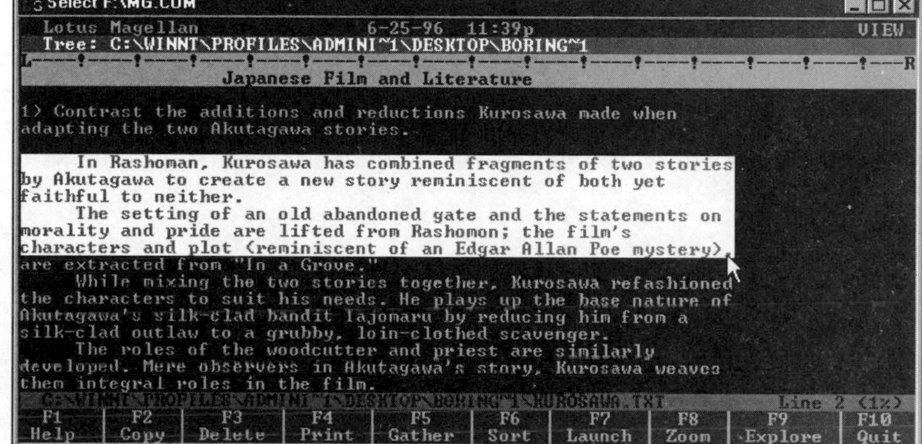

Figure 10-4: As you slide the mouse over the text, it changes color.

- You can't retain any of the special formatting the DOS text may have had, such as boldface or underline. Any adjacent graphics are also left out. In addition, if the text itself is in graphics form, like fancy letters or something, you can't grab it as text.
- This Select mode stuff can be confusing: Your DOS application is frozen on-screen and doesn't respond. It's frozen because you're picking chunks out of it. And you can tell that you're picking chunks out of it by looking at the title bar: The word Select is in front of the program's name.
- If you change your mind and don't want to grab information out of there, press Esc, and everything goes back to normal — as normal as a computer can be, anyway.

Trying to do all this with a keyboard instead of a mouse? Then you must complete the following steps:

1. **Press Alt+Spacebar and choose Mark from the Edit menu.**

   The DOS window goes into Select mode.

2. **Tap the arrow keys until the cursor rests at the beginning of the text you want to grab.**
3. **While holding down Shift, press the arrow keys until the cursor rests at the end of the text you want to grab.**
4. **After the text you're after is highlighted, press Enter.**

   Whew! Windows NT then copies it to the Clipboard.

Pasting text into a DOS program

Most DOS programs are text-based critters. You can't copy any graphics into most of them. You can dump some words into them from the Clipboard, however, by doing the following: With the program running in a window, move the cursor to the spot where you want the text to appear. Next, click on the little icon in the DOS window's upper-left-hand corner. Click on Edit from the menu that appears, and choose Paste.

Any text on the Clipboard is instantly poured into the DOS program, starting where you left the cursor sitting.

Note: You'll probably have to reformat the text after you pour it into the DOS program. The sentences usually break in all the wrong places. Plus, you lose any special formatting, such as boldface or underline. Hey, that's what you get for still clinging to your stubborn old DOS programs!

Stuck with a DOS program that refuses to run in a window? Windows NT can still paste some text into it. Follow these steps:

1. **If the program is running full-screen, click where you want the text to appear.**
2. **Hold down the Alt key and press the Esc key.**

   The DOS program turns into a button on the taskbar at the bottom of your screen.
3. **Click on the DOS program's button with your right mouse button and watch as its Control menu rises eerily from the top of its head.**
4. **Click on the word Edit and then on the word Paste.**

   Presto! The text on the Clipboard jumps into your DOS program, right where you left the cursor sitting.

Using the Clipboard Viewer

Windows NT employs a special program to let you see all the stuff that's being slung around by cutting and copying. Called Clipboard Viewer, it's merely a window that displays anything that has been cut or copied to the Clipboard.

To see Clipboard Viewer, click on the Start button and click on Clipboard Viewer from the Accessories menu (which pops up when you rest the mouse pointer over the Programs area). Inside Clipboard Viewer, you see any information you cut or copied recently. Figures 10-5, 10-6, and 10-7 show some examples.

Figure 10-5: This Clipboard contains a recently copied picture of a chip.

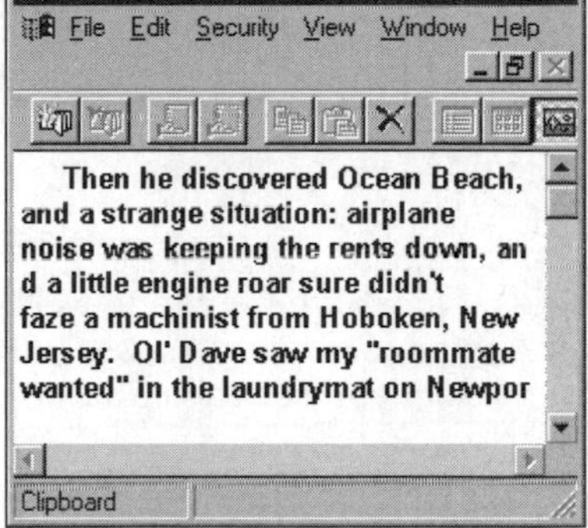

Figure 10-6: This Clipboard contains text recently copied from a boring DOS program.

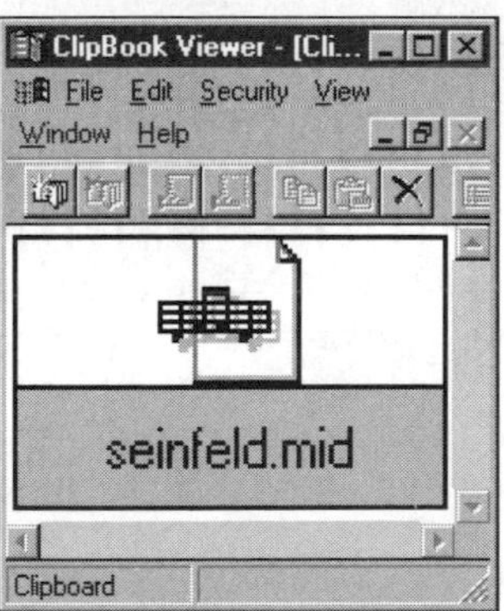

Figure 10-7: This Clipboard contains a sorta-kinda hip TV show's theme song, copied from the Windows NT Media Player.

- Inside the Clipboard Viewer window you can see the Clipboard plus another window called Local ClipBook. They're named that way so you never are quite clear on which is which. In fact, sharp-eyed readers may have noticed the Clipboard windows in the past three figures labeled ClipBook, not Clipboard. (See the next section for some clarity.)
- Sometimes Clipboard Viewer can't show you exactly what you've copied. For example, if you copy a sound from the Windows NT Sound Recorder, you see only a picture of the Sound Recorder's icon. And, at the risk of getting metaphysical, what does a sound look like anyway?
- The Clipboard functions automatically and transparently. Unless you make a special effort, you don't even know it's there. (That's why Clipboard Viewer is handy — it lets you see what the Clipboard is up to.)
- For some confusing reason, when you click the Start menu, choose Programs, and choose Accessories, Windows NT lets you start the Clipboard Viewer. But when that program appears, it's named the *Clipbook* Viewer – not the *ClipBoard* Viewer. Anyway, consider them both to be the same thing.

The *Clipboard* is a special area inside memory where Windows NT keeps track of information that was cut or copied. *Clipboard Viewer* (also called the ClipBook Viewer) is a program that lets you see the information that's currently on the Clipboard.

- The Clipboard Viewer usually contains two windows: the Local ClipBook window and the Clipboard. The Clipboard contains immediately cut or copied information, and the Local Clipbook window lets you save assorted Clipboard tidbits and share them with other computers on the network. (That's covered in the next section.)
- To better track what's being cut and pasted, some people leave Clipboard Viewer sitting open at the bottom of the screen. Then they can actually see what they've cut or copied.
- Most of the time, the Clipboard is used just for temporary operations — a quick cut here, a quick paste there, and on to the next job. But Clipboard Viewer lets you save the Clipboard's contents for later use. Choose File from the menu bar and then choose Save As from the pull-down menu. Type in a filename and click on the OK command button (or just press Enter).
- The Clipboard can hold only one thing at a time. Each time you cut or copy something else, you replace the Clipboard's contents with something new. If you want to collect a bunch of clips for later pasting, use the Save As option described in the preceding paragraph. The Clipboard also starts up empty each time you start Windows NT.

Keeping the Clipboard clear

Whenever you cut or copy something, that information heads for the Clipboard. And it stays there, too, until you cut or copy something else to replace it. But while that information sits there on the Clipboard, it uses up memory.

Windows NT needs all the memory it can get, or it begins running slowly or balking at opening more windows. Big chunks of text, pictures, and sounds can consume a great deal of memory, so clear off the Clipboard when you're through cutting and pasting to return the memory for general Windows use.

To clear off the Clipboard quickly, just copy a single word to the Clipboard: Double-click on a word in a text file, hold down the Ctrl key, and press C.

Or, if Clipboard Viewer is up on-screen, click on the Clipboard window to bring it to the forefront, and then click on the Delete icon: the one with the slashing X on it. That clears off the Clipboard, enabling Windows NT to use the memory for more pressing matters.

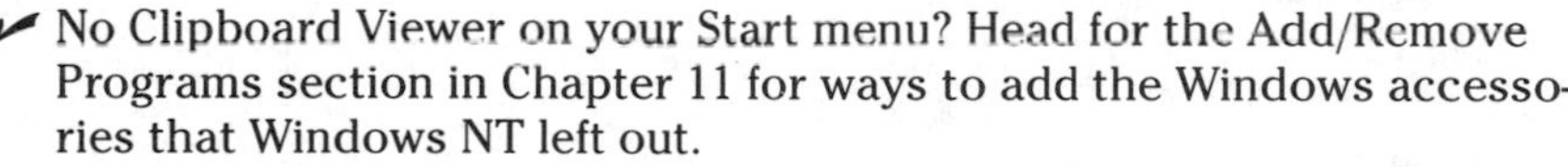

- No Clipboard Viewer on your Start menu? Head for the Add/Remove Programs section in Chapter 11 for ways to add the Windows accessories that Windows NT left out.

- If some programs and settings don't seem exactly as they're described in this book, it's for a special reason: Your Network Administrator has probably been fiddling with your computer's settings. For example, your Network Administrator can remove the solitaire game from your computer just as easily as removing access to ClipBook Viewer. If in doubt, ask 'em.

ClipBook Viewer: Enemy or Foe?

When you open Clipboard Viewer, as described in the preceding section, you find a lurker in the form of a window labeled ClipBook Viewer. It contains your Clipboard's window and a window called Local Clipboard.

Although Clipboard Viewer lets you see the information that you're cutting and pasting on your own computer, ClipBook Viewer shares that information with other people on your network. Anything you copy to the Clipboard can be copied to the ClipBook and passed around to other network users like an hors d'oeuvre with a fancy toothpick (providing you're willing to share, of course). More likely, ClipBooks on other machines offer information you want to see. To see whether any fascinating reading (or eating) is available on other computers, follow these steps:

1. **Click on Clipboard Viewer (or ClipBook Viewer) in the list of programs that cascade out of the Accessories menu.**

(The Accessories menu hides in the Start button's Programs area, by the way.)

2. **Click the File menu and select Connect.**

   A window opens with a list of computers. Double-click on the one that looks the most appetizing.

3. **The ClipBook on the computer in question opens and shows you a list of what's available (see Figure 10-8).**

4. **Double-click on your choice, and you can see what's inside.**

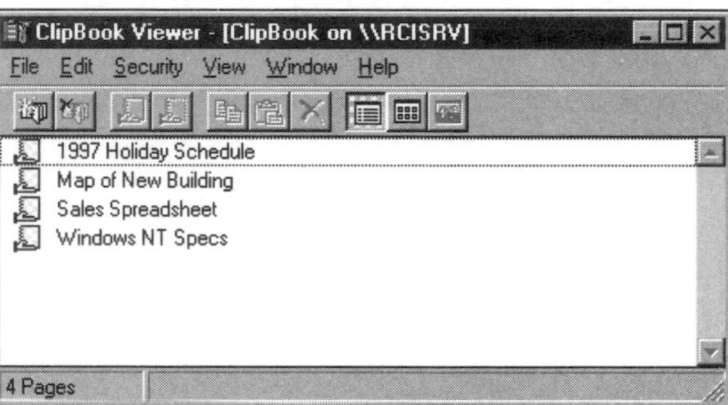

Figure 10-8: ClipBook Viewer lets you use information on the Clipboards of other computers on the network.

- ClipBook may not be used at all on your network because there are other, more slick ways to share information (if your Network Administrator has installed them), such as Exchange and Peer Web Services. (Chapter 16 introduces you to both.)
- The list of items on another computer's ClipBook can be shown as a table of contents or a bunch of little pictures (called Thumbnails). Choose either look from the View menu. Or highlight a particular item and select Full Page from the View menu.

Looking at Cool Object Linking and Embedding Stuff

Because the concepts of cutting and pasting are so refreshingly simple, Microsoft complicated them considerably with something called Object Linking and Embedding, known as OLE. It sounds complicated, so we start with the simple part: the object.

The *object* is merely the information you want to paste into a window. It can be a sentence, a road map, a sneeze sound, or anything else that you can cut or copy from a window.

Normally, when you paste an object into a window, you're pasting the same kind of information. For example, you paste text into a word processor and pictures into the Windows NT Paint program. But what if you want to paste a sound into Write, the Windows NT word processor?

That's where Object Linking and Embedding comes in, offering subtle changes to the paste concept. You'll probably never use them, but they can be fun to fiddle around with on cloudy days. Beware, however: OLE awareness is the first step down those ever-spiraling stairs toward computer-nerd certification.

Embedding

On the surface, embedding an object looks just like pasting it. The object shows up in the window. Big deal. But, when you embed an object, you're also embedding the name of the program that created that object. When you double-click on the object, poof! The program that created it jumps to the top of the screen, ready to edit it.

For example, you can embed a spreadsheet chart showing your current net worth in a letter you're writing to an old high-school friend. Then, if the stock market changes before you mail the letter, you can easily update the letter's chart. Just call up the letter in your word processor and double-click on the chart. The spreadsheet that created the chart pops up, ready for you to make the changes. After you finish, you close the spreadsheet. The spreadsheet disappears, leaving the updated chart in your letter.

Embedding is really pretty handy. You don't have to remember the chart's filename. You don't even have to call up your spreadsheet. Windows NT does all that grunt work automatically. Just double-click on the chart, make the changes after your spreadsheet appears, and then quit the spreadsheet to return to the letter.

As with most things in Windows NT, the OLE concept is easier to use than its name implies.

Linking

Linking looks just like embedding or pasting. Your chart appears in your letter, just as before. But here's where things get weird: You're not really pasting the chart. You're pasting the chart's filename.

The word processor runs over to the file containing the chart, sees what the chart looks like, and then puts a copy of it in the letter.

What's the point? Well, unlike with pasting or embedding, you're keeping only one copy of the chart around. When you call up the chart in your spreadsheet and change it, those changes are automatically reflected in your word processor the next time you load that letter. With only one real version of the object lying around, every copy is always the right version.

- Not all Windows NT programs can handle Object Linking and Embedding. In fact, of the programs that come in the Windows NT box, only WordPad and the obtuse Object Packager are really OLE savvy.
- Object Linking and Embedding can get pretty complex, so the vast majority of Windows NT users simply acknowledge that their computer can do that stuff and let the technicians play with it.

Should you paste, embed, or link your important objects? Here's what to do:

- Use Paste for objects you never want to change.
- Embed objects if you want to be able to easily edit them at a later date.
- Choose the Link option if you want several programs to share the same version of a single object.

Windows NT Workstation 4 tries really, really hard to make Object Linking and Embedding work across networks so, for example, you can send a message with an embedded Excel worksheet to someone who doesn't have Excel on his computer. Sometimes this can be made to work and sometimes it can't. But in either case, you need the help of an expert.

Leaving Scraps on the Desktop Deliberately

The Clipboard's a handy way to copy information from one place to another, but it has a major limitation: Every time you copy something new to the Clipboard, it replaces what was copied there before. What if you want to copy a bunch of things from a document?

If you were cutting and pasting over a real desktop, you could leave little scraps lying everywhere, ready for later use. The same scraps concept works with Windows NT: You can move information from window to window, using the Desktop as a temporary storage area for your scraps of information.

For example, suppose you have some paragraphs in a WordPad document you want to copy to some other places. Highlight the first paragraph, drag it out of the WordPad window, and drop it onto the Desktop. Poof! A small Scrap icon appears on your Desktop. See another interesting paragraph? Drag it onto the Desktop, as well: Another Scrap icon appears.

Eventually, copies of your report's best paragraphs are sitting in little scraps on your Desktop. To move any of the scraps into another document, just drag them into that other document's window and let go.

Any remaining, unused scraps can be dumped into the Recycling Bin, or simply left on the Desktop, adding a nice, comfortable layer of clutter.

To make a scrap, highlight the information you want to move, usually by running the mouse pointer over it while holding down the mouse button. Then, point at the highlighted information and, while holding down the mouse button, point at the Desktop. Let go of the mouse button, and a scrap containing that information appears on the Desktop.

Controlling the Printer

Many of the Windows NT features work in the background. You know that they're there only if something is wrong and weird messages start flying around. The Windows NT print program is one of those programs.

When you choose the Print command in a program, you may see the little Windows NT printer icon appear at the bottom corner of your screen. After your printer stops spitting out pages, the little printer icon disappears.

If everything is running smoothly, the printer icon looks like this in the corner of your taskbar:

Your printer can print only one thing at a time. If you try to print a second memo before the first one is finished, Windows NT jumps in to help. It intercepts all the requests and lines them up in order, just like a harried diner cook.

To check up on what is being sent to the printer, double-click on the taskbar's little printer icon, and you see the print program in all its glory, as shown in Figure 10-9.

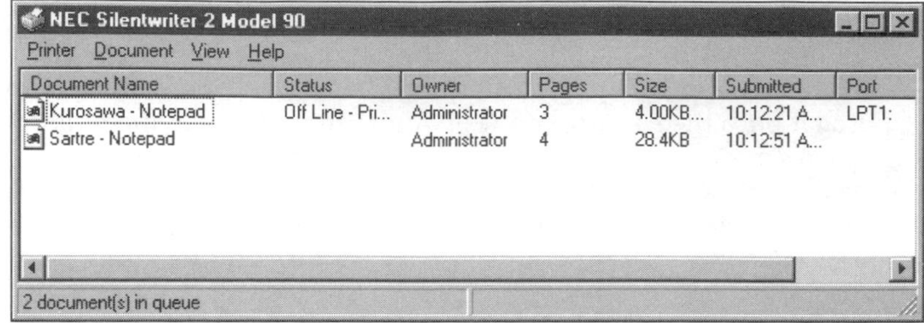

Figure 10-9: Double-click on the taskbar's printer icon to see what files are about to be printed.

- After the printer is through with Kurosawa, it moves to the second file in the lineup, which, in this case, is Sartre.
- Changing the order of the files as they're about to be printed is easy. For example, to scoot Sartre ahead of Kurosawa, click on its name and hold down the mouse button. Then drag the file up so it cuts in front of Kurosawa. Release the button, and Print Manager changes the printing order. (The printing order is called a *queue,* pronounced Q.)
- To cancel a print job, click on the filename you don't like with your right mouse button and then choose Cancel Printing from the menu that pops up.
- If the boss is walking by the printer while you're printing your party flier, choose Document from the menu and select Pause Printing from the menu that drops down. The printer stops. After the boss is out of sight, click on Pause Printing again to continue. Unfortunately, many laser printers have their own memory, so they'll continue printing a few more pages.
- If you're on a network, you may have no control over the order in which files are printed, which printer is used, or whether or not you can pause a print job. It all depends — and you're probably tired of hearing this — on how the network is set up. Yawn.
- If your printer is not hooked up, Windows NT will probably try to send your file to the printer anyway. When it doesn't get a response, it sends you a message that your printer isn't ready. Plug the printer in, turn it on, and try again. Or hit Chapter 19 for more printer troubleshooting tips.

Chapter 11

Switch Flipping in the Windows NT Control Panel

In This Chapter

- Exploring the Control Panel
- Customizing the display
- Changing colors
- Changing video modes
- Adjusting the double-click
- Changing to a different printer
- Hoppin' 'n' jivin' with multimedia sounds
- Installing or removing programs
- Avoiding dangerous and unfriendly icons

In a way, working with Windows NT is like remodeling a bathroom. You can spend time on the practical things, like calculating the optimum dimensions for piping or choosing the proper brand of caulking to seal the sink and tub. Or you can spend your time on the more aesthetic options, like adding an oak toilet paper holder, a marble countertop, or a rattan cover for the Kleenex box.

You can remodel Windows NT, too, and in just as many ways. On the eminently practical side, head for the Windows NT Control Panel, call up the Mouse icon, and spend hours optimizing the way Windows NT recognizes your mouse clicks.

Or check out the Control Panel's more refined options: Change the color of the title bars to teal, for example, or cover the Windows NT Desktop with daisy patterns or argyle wallpaper.

This chapter shows you how to turn Windows NT into that program you've always dreamed of owning someday. (Although you still can't have bay windows. . . .)

Finding the Control Panel

The Control Panel is the cupboard that holds most of the Windows NT switches. Flip open the Control Panel, and you can waste a few hours scratching your head over all the Windows NT options.

To find the Control Panel, click on the Start button, choose Settings, and click on Control Panel. The Control Panel window pops up, as shown in Figure 11-1. (Because different computers often contain different parts, your Control Panel may look a little different than the one in the picture.) Each icon in the Control Panel's window represents a switch that controls part of the computer.

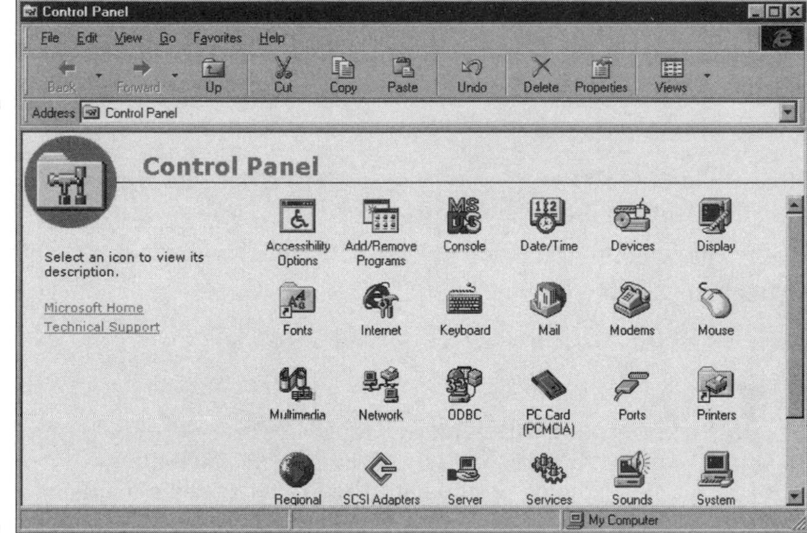

Figure 11-1: Double-click on an icon in the Control Panel to reveal hidden switches controlling that particular icon's subject.

Everybody's Control Panel looks different because everybody (and everybody's corporation) can afford different computer toys. For example, some modem hounds have special icons that control the way their modems collect mail from all their electronic mailboxes. Others have icons that help them agonize over settings for their networks or sound cards. Table 11-1 takes a look at some of the icons you may come across in your copy of Windows NT.

For a quick way to access your Control Panel, double-click on the My Computer icon (it's usually hiding in the upper-left corner of your Desktop). You find a Control Panel folder inside, waiting for you to open it with a double-click.

Your Control Panel may have more icons than the ones described in Table 11-1. Some programs and some hardware plop an icon of their own in the Control Panel when they install.

Table 11-1 Deciphering the Control Panel Icons

This Icon	*Does This*
Accessibility Options	Windows NT can be customized to work more easily for people with physical limitations. The screen can be made more readable, for example, or the numeric keypad can be converted into a makeshift mouse (which is also handy for laptop users).
Add/Remove Programs	Are you eager to install that new (insert name of expensive software here)? Double-click here to make Windows NT automatically install your new software. Use this icon to tell Windows NT to add on any optional components, too, like the FreeCell card game. (You may need to consult the Network Administrator first, though.)
Console	Use a lot of DOS programs? This feature lets you adjust how they look in their window — font sizes, screen colors, and other settings for the detail-oriented.
Date/Time	This area lets you change your computer's date, time, and time zone settings.
Devices	This icon controls how Windows NT reacts to your computer's parts. Don't mess with this one, or you'll be sorry.
Display	Double-click on the Display icon to change your screen's wallpaper, color scheme, number of available colors, resolution, screensaver, and other display-oriented settings. (Or, right-click on a blank part of your Desktop; both methods work.)
Fonts	Windows NT comes with fonts like Arial and Courier. If you head back to the software store and buy more, like Lucida-Blackletter, install them by double-clicking on this icon. (***Nerdly Note:*** This icon is actually a *shortcut* to the real Fonts setting area. Shortcuts are covered in Chapters 4 and 11.)
Internet	Don't mess with this icon until you've had a chance to read up on Internet Explorer in Chapter 16. Even then, you may want to leave the settings alone.

(continued)

Table 11-1 *(continued)*

This Icon	*Does This*
Keyboard	Here you can change how long the keyboard takes to repeat a letter when you hold down a key. Yawn. Rarely used. Or, if you pack up the computer and move to Sweden, double-click here to switch to the Swedish language format (or Belgian, Finnish, Icelandic, and a bunch of other countries' formats). Finally, here's where you tell Windows NT whether you upgraded to a newer 101- or 102-key keyboard.
Mail	E-mail junkies with pen pals from several different sources — Office networks, CompuServe, The Microsoft Network, or even a fax program — direct all their mail into one big Inbox through this program. You need a computer nerd to set this one up, however, and that's where Network Administrators come in. Don't touch this one.
Microsoft Mail Postoffice	If you use Microsoft Mail on your network this is where you can set up what Microsoft calls a *Postoffice*. If you are supposed to do this, someone will show you how.
Modems	Before you can talk to other computers over the phone lines, you need a modem. Double-click here, and Windows NT tries to figure out what sort of modem you have so that it can start bossing it around. If you're working in an office, check with the Network Administrator first — you don't want to fiddle with any settings that are already in place.
Mouse	Make that mouse scoot faster across the screen, change it from right-handed to left-handed, fine-tune your double-click, choose between brands, and change all sorts of mouse-related behaviors.
Multimedia	Sound-card owners can drop by here to tweak their gear settings, adjust playback/record volumes, fiddle with MIDI instruments, and play with other goodies like video capture cards and laser disc players.
Network	Save this one for the office network guru. You aren't missing much, just the mechanics of linking computers so that people can swap information.
PC Card (PCMCIA)	This setting controls how Windows NT talks to those credit card-sized PC Cards that usually fit into laptops and note books. If you're using a laptop, you can click on this icon and see whether your PC Card is working properly. There's nothing here to "set" — the program just reports on settings.

This Icon	Does This
Ports	This area controls how your computer squirts information through its cables. If you fiddle with the settings, the computer can stop sending information, making everybody think you've stopped being a Productive Employee. Save this one for the Network Administrator.
Printers	The Network Administrator comes here to tell Windows NT about a new printer, adjust the settings on an old printer, or choose which printer (or fax card) Windows NT should use. ***Technical Note:*** This isn't really an icon; it's a shortcut that leads to the Printer setup program.
QuickTime 32	Are you using multimedia programs? If you've been watching movies on-screen, you may see this ignorable icon on the screen. It contains settings the Network Administrator frets over if something goes wrong with the movie player.
Regional Settings	Used mostly by laptoppers with Frequent Flyer cards, this area changes the way Windows NT displays and sorts numbers, currency, the date, and the time. (If you changed time zones, just click on the date/time display on the bottom-right corner of the taskbar, a process described in this chapter.)
SCSI Adapters	Boring information about your computer's parts, all designed to make your Network Administrator sweat.
Server	Network Administrators click here to see who's snooping around on which computer. It's much more boring than it sounds.
Services	Administrators can peek in here to check on whether the computer is conducting its appropriate tasks at the right times.
Sounds	This area is the most fun! Make Windows NT play different sounds for different events. For example, hear a cool Pink Floyd riff whenever a Windows NT error message pops up on-screen. Windows NT comes with a few sounds, but you have to record Pink Floyd yourself, unfortunately. Grab a microphone, Sound Recorder, and a copy of *Multimedia and CD-ROMs For Dummies,* 2nd Edition (by some guy you may have heard of named Andy Rathbone) if you're not sure how your sound card works yet.
System	As boring as a mechanic's manual for '74 Pontiacs, this icon lets the Network Administrator tweak incredibly detailed parts of your computer's life. Stay away from it.

(continued)

Table 11-1 *(continued)*

This Icon	*Does This*
Tape Devices	You use this icon to install a tape device used for backing up files. On a network, backups are usually done on one main computer — most likely by the Network Administrator or one of the minions. If, heaven forbid, you need to install a tape device, get help.
	Similar to the Modem icon, Telephony provides Network Administrator-level settings for the advanced pencil chewer.
UPS	By using a gizmo called an *Uninterruptible Power Supply (UPS),* some computers can keep on working even if the power goes off. If you have a UPS (doubtful) or need to configure one yourself (even more doubtful), you need to click here (most unlikely of all).

Customizing the Display

The most-often-used part of the Control Panel is probably the Display icon, which looks like the picture in the margin. When you open this door, you can change the wallpaper, screen saver, and other visual aspects of the Windows NT Desktop (see Figure 11-2).

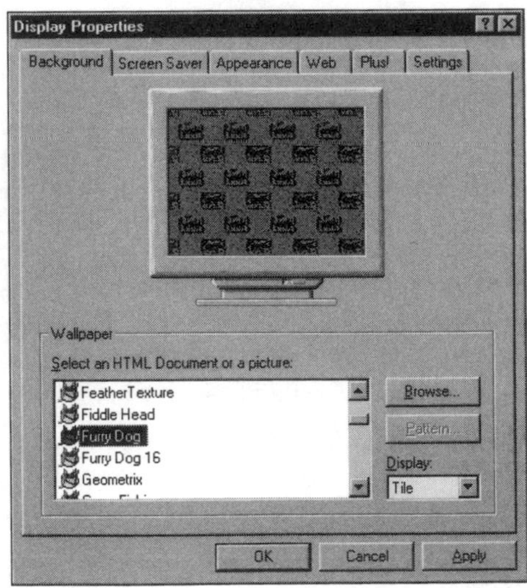

Figure 11-2: When double-clicked, the Display icon brings up a dialog box that lets you change your Desktop's colors, resolution, wallpaper, screen saver, and other display-oriented options.

Unlike several other switches in the Control Panel, the Display icon doesn't control anything too dangerous. Feel free to fiddle around with all the settings. You can't cause any major harm. If you do want to play, however, be sure to write down any original settings. Then you can always return to normal if something looks odd.

Basically, just don't change the color of your text and the color of your background to white, like some poor fellow once did in Minnesota. That makes it much too hard to see what you're doing.

You don't have to root through the Start button and the Control Panel to get to the Display icon's contents. Instead, just click on a blank part of your Desktop using your right mouse button. After the menu pops up out of nowhere, click on Properties. That bypasses the Control Panel and takes you straight to the Display settings area.

The display's background (hanging new wallpaper)

When Windows NT first installs itself, it paints a dull green background across the screen and then starts sprinkling windows and icons over it. Windows NT has to choose that dull green in the beginning, or nobody would think it's a serious business application.

However, Microsoft snuck other backgrounds, known as wallpaper, into the Windows NT box. Those pieces of wallpaper are hiding on the hard disk, just waiting for you to install them. Different wallpaper can reflect different moods. For example, you can turn the window's background into a pattern of leaf fossils or seashells or soap bubbles. You can use a scanned photo of your choice for a cheery day (see Figure 11-3). Or you can create your own wallpaper in Paint, the Windows NT graphics program, and hang your new wallpaper yourself.

To change the wallpaper, do the following:

1. **Double-click on the Display icon from the Control Panel.**

   Or you can click on a blank spot of your Desktop with your right mouse button and choose Properties from the menu that appears from nowhere.

   A rather large dialog box appears (refer to Figure 11-2).

2. **Look for the word Wallpaper hovering over a list of names and click on one of the names.**

   Wham! Windows NT displays a small preview of how your selection would look as wallpaper (see Figure 11-4).

Figure 11-3: Windows wallpaper, the backdrop beneath all the windows and icons can match your mood for the day.

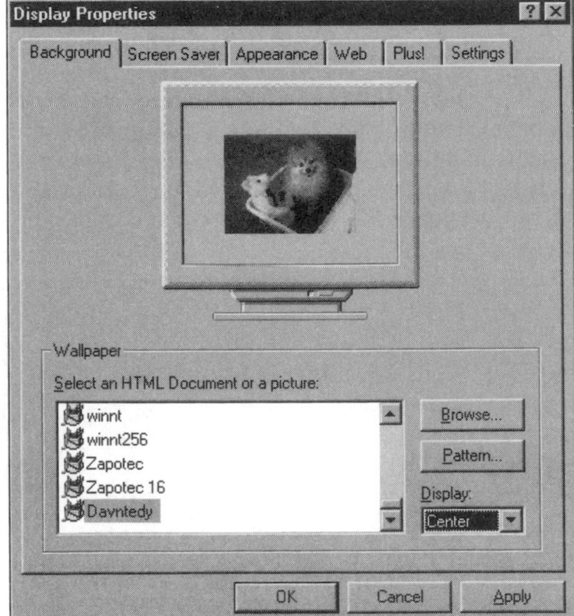

Figure 11-4: Windows NT displays a small preview of how your selection will look as wallpaper.

3. **To see more names on the list, click on the little arrows on the bar next to the names.**

   If you aren't using a mouse, you can select a listed item by using the arrow keys to highlight the item you want and then pressing Enter. In a long list, you can find a certain name more quickly by pressing the name's first letter.

4. **After you see the name of the wallpaper you want, select it and then choose the Apply button to make Windows NT install it.**

5. **Like the way your new wallpaper looks on-screen? Then choose the OK command button. If you don't like the way it looks, go back to Step 4 and choose a new filename.**

   The dialog box disappears, and you are back at your Desktop (with the new wallpaper displayed proudly in the background).

- Wallpaper can be tiled across the screen or centered. Small pictures should be tiled, or painted repeatedly across the screen. Larger pictures look best if they're centered. Select the option button next to your preference; the buttons lurk beneath the list of wallpaper names. Or try them both and then choose the one you like best.
- Wallpaper files are merely bitmaps, or files created in Windows NT Paint. (Bitmap files end with the letters BMP.) Anything you create in Windows NT Paint can be used as wallpaper. In fact, you can even use Paint to alter the wallpaper Microsoft provides with Windows NT.
- See a pretty picture you like while browsing on the World Wide Web with Windows NT Explorer? Then click on the picture with your right mouse button and choose Set as Wallpaper from the pop-up menu. (You may need to save the file onto your hard disk first.)
- Windows NT only lists wallpaper that's stored directly in the Windows NT folder. If you create some potential wallpaper in Paint, you have to move the file to the WinNT folder before the file's name shows up in the Desktop dialog box's master list, or you must choose the file by clicking on the Browse button. If this concept seems strange, foreign, confusing, or all three, check out Chapter 12 for more information about folders and moving files between them.

Wallpaper looks like a lot of fun, but it may be too much fun if your computer is running big programs and trying to display complicated wallpaper at the same time. Large chunks of wallpaper can use up a great deal of the computer's memory, consistently slowing Windows NT down. If you find yourself running out of memory, change the wallpaper to the (None) option. The screen won't look as pretty, but Windows NT may work better.

Small files that are tiled across the screen take up much less memory than large files that are centered on-screen. If Windows NT seems slow or it sends you furtive messages saying it's running out of memory, try tiling some smaller bits of wallpaper. Also, try black-and-white wallpaper; it doesn't slow down Windows NT as much.

- The Pattern option sprinkles tiny lines and dots across the screen, providing a low-budget alternative to wallpaper. To add or change those sprinkles, click on one of the names listed in the Pattern section, right next to the list of Wallpaper names (refer to Figure 11-2). Choose from the patterns Microsoft provided; or if you're desperate for something to do, click on the Edit Pattern button to create your own little patterns.
- Patterns are a poor-man's wallpaper. They're only one color, and they don't vary much. If Windows NT keeps complaining about needing more memory, dump your wallpaper and switch to patterns. They don't eat up nearly as much memory. (They're pretty ugly, though.) And remember, your best bet is to buy as much memory as possible — especially while memory costs so little.
- To see patterns across the back of Desktop, you need to change the wallpaper option to (None); otherwise, the patterns won't show up.

The display's screen saver

In the dinosaur days of computing, computer monitors were permanently damaged when an oft-used program burned its image onto the screen. The program's faint outlines showed up even if the monitor was turned off.

To prevent this burn-in, people installed screen savers to jump in when a computer hadn't been used for a while. The screen saver would either blank the screen or fill it with wavy lines to keep the program's display from etching itself into the screen.

Today's monitors don't really have this problem, but people use screen savers anyway — mainly because they look cool.

Windows comes with several screen savers built in, although none of them is activated at first. To set one up, do the following:

1. **Click on the Screen Saver tab along the top of the Display Properties dialog box (refer to Figure 11-2).**
2. **Then click on the downward-pointing arrow in the Screen Saver box.**
3. **Select the screen saver you want.**

   Immediately after choosing a screen saver, you should click on the Preview command button to see what the screen saver looks like. Wiggle the mouse or press the spacebar to come back to Windows NT.

- Fiddlers can click on Settings for more options. For example, you can control the colors and animation speed.
- If you click on the Password protected box, your workstation locks up when the screen saver kicks in. You unlock it by typing your password (the one you use to log on with). If you forget your password, you have to make your feeble excuses to the Network Administrator and get that oh-so-jolly soul to unlock it.
- Click on the up or down arrows next to Wait to tell the screen saver when to kick in. If you set the option to 5, for example, Windows NT waits until you haven't touched the mouse or keyboard for five minutes before letting the screen saver out of its cage.
- Windows NT comes with more screen savers than it initially installs. To make Windows NT install all its screen savers, use the Control Panel's Add/Remove Programs icon, described later in this chapter. (Hint: The 3D Pipes screen saver looks way cool.)

The display's appearance (getting better colors)

If you paid extra for a fancy color monitor and video card, the time has come to put them to use. You can make Windows NT appear in any color you want by clicking on the tab marked Appearance, found along the top of the Display Properties menu.

You can find the Display Properties menu (refer to Figure 11-2) by either double-clicking on the Control Panel's Display icon or right-clicking on a blank part of the Desktop and choosing Properties from the pop-up menu.

The Appearance dialog box opens, enabling you to choose between several Microsoft-designed color schemes or to create your own. (Tell your boss that a more pleasant color scheme will enhance your productivity.) Figure 11-5 shows the Appearance dialog box.

To choose among previously designed color schemes, do the following:

1. **Click on the arrow next to the box beneath Scheme.**
2. **After the list drops down, click on the name of the scheme you want to try out.**

   Each time you select a new color scheme, the sample window shows you how the colors will look.

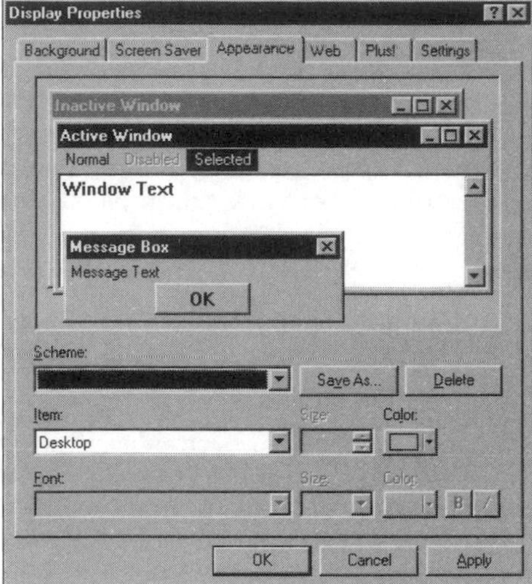

Figure 11-5: Windows NT lets you personalize your computer by choosing different color schemes.

If you want to change one of the color schemes slightly, go for it: Click on the box beneath Item to see a list of areas you can fiddle with. For example, to change the font Windows NT uses for icon titles, choose Icon Title from the list and select a different font from the ones listed in the Font box.

And, if you want even more choices, you can mix your own colors by selecting Other from the Color menu and clicking on the Define Custom Colors command button.

Feel free to play around with the colors by trying out different schemes or designing your own combinations. Playing with the colors is an easy way to see what names Windows NT uses for its different components. It's also a fun way to work with dialog boxes. But if you goof something awful, and all the letters suddenly disappear, click on the Cancel button. (It's in the middle of the three buttons along the bottom.)

- Color schemes don't refer to color alone; they can change the appearance of Windows NT in other ways. For example, the Horizontal Icon Spacing setting listed in the Item box determines how closely your icons sit next to each other. Also in the Item box, the Scrollbar setting determines the width of the scroll bars and their elevator-like buttons you click on to move around in a document.

- Created an outstanding new color scheme? Then click on the Save As button and type in a new name for your creation. If you ever grow weary of your creative new color scheme, you can always return to the Windows NT original colors by selecting Windows Default from the Scheme box.

- Windows NT continues to display your newly chosen colors until you head back to the Appearance icon and change them again.
- All this talk of "dialog boxes," "command buttons," and "funny arrow things" got you down? Then head to Chapter 6 for a field guide to figuring out Windows NT menus.

Display settings (playing with new video modes)

Just as Windows NT can print to hundreds of different brands of printers, it can accommodate zillions of different monitors, too. It can even display different video modes on the same monitor.

For example, Windows NT can display different amounts of color on-screen, or it can slightly shrink the size of everything, packing more information onto the screen. The number of colors and the size of the information on-screen comprise a video mode, or video resolution.

Some Windows NT programs only work in a specific video mode, and those programs casually ask you to switch to that mode. Huh?

Here's what's happening: Monitors plug into a special place on the back of the computer. That special place is an outlet on a video card — the gizmo that translates your computer's language into something you can see on the monitor. That card handles all the video-mode switches. By making the card switch between modes, you can send more or fewer colors to your monitor or pack more or less information onto the screen.

To make a video card switch to a different video mode, do the following:

1. **Head for the Control Panel's Display icon and give it a double-click.**
2. **Then click on the Settings tab — one of the tabs along the top of the Display Properties dialog box (refer to Figure 11-2).**

   Can't find the Display Properties dialog box? Click on a blank part of your Desktop by using the right mouse button and choose Properties from the menu that springs up.

As shown in Figure 11-6, the Display Properties Settings tab lets you select the video mode you want Windows NT to display on-screen.

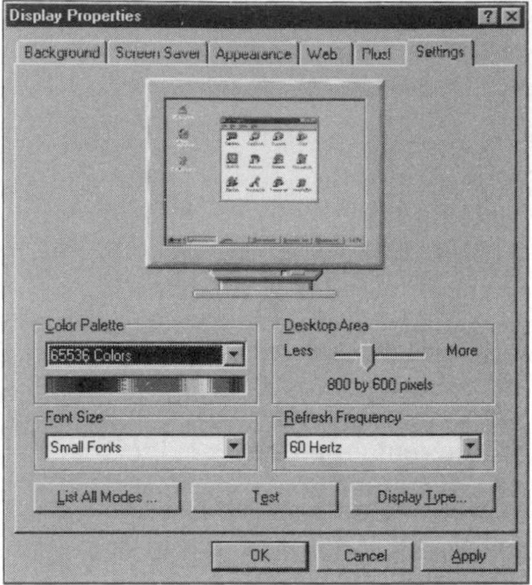

Figure 11-6: The Settings tab of the Display Properties box lets you select the video mode you want to display on-screen.

To change the number of colors Windows NT currently displays on the screen, do the following:

1. **Click on the arrow next to the Color Palette box.**
2. **Choose the desired number of colors from the drop-down menu.**
3. **Click on the Test button to see if your monitor can handle the load.**

   Windows NT displays those colors for 15 seconds, and then returns to the previous number of colors.
4. **If the test looks okay, click on the Apply button to change to the tested number of colors. Doesn't look okay? Don't click Apply, and your amount of color remains the same.**

To change the amount of space you have on your Desktop for displaying programs, follow these steps:

1. **Slide the lever in the Desktop Area box.**

   Sliding the lever to the side marked More lets you fit more information onto the screen; sliding to the Less side fits less information on the screen, but makes the windows larger and easier to see.
2. **Click on the Test button to make sure that your monitor and card can handle the new settings.**

   Windows NT displays the new screen resolution for 15 seconds, and then returns to the previous number of colors.
3. **If the test looks okay, click on the Apply button to apply the changes.**

Windows NT subsequently gives you a chance to back out if you choose a video mode your computer can't handle, thank goodness.

Changing the Refresh Frequency to an incorrect setting can turn your monitor into toast. Don't make changes here.

- Monitors and cards can display Windows NT in different resolutions. The higher the resolution, the more information Windows NT can pack onto the screen. (And the smaller the windows become, too.) Windows NT refers to resolution as Desktop area. For more information about this monitor/card/resolution stuff, troop over to Chapter 2 and read the section about computer parts that I told you to ignore.
- Earlier versions of Windows made users shut down Windows while changing resolution. Windows NT isn't nearly as rude. You can change resolution while all your programs are still running. (Make sure that you save your work anyway, however. Who really trusts their computer to be polite these days?)
- New video cards usually come with a disk that contains special information called a driver. If Windows NT doesn't recognize your breed of video card, it may ask you to insert this disk when you're changing video modes.
- The more colors you ask Windows NT to display, the slower it runs. Usually, it's best to stick with 256 colors unless you have a fancy video card, a fancy monitor to go with it, and want to look at ultra-realistic photos on-screen.
-  If you'll be looking at pictures stored through Kodak's PhotoCD technology, you'll probably want Windows NT to display as many colors as possible — often 65,000 (16-bit) or 1.6 million (24-bit). Switch back to fewer colors after you're done, however, if Windows NT starts running too slowly.
- If Windows NT acts goofy with your video card or monitor — or you recently installed new ones — head for the "Adding New Hardware" section later in this chapter. Windows NT probably needs to be formally introduced to your new equipment before it will talk to it.

Understanding the Fuss about TrueType Fonts

In the first few versions of Windows, the *fonts,* or sets of letters, numbers, and other characters, produced individual letters and numbers that looked kind of jagged. A capital A, for example, didn't have smooth, diagonal lines.

Instead, the sides had rough ridges that stuck out. They usually looked fine on the printer but pretty awful on-screen, especially if the headlines were in large letters.

A few years later, Windows introduced a font technology called TrueType fonts to eliminate the jaggies and make the screen match more closely what comes out of the printer. The technology is still around in Windows NT.

Double-click on the Control Panel's Fonts icon to see what fonts come with Windows NT, to install additional fonts, or to delete the ugly ones you don't like anymore.

Double-click on any of the Font icons, and you see what that particular font looks like. For example, a double-click on the icon marked Courier New Italic brings up an eye chart displaying how that font would look on the printed page, as shown in Figure 11-7.

Figure 11-7: Double-click on a Font icon to see what it looks like.

- Icons marked with the letters TT are TrueType fonts, so they always look better than the fonts marked with the letter A.
- ***Note:*** You'll probably never need to fiddle with the Fonts icon. Just know that it's there in case you ever want to get fancy and install more fonts on your computer.

Fonts can eat up a great deal of hard disk space. If you installed some fonts that you no longer use, delete them using the following steps:

1. **Double-click on the Control Panel's Fonts icon.**
2. **Click with your right mouse button on the name of the font you no longer use.**
3. **Then choose Delete from the pop-up menu.**

   A box appears, asking whether you're sure that you want to remove that font.
4. **Click the Yes button if you really want to give it the purge.**

   Changed your mind? Click the No button instead.

To be on the safe side, don't delete any fonts that come with Windows NT; only delete fonts that you installed yourself. Windows programs often borrow Windows NT fonts for menus; if you delete those fonts, your menus mysteriously vanish.

Making Windows NT Recognize Your Double-Click

Clicking twice on a mouse button is called a double-click; you do a great deal of double-clicking in Windows NT. But sometimes you can't click fast enough to suit Windows NT. It thinks your double-clicks are just two single clicks. If you have this problem, head for the Control Panel's Mouse icon.

Mouse

When you double-click on the Mouse icon, the Mouse Properties dialog box pops up (see Figure 11-8). If your mouse dialog box doesn't look like the one in Figure 11-8, the company that made your mouse slipped its own software into the Control Panel. The following instructions may not work for you, but you can generally access the same types of options for any mouse. If your menu looks weird, try pressing F1 for help.

To check the double-click speed, do the following:

1. **Double-click on the box marked Test area.**

   Each time Windows NT recognizes your double-click, a little puppet with water buffalo horns pops out of the jack-in-the-box. Double-click again, and the puppet disappears.
2. **Slide the scroll box toward the words Fast or Slow until Windows NT successfully recognizes your double-click efforts.**

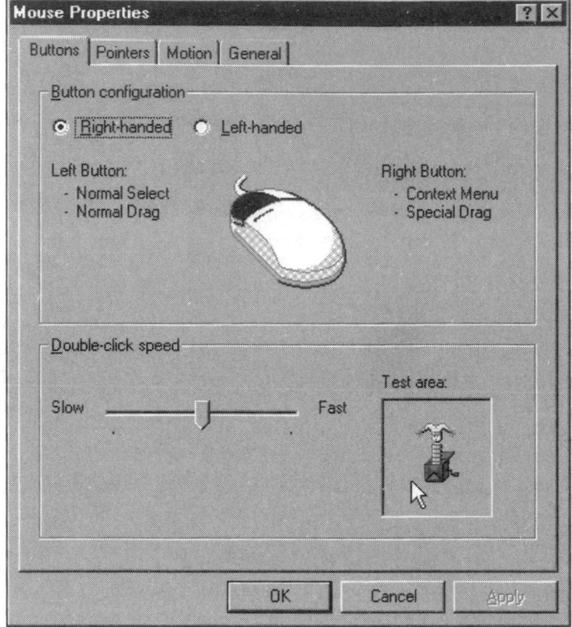

Figure 11-8: Double-click on the Test area box to check your current settings.

3. **Click on the OK command button after you're through, and you're back in business.**

- Can't double-click on the Mouse icon quickly enough for Windows NT to open the darn thing up? Then just click once, and poke the Enter key with your finger. Or, click once with the right button and choose Open from the menu that shoots out of the mouse icon's head. Yep, Windows NT offers many ways to do the same thing.
- If you're left-handed, click on the little circle marked Left-handed, shown along the top of Figure 11-8, and click on the Apply button. Then you can hold the mouse in your left hand and yet still click with your index finger.
- Looking for some fun? Click on the Pointers tab, click on the arrow next to the Scheme box, and choose some of the different point schemes for your mouse pointers. Yep, the Serious Windows NT software lets you substitute dinosaur cartoons for your mouse pointer. Fun!

Setting the Computer's Time and Date

Many computer users don't bother to set the computer's clock. They just look at their wristwatches to see when it's time to stop working. But they're missing out on an important computing feature: Computers stamp new files with the current date and time. If the computer doesn't know the correct date, it stamps files with the wrong date. Then how can you find the files you created yesterday? How about the ones from last week?

Also, Windows NT sometimes does some funny things to the computer's internal clock, so you may want to reset the date and time if you notice that the computer is living in the past.

To reset the computer's time or date, click on the Control Panel's Date/Time icon.

A double-click on the Date/Time icon brings a little calendar to the screen, shown in Figure 11-9. To change the date, just click on the correct date as listed on the on-screen calendar. If the date's off by a month or more, click on the little arrow next to the currently listed month. A list drops down, letting you select a different month. To change the year or the hour, click on the number you want to change and then click on the up or down arrows to make the number bigger or smaller. After the number is correct, click on the OK button for Windows NT to make the changes.

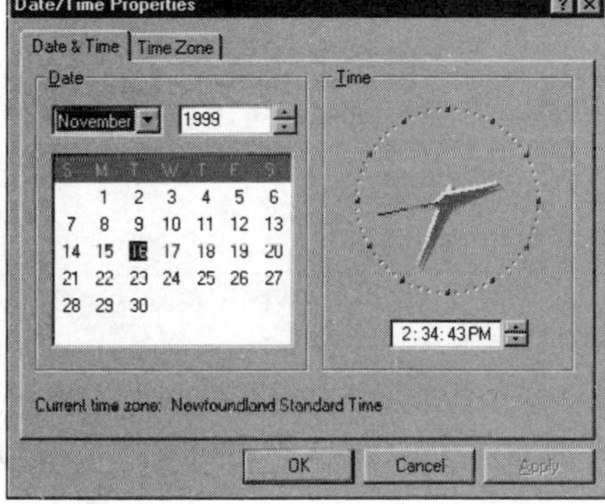

Figure 11-9: To change the time, click on the numbers beneath the clock; then click on the little arrows next to the numbers.

For an even quicker way to change your computer's time or date, double-click on the little clock Windows NT puts on the taskbar that lives along the edge of the screen. Windows NT brings up the Date/Time menu, just as if you waded through the Control Panel and double-clicked on the Date/Time icon.

Fiddling with the Printer

Most of the time, the printer works fine — especially after you turn it on and try printing again. In fact, most people never need to read this section. (And if you're working in a corporation, the network folks are in charge of fiddling with a malfunctioning printer.)

Occasionally, however, you may need to tweak some printer settings. You may need to install a new printer or remove an old one that died (so it doesn't keep cluttering up the list of printers). Either way, start by clicking on the Control Panel's Printers icon.

The Printers dialog box surfaces, as shown in Figure 11-10.

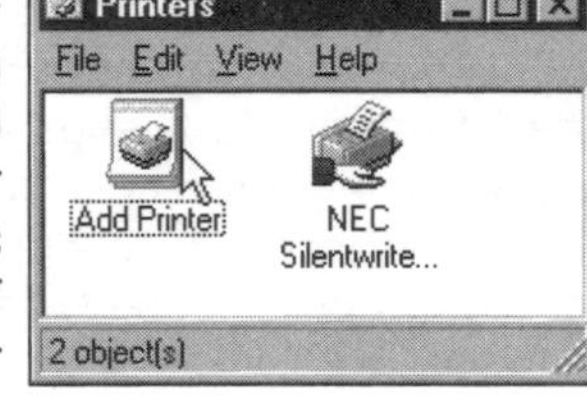

Figure 11-10: Double-clicking on the Add Printer icon tells Windows NT about your new printer.

If you're installing a new printer, grab the Windows NT compact discs that came in the box; you may need them during the installation. To add a new printer, follow these steps:

1. **Double-click on the Add Printer icon.**

   Déjà vu! You see the same Add Printer Wizard that appeared when you first installed Windows NT.

2. **Select the My Computer or Network printer server options.**

   If you're plugging the printer into the back of your own computer, select the My Computer option. If you'll be using a computer on a network, jump to the section "Adding a Network Printer" later in this chapter.

3. **Click on the Next button and click on the LPT1 box.**

   Windows NT must keep up a reputation for being the best, so it offers zillions of options for printer ports. Just about every printer you may come across in your lifetime uses LPT1:, however, so start by selecting that one.

4. **Just as before, click on the Next button and then use the PgUp and PgDn keys to choose your printer's manufacturer and model number.**

   The Add Printer Wizard box lists the names of printer manufacturers on the left; click on the name of your printer's manufacturer. The right side of the box lists the models of printers that the manufacturer makes.

5. **After you see your printer listed, press Enter or double-click on the printer's name.**

Windows NT asks you to stick the appropriate setup disks into a drive, and the drive makes some grinding noises. After a moment, you see the new printer listed in the box.

6. **Click on the new printer's icon and choose the Set As Default Printer option from the window's Printer menu.**

   That's it. If you're like most people, your printer works like a charm. If it doesn't, you may have to wade through the technical stuff in the sidebar about printer ports and such.

If you have more than one printer attached to your computer, choose your most-often-used printer as the default printer. That choice tells Windows NT to assume that it's printing to that often-used printer.

Also, if you feel generous enough to let other computers on your network use your printer, select the Shared option after that page comes up toward the end of the installation process. Windows NT then asks you what operating systems the mooches are using — various incarnations of Windows NT or Windows 95 and Windows 98. Pick them from the list, and finally, be sure to click on the Yes button when Windows NT asks whether you want to see a test page.

Adding a Network Printer

Installing a network printer so that you can use it is even easier than installing a printer connected directly to your computer. The setup is easy because Windows NT and the Network Administrator do all the heavy lifting.

1. **To add a network printer, double-click on the Printers folder in the Control Panel.**
2. **Double-click on the Add Printer icon to start up the Add Printer Wizard.**
3. **Select Network Printer Server and then click on the Next button.**
4. **A window called Connect to Printer opens. In the area called Shared Printers, double-click on computer names until you find the printer you want.**

   The printer is shown attached to a particular computer — called a printer server.

5. **Highlight the printer by clicking on it once so that the name appears in the box labeled Printer at the top of the Connect to Printer window.**
6. **Click on the OK button, and you're done.**

   See the end of Chapter 9 for a section on selecting which printer you'll use most of the time and how to make exceptions.

Printer ports and configuration nonsense

Windows NT shoots information to printers through *ports* (little metal outlets on the computer's rump). Most printers connect to a port called *LPT1:*, or the *first line printer port.*

Always select this option first. If it works, skip the rest of this technical chatter. You've already found success!

Some people, however, insist on plugging printers into a *second line printer port,* or *LPT2:*. (If you meet one of these people, ask them why.) Still other people buy *serial* printers, which plug into *serial ports* (also known as *COM ports*).

Different brands of printers work with Windows NT in different ways, but here are a few tips:

1. **To connect a printer to a different port, click on the Printers icon with your right mouse button and choose Properties from the pop-up menu.**
2. **Click on the tab marked Details, and you can select the port you want.**
3. **Look to see what port you're plugging the printer into, and select that port from the menu.**

   Computer ports are rarely labeled, so you probably have to bribe a computer guru to help you out. Start tossing Cheetos around your chair and desk; computer gurus are attracted by the smell.
4. **If you're connecting a printer to a serial port, you need to do one more little chore: Configure the serial port.**
5. **Click on the Port Settings box and make sure that the following numbers and characters appear, in this order:** `9600, 8, N, 1, Xon/Xoff.`

The printer should be all set. If not, call over a computer guru. At least you only have to go through all this printer hassle once — unless you buy another printer.

- To remove a printer you no longer use, call up the Control Panel, double-click on the Printer icon, and click on the icon for the printer you don't like anymore. Then press the Del key on the keyboard. Windows NT asks if you're sure that you want to delete the printer before removing it from your options.
- You can change most of the printer options from within the program you're printing from. Click on Files in the program's menu bar and then click on Print Setup. From there, you can often access the same box of printer options as you find in the Control Panel.
- Some printers offer a variety of options. For example, you can print from different paper trays or print at different resolutions. To play with these options, click on the Printers icon with the right mouse button and choose Properties from the menu that pops up. Although different models of printers offer different options, most let you change paper size, fonts, and types of graphics.

- If your printer isn't listed in the Windows NT master list, you have to contact the printer's manufacturer for a driver. After it comes in the mail, repeat the process for adding a printer, but click on the Have Disk button. Windows NT asks you to stick in the manufacturer's disk so that it can copy the driver onto the hard disk. (For more information, check out the section on adding new hardware later in this chapter; impatient searchers may be able to download files from the manufacturer's World Wide Web page.)
- Working with printers can be more complicated than trying to retrieve a stray hamster from under the kitchen cupboards. Feel free to use any of the Help buttons in the dialog boxes. Chances are they'll offer some helpful advice, and some are actually customized for a particular brand of printer. Too bad they can't catch hamsters.

Stirring Things Up with Sound and Multimedia

The term multimedia means mixing two or more media — usually combining sound and pictures. A plain old television, for example, could be called a multimedia tool, especially if you're trying to impress somebody.

Windows NT can mix sound and pictures if you have a sound card: a gizmo costing from $20 to $200 that slips inside the computer and hooks up to a pair of speakers or a stereo.

Macintosh computers have had sound for years. And for years, Mac owners have been able to assign sounds to system events. In lay language, that means having the computer make a barfing sound when it ejects a floppy disk. Windows NT doesn't normally let you assign sounds to the floppy disks, but you can assign noises to other events by double-clicking on the Control Panel's Sounds icon.

Sounds

The Sounds Properties dialog box appears (see Figure 11-11). Windows NT automatically plays sounds for several system events. An event can be anything as simple as when a menu pops up or when you first log on to Windows NT in the morning.

Windows NT lists the events on the top of the box and lists the possible sounds directly below them in the box called Name. To assign a sound, click on the event first and then click on the sound you want to hear for that event. In Figure 11-11, for example, Windows NT is set up to make a barfing sound whenever it sends out an urgent dialog box with an exclamation point in it.

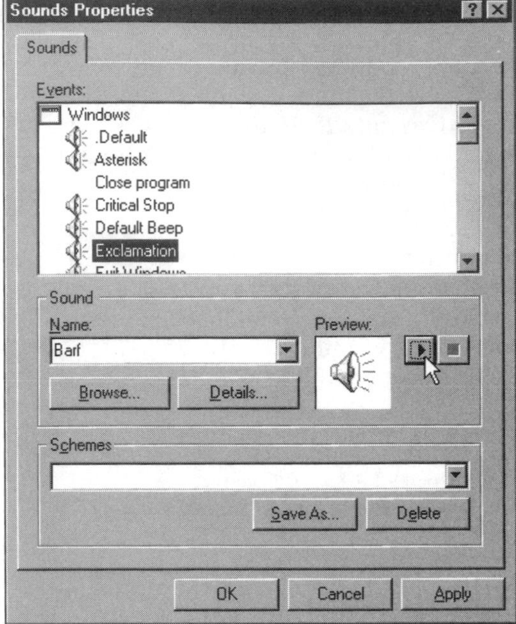

Figure 11-11: Windows NT can play back different sounds when different things happen on your computer.

- Are you satisfied with your new choices of sounds? Then click on the box marked Save As, and change the words in the box to something else, like My Sound Settings. That way you can still change back to the more polite Windows NT Default sounds if you don't want houseguests to hear your computer barf. (You can change back to My Sound Effects after they leave.)
- To take advantage of this multimedia feature, you must buy and install a sound card. Then you have to tell Windows NT about your new card by clicking on the Control Panel's Multimedia icon, described in this section's ugly technical sidebar.

- To hear a sound before you assign it, click on its name and then click on the Preview button (the little black triangle next to the speaker).
- You can record your own sounds through most sound cards. You can probably pick up a cheap microphone at Radio Shack; many sound cards don't include one.
- Be forewarned: Sound consumes a lot of disk space (especially when recorded in 16-bit stereo) so stick with short recordings — short and sweet B. B. King guitar riffs, for example, or the sound of a doorbell ringing work well.
- Is your sound card not working right? You may have to muddle through the Multimedia icon, described in the dreary technical sidebar in this section.

Multimedia setup problems

Multimedia gadgetry inevitably brings a multitude of setup problems. Too many file formats and program settings exist for an easy ride. Although Windows NT tries to set up your computer's hardware automatically, the Control Panel's Multimedia icon lets techno-fiddlers change some of the settings. Because different computers use different parts, the settings listed under the Multimedia icon vary, but here's a general look at what they can do:

- **Audio:** This page controls your sound card's volume settings as well as its recording quality. The better the quality of the recording, the more hard disk space your recordings consume. A quicker way to adjust the volume is to click on the little speaker in the corner of the taskbar.
- **Video:** Click here to decide whether your videos should play back kinda blurry (but filling the full-screen) or sharp and crisp (but in a tiny window).
- **MIDI:** Musicians can tell Windows NT about new MIDI instruments on this page.
- **CD Music:** Mostly useful for adjusting the volume of headphones that plug into a CD-ROM's headphone jack.
- **Devices:** Here Windows NT lists all the multimedia devices attached to your computer (as well as a few devices you may want to add to your computer in the future). By clicking on a device and clicking on the Properties button near the bottom, you can turn a device on or off. Also, click on the Add button to add new drivers for currently (or recently) installed multimedia devices.

Adding and Removing Programs

By adding an Add/Remove Programs icon to the Control Panel, Windows NT is trying to trick you into thinking it's easier than ever to install or remove a program. Nope.

Here's how the installation programs work — if you're lucky:

1. **After you get a new program, look for a disk marked Install or Installation and stick the disk into any disk drive that it fits.**

   If the program came on a compact disc, put the disc into your compact disc drive.

2. **Next, double-click on the Control Panel's Add/Remove Programs icon.**

3. **Click on the Install button, and click on Next from the next screen.**

   Windows NT searches all your disk drives for a disk containing an installation program; if it finds an installation program, it runs it, effectively installing the program. If it doesn't find one, it just gives up. What to do? Search for a file named SETUP.EXE on your floppy disk or CD-ROM disc, and double-click on that file.

   - Most programs you buy at software stores come with installation programs, so Windows NT can install them without too much trouble. Some of the smaller shareware programs found on online services don't come with installation programs, unfortunately, so you have to install them yourself.

   - Forced to install a DOS or Windows program yourself? Make a new folder somewhere on your hard disk and copy all the files from the program's disk to the new folder. Then to load the program, double-click on the program's icon from within that folder. Chapter 13 is filled with tips on creating folders, copying files, and sticking new programs on the Start menu.
   - The Add/Remove Programs icon can uninstall programs, but only if those programs were designed with the uninstall feature in mind. Therefore, you won't find very many — if any — of your programs listed on the uninstall menu.

   - Until the built-in uninstall feature of Windows NT catches on, the easiest way to remove old or unwanted Windows programs is to buy a third-party uninstaller program, such as Quarterdeck's CleanSweep.

Finding Out Which Icons to Avoid

Unless you have a very pressing reason, avoid these icons in the Control Panel: Devices, Keyboard, Internet, Mail, Modems, Network, PC Card (PCMCIA), Ports, Regional Settings, SCSI Adapters, Server, Services, System, Tape Devices, Telephony, and UPS.

- The Devices icon starts and stops devices — and that's only something experts should be doing.
- The Keyboard icon doesn't do any major damage, but it doesn't do any major good, either. It controls how fast a key repeats if you hold it down. Big deal.
- Just as you don't need to climb a telephone pole to make a phone call, you probably won't need to use the Internet icon to "surf the Web." Zip over to Chapter 16 for the basics on using the Internet features.

- The Mail icon is for setting up a Microsoft Mail postoffice, or for administering one. If you have Microsoft Mail on your network, ask for help.
- **Exception Department:** If you don't want to bother the Network Administrator, feel free to double-click on the Modems icon when you need to adjust your modem's settings (or install a new modem). Windows NT usually does a surprisingly good job of automatically detecting your modem and setting it up for you.
- The Network icon controls how Windows NT talks to other computers through your office's network — those cables meandering from PC to PC. Talk to your Network Administrator before playing with this icon "just to see what it does."
- Don't bother with the PC Card (PCMCIA) icon unless you have a laptop. (And even then, the program usually just indicates whether or not you have a PC Card in your laptop's PC slot. Yawn.)
- Don't fiddle with your Ports settings; they don't need changing.
- The Regional Settings icon changes the keyboard layout to the one used by people in other countries. This icon doesn't make the Windows NT dialog boxes appear in German (although you can order the German version of Windows NT from Microsoft). Instead, a foreign keyboard layout makes certain keys produce foreign characters.
- The information listed in the System icon turns on network hounds and techno-nerds. Your Network Administrator puzzles over this stuff, not you.

Adding New Hardware

After you wolf down a sandwich for lunch, you know what you ate. After all, you picked it out at the deli counter, chewed it, swallowed it, and wiped the breadcrumbs away from the corners of your mouth.

But when you add a new part to your computer, it's turned off; Windows NT is asleep. And when you turn the computer back on and Windows NT returns to life, it may notice the new part, and it may not.

Here's the good news, however: If you tell Windows NT to look for the new part, it will probably find it. In fact, Windows NT not only spots the new part, but it introduces itself and starts a warm and friendly working relationship using the right settings.

The problem is knowing where to tell Windows NT to start looking. Here are a few tips:

- **Video card:** First look at the box your card came inside — you need to know what model of video card you installed. Next, double-click on the Control Panel's Display icon and click on the Settings tab from the top, right side. Click on the Display Type button near the bottom, right corner, and click on the Change button. Breathe heavily. Select the card's manufacturer from the list on the left; select the card model from the list on the right, and then click on the Have Disk button. Insert the disk that came with the card and follow the instructions on the screen. Exhale.
- **Multimedia cards:** Did you add a sound card, video capture card, or something similar? You'll want to head for the Multimedia icon and click on the Devices tab, as described earlier in this chapter.
- **Printer:** Double-click on the Control Panel's Printer icon and double-click on the Add Printer icon. (This chapter's Printer section has more specific information.)
- **Modem:** Double-click on the Control Panel's Modems icon and click on the Add button. (The process is a great deal easier than you may expect, actually.)
- Are you adding a new modem? Windows NT will want to know your current country and area code, as well as whether you dial a special number (such as a 9) to reach an outside line.

Are you moving from Windows 95 or Windows 98? Windows NT doesn't have true "Plug and Play," but it does have a modified version. So hardware sometimes installs without a glitch, and sometimes a little prodding is necessary. Also, some companies haven't released Windows NT drivers for their gear, so shop carefully before buying new parts. (The stuff that works best for Windows NT has a special "Windows NT" sticker on the box.)

Part III
Using Windows NT Applications

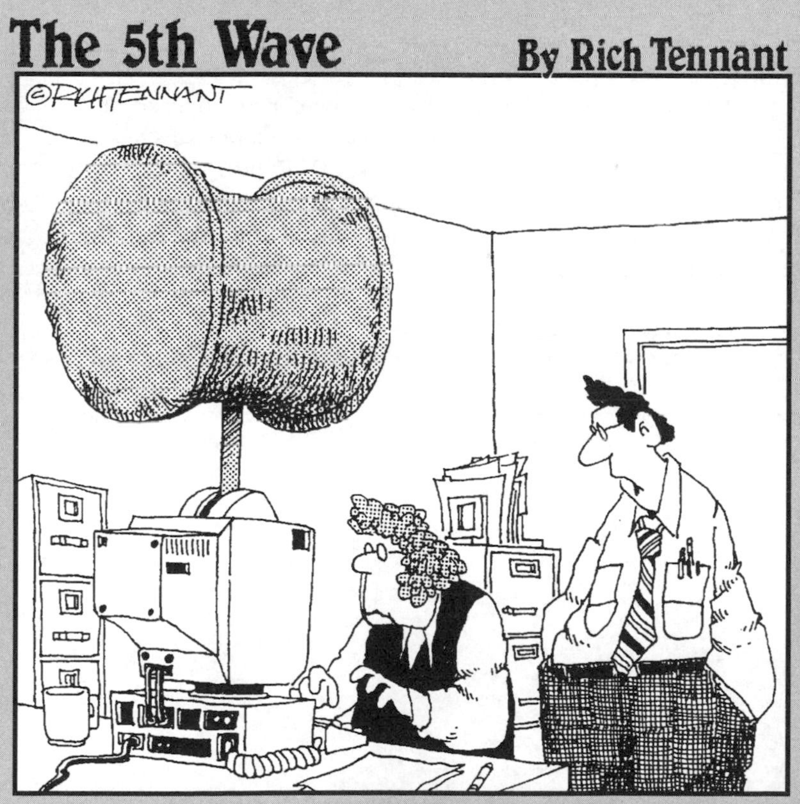

"OH YEAH, AND TRY NOT TO ENTER THE WRONG PASSWORD."

In this part . . .

Did you know that

- Fish have no eyelids?
- A dime has 118 ridges around it? (Count 'em!)
- Scientist Percy LeBaron Spencer discovered in 1942 that microwaves could cook food after the waves melted a chocolate bar in his pocket?
- Windows NT comes with a bunch of free programs that aren't even mentioned on the outside of the box?

This part takes a look at all the stuff you're getting for nothing. Well, for the price on the sales receipt, anyway.

Chapter 12

The Windows NT Desktop, Start Button, and Taskbar

In This Chapter

- Using the Desktop
- Making shortcuts
- Deleting files, folders, programs, and icons
- Retrieving deleted items from the Recycle Bin
- Finding out the Start button's reason for living
- Putting programs on the Start button menu
- Using the taskbar

In the old days of computing, pale technoweenies typed disgustingly long strings of code words into computers to make the computers do something. Anything.

Windows NT brings computers to the age of modern convenience. To start a program, simply click on a button. A slight complication exists, however: The buttons no longer look like buttons. In fact, some of the buttons are hidden, revealed only by the push of yet another button (if you're lucky enough to stumble upon the right place to push).

This chapter covers the three main Windows NT buttonmongers: the Desktop, the taskbar, and that mother of all buttons — the Start button.

Making Piles of Junk on the Windows NT Desktop

Normally, nobody would think of mounting a desktop sideways. Keeping the pencils from rolling off a normal desk is hard enough.

But in Windows NT, your computer monitor's screen is known as the Windows Desktop, and it's the area where all your work takes place. When working with Windows NT, you create files and folders right on your new electronic Desktop and scatter those files and folders across the screen.

For example, need to write a letter asking the neighbor to return the circular saw she borrowed? Here's how to put the Desktop's functions to immediate use.

Point at just about any Windows NT item and click your right mouse button to see a menu listing the things you're allowed to do with that item.

1. **Click on the Desktop with your right mouse button.**

   A menu pops up, as shown in Figure 12-1.

   Too much clutter to even spot the Desktop? Try this tip:

   With your right mouse button, click on the taskbar — the strip of buttons along an edge of your screen — and choose Minimize All Windows from the menu that appears. Windows NT will instantly clear off your Desktop. (***Hint:*** Click on the taskbar's buttons to make the clutter reappear, program by program.)

2. **Point at the word New and click on WordPad Document from the menu that appears.**

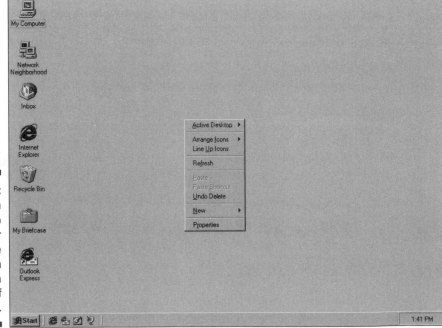

Figure 12-1: Clicking on the Desktop with your right mouse button brings up a list of options.

Because you're creating something new — a new letter — you should point at the word New. Windows NT lists the new things you can create on the Desktop. Choose WordPad Document, as shown in Figure 12-2.

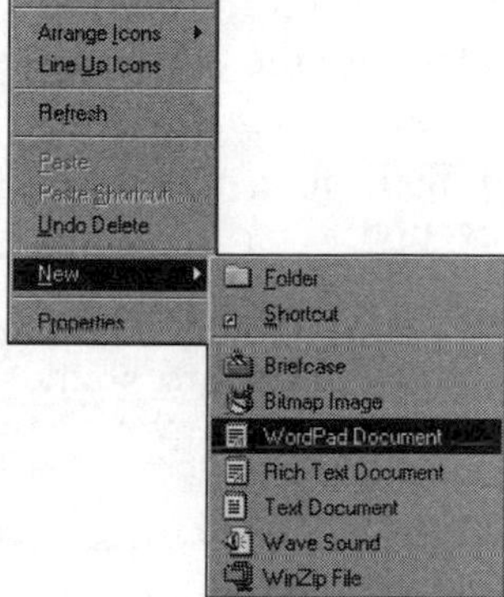

Figure 12-2: Point at the word New and choose WordPad Document from the menu.

3. **Type a title for your letter and press Enter.**

   When an icon for a WordPad Document appears on the Desktop, Windows NT doesn't want you to lose it. So the first step is to give it a name of up to 255 characters. As soon as you start typing, your new title replaces the old name of New WordPad Document, shown in Figure 12-3.

Figure 12-3: Start typing to create the icon's new name.

4. **Double-click on your new icon, write your letter, save it, and print it.**

   Double-clicking on the new icon calls up WordPad, the word processor, so you can write the letter requesting the return of your circular saw. Done writing? Then move on to Step 5.

5. **Click on Save from WordPad's File menu to save the letter.**

6. **Head back to WordPad's File menu and choose Print to send the letter to the printer.**

7. **To store the file, drag the icon to a folder. To delete it, drag the file to the Recycle Bin.**

   After you finish writing and printing the letter, you need to decide what to do with the file. You can simply leave its icon on your desk, but that clutters things up. If you want to save the letter in a folder, click on the Desktop with your right mouse button and choose Folder from the New menu. Windows NT tosses a new folder onto the Desktop, ready for you to drag your letter into.

   Or, if you want to delete the letter, drag the icon into the Desktop's Recycle Bin (described in the next section).

- Windows NT is designed for you to work right on the Desktop. From the Desktop, you can create new things like files, folders, sounds, and graphics — just about anything. After working with your new file or folder, you can store it or delete it.
- You can store your favorite files and folders right on the Desktop. Or, to be more organized, you can drag your files and folders into the folders listed in the My Computer window. (The My Computer program gets a great deal more coverage in Chapter 13.)

- Confused about what something is supposed to do? Click on it with your right mouse button. Windows NT tosses up a menu listing just about everything you can do with that particular object. This trick works on the Desktop or just about any icon you come across.
- Is your Desktop looking rather cluttered? Make Windows NT line up the icons in orderly rows: Click on the Desktop with the right mouse button, point at the Arrange Icons option, and choose Auto Arrange from the menu.

Using the Recycle Bin

The Recycle Bin, that little wastebasket with green arrows on the Desktop, is supposed to work like a real Recycle Bin — something you can fish the Sunday paper out of if somebody pitched the comics section before you had a chance to read it.

If you want to get rid of something in Windows NT — a file or folder, for example — simply drag it to the Recycle Bin: Point at the file or folder's icon with the mouse and, while holding down the left mouse button, point at the Recycle Bin. Let go of the mouse button, and your detritus disappears. Windows NT stuffs it into the Recycle Bin.

But if you want to bypass that cute metaphor, Windows NT offers another way to delete stuff: Click on your unwanted file or folder's icon with the right mouse button and choose Delete from the menu that pops up. Whoosh! Windows NT asks cautiously whether you're sure that you want to delete the icon. If you click on the Yes button, Windows NT dumps the icon into the Recycle Bin, just as if you dragged it there.

So, if you like to drag and drop, feel free to drag your garbage to the Recycle bin and let go. If you prefer the menus, click with your right mouse button and choose Delete. Or if you like alternative lifestyles, click on the unwanted icon with your left button and push your keyboard's Delete key. All three methods toss the file into the Recycle Bin, where it can be salvaged later or, after it fills up, purged for good.

- Want to retrieve something you deleted? Double-click on the Recycle Bin icon, and a window appears, listing deleted items. See the name of your accidentally deleted icon? Drag it to the Desktop. Point at the icon's name and, while holding down the left mouse button, point at the Desktop. Let go of the mouse button, and the Recycle Bin coughs up the deleted item, good as new.

- The Recycle Bin's icon changes from an empty wastepaper basket to a full one as soon as it's holding a deleted file.
- A full Recycle Bin usually eats up 10 percent of your hard disk space. To free up some space, empty the bin by purging the deleted files for good. Click on the Recycle Bin with your right mouse button and choose Empty Recycle Bin from the menu. Then click on the Yes button after Windows NT asks if you're sure that you want to really delete those files and folders that you already deleted once. Cautious program, that Windows NT.

- You can control how long the Recycle Bin holds on to your deleted files. Click on the Recycle Bin with your right mouse button and choose Properties from its menu. Normally, Recycle Bin waits until your deleted files consume 10 percent of your hard disk before it begins purging your oldest deleted files. If you want the Recycle Bin to hang on to more deleted files, increase the percentage. If you're a sure-fingered clicker who never makes mistakes, decrease the percentage.

Making a shortcut

Some people like to organize their Desktop, putting a pencil sharpener on one corner and a box of Kleenex on the other corner. Other people like their tissue box in the top desk drawer. Microsoft knew that one Desktop design could never please everybody, so Windows NT enables people to customize their Desktops to suit individual tastes and needs.

For example, you may find yourself frequently copying files to a floppy disk in drive A. Normally, to perform that operation, you open the My Computer icon and drag your files to the drive A icon living in there. But a quicker way exists, and it's called a Windows NT shortcut. A shortcut is simply a push button — an *icon* — that stands for something else.

For example, here's how to put a shortcut for drive A on your Desktop; these same steps work when creating any ol' shortcut:

1. **Double-click on the Desktop's My Computer icon.**

   The My Computer folder opens up, showing the icons for your disk drives as well as folders for your Control Panel and Printer. (My Computer gets more coverage in Chapter 13.)

2. **With your right mouse button, drag the drive A icon to the Desktop.**

   Point at the drive A icon (or any icon you want to create a shortcut to) and, while holding down your right mouse button, point at the Desktop, shown in Figure 12-4. Let go of your mouse button.

Figure 12-4: Dragging the drive A icon to the Desktop creates a shortcut.

3. **Choose Create Shortcut(s) Here from the menu.**

   Windows NT puts an icon for drive A on your Desktop, but it looks a little different from the drive A icon you dragged. Because it's only a shortcut — not the original icon — it has a little arrow in its corner, shown in Figure 12-5.

Figure 12-5: The icon on the left is a shortcut that stands for the icon on the right.

That's it. Now you don't need to root through the My Computer or Explorer folders and programs to access drive A. The drive A shortcut on your Desktop works just as well as the real drive A icon found in My Computer and Explorer.

- A shortcut is the equivalent of an icon in the Windows NT 3.51 Program Manager — a push button that starts a program or loads a file. A shortcut for a disk drive is just like the disk drive icons along the top of the Windows NT 3.51 File Manager, too.
- Feel free to create Desktop shortcuts for your most commonly accessed programs, files, or disk drives. Shortcuts are a quick way to make Windows NT easier to use.

- If your newly dragged icon doesn't have an arrow in its bottom corner, it's not a shortcut. Instead, you dragged the real program to your Desktop, and other programs may not be able to find it. Drag the icon back to where it was and try again. (You probably mistakenly held down the left mouse button rather than the correct button — the right button.)
- Grown tired of a shortcut? Feel free to delete it. Deleting a shortcut has no effect on the original file, folder, or program that it represents.

- Windows NT's shortcuts aren't very good at keeping track of moving files. If you create a shortcut to a file or program and then move the file or program to a different spot on your hard disk, the shortcut isn't able to find that file or program anymore.

Uh, what's the difference between a shortcut and an icon?

An icon for a file, folder, or program looks pretty much like a shortcut, except that the shortcut has an arrow wedged in its lower reaches. And double-clicking on a shortcut does pretty much the same thing as double-clicking on an icon: starts a program or loads a file or folder.

But a shortcut is only a servant of sorts. After you double-click on the shortcut, it runs over to the program, file, or folder that the shortcut represents and kickstarts that program, file, or folder into action.

You could do the same thing yourself by rummaging through your computer's folders, finding the program, file, or folder you're after, and personally double-clicking on its icon to bring it to life. But creating a shortcut so that you don't have to rummage so much is often more convenient.

- If you delete a shortcut — the icon with the little arrow — you're not doing any real harm. You're just firing the servant that fetched things for you, probably creating more work for yourself in the process.
- If you accidentally delete a shortcut, you can pull it out of the Recycle Bin, just like anything else that's deleted in Windows NT.

The Eager-to-Please Start Button

The Start button lives on your taskbar, and it's always ready for action. By using the Start button, you can start programs, adjust the Windows NT settings, find help for sticky situations, or, thankfully, shut down Windows NT and get away from the computer for a while.

The little Start button is so eager to please, in fact, that it starts shooting out menus full of options as soon as you click on it. Just click on the button once, and the first layer of menus pops out, as shown in Figure 12-6.

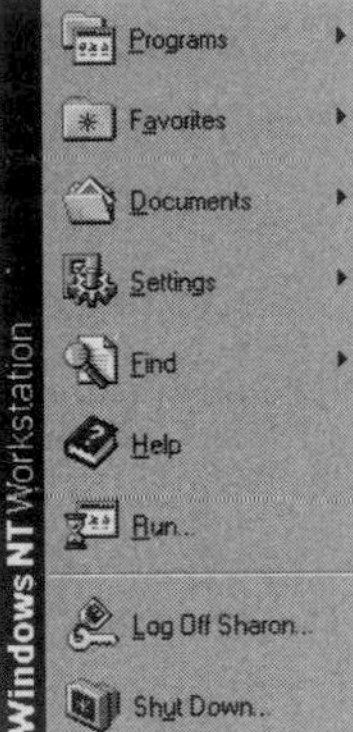

Figure 12-6: Click on the taskbar's Start button to see a list of options.

The explosive Table 12-1 shows what the different parts of the Start button do when you point at them.

Table 12-1 The Start Button

This Part	*Does This When You Point At It*
Programs	Probably the most used spot. Point here, and a second menu appears, listing available programs and folders containing related programs.
Favorites	Here's where your favorite Internet connections hide out. Chapter 16 has all the news on how to add and subtract from this list.

This Part	Does This When You Point At It
Documents	Point here to see the names of the last 15 files you played with. Spot one you want to open again? Click on its name to reopen it.
Settings	Allows access to the Control Panel and Printer settings, as well as ways to customize the Start button menus and taskbar.
Find	Lost a program or file? Head here to make Windows NT search for it.
Help	Clicking here does the same thing as pressing F1 — it brings up the Windows NT Help menu.
Run...	Used mostly by old-school, "stick-shift" computer users, it lets you start a program by typing in the program's name and *path*.
Shut Down...	Click here to shut down or restart Windows.
Log Off Sharon...	Use this icon to sign yourself off — but not shut down the computer.
Start	Clicking on the Start button makes the Start menu shoot out of the button's head.

- Microsoft boiled down the Windows NT 3.51 Program Manager and came up with the Start button. The Start button can handle just about everything the Program Manager does. Those folders listed on the Start button's Programs menu would be program groups in the Program Manager. Imagine!
- The Start button's menu changes as you add programs to your computer. That means that the Start button on your friend's computer probably offers slightly different menus than the ones on your own computer.
- See the little arrows on the menu next to the words Programs, Documents, Settings, and Find? The arrows mean that when you point at those words, another menu pops up, offering more detailed options.

- Need to open a file yet another time? Before you spend time clicking your way through folders, see if it's listed under the Start button's Documents area. You can find the last 15 documents you had open listed there, ready to be opened with a click.

Is Run a *real* DOS command line?

For the most part, Windows NT treats the Start button's Run command just like a regular ol' DOS command line. When you type in the name of a Windows or DOS program, Windows NT tries to run it. Windows NT first searches the current directory, and then it looks along the path. If Windows NT can't find the program, it sends out a message of complaint. (Just click on the OK button and start over.)

If Windows NT doesn't find the program, you have to type in the path name along with the program's name. For example, to load WordPerfect for Windows, these days, you must type something like the following:

```
c:\Office\Wpwin\Wpwin.exe
```

The Start button's Run command line differs from the DOS command line in one key area: It can't handle DOS commands like DIR and TYPE.

If you're salivating at the thought of a command line, you can make a shortcut to the Command Prompt and put it on your Desktop. But, if you're looking for a quick, menuless way to call up a program, you may want to give the Run command an occasional shot.

Starting a program from the Start button

This one's easy. To start a program from the Start button, follow these steps:

1. **Click on the Start button.**
2. **After the menu pops out of the button's head, point at the word Programs.**

   Yet another menu pops up, this one listing the names of programs or folders full of programs.
3. **If you see your program listed, click on the name.**

   Wham! Windows NT kicks that program to the screen.
4. **If you don't see your program listed, try pointing at the folders listed on the menu.**

   New menus fly out of those folders, listing even more programs.
5. **When you spot your program's name, just click on it.**

   In fact, you don't have to click until you see the program's name: The Start button opens and closes all the menus automatically, depending on where the mouse arrow is pointing at the time.

Still don't see your program listed by name? Head for Chapter 8. You can tell Windows NT to find your program for you.

There's another way to load a program that's not listed — if you know where the program is living on your hard disk. Follow these steps:

1. **Choose Run from the Start button menu.**
2. **Type in the program's name.**
3. **Press Enter.**

   If Windows NT finds the program, it runs it.

4. **If it can't find the program, though, click on the Browse button.**

   Shazam! Yet another box appears, this time listing programs by name.

5. **Pick your way through the dialog box until you see your program; then double-click on its name.**
6. **Click on the OK button to load it.**

If you don't know how to pick your way through this particular dialog box, head to the section of Chapter 6 on opening a file. (This particular dialog box rears its head every time you load or save a file or open a program.)

Adding a program to the Start button

The Windows NT 4 Start button works great — until you're hankering for something that's not listed on the menu. How do you add things to the Start button's menu?

If you're installing a Windows program that comes with its own installation program, breathe a sigh of relief. Those programs automatically put themselves on the Start button's menu — even if they say they're putting themselves on the "Program Manager" that served as the mainstay for earlier versions of Windows. But what if your program comes from a simpler household and doesn't have an installation program? Well, it means more work for you, as described here:

1. **Copy the program to your hard disk.**

   Create a new folder somewhere on your hard disk and copy your new program and its files to that folder. (And turn to Chapter 13 if you're a little sketchy about creating folders and copying files.)

2. **Click on the Start button and then point at Settings.**

   A menu shoots out from the right side of the Start menu.

3. **Click on Taskbar and then click on the Start Menu Programs tab.**

   The tab lurks along the top, on the right side.

4. **Click on the Add button and then click on Browse.**

   A new box pops up, as shown in Figure 12-7.

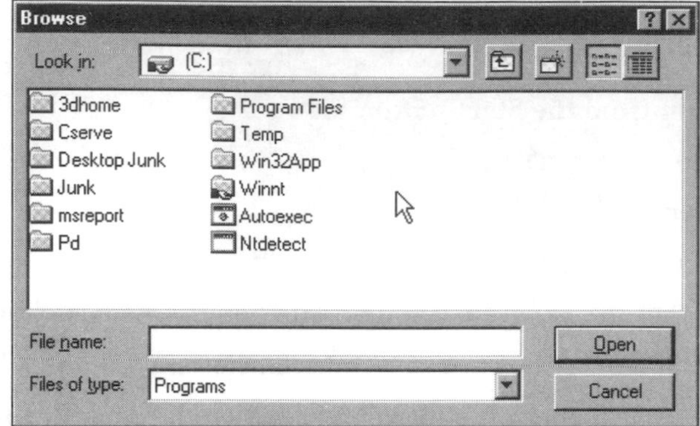

Figure 12-7: Click on a folder, and the Browse box lists the programs inside that folder.

5. **Click on the folder to which you copied the program and its files.**

   Hint: If you can't find that folder, click on the icon of the little folder with the arrow inside, up near the top. Doing so tells Windows NT to work its way up the folder listings, eventually showing you a list of your computer's disk drives. From there, you can once again start clicking your way down into the depths of folderdom.

6. **Double-click on the icon of the program you want to add.**

   The program's filename appears in the Command line box. (By double-clicking on the program's name, you are able to avoid typing in the name yourself.)

7. **Click on the Next button and then double-click on the folder where you want your program to appear on the Start menu.**

   For example, if you want your new program to appear under the Programs heading, simply click on the Programs folder. In fact, Windows NT automatically highlights the Programs folder, assuming that you want to install your new program there.

8. **Type the name that you want to see on the menu for that program and then click on the Finish button.**

   Most people just type the program's name. (Just as many people have nicknames, most program's filenames are different from their real names. For example, you probably want to change WPWIN — the filename — to WordPerfect — the program's real name.)

9. **Click on the OK button at the bottom of the box.**

   Doing so gets rid of the Taskbar Properties box and really finishes the job. Now, after you click on the Start button, you see your new program listed on the menu.

A quicker, but dirtier, way to add programs to the Start menu

A quicker way to add a program to the Start menu exists, but it's not as versatile. The preceding steps enable you to add a program's icon anyplace on the menu. But if you simply want the program's icon on the menu *now,* and you don't care about location, try this:

1. **Open the My Computer or Explorer program and find the folder where you copied your program.**
2. **Drag the program's icon over to the Start button and let go.**
3. **Point at the program and, while holding down the mouse button, point at the Start button.**
4. **When the icon hovers over the Start button, let go of the mouse button.**

Now, after you click on the Start button, you see your newly installed program's icon at the very top.

- These steps can put both Windows and DOS programs on your Start menu. (If your DOS program doesn't work, head for Chapter 15, which is full of ways to doctor your DOS programs into health under Windows NT. Plus, it shows how to change the program's icon.)
- Windows NT lets you add programs to the Start menu in several ways. The one I just listed is probably the easiest one to follow step-by-step.
- To get rid of unwanted menu items, follow these steps but choose the Remove button instead of the Add button in Step 4.

Shutting down Windows NT

Although the big argument used to be about whether pasta is fattening, today's generation has found a new source of disagreement: Should a computer be left on all the time or turned off at the end of the day? Both camps have decent arguments, and no real answer exists (except you should always turn off your monitor if you won't be using it for a half hour or so).

However, if you want to turn off your computer, don't just head for the Off switch. First, you need to tell Windows NT about your plans by following these steps:

1. **From the Start menu, choose Shut Down.**
2. **Click on the Shut down button from the box that appears.**

3. **Finally, click on the OK button.**

   That action tells Windows NT to put away all your programs and make sure that you saved all your important files.

   You may not even be allowed to shut down the computer you're working on. (Yes, Windows NT has rules even for that!)

Don't turn off your computer unless you use the Shut Down command from the Start button. Windows NT needs to prepare itself for the shutdown, or it may accidentally eat some of your important information.

Organizing the Desktop Mishmash with the Taskbar

Put a second or third window onto the Windows NT Desktop, and you'll immediately see the Big Problem: Windows and programs tend to cover each other up, making them difficult to locate.

The solution is the taskbar. Shown in Figure 12-8, the taskbar is that little bar running along the bottom edge of your screen.

Figure 12-8: The taskbar lists the names of all currently running programs and open folders.

The taskbar keeps track of all the open folders and currently running programs by listing their names. And, luckily, the taskbar is almost always visible, no matter how cluttered your Desktop becomes.

- When you want to bring a program, file, or folder to the forefront of the screen, click on its name on the taskbar.
- If the taskbar does manage to disappear, press Ctrl+Esc; that usually brings it to the surface.

- If you can only see part of the taskbar — it's hanging off the edge of the screen, for example — point at the edge you can see. When the mouse pointer turns into a two-headed arrow, hold down your mouse button and move the mouse to drag the taskbar back into view.
- If the taskbar looks too bloated, try the same trick: Point at its edge until the mouse pointer turns into a two-headed arrow and then drag the taskbar's edge inward until it's the right size.

The taskbar works somewhat like the minimized icons Windows NT 3.51 loads along the bottom of your screen. A few key differences exist, however: Windows NT 3.51 only displays icons of minimized programs; the taskbar displays icons for any currently running program or open folder. Also, Windows NT 3.51 lets you drag and drop files onto minimized icons — you can hear a WAV file by dragging and dropping it onto a minimized Media Player icon, for example. But you can't drag and drop anything onto the taskbar's program icons; you can only drag and drop files onto open windows.

Want to drag and drop a file onto a program or folder that's resting lazily along the screen's taskbar? Here's the secret: Drag the file until it hovers over the program or folder, but don't let go of the mouse button. After a few moments, the taskbar kickstarts the folder or program into action, making it jump into a window on the screen. Then, you can drag and drop your file onto the window to put it inside the program or folder.

Clicking on the taskbar's sensitive areas

Like a crafty card player, the taskbar comes with a few tips and tricks. For one thing, it has the Start button. With a click on the Start button, you can launch programs, change settings, find programs, get help, and order pizza. (Well, you can't order pizza, but you can do all the things mentioned in the Start button section earlier in this chapter.)

But the Start button is only one of the taskbar's tricks; some others are listed in Figure 12-9.

Hover the mouse pointer over the clock, and Windows NT shows the current day and date. Or if you want to change the time or date, a double-click on the clock summons the Windows NT time/date change program.

If you have a sound card installed, a click on the little speaker brings up the volume control, shown in Figure 12-10. Slide the volume knob up for louder sound; slide it down for peace and quiet. (Or click on the Mute box to turn the sound off completely.)

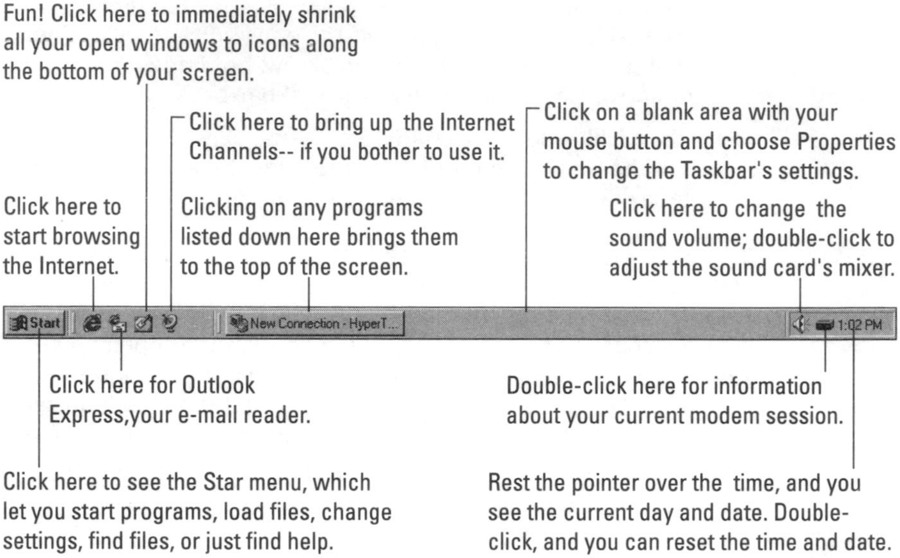

Fun! Click here to immediately shrink all your open windows to icons along the bottom of your screen.

Click here to bring up the Internet Channels-- if you bother to use it.

Click on a blank area with your mouse button and choose Properties to change the Taskbar's settings.

Click here to start browsing the Internet.

Clicking on any programs listed down here brings them to the top of the screen.

Click here to change the sound volume; double-click to adjust the sound card's mixer.

Start

New Connection - HyperT...

1:02 PM

Click here for Outlook Express,your e-mail reader.

Double-click here for information about your current modem session.

Click here to see the Star menu, which let you start programs, load files, change settings, find files, or just find help.

Rest the pointer over the time, and you see the current day and date. Double-click, and you can reset the time and date.

Figure 12-9: Clicking on or double-clicking on these areas on the taskbar performs these tasks.

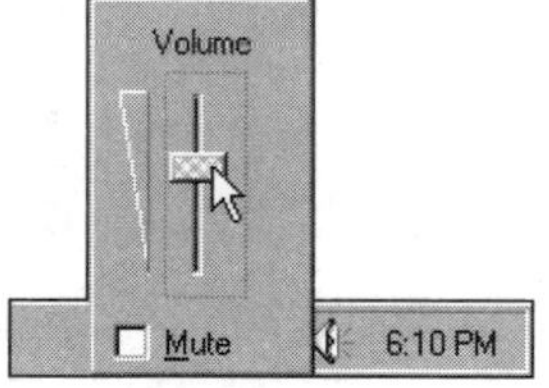

Figure 12-10: Clicking on the little speaker lets you adjust the sound card's volume.

Double-click on the little speaker to bring up a more advanced mixer program, shown in Figure 12-11, if your sound card offers that feature. Mixers let you adjust volume levels for your microphone, line inputs, CD players, and other features.

If you're running a modem, a little picture of a modem often appears next to the clock, as shown in Figure 12-12. Double-click on the modem to see statistics on the amount of data your modem is pushing and pulling over the phone lines.

- Other icons often appear next to the clock, depending on what Windows NT is up to. If you're printing, for example, you'll see a little printer down there. Laptops sometimes show a battery monitor. As with all the other icons, a double-click on the printer or battery monitor brings up information about the printer's or battery's status.

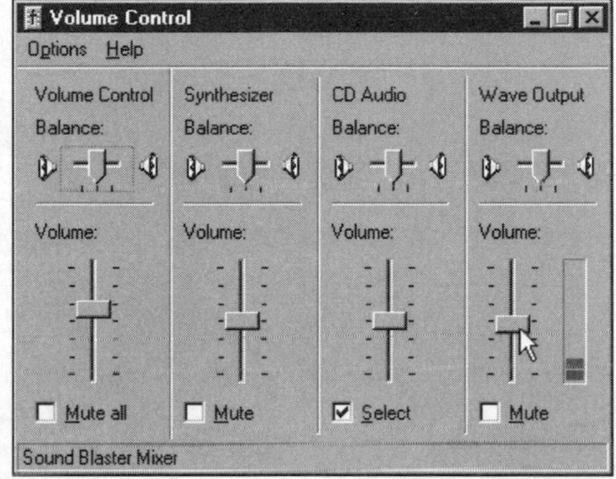

Figure 12-11: Double-clicking on the little speaker brings up a mixer program for the sound card.

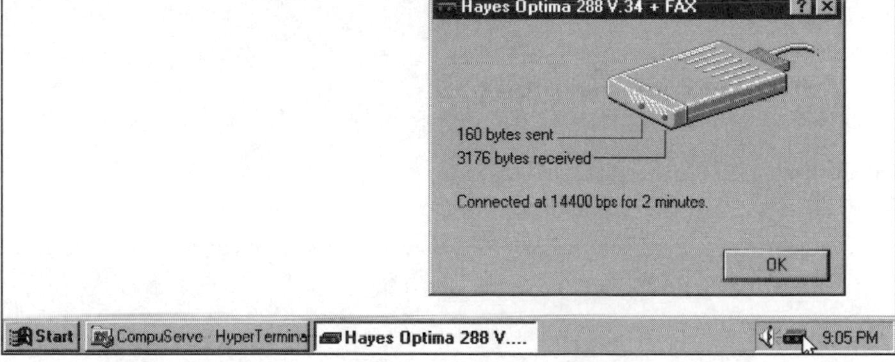

Figure 12-12: If you have a modem installed, you see this dialog box.

- Want to minimize all your Desktop's open windows in a hurry? Simply click on that tiny icon that looks like a pad and paper just to the right of the Start button. Can't find that icon? Then click on a blank part of the taskbar with your right mouse button and choose the Minimize All Windows option from the pop-up menu. All the programs keep running, but they're now minimized to icons along the taskbar. To bring them back to the screen, just click on their names from the taskbar.

Customizing the taskbar

Although Windows NT starts the taskbar along the bottom of the screen, it doesn't have to stay there. If you'd prefer that your taskbar hang from the top of your screen like a bat, just drag it there. Point at a blank spot of the taskbar and, while holding down your mouse button, point at the top of the screen. Let go of the mouse button, and the taskbar dangles from the roof, as shown in Figure 12-13.

Figure 12-13: The taskbar can be moved to any side of the screen by dragging it there.

Figure 12-14: The taskbar's buttons become harder to read when placed along one side.

Prefer it along one side? Then drag it there, as shown in Figure 12-14. (The buttons become more difficult to read, however.)

If the taskbar is starting to look too crowded, you can make it wider by dragging its edges outward, as shown in Figure 12-15.

To change other taskbar options, click on a bare taskbar area with your right mouse button and choose Properties from the pop-up menu. From there, you can make the taskbar always stay on top of the current pile of windows, make the taskbar automatically hide itself, hide the clock, and shrink the Start menu's icons. Whenever you click on an option button, a handy on-screen picture previews the change. If the change looks good, click on the OK button to save it.

Toolbars on the taskbar

You can do even more to set up the taskbar so that it suits you by adding a toolbar or two. *Toolbars* are little collections of your most used icons and commands: By gathering your favorites and placing them along the taskbar at the bottom of your screen, you can reach them over and over again. Ain't repetition grand?

To display a toolbar, right-click on a blank spot in the taskbar along the screen's bottom edge and select Toolbars from the pop-up menu. A list of available toolbar names appears; click on a toolbar name to select it. (Toolbars with checkmarks are already alive and kicking on your taskbar.) To remove a toolbar, click on the name to remove the checkmark.

The Desktop toolbar (shown to the left) is particularly handy.

If you have a bunch of open windows and need to get at an icon or something on your Desktop, just click the Desktop icon, and everything open is minimized to the taskbar — even windows that don't have a minimize button. Windows NT forces them to the taskbar — out of the way — until you click on a minimized icon to open it again.

You can add your own favorite programs to Quick Launch. Just find the program's icon and click it with your mouse. Hold the mouse button down and drag the icon to the Quick Launch pad. Leggo of the mouse.

Figure 12-16 shows the CD Player icon being dragged onto Quick Launch. After the mouse lets go, the CD Player is ready for action. Click on it and the program starts.

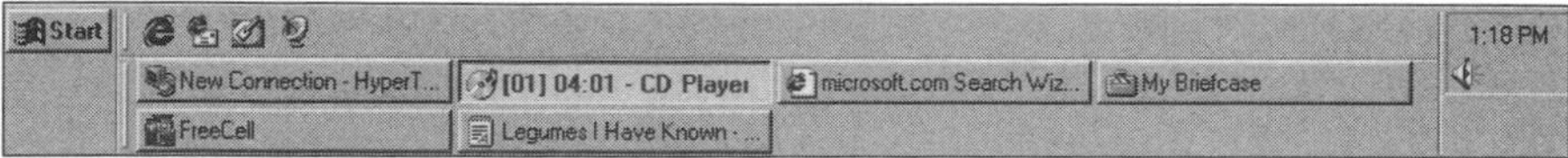

Figure 12-15: Dragging the taskbar's edge upward gives the icons more room to display their titles.

Figure 12-16: Drag an icon to the Quick Launch toolbar and a shortcut to the program is added.

Not interested in Channels or something else on the Quick Launch toolbar? Just click on it with your right mouse button and select Delete from the pop-up menu. It's just a shortcut, so you can always replace it if you want. *Except* don't delete the Desktop icon — you won't be able to get it back.

Adding a toolbar to the taskbar

Quick Launch is just one of the toolbars that can be shown on the taskbar. Right click on a blank spot on the taskbar and select Toolbars. Out springs a list of the possible toolbars that can be shown on the taskbar. (See Figure 12-17).

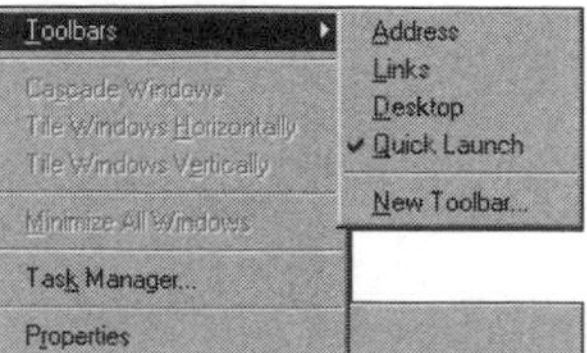

Figure 12-17: Pick the toolbar you want from this menu.

Address toolbar

Select the Address toolbar and a box like the one in Figure 12-18 will pop open on your taskbar.

Figure 12-18: Use the Address toolbar to make those essential Internet connections.

You can type in local intranet addresses here or Internet addresses for a quick connection. You can even enter local addresses to open a folder on your hard drive. Click the arrow to the side of the text box to open a list of past addresses you entered.

Links toolbar

Select the Links toolbar to display the links that are ordinarily shown at the top of your Internet Explorer window. Like the Address toolbar, this is another way to make quick connections — in this case to the sites represented by the links.

Links are properly a part of Internet Explorer, so check out Chapter 16 for information on how to make and use links.

Desktop toolbar

Yes, it's true that you can always get to your Desktop by clicking the Desktop icon in the Quick Launch toolbar, but you can also make a toolbar where every icon on your Desktop is represented.

The Desktop toolbar looks like Figure 12-19.

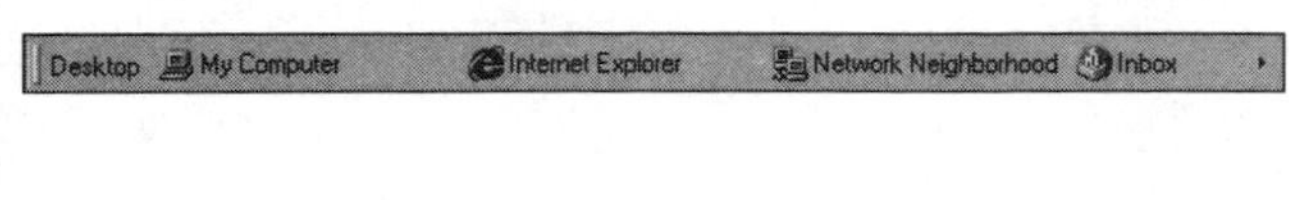

Figure 12-19: The Desktop toolbar is sort of ungainly in its natural state.

As you can see, this toolbar isn't very useful because each button is so large. However, if you right click directly on the Desktop label and then click Show Text (which turns the text labeling off), you get a toolbar that looks like Figure 12-20.

Figure 12-20: The Desktop toolbar with the text turned off. Can't remember what an icon controls? Just point the mouse at it and a magical box tells you.

Just to make things complicated, Windows NT has two different kinds of toolbars. (The more famous ones are the rows of buttons at the top of various windows. There's more about those guys in Chapter 23.)

Remember this, too: A toolbar and a taskbar are different creatures. The taskbar always contains the Start button. The toolbars are ways to add additional handy items to the taskbar.

Chapter 13

The Frightening Windows Explorer and My Computer Programs

In This Chapter

- Understanding why file managers are so scary
- Looking at folders
- Loading a program or file
- Deleting and undeleting files
- Copying and moving and renaming files
- Using legal filenames
- Copying a whole floppy disk
- Getting information about files
- Finding files that aren't shown
- Formatting new floppy disks

Exploring has always been a perilous business (consider the sorry fates of Magellan, Hudson, and La Salle for example) so it's all-too-appropriate that the program for figuring out everything on your computer is called the Windows NT Explorer. With this Explorer, it's definitely possible to get lost and wander around for a while but at least it's not actively dangerous. In this chapter, we'll take a look at Explorer and its cousin, My Computer (which lives on your Desktop). Though they have a few minor differences, Explorer and My Computer are just two different doors into the same place.

Regardless of which door you choose to enter, though, be prepared: These roads can be some of the most difficult Windows NT areas to navigate.

Why Are the Windows Explorer and My Computer Programs So Scary?

Everybody organizes his or her computer differently. (Some people don't organize their computers at all.) And whether you use Explorer or My Computer to poke around your computer's innards depends completely on which one you like the best. To start with Explorer, click once on the Start button with your right mouse button, then choose the word Explore from the pop-up menu. The Explorer window that opens may look something like the one in Figure 13-1 — or it may not.

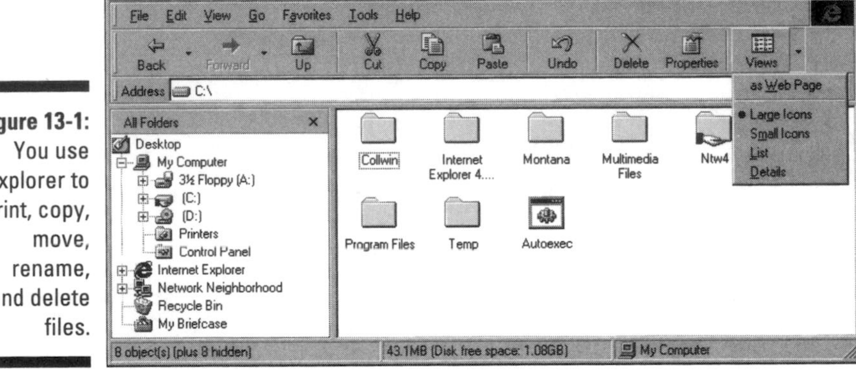

Figure 13-1: You use Explorer to print, copy, move, rename, and delete files.

If you like the way your Explorer looks — you can keep it. But if you'd like another view, well, click once on the word View at the top of the window and slide down to the part of the menu that reads

- Large Icons
- Small Icons
- List
- Details

and choose one. Each of the four View options (on the right end of the toolbar, as shown in Figure 13-1), arranges the icons in a different way, showing different amounts of information. Clicking on those options simply changes the way Windows NT displays the icons — it doesn't hurt anything.

The toolbar isn't living on top of your window? Then put it there by selecting Toolbar from the View menu. That little bar of buttons that you see in Figure 13-1 now appears atop your window like a mantel over a fireplace.

When you create a file or folder, Windows NT scrawls a bunch of secret hidden information on the file: its size, the date you created it, and even more trivial stuff. To see what Windows NT is calling these files and folders behind your back, select View from the menu bar and then select Details from the menu (Figure 13-2).

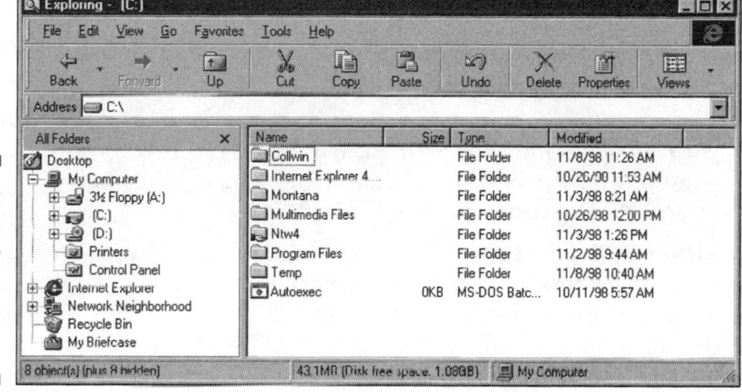

Figure 13-2: This is the Details view when you're Exploring.

You can get an Explorer-like view of most folders. Just right click on the folder and select Explore from the menu that pops up (see Figure 13-3).

Figure 13-3: Open a folder by double-clicking it and you get a window with just one pane.

The My Computer program lets you sling files around, just like Explorer, with one difference. My Computer defaults to the Open view. Double-click the My Computer icon and it opens to a window with just one pane. Wanna see My Computer in Explore style? Just right click the My Computer icon and then select Explore.

My Computer has the same View menu as Windows NT Explorer so you can choose to swap your large icons for small ones or get all the details you'd ever want.

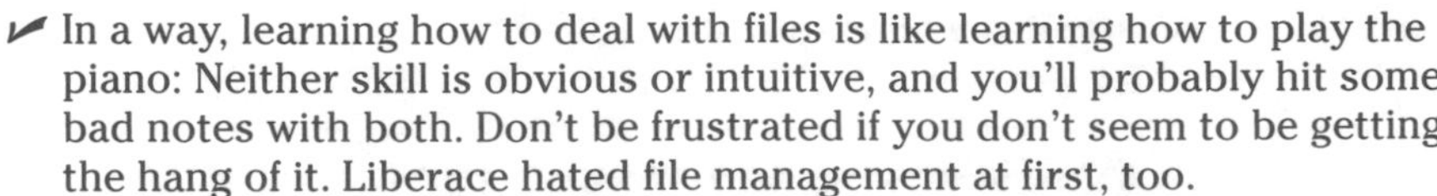

- In a way, learning how to deal with files is like learning how to play the piano: Neither skill is obvious or intuitive, and you'll probably hit some bad notes with both. Don't be frustrated if you don't seem to be getting the hang of it. Liberace hated file management at first, too.

- Tired of using a menu to get the Explorer view? Then press the Shift key while double-clicking on any folder you want to explore.

- If you can't remember what those little tool buttons in Explorer do, rest your mouse pointer over them. Windows NT pops up with a helpful box summing up the button's mission, and a further explanation often appears along the bottom of the window.
- Although some of the additional file information available when using the Details view is handy, it can consume a lot of space on your screen, limiting the number of files you can see in the window. Displaying only the filename is often a better idea. If you want to see more information about a file or folder, try the following tip.

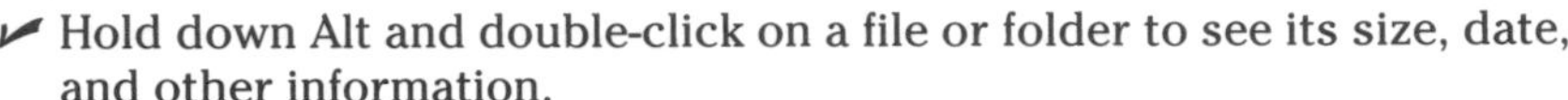

- Hold down Alt and double-click on a file or folder to see its size, date, and other information.

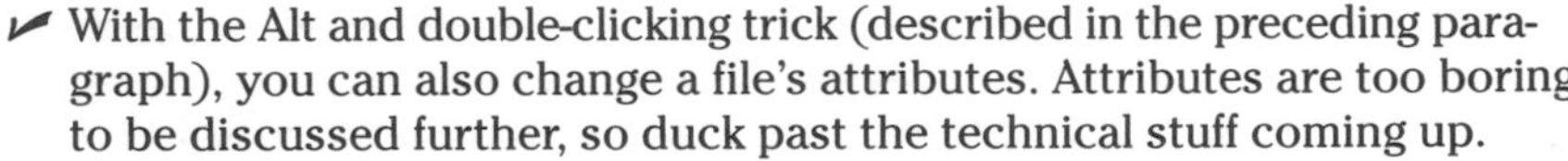

- With the Alt and double-clicking trick (described in the preceding paragraph), you can also change a file's attributes. Attributes are too boring to be discussed further, so duck past the technical stuff coming up.

Who cares about this attribute stuff, anyway?

Windows NT gives each file four special switches called *attributes.* The computer looks at the way those switches are set before it fiddles with a file.

- **Read Only:** Choosing this attribute allows the file to be read but not deleted or changed in any way.
- **Archive:** The computer sets this attribute if a file has changed since the last time it was backed up with a special Windows NT Backup command.
- **Hidden:** Setting this attribute makes the file invisible during normal operations.
- **System:** Files required by a computer's operating system have this attribute set.

The Properties box makes it easy — perhaps too easy — to change these attributes. In most cases, you should leave them alone. They're just mentioned here so you'll know what computer nerds mean when they tell cranky people, "Boy, somebody must have set *your* attribute wrong when you got out of bed this morning."

At first, Windows NT displays filenames sorted alphabetically by name in the Explorer and My Computer windows. But by right clicking on a folder and choosing the different sorting methods in the Arrange Icons menu, you display the files in a different order. Windows NT puts the biggest files at the top of the list, for example, when you choose sort by Size. Or you can choose sort by Type to keep files created by the same application next to each other. You can also choose sort by Date to keep the most recent files at the top of the list.

Fiddling Around with Folders

This stuff is really boring, but if you don't read it, you'll be just as lost as your files.

A *folder* is a workplace on a disk. Hard disks are divided into many folders to separate your many projects. You can work with the spreadsheet, for example, without having all the word-processing files get in the way.

Any disk can have folders, but hard disks need them the most because they need a way to organize their thousands of files. By dividing a hard disk into little folder compartments, you can more easily see where everything sits.

The Explorer and My Computer programs enable you to move around to different folders and peek at the files you've stuffed inside each one. It's a pretty good organizational scheme, actually. Socks never fall behind a folder and jam the drawer.

Folders used to be called directories and subdirectories. But just as soon as people were getting used to those terms, the industry switched to the term folders.

- Folders can be inside folders to add a deeper level of organization, like adding drawer partitions to sort your socks by color. Each sock color partition is a smaller, organizing folder of the larger, sock-drawer folder.
- Of course, you can ignore folders and keep all your files right on the Windows NT Desktop. That's like tossing everything into the back seat of the car and pawing around to find your tissue box a month later. Stuff you've organized is a lot easier to find.
- If you're eager to create a folder or two (and it's pretty easy), page ahead to this chapter's "Creating a Folder" section.
- Windows NT creates several folders when it installs itself on your computer. It creates a Windows NT folder to hold most of its programs and a bunch of folders inside that to hold its internal engine parts.
- Just as manila folders come from trees, computer folders use a tree metaphor, as shown in Figure 13-4, as they branch out from one main folder to several smaller folders.

Figure 13-4: The structure of folders inside your computer is tree-like, with main folders branching out to smaller folders.

What's all this path stuff?

Sometimes Windows NT can't find a file, even if it's sitting right there on the hard disk. You have to tell Windows NT where the file is sitting — a process it calls *browsing* — and in order to do that, you need to know that file's *path name.*

A path name is like the file's address. A typical mailing address uses generalities (your home state) before getting to the specifics (your apartment number). A computer path does the same thing. It starts with the letter of the disk drive and ends with the name of the file. In between, the path name lists all the folders the computer must travel through in order to reach the file.

For example, look at the folder named Homes in Figure 13-4. For Windows NT to find a file stored in the Homes folder, it starts from the C:\ folder, travels through the 3dhome folder and then goes into the Homes folder. Only then does it find the files stored inside that folder.

Take a deep breath. Exhale. Run your hand through your hair. Now, the *C* in C:\ stands for disk drive C. (In the path, a disk drive letter is always followed by a colon.) The disk drive letter and colon make up the first part of the path. All the other folders are inside the big C: folder, so they're listed after the C: part. DOS separates these nested folders with something called a backslash, or (\). The name of the actual file — let's say adobe.wav — comes last in this string.

C:\3dhome\Homes\adobe.wav is what you get when you put it all together, and that's the official path of the adobe.wav file in the Homes folder.

This stuff can be tricky, so here it is again: The letter for the drive comes first, followed by a colon and a backslash. Then come the names of all the folders, separated by backslashes. Last comes the name of the file (with no backslash after it).

When you click on a folder, Windows NT puts together the path for you. Thankfully.

Want all your folders to look the same? Open a folder and use the View menu to set it up the way you like: Click the View menu and select Folder Options. Click the View tab. At the top of the page is a button that reads Like Current Folder. Click it and then the OK button.

Peering into Your Drives, Folders, and Network Storage Tanks

Knowing all the folder stuff described in the previous section can help you blend in with the people behind the counter at the computer store. But what really counts is knowing how to use Windows NT Explorer and My Computer to flip through the folders and get to a file you want. Never fear. Just read on.

Seeing the files on a disk drive

Like everything else in Windows NT, disk drives are represented by buttons, or icons, shown in Table 13-1.

Table 13-1 Disk Drives, Networked Drives, and Other Containers

This Icon	*Stands for This*	*Use It Like This*
3½ Floppy (A:)	Floppy disk	Double-click here to see the files stored on a floppy disk in a floppy disk connected to your computer or network.
(C:)	Hard disk	Double-click here to see the files. stored on a hard disk that lives inside your computer or on the network.
(C:)	Shared Hard Disk	The little hand shows that you're sharing this hard disk with others on the network
(D:)	CD-ROM drive	Double-click here to see the files stored on a compact disc in a CD-ROM drive connected to your computer or network.
	Folder on your computer or network	Double-click here to see the files in a folder.
D on 'Rci2' (H:)	Folder or hard disk your network	Double-click here to see the files in a folder or hard disk that's being shared on your network.

The little icons resemble the types of disk drives they represent — if you sort of squint a little. For example, a floppy disk icon floats above the floppy drive in Table 13-1; a floating compact disc represents your CD-ROM drive. Double-click on either of those icons to see the files and folders stored on those disks and drives.

Hard disks — the little rectangles — don't have anything hovering over them except that nagging suspicion that they'll fail horribly at the worst possible moment.

- If you're kinda sketchy on those disk drive things, then you probably haven't read Chapter 2. Trot back there for a refresher course.
- Double-click on a drive icon in My Computer, and a window comes up to display the drive's contents. For example, put a disk in drive A: and double-click on My Computer's drive A: icon. A new window leaps up, showing what files and folders live on the disk in drive A:.
- Click on a drive icon in Explorer, and you see the drive contents displayed on the right side of the window.

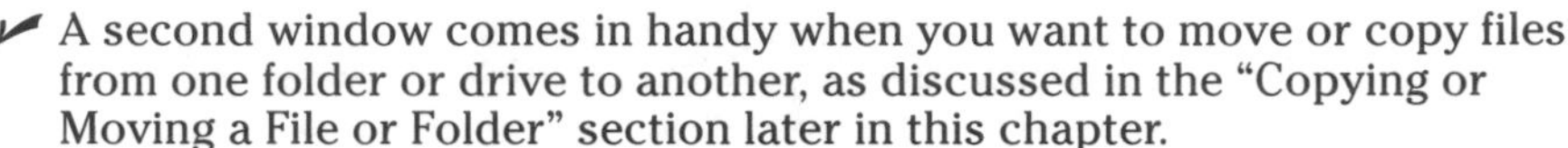

- A second window comes in handy when you want to move or copy files from one folder or drive to another, as discussed in the "Copying or Moving a File or Folder" section later in this chapter.
- If you click on a floppy drive icon when no disk is in the drive, Windows stops you gently, suggesting that you insert a disk before proceeding further.

Seeing what's inside a folder

Because folders are really little storage compartments, Windows NT uses a picture of a little folder to stand for each separate place for storing files.

To see what's inside a folder (whether you've viewing the folder icon in My Computer, Explorer, or on the Desktop itself), just double-click on the folder's picture. A new window pops up, showing that folder's contents.

Folder opening looks a little different in Windows Explorer. In Explorer, folders line up along the left side of a window. One folder, the one you're currently exploring, has a little box around its name, as shown with the Winnt folder in Figure 13-5.

The files living inside that particular folder appear on the right side of the window.

It all looks somewhat like Figure 13-5.

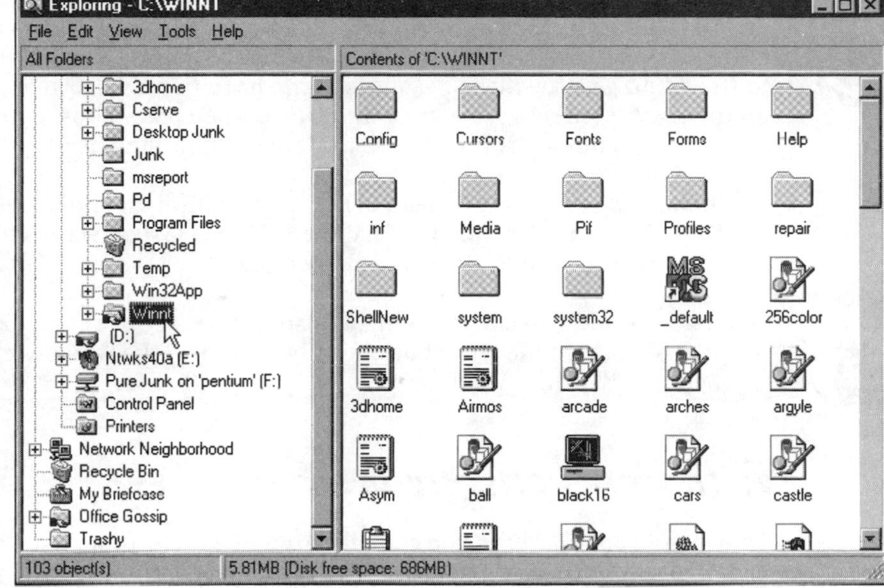

Figure 13-5: When you click on a folder on Explorer's left side, that folder's contents appear on the right side of the window.

To peek inside a folder while in Explorer, click on the folder name on the left side of the window. You see two things: That folder's next level of folders (if it has any) appear beneath it on the left side of the window, and that folder's filenames spill out into the right side of the window.

- As you keep climbing farther out on a branch and more folders appear, you're moving toward further levels of organization. If you climb back inward, you reach files and folders that have less in common.

- Yeah, this stuff is really confusing, but keep one thing in mind: Don't be afraid to double-click, or even single-click, on a folder just to see what happens. Clicking on folders just changes your viewpoint; nothing dreadful happens, and no tax receipts fall onto the floor. You're just opening and closing file cabinet drawers, peeking into folders along the way.
- To climb farther out on the branches of folders, keep double-clicking on new folders as they appear.
- To move back up the branches in Explorer, double-click on a folder closer to the left side of the window. Any folders beneath that folder are now hidden from view.
- Sometimes a folder contains too many files to fit in the window. To see more files, click on that window's scroll bars. What's a scroll bar? Time to whip out your field guide, Chapter 6.

While in Explorer, move the mouse pointer over the bar separating a folder on the left from its filenames on the right. When the pointer turns into a mutant two-headed arrow, hold down the mouse button. Then move the bar to the left to give the filenames more room, or to the right to give the folders on the right more room. Let go of the mouse when the split is adjusted correctly and the window reshapes itself to the new dimensions.

Can't find a file or folder? Instead of rummaging through folders, check out the Find command described in Chapter 8. It's the fastest way to find files and folders that were "there just a moment ago."

To close a window — and subsequently shut down the program inside that window — click on the close button — the little X in the window's upper-right corner. Closing a window helps clear a crowded screen.

A thumb's eye view

There's still another view you can play around with — though it's only useful for pictures. If you have a folder containing graphic files, right click the folder and select Properties. On the Properties page, click the box next to Enable thumbnail view. Click the OK button.

Now open the folder and click the View menu and select Thumbnails. In the Thumbnail view, your graphics files show up as little pictures like the ones shown in Figure 13-6.

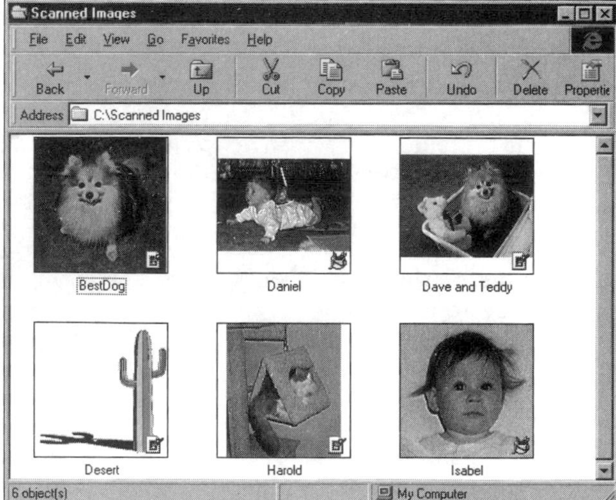

Figure 13-6: For graphics files, the Thumbnail view can be very handy.

Don't bother reading this hidden technical stuff

Sometimes programs store their own special information in a data file. These special programs may need to store information about the way the computer is set up, for example. To keep people from thinking that those files are trash and deleting them, the program hides those files.

You can view the names of these hidden files and folders in My Computer, however, if you want to play voyeur. Select Folder Options from the View menu bar. When the dialog box appears, click on the tab marked View, select the Show all files button and then click on the OK button.

The formerly hidden files appear alongside the other filenames. Be sure not to delete them, however: The programs that created the hidden files will gag, possibly damaging other files.

When you're done peeking, click the Do not show hidden or system files just beneath the Show all files button, and click the OK button. Doing so stashes the files away, hidden from view.

As you can see, the View page gives you many opportunities for poking around and trying different settings. Fortunately for those of us who tend to forget where we were when we started, there's a Restore Defaults button on the same page. Click that button and all the settings go back to the way they were when Windows NT was installed (and you can start fiddling all over again).

Loading a Program or File

A file is a collection of information on a disk. Files come in two basic types: program files and data files.

- *Program files* contain instructions that tell the computer to do something: balance the national budget or ferret out a fax number.
- *Data files* contain information created with a program, as opposed to computer instructions. If you write a letter to the grocer complaining about his soggy apricots, you're creating a data file.

To open either kind of file in Windows NT, double-click on the icon next to the filename. A double-click on a program file's icon brings the program to the screen, whether that file's listed in My Computer, Explorer, or even the Find program. When you double-click on a data file, Windows NT loads the file and the program that created it. Then Windows NT brings both the file and the program to the screen at the same time.

- Windows NT sticks little icons next to filenames so you know whether they're program or data files. In fact, even folders get their own icons so you won't confuse them with files. Chapter 25, at the tail end of the book, provides a handy reference for figuring out what icon is what. (That's because the tail end of this book is much easier to find than this particular chapter.)

- Because of some bizarre New School of Computing mandate, any data file that Windows recognizes is called a document. A document doesn't have to contain words; it can have pictures of worms or sounds of hungry animals.

If the program or folder you're after is already highlighted, just give the Enter key a satisfying little pound with your index finger. That not only keeps your computer from getting out of line, but it shows you how many different ways Windows NT lets you do things (which means that you don't need to worry about remembering them all).

Deleting and Undeleting Files and Folders

Sooner or later, you'll want to delete a file that's not important anymore — yesterday's lottery picks, for example, or something you stumble on that's too embarrassing to save any longer. But suddenly you realize that you made a mistake and deleted the wrong file. Not to worry: The Windows NT Recycle Bin can probably resurrect that deleted file — if you're quick enough. The next two sections show how to delete a file and retrieve it quickly.

Getting rid of a file or folder

To permanently remove a file from the hard disk, click on its name. Then press the Delete key. This surprisingly simple trick works for files, programs, and even folders.

The Delete key deletes entire folders, as well as any additional folders lurking inside them. Make sure that you select only the file or folder that you want to delete before you press the Delete key.

- When you press Delete, Windows tosses a box in your face, asking whether you're sure. If you are, click the Yes button.
- As soon as you learn how to delete files, you'll want to read the very next section, "How to undelete a file or folder."

Deleting a shortcut from the Desktop, My Computer, or Explorer just deletes a button that loads a program. You can always put the button back on later. Deleting an icon that doesn't have the little shortcut arrow removes that file from the hard disk and puts it into Recycle Bin, where it will eventually disappear. See the following section to find out which file has to walk the plank first.

How to undelete a file or folder

Sooner or later, your finger will push the Delete key at the wrong time, and you'll delete the wrong file. A slip of the finger, the wrong nudge of a mouse, or if you're in Southern California, a small earthquake at the wrong time can make a file disappear. Zap!

Scream! When the temblors subside, double-click the Recycle Bin, and the Recycle Bin box drops down from the heavens, as shown in Figure 13-7.

The files listed in Recycle Bin can be brought back to life simply by dragging them out of the Recycle Bin box: Point at the name of the file you want to retrieve and while holding down the mouse button, point at the Desktop. Then let go of the mouse. Windows NT moves the once-deleted file out of Recycle Bin and places the newly revived file onto your Desktop.

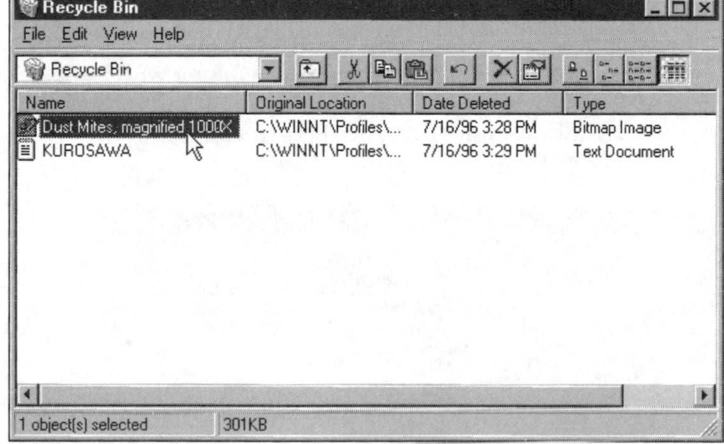

Figure 13-7: Recycle Bin drops down from the heavens to save the day.

- After the file's on your Desktop, it's as good as new. Feel free to store it in any other folder for safekeeping.
- Recycle Bin normally holds about 10 percent of your hard disk's space. For example, if your hard disk is 800MB, the Recycle Bin holds on to 80MB of deleted files. When it reaches that limit, it starts deleting the oldest files to make room for the incoming deleted files. (And the old ones are gone for good, too.)

Copying or Moving a File or Folder

To copy or move files to different folders on your hard disk, use your mouse to drag them there. But first, a warning.

After installing a program to your hard disk, don't move the program or its folders around. An installation program often wedges a program into Windows NT pretty securely; if you move the program, it may not work anymore.

Now that the warnings have been issued, here's how to move a file to a different folder on your hard disk:

1. **Move the mouse pointer until it hovers over the file you want to move and then press and hold down the mouse button.**
2. **While holding down the mouse button, point at the folder to which you'd like to move the file.**

   The trick is to hold down your mouse button the whole time. As you move the mouse, its arrow drags the file along with it. For example, Figure 13-8 shows how Explorer looks when Andy drags the arcade file from his Windows folder on the right to his Junk folder on the left.

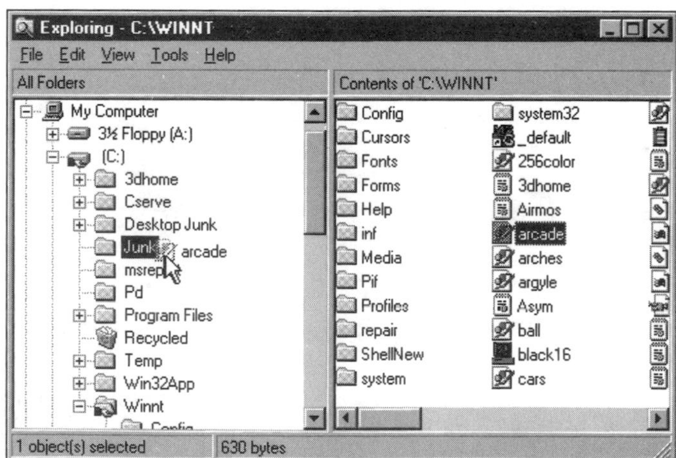

Figure 13-8: Drag the arcade icon from the Explorer window's right side to the Junk folder on the left side.

3. **Release the mouse button.**

   When the mouse arrow hovers over the place to which you'd like to move the file, take your finger off the mouse button. The file drops into its new home.

Moving a file by dragging its name is pretty easy, actually. The hard part often comes when trying to put the file and its destination on-screen at the same time. You often need to use both Explorer and My Computer to put two windows on-screen. When you can see the file and its destination, start dragging.

However, both Explorer and My Computer do some awfully dumb things that confuse people. For instance, when you drag a file from one folder to another on the same drive, you move the file. When you drag a file from one folder to another on a different drive, you copy that file.

I swear I didn't make up these rules. And it gets more complicated: You can click on the file and hold down Shift to reverse the rules. Table 13-2 can help you keep these oafish oddities from getting too far out of control.

Table 13-2 Moving Files Around

To Do This	*Do This*
Copy a file to another location on the same disk drive	Hold down Ctrl and drag it there.
Copy a file to a different disk drive	Drag it there.
Move a file to another location on the same disk drive	Drag it there.
Move a file to a different disk drive	Hold down Shift and drag it there.
Make a shortcut while dragging a file	Hold down Ctrl+Shift and drag it there.
Remember these *obtuse* commands	Refer to the handy Cheat Sheet at the front of this book.

Here's an easy way to remember this stuff when the book's not handy: Always drag icons while holding down the right mouse button. Windows NT is then gracious enough to give you a menu of options when you position the icon, and you can choose among moving, copying, or creating a shortcut.

- To copy or move files to a floppy disk, drag those files to the icon for that floppy disk, which you should find along the top of the Explorer window.

- When dragging a file someplace in Windows NT, look at the icon attached to the mouse pointer. If the document icon has a plus sign in it, you're copying the file. If the document icon is blank, you're moving the file. Depending on where the file's being dragged, pressing Ctrl or Shift toggles the plus sign on or off, making it easier to see whether you're currently copying or moving the file.

Selecting More than One File or Folder

Windows NT lets you grab an armful of files and folders at one swipe; you don't always have to piddle around, dragging one item at a time.

To pluck several files and folders from a list, hold down Ctrl as you click on the names. Each filename stays highlighted as you click on the next one.

To gather several files or folders that appear next to each other, click on the first one. Then hold down the Shift key as you click on the last one. Those two items are highlighted, along with every file and folder between them.

Windows NT also lets you lasso files and folders: Point slightly above the first file or folder you want to select. Then, while holding down the mouse button, point at the last file or folder. The mouse creates a lasso to surround your files. Let go of the mouse button, and the lasso disappears, leaving all the surrounded files highlighted.

- You can drag these armfuls of files in the same way as you drag one file.
- You can delete these armfuls, too. Just press the Delete key while they're all lassoed.
- You can't rename an armful of files all at one time. To rename the files, you have to go back to piddling around with them one file at a time.

Renaming a File or Folder

If you're a he-man stuck with a name like Pink Gardenia, you can petition the courts to change it to something more masculine like Blue Gardenia. Changing a filename requires even less effort:

1. **Click on the file or folder's name to select it.**
2. **Wait a second, and then click on the file's name — its title — running beneath or next to it.**

   The old filename appears highlighted.
3. **Start typing the new filename in the text box.**

   The filename disappears when you do this. If something awful happens, read the section about Legal Filenames coming up next.
4. **Press Enter or click on the Desktop when you're through — and you're off.**
   - When you rename a file, only its name changes. The contents are still the same, the file remains the same size, and it's still in the same place on your hard disk.

- You can't rename groups of files this way. The programs spit in your face if you even try.
- You can rename folders this way, too, although you should only rename folders that you created yourself. In particular, don't rename a folder that a program created for itself upon installation; Windows NT often grows accustomed to that folder's name, and doesn't like changes.

Sometimes clicking on filenames to rename them is tricky business. If you're having trouble renaming a file, just click on the file or folder with your right mouse button and choose Rename from the menu that pops up. Handy button, that right mouse button.

Using Legal Folder Names and Filenames

In the Cro-Magnon days of computing, DOS was pretty picky about what you could and couldn't name a file or folder, and Windows NT still plays along. If you stick to plain old letters and numbers, you're fine. But don't try to stick any of the following characters in a filename:

```
: / \ * | < > ? "
```

In fact, if you try to use any of those characters, Windows NT bounces an error message to the screen, and you have to try again.

For example, these names are illegal:

```
1/2 of my Homework
JOB:2
ONE<TWO
He's no "Gentleman"
```

These names are legal:

```
Half a Term Paper
JOB2
Two is Bigger than One
A #@$%) Scoundrel
```

- Unlike third graders who must face those ghastly multiplication tables, you have no major reason to memorize the characters you can't use. Just type in the filename you want, and Windows NT immediately lets you know if you've transgressed, so you can try again.

- Just as in earlier versions of Windows, Windows NT programs tack three identifying letters onto the end of all the files they create. By looking at that three-letter filename extension, Windows NT knows what program created that particular file. Normally, Windows NT hides those extensions so they're not confusing. But if you happen to spot filenames like savvy.doc, readme.txt, and nude.bmp on the hard disk, you know that those filename extensions have been added by the Windows NT programs WordPad (doc), Notepad (txt), and Paint (bmp). The picture on the file's icon provides the biggest clue to the file's contents.

If you really want to see a filename's extension, click on File Options from the folder's View menu and then click on the tab marked View. Finally, make sure that no check mark shows up in the little box that says Hide file extensions for known file types. Windows NT then reveals your file's extensions. (Click on the box again to remove the extensions from your sight.)

If you ever see a filename with a squiggly tilde thing in it, like in wigwam~1.txt, you are witnessing Windows NT's special way of making file names that older programs can use. Programs that predate Windows 95 expect files to have names no longer than 8 characters; Windows NT whittles down long filenames so those older programs can use them. (Windows NT remembers the long filename for itself.)

Copying a Complete Floppy Disk

To copy files from one disk to another, drag 'em over to their new home, as described a few pages back in the section "Copying or Moving a File or Folder." To copy an entire disk, however, you can use the Copy Disk command.

What's the difference? When you copy individual files, you're dragging specific filenames. But when you copy a disk, the Copy Disk command duplicates the entire floppy disk exactly: This command even copies the empty parts of the source disk! (That's why it takes longer than just dragging the files over.)

The Copy Disk command has three main features:

- First, the Copy Disk command can copy only floppy disks that are the same size or capacity. Just as you can't pour a full can of beer into a shot glass, you can't copy one disk's information onto another disk unless they hold the same amount of data.
- Second, the Copy Disk command can't copy the hard disk or a RAM drive. Luckily, you really have no reason to copy them, even if you know what a RAM drive is.

- Finally, the Copy Disk command is most often used when you only have one floppy drive — but you want to make a complete copy of one floppy disk to another. (Some disks have secret hidden files, and the Copy Disk command is the best way to ensure that all those important files are copied.)
- All this capacity and size stuff about disks and drives is slowly digested in Chapter 2.

Here's how to make a complete copy of a floppy disk:

1. **Put your floppy disk in the disk drive.**
2. **Click on the disk drive's icon with your right mouse button and choose Copy Disk from the menu.**

   A window appears, listing Copy from: on the left side and Copy to: on the right side.
3. **Click on the letters of the disk drives you're copying to and from.**
4. **Follow the instructions on the screen.**

   In a few moments, your computer creates an exact duplicate of your floppy disk, and then politely asks whether you'd like to create another.

You can't copy a floppy if the contents of the floppy are being displayed in the right-hand pane of Explorer. When the contents are displayed, Windows NT gets befuddled, thinks the disk is being used by a program, and sends a confusing error message to the screen. So to make the copy, make sure that no programs are displaying the floppy's contents when you try to copy it.

Creating a Folder

To store new information in a normal file cabinet, you grab a manila folder, scrawl a name across the top, and start stuffing it with information.

To store new information in Windows NT — for example, a new Exercise Tracking program or a ginseng root diet — you do the same thing: Create a new folder, think up a name for the new folder, and start moving or copying files into it.

New, more organized folders make finding information easier, too. For example, you can clean up a crowded Letters folder by dividing it into two folders: Business Letters and Personal Letters.

Here's how to use Explorer to create a new folder called Business Letters, which lives in your Letters folder:

1. **On the left side of the Explorer window, click on the folder where you want the new folder to appear.**

   In the Letters example, you click on the Letters folder, as shown in Figure 13-9, because you want the Business Letters folder to appear in the Letters folder.

   Click on the Letters folder, and its current contents spill out into Explorer's right side.

2. **Click on Explorer's right side with your right mouse button and choose New. When the menu appears, select Folder.**

   The My Computer window lets you create a folder when you right-click in any window. Explorer lets you create a folder only when you right-click within its right-hand side. A box pops up and asks you to think of a name for your new folder.

3. **Type the new folder's name and press Enter.**

   For example, type the name for your first new folder: Business Letters.

   Remember, Windows NT can sometimes be picky about the names you give to folders and files. For the rules, check out the "Using Legal Folder Names and Filenames" section earlier in this chapter.

After you type the folder's name and press Enter, the new Business Letters folder is complete and ready for you to start moving your business letter files there. For impeccable organization, follow the same steps to create a Personal Letters folder and move your personal letter files there. For

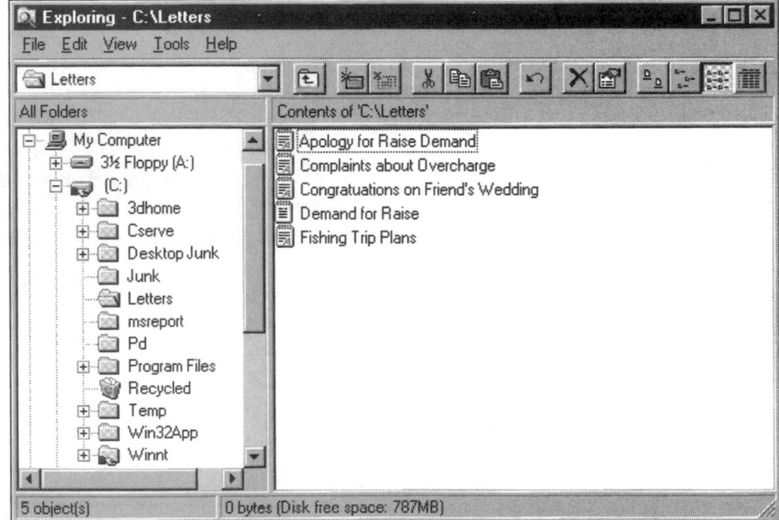

Figure 13-9: Organize the Letters folder by creating a new folder for business letters and one for personal letters.

example, as shown in Figure 13-10, you can drag the file called Fishing Trip Plans to your new Personal Letters folder. Check out the "Copying and Moving a File or Folder" section earlier in this chapter if you need some pointers on moving files.

- Want to install a new Windows-based program that doesn't come with an installation program? Create a new folder for it and copy its files there. Then head to Chapter 12 to see how to put the new program's name in the Start menu for easy clicking.
- To move files into a new folder, drag them there. Just follow the directions in the "Copying or Moving a File or Folder" section.
- When copying or moving lots of files, select them all at the same time before dragging them. You can chew on this stuff in the "Selecting More than One File or Folder" section.
- Just as with naming files, you can use only certain characters when naming folders. (Stick with plain old letters and numbers, and you'll be fine.)

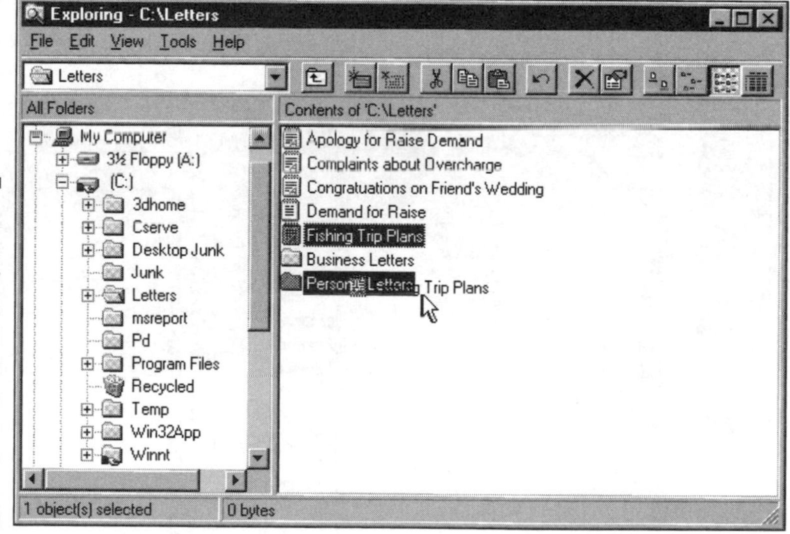

Figure 13-10: Drag files into the new Business Letters and Personal Letters folders to organize your work.

Dragging, Dropping, and Running

You can drag files around in Windows NT to move them or copy them. But there's more: You can drag a file outside of the Explorer or My Computer window and drop the file into other windows. This action loads the file into other files and programs. For example (as shown in Figure 13-11), you can drag the egypt file into the Paint window and let go of the mouse button. Paint loads the egypt file, just as if you'd double-clicked on it in the first place.

This feature brings up all sorts of fun possibilities. If you have a sound card, you can listen to sounds by dropping sound files into the Media Player or Sound Recorder windows. You can drop text files into Notepad to load them quickly. Or you can drop WordPad files into WordPad.

- Okay, the first thing everybody wants to know is what happens if you drag a sound file into WordPad? Or a WordPad file into Notepad? Or any other combination of files that don't match? Well, Windows NT either embeds one file into the other — a process described in Chapter 10 — or displays a box that says it's getting indigestion. Just click on the OK button, and things return to normal. No harm done, either way.
- The second question everybody asks is why bother? You can just double-click on a file's name to load it. That's true. But this way is more fun and occasionally faster.
- Never dragged and dropped before? Chapter 3 contains complete instructions.

- Old-time Windows users will want to know whether they can load files by dropping them onto taskbar icons along the screen's bottom. Not anymore; Windows NT lets you drop files into open windows only. But if you hover your mouse pointer over the taskbar icon you're interested in, the icon turns into an open window, ready to receive. (Yep, a lot of mouse-pointer-hovering happens in Windows NT.)

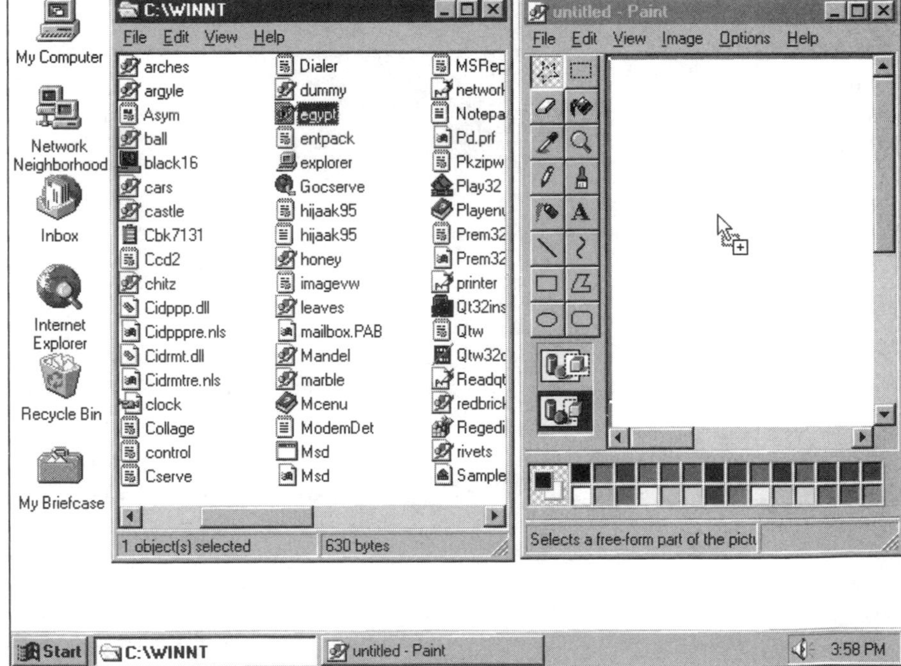

Figure 13-11: To make things easier when loading files, Windows NT lets you drag files from one window into another.

Making Windows Explorer and My Computer List Missing Files

Sometimes Windows NT snoozes and doesn't keep track of what's really on the disk. Oh, it does pretty well with the hard disk, and it works pretty well if you are just running Windows NT programs. But Windows NT can't tell when you've just inserted a new floppy disk. Also, if you create a file from within a DOS program, Windows NT may not know that the new file is there.

If you think the Windows NT Explorer or My Computer window is holding out on you, tell it to refresh, or take a second look at what's on the floppy disk or hard disk.

You can click on View from the menu bar and choose Refresh from the pull-down menu, but a quicker way is to press the F5 key. (It's a function key along the top or left side of the keyboard.) Either way, the programs take a second look at what they're supposed to be showing and update their lists if necessary.

Press the F5 key whenever you stick in a different floppy disk and want to see what files are stored on the disk. Windows NT then updates the screen to show that new floppy's files, not the files from the first disk.

Formatting a New Floppy Disk

New floppy disks don't work straight out of the box; your computer burps out an error message if you even try to use them fresh and unformatted. Floppy disks must be formatted before you can use them. (Flip to Chapter 2 for a quick course in floppy disk basics.) Unless you paid extra for a box of preformatted floppy disks, you must format them yourself. The My Computer icon handles this particularly boring chore quite easily. It's still boring, though, as you'll discover when repeating the process 12 times — once for each disk in the box.

Here's the procedure:

1. **Place the new disk into drive A: or drive B: and close the latch (if necessary).**
2. **In either Explorer or the My Computer window, click on the disk drive's icon with your right mouse button and choose Format from the menu.**
3. **In the Capacity box, select the type of disk you're formatting, and click on the Start button.**

Almost everybody will be selecting the 3.5", 1.44MB, 512 bytes/sector option. If you're in doubt, check the disk's box.

Your disk drive whirs for several minutes as your disk is formatted. Then Windows NT asks whether you want to format another disk. If you do, remove the floppy disk and return to Step 1. If you're through, move on to Step 4.

4. **Click on the Close button when Windows NT is through.**

- You can format disks in your drive B: by clicking on the drive B: icon with your right mouse button. Likewise, you can change a disk's capacity by clicking on the little arrow in the Capacity: box. Don't know the capacity of your disks? Then head for the handy chart in Chapter 2.
- Don't get your hopes up: The Quick Format option won't speed things up unless your disk has already been formatted once before.

- Windows NT Workstation won't let you format a floppy that it thinks is busy doing something else, so don't try to format a floppy whose contents are being displayed. To make the format happen, click on the C: drive icon, then right-click on the floppy drive's icon and select Format from the menu.

Chapter 14

Little Accessories that Clog the Start Button's Programs Menu

In This Chapter

- Getting to know Windows NT accessories
- Figuring out differences between NT 3.51 and NT 4

Windows NT 4 comes with a lot of other free programs, but not all of them will appear on your particular computer. You may have some leftover Windows NT 3.51 freebies, too. The point? Depending on the generosity of your Network Administrator, the programs described in this chapter may differ from the number of programs installed on your particular computer.

Don't expect these little programs to work wonders. Microsoft programmers squirm a little in their chairs if you even call them programs. No, Microsoft calls these things *applets* — mini-programs designed to demonstrate what a real Windows NT program could do if you would just head back to the software store and buy one. However, if your needs are simple, these simple programs may just fill those needs. But when your needs start growing, your software budget will probably have to grow, too.

Either way, this chapter explains what comes free in the Windows NT box. And if you don't find a confusing little freebie program covered here, check out Chapter 16, where you find more of the network-related goodies explained in fuller detail.

ActiveMovie Control

What it does: Actually, nothing. This item may still show up on the Multimedia menu, but it's been replaced by the new Media Player (just mosey to the M part of the alphabet in this chapter).

To get rid of this useless listing, right-click on the Start button and select Open. Then double click Programs, double click Accessories, double-click Multimedia (see a pattern here?) until you at last see the ActiveMovie shortcut icon. Right-click on the shortcut and select Delete from the pop-up menu.

Calculator

What it does: Calculator is, well, a calculator — as shown in Figure 14-1. It looks simple enough, and it really is — unless you've mistakenly set the view to Scientific mode and see some nightmarish logarithmic stuff. To bring the calculator back to normal, choose View and select Standard.

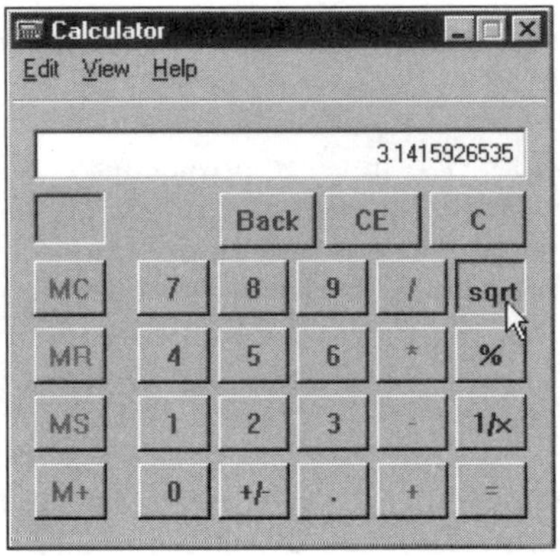

Figure 14-1: Calculator works like those simple calculators given away free at trade shows.

Where it lives: Open the Start menu, choose Programs, choose Accessories, and click on the Calculator icon.

How to use it: To punch in numbers and equations, click on the little number buttons, just as if it were a normal calculator. When you click on the equal sign (=), the answer appears at the top in the display window. For an extra measure of handiness, you can copy the answers to the Clipboard by pressing Ctrl+C (holding down the Ctrl key and then pressing C). Then click in the window where you want the answer to appear and paste the answer by pressing Ctrl+V. This method is easier than retyping a number like 3.14159265.

- Unlike in other Windows programs, you can't copy Calculator's answer by running the mouse pointer over the numbers. You have to press Ctrl+C or click on the Edit menu item and choose Copy.

- If the mouse action is too slow, press the Num Lock key and punch in numbers with the numeric keypad.
- The asterisk is the multiply sign, and the forward slash (located under the question mark key) means division.

- The Windows NT Calculator fixes the subtraction and decimal point problems found in the Windows NT 3.51 version. The new version has been verified to be at least as accurate as the Star Trek key chain calculators.

CD Player

What it does: Adding a CD-ROM drive to a computer doesn't always add multimedia capabilities as much as it adds a little Bachman Turner Overdrive to your lunch hour. Most multimedia computer owners tend to pop a music CD into their computer's CD-ROM drive now and then. CD Player, shown in Figure 14-2, lets you keep track of which songs are playing, arranges the song order, fast-forwards past the bad stuff, and performs other basic CD player tasks.

Figure 14-2: CD Player lets you play CDs and hear music using your computer's CD-ROM drive.

Where it lives: Open the Start menu, choose Programs, choose Accessories, choose Multimedia, and then double-click on the CD Player option.

How to use it: The CD Player lets you add song titles to the menu, as well as create your own play lists. If you're feeling random, choose Options and then select the Random Order setting to make Windows NT act like a jukebox. Now, if Windows NT would just come with a pool table. . . .

- Music too loud? Click on the little speaker in the corner of the taskbar. An easy-to-use sliding bar lets you raise or lower the volume — no more frantic searching to save your ears.

  Don't forget — most CD-ROM drives come with a headphone jack along the front of the computer so your Beethoven symphonies don't disturb your coworkers.

- Don't remember what some of those buttons do? Just rest your mouse pointer over the button, and Windows NT sends a message to the screen to help you out.
- Looking for a certain song, but can't remember which one it is? Choose Options and then select the Intro Play option. CD Player automatically plays the first few seconds of each song on the CD until you recognize the one you're after.

- As soon as you insert an audio CD, Windows NT automatically begins playing it — as long as your CD-ROM drive supports that feature. To stop Windows NT from immediately playing the CD, hold down the Shift key while inserting the CD into the CD-ROM drive.

Character Map (Adding the à in Voilà)

What it does: To add weird foreign characters, such as à, É, or even $, open the Start menu, choose Program Accessories, and then select Character Map. A box like the one shown in Figure 14-3 appears, listing every available character and symbol.

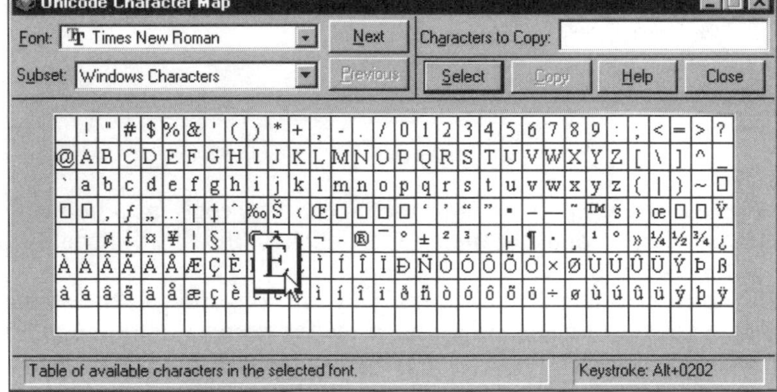

Figure 14-3: Character Map makes it easier to find and use foreign symbols.

That weird Alt+0233 stuff is too trivial to bother with

In the bottom right-hand corner, Character Map flashes numbers after the words `Keystroke: Alt+`. Those numbers hail back to the stone-tablet days of inserting foreign characters when word processing. Back then, people had to look up a character's code number in the back of a boring manual.

If you remember the code numbers for your favorite symbols, however, you can bypass Character Map and add them directly to documents. For example, the code number listed in the bottom corner for é is 0233.

Here's the trick: Turn on the Num Lock key by pushing it until its little light goes on. Then hold down Alt and type 0233 with the numeric keypad. Let go of the Alt key, and the é symbol appears.

If you consistently use one special character, this method may be faster than using Character Map.

Where it lives: Open the Start menu on the taskbar, choose Programs, choose Accessories, and click on Character Map.

How to use it: Follow these steps to put a foreign character in your work:

1. **Make sure that the current font — the name for the style of the characters on the page — shows in the Character Map's Font box.**

   Not showing? Then click on the down arrow and select the font when it appears in the drop-down list.

2. **Scan the Character Map box until you see the symbol you're after; then pounce on that character with a double-click.**

   The symbol you select appears in the Characters to Copy box.

3. **Click on Copy to send that character to the Clipboard.**
4. **Click on the Close button to close the Character Map.**
5. **Click in the document where you want the new symbol or character to appear.**
6. **Press Ctrl+V, and the new character pops right in there.**

   (Give it a second. Sometimes it's slow.)

The symbols in the Character Map box are easier to see if you hold down the mouse button and move the pointer over them.

- When working with foreign words, keep the Character Map handy as an icon, ready for consultation.
- For some fun symbols like ✌, 📪, &, ✍, 💣, ☠, and check box symbols, switch to the Wingdings font. It's full of little doodads to spice up your work.
- You can grab several characters at a time by double-clicking on each of them and then copying them into your work as a chunk. You don't have to keep returning to the Character Map for each one.

Chat

What it does: Chat serves as an electronic water cooler, letting everybody swap chatter through their keyboards. In fact, you're not only allowed to chat on a network, you're supposed to.

Where it lives: Open the Start menu, choose Programs, choose Accessories, and click on Chat. The program appears, as shown in Figure 14-4.

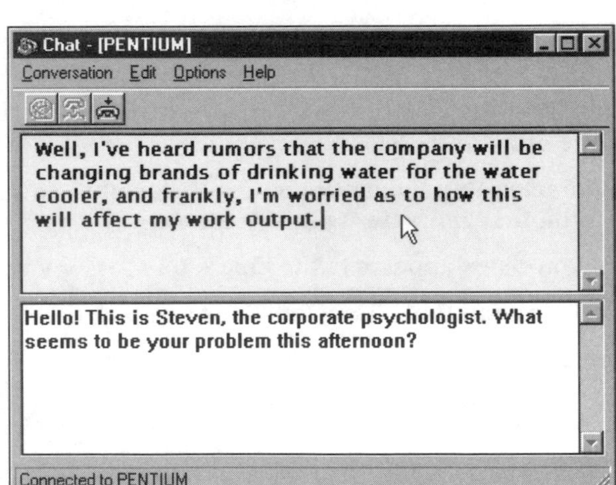

Figure 14-4: Chat lets you correspond with other members on the network; as you type in the top part of the window, the responses appear in the bottom part.

How to use it: Chat works about as easy as a traditional telephone. Just follow these steps:

1. **Load the program and then click on the icon of the finger dialing on a telephone.**

   The "dialing finger" icon is in the program's upper-right-hand corner. A window appears, listing the other computers available on your network.

2. **Double-click on the name of the computer you want to reach.**

   The Chat program attempts to reach the other person's computer. If that person's computer has their own Chat program up and running, they hear a "ringing" sound on their sound card, and the little Chat icon flashes along their taskbar.

3. **Start typing your message.**

   Your words appear in the top half of the window; your buddy's responses appear in the window's bottom half.

4. **Done talking? Click the icon of the telephone with the little arrow pointing down at the receiver to hang up.**

Chat usually works even if the person on the receiving end doesn't have their Chat program open. When you call the computer you want to talk to, their Chat program starts itself. If this doesn't happen on your network, you or someone braver than you should go to the Network Administrator and say these words, "Would you please set up the Network DDE service so it starts automatically?"

By default, Chat runs manually. This means that you have to start up Chat after you log on in the morning. You'll see a little box for a few seconds that says Starting NetDDE Related services. After that, Chat receives calls even if you close it because the DDE Services continue to run until you turn off the computer. Changing the setting to automatic just means that you (and everyone else) no longer have to remember to start up Chat to get it activated.

Clipboard Viewer

What it does: As shown in Figure 14-5, Clipboard Viewer lets you see the things that you've cut or copied and are preparing to paste. It's almost identical to ClipBook Viewer, which is discussed in the next section. (In fact, even the icons and programs look identical.)

Where it lives: Open the Start menu on the taskbar, choose Programs, choose Accessories, and then click on Clipboard Viewer.

How to use it: Clipboard Viewer gets its due in Chapter 10.

Figure 14-5: Clipboard Viewer lets you see items that have been cut or copied and are ready to be pasted.

ClipBook Viewer

What it does: ClipBook Viewer is a way of posting documents for others on your network to view. It looks just like the ClipBook Viewer shown in Figure 14-5.

Where it lives: Open the Start menu on the taskbar, choose Programs, choose Accessories, and then click on Clipboard Viewer.

How to use it: Using the ClipBook Viewer is covered in Chapter 10.

HyperTerminal

What it does: The old Windows NT 3.51 modem program, Terminal, could handle the basics of logging on to a BBS and grabbing files, but it wasn't fancy enough for today's more sophisticated Internet surfers. Terminal's replacement, HyperTerminal, is slightly easier to use, but you probably won't be using it much. HyperTerminal can't handle the graphics of the World Wide Web, severely limiting its fun. Figure 14-6 shows HyperTerminal in action.

Where it lives: Open the Start menu on the taskbar, choose Programs, choose Accessories, and click on HyperTerminal.

How to use it: HyperTerminal can automatically figure out what settings to use for most places you call. And because Windows NT tells HyperTerminal what brand of modem your computer's using, HyperTerminal automatically knows your modem's language — you no longer have to play the part of translator.

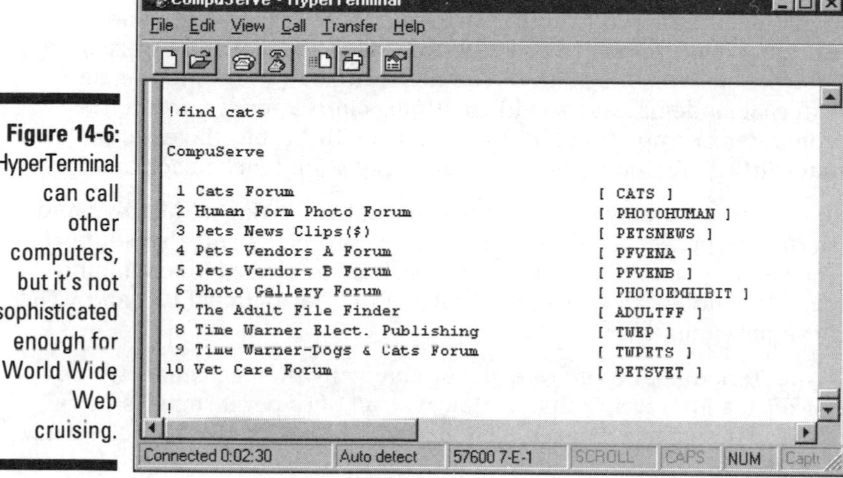

Figure 14-6: HyperTerminal can call other computers, but it's not sophisticated enough for World Wide Web cruising.

HyperTerminal is used for calling computers that display text — not graphics. It's not for jumping on the Web and looking at pictures of goldfish, nor will it work with Prodigy or America Online. HyperTerminal is most useful for downloading files and swapping e-mail with some of the older, more complicated online services. That means it's more advanced than most programs, and you may need help with it.

If you know the phone number of a computer you want to call, follow these steps to put HyperTerminal to work:

1. **Load HyperTerminal.**

   Watch the cute little spinning globe as the program starts up.

2. **Type a name to describe the place you're calling — the Microsoft BBS, for example — and select an icon to represent that location for future calls.**

3. **Click on the OK button.**

4. **Type the phone number into the next page's Phone number box.**

   Change the area code and country code, if HyperTerminal hasn't already guessed them right.

5. **Click on OK and then click on Dial on the next page.**

   HyperTerminal calls the other computer — and the other computer takes over, asking you to type in various commands to boss it around. You usually can grab files, as well as send and receive messages to other people.

- Modems are computer gizmos that can translate the computer's digital information into sound and squirt it over the phone lines to other modems. Modems come in two types: internal and external. Internal modems plug into the nether regions of the computer, and external modems have a cable that plugs into a serial port on the computer's rump. Both types do the same thing, but the external ones have little lights on them that blink as the sound flows back and forth.

- Terminal could only download files using two settings: XMODEM and Kermit. HyperTerminal can handle those protocols and also supports the much speedier ZMODEM and YMODEM formats. Modem hounds can also choose among ANSI, Minitel, TTY, Viewdata, VT100, and VT52 terminal emulations.
- HyperTerminal does more stuff automatically than Terminal, which makes it a little easier to use. However, all of HyperTerminal's extra capabilities brings its user-friendliness level back down by quite a few notches.
- World travelers with Windows NT on their laptops will appreciate HyperTerminal's support for dialing codes used by a wide variety of countries, from Afghanistan to Zimbabwe.

If your modem and telephone share a single line, don't pick up the phone while the modem is using it to transmit information. Just picking up the handset can garble the modem signal and possibly break the connection.

Imaging

What it does: Imaging lets you peek inside a file containing graphics and see the file's contents. Imaging is the program that Internet Explorer often uses to look at pictures while you're browsing the Internet's World Wide Web.

Where it lives: Open the Start menu on the taskbar, choose Programs, choose Accessories, and click on Imaging.

How to use it: Internet Explorer brings up Imaging automatically when it needs it. But if you want to peek inside a picture, double-click on the picture's icon from within My Computer or Explorer. If it's capable, the Imaging program usually loads the picture and brings it into view.

- Imaging can peer inside files saved in various graphics formats: TIF, BMP, JPG, and PCX. However, it can only save files in two formats: BMP and TIF.

- Sharon likes Imaging's Annotation feature, as shown in Figure 14-7. With this feature, she can make a "rubber stamp" that says "THIS PROJECT IS DOOMED," and stamp it all over her favorite images.
- If you find yourself using Paint a lot, give Imaging a try.

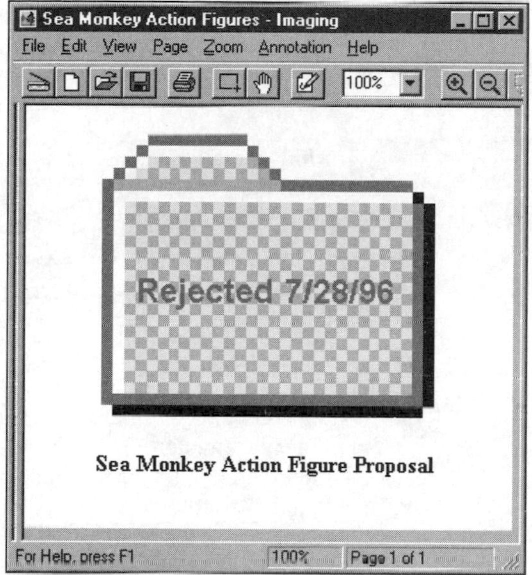

Figure 14-7: Imaging can "tweak" images created in Paint or grabbed from the Internet.

Media Player

What it does: Media Player can play sounds from a sound card, connect to MIDI keyboards, and can access CD-ROM drives for both sound and data. Media Player can even play video stored in files or on video discs.

Where it lives: Open the Start menu on the taskbar, choose Programs, choose Accessories, choose Multimedia, and click on Media Player.

How to use it: From within Explorer or My Computer, double-click on the media file you want to play; Media Player rises to the task. (You can find pictures of icons containing videos, sounds, and music in Chapter 25.)

- Windows NT comes ready to run with some of the most popular sound cards. Other sound cards or CD-ROM drives come with special drivers on a floppy disk that is boxed with the package.
- Sound cards and CD-ROM drives are covered in Chapter 2.

Getting the latest Media Player

The easiest way to get the latest Media Player is, of course, to get someone else to fetch it for you. And if you're on a network with an administrator, that's precisely what you should do. (In fact, ask the administrator to install Windows NT Service Pack 4, which contains that new Media Player.) If that isn't an option and you have an connect to the Internet, take a deep breath and follow these steps:

1. **Open Internet Explorer and type in the address:**

   `www.microsoft.com/windows/downloads`

   Then press the Enter key.

2. **Scroll down the page until you find the Windows NT Workstation heading, and under that, Windows Media Player.**

3. **Click Windows Media Player. Click the links for downloading — reading the accompanying information as you go.**

   Working in cooperation, Windows NT and the Microsoft Web site transfer the new Media Player software to your computer. You have to provide a little bit of information such as a temporary location for the file. (The system suggests the Temp folder which is as good a place as any.)

4. **After the file download is completed, open the Windows NT Explorer and root around until you find the Temp folder.**

5. **Double-click the file `mpie4ful` (or it may show itself as `mpie4ful.exe`).**

   The new Media Player installs itself and even puts a shortcut on your Desktop.

If you need help getting Internet Explorer going, consult Chapter 16 which has plenty of information on getting that all-important connection to the Internet.

My Briefcase

What it does: Want to move files between your laptop and desktop computers — and not get the different versions of the files mixed up? The Windows NT My Briefcase lets you connect two computers with a serial or parallel cable and shoot files between them. Or, you can simply copy files back and forth with a floppy disk. Best yet, My Briefcase can tell which file is most up-to-date, so you always keep the current copy.

Where it lives: The My Briefcase icon lives directly on the Desktop.

How to use it: My Briefcase works as a specialized folder that keeps track of the dates and times on your files. Start by dragging the desired files directly onto the My Briefcase icon on the Desktop.

Working with floppies? Just drag the My Briefcase icon onto a floppy's disk drive icon, and take that floppy to your other computer. Then open the floppy on the other computer, open the My Briefcase icon, and work on the files from within the My Briefcase icon. When you're done, reinsert the floppy into your main computer and drag the My Briefcase icon back onto that computer. My Briefcase looks at the files and constantly makes sure that you're replacing older files with newer ones.

If you're working with cables or networks, drag the My Briefcase icon onto the other computer's icon on the Desktop, and work from there. Either way, by always working on the files inside the My Briefcase icon, you can keep from accidentally overwriting your new files with old ones — a common occurrence when moving files from computer to computer.

My Briefcase depends on both computers to display the correct time and date. If you're counting on using My Briefcase, make sure that the clocks on both computers are accurate.

If you want more full-featured software, stick with Traveling Software's LapLink, a program that's been doing the same thing for years — and it comes with the cables you need, too. Traveling Software can be reached at 18702 North Creek Parkway, Bothell, WA 98011; (206) 483-8088; (800) 343-8080, Fax: (206) 487-1284. Or, head for their Web site at `www.travsoft.com/`.

Notepad

What it does: Windows comes with two word processors, WordPad and Notepad. WordPad is for the letters you're sprucing up for other people to see. Notepad is for quick notes you're going to keep for yourself.

Where it lives: Open the Start menu on the taskbar, choose Programs, choose Accessories, and select Notepad.

How to use it: Notepad loads more quickly than WordPad. Double-click on the Notepad icon, and it leaps to the screen more quickly than you could have reached for a notepad in your back pocket. You can type in some quick words and save them on the fly.

Notepad's speed comes at a price, however — it stores only words and numbers. Notepad doesn't store any special formatting, such as italicized letters, and you can't paste any pictures into it, as you can with WordPad. It's a quick, thrown-together program for your quick, thrown-together thoughts.

- Notepad tosses you into instant confusion: All the sentences head right off the edge of the screen. To turn one-line, runaway sentences into normal paragraphs, turn on the Word Wrap feature by choosing the Edit menu and selecting Word Wrap. You have to turn on Word Wrap each time you start Notepad, strangely enough.

- Notepad prints kind of funny, too: It prints the file's name at the top of every page. To combat this nonsense, choose File and then select Page Setup. A dialog box appears, with a funny code word in the Header box. Delete the word and click on the OK button. If you want to get rid of the automatic page numbering, clear out the Footer box as well.
- Here's another printing problem: Notepad doesn't print exactly what you see on-screen. Instead, it prints according to the margins you entered in Page Setup under the File menu. This quirk can lead to unpredictable results.
- Although Notepad leans toward simplicity, it has one fancy feature that not even WordPad can match. Notepad can automatically stamp the current time and date at the bottom of your page whenever you open it. Just type **.LOG** in the very top, left-hand corner of a file and then save the file. Then whenever you open it again, Notepad stamps the bottom of the file with the current time and date, and you can jot down some current notes.
- Don't try the .LOG trick by using lowercase letters and don't omit the period. It doesn't work.

- To stick in the date and time manually, press F5. The time and date appear, just as they do in the .LOG trick.

Paint

What it does: Love the smell of paint and a fresh canvas? Then you'll hate Paint. After working with real fibers and pigments, you'll find the Windows NT computerized graphics program, Paint, to be a little sterile. But at least you don't have any mess. Paint creates pictures and graphics to stick into other programs.

Where it lives: Open the Start menu, choose Programs, choose Accessories, and click on the Paint icon.

How to use it: Paint offers more than just a paintbrush. It has a can of spray paint for that airbrushed look, several pencils of different widths, a paint roller for gobbing on a bunch of paint, and an eraser for when things get out of hand.

In addition to capturing your artistic flair, Paint can team up with a digital camera or scanner to touch up pictures in your PC, as shown in Figure 14-8. You can create a flashy letterhead to stick into the letters you create in WordPad. You can even create maps to paste into your party fliers.

Figure 14-8: With Paint, you can create pictures (like this one) and touch up scanned-in photos and faxes.

- You can copy drawings and pictures from Paint and paste them into just about any other Windows NT program.
- Remember that cut and paste stuff from Chapter 10? Well, you can cut out or copy chunks of art from the Paint screen using the select or free-form select tools described later in this section. The art goes onto the Windows NT Clipboard, where you can grab it and paste it into any other Windows program. (Paint doesn't support "Scraps," also covered in Chapter 10.)
- Paint enables you to add text and numbers to graphics, so you can add street names to maps, put labels inside drawings, or add the vintage year to your wine labels.

Paint replaces Paintbrush that came with Windows NT 3.51. Unlike Paintbrush, the Windows NT Paint program is a lot pickier about opening PCX files. If you use a lot of PCX files, you may want to copy your old version of Paintbrush back onto your hard disk. (Paintbrush can also do a few other things that Paint can't do, like erasing in straight lines when you hold down the Shift key.)

Anything you create in Paint can be turned into wallpaper and used as a backdrop for your Desktop. Just save your fun new file, open the File menu and then select the Set as Wallpaper (Tiled) or Set as Wallpaper (Centered) options. More detailed information about wallpaper installation lurks in Chapter 10.

Sound Recorder

What it does: Records and plays back sounds.

Where it lives: Open the Start menu from the taskbar, choose Programs, choose Accessories, choose Multimedia, and then click on Sound Recorder.

How to use it: If you have a microphone or a CD-ROM drive, you can make your own sound files that you can associate with a Windows event or even send with e-mail. Here's how you do it:

1. **Open Sound Recorder then select New from the File menu. To begin recording, click the button with the big red dot.**
2. **Start the CD or start speaking into the microphone.**
3. **Click the button with the black square to stop recording.**

   Figure 14-9 shows the Sound Recorder recording from the CD-ROM drive.
4. **Select Save from the File menu, give your new file a name, and then click the Save button.**

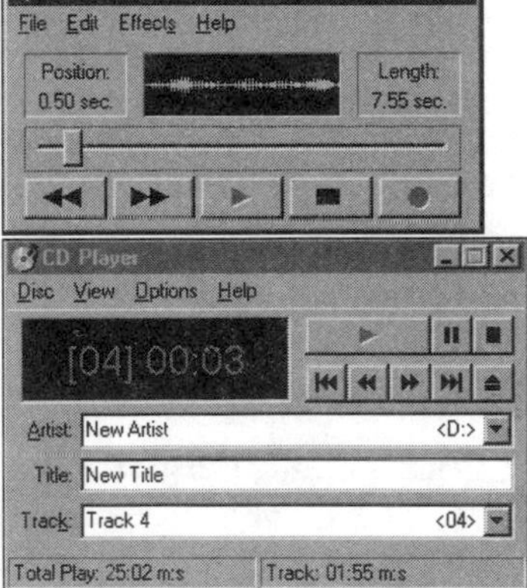

Figure 14-9: Sound Recorder records what the CD is playing.

- To record from a microphone, you'll need a sound card because that's what the microphone plugs into.
- You don't need a sound card to *record* from a CD-ROM drive — but a sound card and speakers are required if you want to *hear* a playback of what you've recorded.

Telnet

What it does: Telnet is a graphical version of the old Internet program of the same name. It lets you connect to another computer (using either a modem or your network connection to the Internet) and operate the other computer from your own keyboard.

Telnet has long been used to access library catalogs and other public information services that do not have a nice, easy-to-use location on the World Wide Web (you know, those colorful, fancy home pages that you can visit using Internet Explorer, which we cover in Chapter 16).

Where it lives: Open the Start menu on the taskbar, choose Programs, choose Accessories, and select Telnet.

How to use it: If you've used Telnet before, you can easily pick your way through the menus to get what you want. If you're not familiar with Telnet, you're going to need help deciphering the terms and seeing how they translate into your situation. Better flag down the Network Administrator before trying to use this program.

WordPad

What it does: WordPad isn't quite as fancy as some of the more expensive word processors on the market. For example, you can't create multiple columns like the ones in newspapers or newsletters, nor can you double-space your reports. But WordPad works fine for letters, simple reports, and other basic documents.

Where it lives: Open the Start menu, choose Programs, choose Accessories, and select WordPad.

How to use it: Double-click on the WordPad icon, and you're ready to start typing in a new document. And in a refreshing change of pace, all Windows NT programs enable you to open and save a file in exactly the same way: Select the word File at the top of the program's window, and a menu tumbles down. Choose Open or Save, depending on your whim.

A dialog box pops up, listing the files in the current folder. Select the name of the file you want to open (click on it) or type the name of a new file. Then select OK. That's it.

- If you want to open a file that you spot listed in Windows Explorer or the My Computer window, double-click on the file's name. Windows NT yanks the file into the right program and brings both the program and the file to the screen.
- You can find more explicit instructions on opening a file in Chapter 6. Folders and equally mind-numbing concepts are browbeaten in Chapter 12.
- When you save a file for the first time, you have to choose a name for the file, as well as a folder to put it in. WordPad subsequently remembers the file's name and folder, so you don't have to keep typing the filename each time you save the current version of the file.
- WordPad can save files in three different formats: A plain text file known as ASCII, a Word 6 file, or a Rich Text Format. All three file formats are covered in the sidebar titled "Saving a WordPad file in different formats," later in this chapter.
- Sometimes you'll want to open a file, change parts of it, and save the file with a different name or in a different folder. Choose Save As, not Save, and WordPad then treats your work as if you were saving it for the first time. It asks you to enter a new filename and a new location.
- Although you can make up filenames on the fly in WordPad, you can't use WordPad to create new folders. That duty falls to the Windows NT Explorer or My Computer programs, which we discuss in Chapter 13.

Saving a WordPad file in different formats

Just as you can't drop a Ford engine into a Volvo, you can't drop a WordPad file into another company's word processor. All brands of word processors save their information in different ways in order to confuse the competition.

WordPad can read and write in three file formats. As soon as you try to create a new file, WordPad forces you to choose between four formats: a Word for Windows 6.0 document, a Rich Text Format (RTF), a Text Document, and a Text Document-MS-DOS Format. Each format meets different needs.

- **Word for Windows 6.0 Document:** This option creates files that can be read by Microsoft's *real* (and expensive) word processor, Microsoft Word for Windows. Many of the most popular competing word processors can read Word for Windows 6.0 files, too. You'll probably be safe with this format.
- **Rich Text Document (RTF):** These files can also be read by a variety of word processors. Like the Word 6 documents, Rich Text documents can store boldfaced and *italicized* words, as well as other special formatting. These files can be *huge*, however. Don't choose this format unless it's the only format your friend's word processor will accept.
- **Text Document or Text Document - MS-DOS Format:** Almost all brands of word processors can read plain old text, making Text Document the safest format if you plan on exchanging files with friends. Use the MS-DOS format to save files for older,

MS-DOS programs. Either way, the Text Document can't have any boldface type, italic type, columns, or any other fancy stuff, however. **Nerdly note:** Text Document files are also called *ASCII* files (pronounced *ASK-ee*).

If somebody asks you to save a WordPad file in a different format, do the following:

1. **Choose File and select Save As.**
2. **Click on the arrow next to the Save file as type box and choose the new format from the drop-down list.**
3. **Type a new name for the file into the File name box and press Enter.**

Voilà! You've saved your file in the new format.

- The other Windows NT word processor, Notepad, can't handle anything *but* Text Only files. Notepad can't load WordPad's Word 6 files, and if it opens the Rich Text Documents, the files look *really* weird. (WordPad can easily read Notepad's files, though.) Notepad gets its due earlier in this chapter.
- Although most word processors can read and write ASCII files, problems still occur. When you save a file as an ASCII file, you lose any formatting such as italicized words, special indents, or embedded pictures of apples.

- If you're ditching your typewriter for Windows, remember this: On an electric typewriter, you have to press the Return key at the end of each line or else you start typing off the edge of the paper. Computers, in contrast, are smart enough to sense when words are about to run off the end of the screen. They automatically drop down a line and continue the sentence. (Hip computer nerds call this phenomenon *word wrap.*)

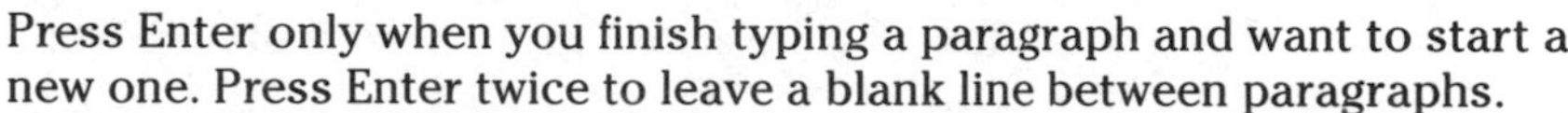

  Press Enter only when you finish typing a paragraph and want to start a new one. Press Enter twice to leave a blank line between paragraphs.

- WordPad works well for most word processing needs: writing letters, reports, or term papers on somber philosophers with weird last names. Unless you're a lousy speller, you'll find WordPad easy to use, and you'll like its excellent price.

- WordPad replaces the old Write word processor from Windows NT 3.51, and it does almost everything Write could do. You won't find any way to add headers or footers, however, nor will WordPad let you double-space your documents. Finally, none of the new Windows NT applications let you search for funny characters like Tabs or paragraph marks.

My Version of Windows NT Doesn't Have the Right Programs!

Windows NT doesn't automatically install all of its possible freebie programs. Depending on the buttons you punched when installing Windows NT, you'll find different varieties of programs installed on your hard disk. Very few people get all the programs installed. If you feel left out and want some of the optional programs mentioned in this chapter, follow these steps:

1. **Open the Start menu, choose Settings, and then choose Control Panel.**
2. **Double-click on the Control Panel's Add/Remove Programs icon.**
3. **Click on the Windows NT Setup tab.**

   A box appears showing the various components of Windows NT, as well as the amount of space those components need to nestle onto your computer's hard disk.
4. **Click on the check box by the programs or accessories you want to add.**

   A check mark appears in the boxes of the items you've selected. To select part of a category — a portion of the accessories, for example — click on the category's name and click on the Details button. Windows NT lists the items available in that category so that you can click on the ones you want. If you clicked the Details button, click on the OK button to continue back at the main categories list.
5. **Click on the OK button and insert your installation discs when asked.**

   Windows NT copies the necessary files from your installation CD-ROM onto your hard disk. You can remove Windows NT accessories the same way, but by removing the check mark from the box next to the accessory's name (you don't need the CD to remove programs, however).

Adding and removing parts of Windows NT can be a serious matter. You may have to flag down the Network Administrator on this one — especially if you don't have any of the discs Windows NT asks for.

How Did Windows NT 3.51 Hold Up?

Like an evolving creature, Windows NT 4 has changed Windows NT 3.51 fairly drastically. To see whether your favorite programs have been improved, removed, or destroyed, check out Table 14-1; it lists Windows NT 3.51 programs and their Windows NT 4 replacements. (Chapter 15 contains even more information to help Windows NT 3.51 users make their move.)

Table 14-1 Windows NT 3.51 Programs and Their Windows NT 4 Replacements

Windows NT 3.51 Program	*Its Windows NT 4 Equivalent*
Program Manager	Start Button. (Program Manager is still included, if you'd prefer to stick with it.)
File Manager	Explorer and My Computer programs. (File Manager is still included, if you like it better.)
Write	WordPad; both adds and removes features.
Paintbrush	Paint; both adds and removes features.
Cardfile	Gone with no replacements, although Windows NT 4 often leaves the Windows NT 3.51 versions on the hard disk if you've upgraded.
Calculator, Character Map, ClipBook Viewer, Clock, MS-DOS prompt, Notepad, Solitaire, Sound Recorder	Still the same in Windows NT.
Terminal	HyperTerminal; adds many more features.
Control Panel	Control Panel window, a similar collection of icons.
PIF Editor	Properties sheet: Click on a DOS program's icon with the right button and choose Properties from the menu to tweak the program's settings.
Schedule+	Gone. To get Schedule+ in Windows NT 4, you have to install Exchange Server on the network. (Exchange Server comes with a full and updated version of Schedule+.)

Administrative Tools for the TechnoProbics

Windows NT comes with several technical programs designed to make the nerd feel at home. The Windows NT installation program doesn't automatically install all of these technical programs, however. If you want to go back and add them, check out the "My Version of Windows NT Doesn't Have the Right Programs!" section earlier in this chapter. That section explains how to use Control Panel's Add/Remove Programs feature to make Windows NT toss a few more goodies onto your hard disk. Meanwhile, the next few sections describe some of the more technical programs in Windows NT.

Backup

What it does: Copies all of your computer's files to another area for safekeeping.

Where it lives: Open the Start menu, choose Administrative Tools (Common), and click on Backup.

How to use it: Everybody knows he's supposed to make backup copies of their computer's information. The problem is finding the time to do it.

The Windows NT Backup program isn't anything really special except in one key area: It can handle long filenames. Because the old-school, DOS-based backup programs can only handle eight-character filenames, they can't make reliable Windows NT backups.

To keep Windows NT users from treading dangerously, Microsoft tossed a Backup program in with Windows NT until all the other companies update their backup programs. After you tell the Backup program which files to save, Backup copies them to floppy disks or a tape backup unit.

If you haven't bought a tape backup unit yet for your home computer, now may be a good time to put one on your shopping list — especially because you're using Windows NT. Tape backup units have come way down in price, and copying huge hard disks onto hundreds of floppies is a bore, even if Windows NT does let you play FreeCell while you're doing it.

Disk Administrator

What it does: Disk Administrator lets knowledgeable computer gurus examine the status of their computers' disk drives.

Where it lives: Click on the Start button, choose Administrative Tools (Common), and click on Disk Administrator.

How to use it: Don't bother trying. This one's for the person flying the airplane, not the person eating the salted almonds in the back.

Event Viewer

What it does: Provides a detailed list of what's been happening on the computer at what times.

Where it lives: Click on the Start button, choose Administrative Tools (Common), and click on Event viewer.

How to use it: Another yawner. Network gurus need to watch these charts so they can tell when the computer's screwing up and how they can fix it. To everybody else, the Event viewer charts look like boring inventory lists.

Performance Monitor

What it does: Creates a constantly updated chart of your computer's inner workings.

Where it lives: Click on Start button, choose Administrative Tools (Common), and click on Performance monitor.

How to use it: This chart doesn't mean much, but the little graph looks sort of cool — sort of an Emergency Room EEG of your computer's internal organs. Feel free to fiddle with it — you can't get into much trouble — but remember to shut it down when the novelty wears off.

User Manager

What it does: Your Network Administrator uses a grown-up version of this program. This version can show you the users and groups that are local to your computer and lets you create your own local groups, should you have a mind to.

Where it lives: Click on the Start button, choose Administrative Tools (Common), and click on User Manager.

How to use it: Chapter 9 has a whole section on making obedient workgroups (also called local groups) through User Manager.

Windows NT Diagnostics

What it does: Lists information for computer mechanics.

Where it lives: Click on the Start button, choose Administrative Tools (Common), and click on Windows NT Diagnostics.

How to use it: Don't bother trying. This stuff is too complicated. Leave it for the Network Administrator to chew his lower lip over.

Chapter 15

Uh, How Do I Run My Older Programs?

In This Chapter

- Running DOS programs under Windows NT
- Making your own PIFs for DOS programs
- Changing fonts in a DOS window
- Halting runaway DOS programs

Windows programs are accustomed to a communal lifestyle where they all eat from the same granola trough. They can share the computer's memory without bickering. Age-old DOS programs, however, hail from a different computing era. Windows NT must nurse DOS programs along, or the DOS programs won't run.

In fact, Windows NT keeps a special chart called a *PIF* (an acronym for program information file) for each problem-causing DOS program. A PIF (rhymes with *sniff*) contains the care and feeding instructions that Windows NT needs to make that particular DOS program happy.

The information in these PIFs can include some pretty meaty stuff. This chapter chops it into easily digestible chunks, but you may want to keep a napkin around, just in case.

Running DOS Programs under Windows NT

Some DOS programs are easy to run under Windows NT. Just head for the Start menu (or Windows NT Explorer or the My Computer window), double-click on the DOS program's icon, and stand back while it heads for the screen. Sometimes the DOS program fills the entire screen while Windows NT waits in the background. Other times, the program runs happily in its own window, oblivious to everything around it.

But some DOS programs refuse to run under Windows NT at all. Those particular DOS programs were designed to use *all* of a computer's resources, so they balk if they think that Windows NT is just tossing them a few scraps.

To trick these malcontents into feeling at home, Windows NT gives each problem-causing DOS program its own PIF containing the special instructions needed to trick the program into running under Windows.

For example, a PIF may tell Windows NT to put the DOS program in a window or to make the program fill the entire screen. PIFs tell Windows NT the type of memory that the DOS program craves and how much of that memory the DOS program wants. Other settings are cosmetic, such as specifying what type of font to use.

Windows NT can automatically create PIFs for the most popular DOS programs. In fact, when you're double-clicking on a DOS program's icon, you're probably double-clicking on that program's PIF. Windows NT consults the PIF and then runs the DOS program accordingly.

- If you installed Windows NT 4 over Windows NT 3.51, Windows NT 4 peeks inside the old NT 3.51 "DOS program list" to see what programs you already installed on the computer. When it finds a troublesome DOS program that it recognizes, it tosses a PIF for that program onto the computer and puts an icon for that PIF on the Start menu, as well as on the My Computer and Explorer programs. The PIF also serves as a shortcut, telling Windows NT where the DOS program lives on the computer.

- That official Windows NT 3.51 "DOS program list" is part of what's called the *Registry* — a big part of Windows NT that keeps track of important computing details.
- If you installed a favorite DOS program and want to run it under Windows NT, check out the section in Chapter 12 about putting a favorite program into the Start menu. If Windows NT recognizes that new DOS program, it creates a PIF, and everything is hunky-dory.
- Some DOS programs come with their own Windows PIFs. When you install such a program, it tosses its PIF onto the hard drive. PIF names usually start with the program's filename and end in the letters PIF. When Windows NT searches the hard drive, it updates that PIF and uses it as its own PIF and shortcut for the DOS program.
- If you double-click on a DOS program that doesn't have a PIF, Windows NT uses general-purpose settings that allow almost any DOS program to run without problem. If there is a problem, however, you can fiddle with the DOS program's settings — a process touched on in the rest of this chapter.

Adjusting a DOS Program's Diet

If your DOS program isn't working under Windows NT, call the software company that made the program and tell them that you need the program's PIF for Windows NT. If the company doesn't have a PIF for that DOS program, bribe a Network Administrator to make one for you — if you're supposed to be using the program, the Network Administrator should be able to fix it up for you.

Although you can probably make a few changes to some minor settings, don't bother trying to make big changes to a DOS program's PIF. This is heavy stuff, meant for advanced users who *enjoy* fiddling with PIFs. Besides, some DOS programs don't run under Windows NT no matter how much PIF coddling they get. Until you become a PIF manufacturer, you're better off sticking with Windows NT or Windows 95 programs when running Windows NT. Most companies have already written Windows versions of their DOS programs, so you have less need to run a DOS program in Windows NT, anyway.

Making Text Bigger or Smaller in a DOS Program Window

DOS programs are used to roaming free and wild, having the whole screen to themselves. Windows NT, however, can force the DOS program to run inside a window just like any Windows NT program. A DOS window functions pretty much like any other window: You can move it around, tug on its borders to change its size, or shrink it into an icon if it's getting in the way.

If the DOS program normally fills the whole screen under Windows NT, try this to run it inside a window: Press the Alt key and then press Enter. The DOS program hops obediently into a window on the screen.

Unfortunately, a DOS window sometimes won't fit comfortably on the screen. To remedy that oversight, you can change the size of the font used by the window. This action makes the letters larger or smaller so the information fits better on the screen. Follow these steps to change the font size in a DOS window:

1. **Click on the icon in the DOS window's uppermost, left corner and then choose Properties from the drop-down menu, as shown in Figure 15-1.**
2. **Click on the Font tab from the Properties menu.**

   The Font tab is the second tab from the left.

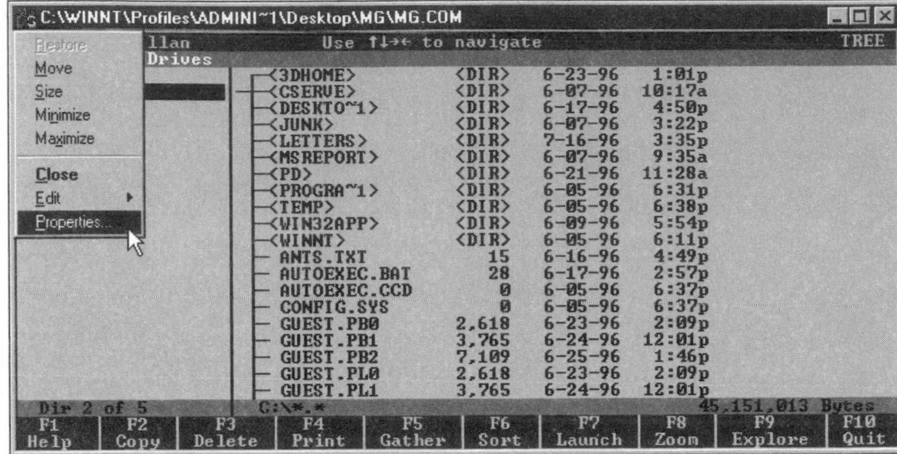

Figure 15-1: Choose Properties to change the font size — and the program's window size along with it.

3. **Choose the new dimensions from the Size window, as shown in Figure 15-2.**

   A smaller dimension (like 4 × 6) makes for small fonts and small windows. A larger dimension (like 12 × 16) makes for enormous fonts and larger windows.

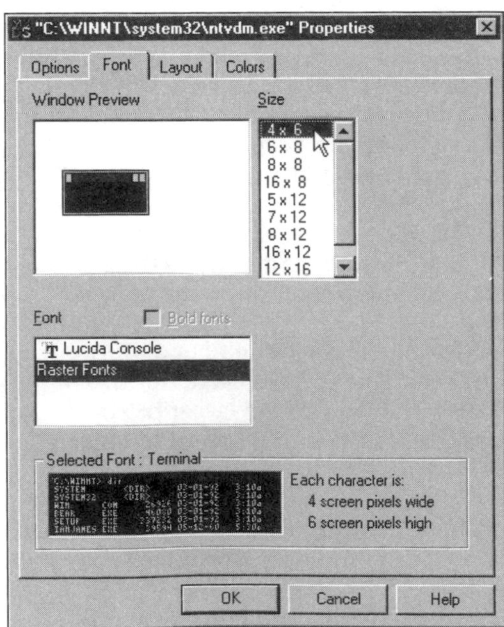

Figure 15-2: Smaller fonts make for a smaller window; larger fonts make a window larger and easier to view; the Window Preview area shows the window's new size in relation to the Desktop.

4. **Click on the OK button.**

   Your DOS program appears, sporting its new fonts and window size, shown in Figure 15-3.

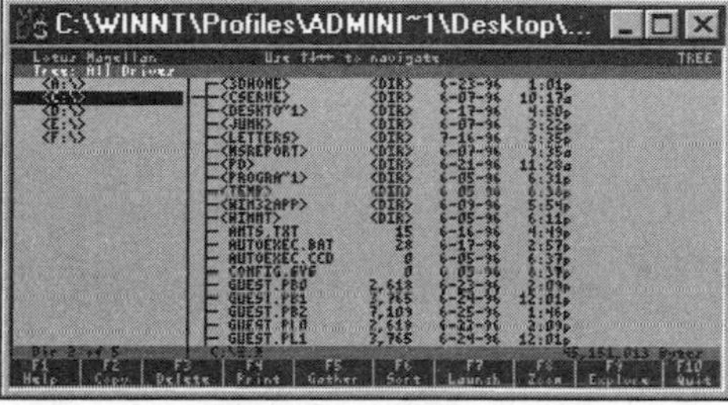

Figure 15-3: Changing a DOS window's font size changes the entire window size.

You can make the fonts larger, too, so that they're easier to read. If you're using a laptop on an airplane, try some of the larger fonts so that the passenger sitting next to you doesn't have to strain so hard to see what you're writing.

- The changing-fonts trick works only with DOS programs that display mostly text — like spreadsheets and word processors. DOS programs that use graphics don't work too well in windows. Their displays don't completely fit in a window, and the colors almost always look weird.
- You can change a DOS window's size by dragging its borders, but that's pointless. A DOS program's display doesn't shrink or grow in size like a Windows NT program does. If you drag the border in, you just cover up your view of the program.
- If you want to cut or paste anything from a DOS program in a window, head back to Chapter 10 for information about the DOS window versions of cut, copy, and paste.

You'll probably want to keep both the TrueType and Bitmap fonts options selected. Although TrueType fonts usually look better than Bitmap fonts, that doesn't hold true as often with DOS programs. Leave the Both font types option selected so you'll have the most fonts to choose from.

Stopping a DOS Program that Won't Stop

Like a startled Arkansas farmer who wakes up in the belly of a spaceship, some DOS programs simply freak out when they find themselves running under Windows NT. For example, some freeze up solid, stubbornly beeping each time you press a key.

To halt a runaway DOS program, first look at the top of the DOS window. If the first word along the top says `Mark` or `Select`, then Windows NT thinks that you're trying to copy information from the DOS window. Press Esc to restore order. If you really are trying to copy something, head for Chapter 10 to see how to do it the *right* way.

If pressing Esc doesn't work, try holding the Alt key and then pressing Enter. This action tells Windows NT to let the temperamental program have the entire screen. For example, if a program suddenly switches from text to graphics in a window, Windows NT sometimes freezes the program until you use the Alt+Enter trick.

That didn't work, either? Then things are getting serious. If the confused DOS program is in a window, follow these steps:

1. **Double-click on the little x in the window's upper-right corner.**

   Or you can click on the icon in the window's upper-left corner and choose Close from the drop-down menu. Either action does the same thing: It tells the program to get the heck off your screen.

2. **Click on the Wait or End Task buttons.**

   Windows NT sends up a box, basically saying that your program is stuck. It offers two options: You can be nice and wait five seconds to see if the program jumps back into shape. Or, you can click End Task to wipe the program off the screen, then and there.

   If your DOS program is stuck on the screen and you choose the End Task button, you lose any unsaved work left in that program. Use the End Task button as a last resort.

Hopefully, these steps will rip the DOS program from the computer's memory.

If the frozen DOS program is running full-screen, press the Alt+Tab keys simultaneously to put the program into a window, and then follow the preceding steps.

- Only use the End Task button if you have to — as a last resort. If at all possible, quit the DOS program in an orderly fashion. To quit some DOS programs, you press Alt+X; in others, you press F10 or Esc. Almost all DOS programs are different.
- After you use End Task, save any work in the other windows. Then exit Windows NT and start it up again. DOS programs occasionally try to sabotage things on the way out.

Chapter 16

Talking to Computers Everywhere

In This Chapter

- Setting up Outlook Express or Windows Messaging
- Getting your Internet mail going
- Exploring the Internet (and intranet)

When it comes right down to it, work is rarely very exciting in an office cubicle because you're seeing the same ol' things, over and over. Excluding those lunches out, the new blond sales manager, and the latest Dilbert cartoon — things can get downright dull.

However, Windows NT comes to the rescue with features that not only help you get your job done but can also perk up your day. The Windows NT mail feature lets you plan exciting lunches and discuss Dilbert's most recent sociopolitical statement; plus, a mountain of trendy stuff is available for you to explore on the Internet.

This chapter shows you how to open some of the doors in Windows NT and start talking to the people on the other side. But be forewarned: This stuff can be downright complicated. Until you learn how to open and close the right computerized doors at the right time, don't be surprised if you find yourself with a few bumps and bruises.

Mail Basics

You can send and receive mail a lot of different ways. If your network is using a program other than Outlook Express, Windows Messaging (the Inbox on your Desktop), or Outlook (without the Express), then the mail instructions in this chapter won't do you a lot of good. The Network Administrator (or more likely, one of your co-workers) will brief you on how your particular system works.

Installing Internet mail is really easy, but you have to follow tons of steps. So if the sight of oodles of installation steps makes you feel a little queasy, politely ask the Network Administrator for help. That's what she's paid for.

In this chapter, we describe Windows Messaging, an older e-mail program, and Outlook Express, which became available around Service Pack 2. Outlook Express handles e-mail and Internet newsgroups. Outlook Express is preferred. You may not even have Windows Messaging available on your Desktop. If not, don't worry about it. Use the Outlook Express icon instead.

Getting on the Outlook Express

Outlook Express is the new e-mail program that comes as part of Internet Explorer 4. Getting your e-mail set up in Outlook Express is not very different from setting up Windows Messaging, except for slight differences in the windows. But you should read through the steps below to make sure you have all the pieces of information before you start.

1. **Double-click the Outlook Express icon.**

   Outlook Express Opens.

2. **In Outlook Express, choose Tools and then Accounts.**

   The Internet Accounts dialog box appears.

3. **Click the Mail tab.**

   Any existing accounts are listed here, as shown in Figure 16-1.

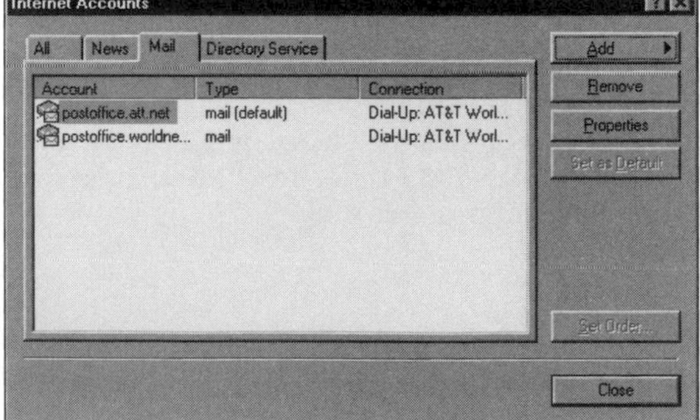

Figure 16-1: Mail accounts in Outlook Express.

4. **Click Add and choose Mail to set up a new account.**

   The Internet Connection Wizard starts.

5. **Enter the name you want to appear at the end of messages you send from this account in the From field. Click Next.**

6. **Enter your e-mail address for this account. Your service provider assigns this address to you when you establish a new account. Click Next.**

Your e-mail address looks like *yourname@yourplace.com*. Except that in place of *yourname*, your actual name appears in some form. Instead of *yourplace*, substitute the name of your company or Internet provider. (It's also possible that instead of *com*, the extension will be *net* or *org* or some other nonsense syllable.)

7. **Enter the e-mail server names given to you by your service provider.**

   There may be separate servers for incoming and outgoing mail. Set the incoming mail server type (in the drop-down box) to either POP3 or IMAP, to match the beginning of the server name. Click Next.

8. **Enter your logon name and password for this e-mail account. Click Next.**

   On a well-run network, your e-mail logon name and password should be the same as your network logon name and password. If they are not, please don't quote our book to the network administrator — just enter the e-mail name and password you've been assigned.

   If you're not on a network, you chose the e-mail logon name and password when you signed up with the Internet service provider.

9. **Enter a "friendly name" for this Internet mail account.**

   If you have multiple accounts, this name will help you tell them apart. For example, use names like "Office Mail" or "MSN Mail." Click Next.

10. **Choose your method for connecting to the Internet.**

    If you connect via a local area network or connect manually, this is your last entry. Click Next, and then Finish. Or, if you want Outlook Express to dial automatically to connect, choose Connect Using My Phone Line, and then click Next. (You may have to provide your Windows NT Workstation installation CD).

11. **To use a connection that's already set up on your computer, choose the connection from the list, click Next, and then click Finish.**
    Or, if you need to set up a new connection, choose Create a New Dial-up Connection, and click Next.

12. **Continue through the wizard.**

    You have to enter the phone number used to connect to your Internet service provider, your user name and password, and a name (that you assign) for the connection. Don't change the advanced properties. Finally, click Finish.

Outlook Express can now connect to your Internet mail account to send and receive mail. If you need to change (or just check) any of the information you entered, re-open the Internet Accounts dialog box (see Step 2), highlight the account name, and click the Properties button.

But I Really Need to Use Windows Messaging

If Outlook Express isn't for you, you can still use Windows Messaging. Double-click on the Inbox icon, the first screen you see announces Windows Messaging, as shown in Figure 16-2.

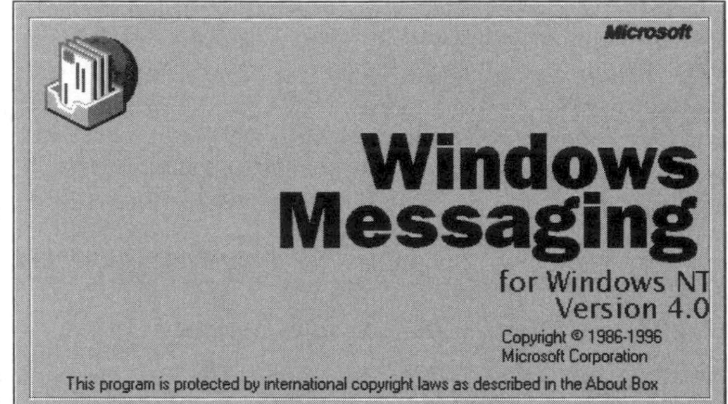

Figure 16-2: The opening of the built-in e-mail program.

Running the Windows Messaging Setup Wizard

After double-clicking on the Inbox icon for the first time, follow these steps. (Depending on the services you select, you may not see all of these steps.) Every box offers a Back button to retrace your steps if you think that you made a wrong move, as well as a Next button that you click on when you're ready to move on.

1. **When you see a list of what the Setup Wizard calls services, check the boxes in front of the services you want to use.**

   The list may be a very short one, listing only Microsoft Mail or Internet Mail, as shown in Figure 16-3. This box may also contain other services.

   In Windows NT, a *service* is any of the various ways you connect to other people. A service may include Internet Mail or Outlook Network Administrator.

   If you're setting up Internet Mail and not Microsoft Mail (or vice versa) just ignore the steps that don't relate to you.

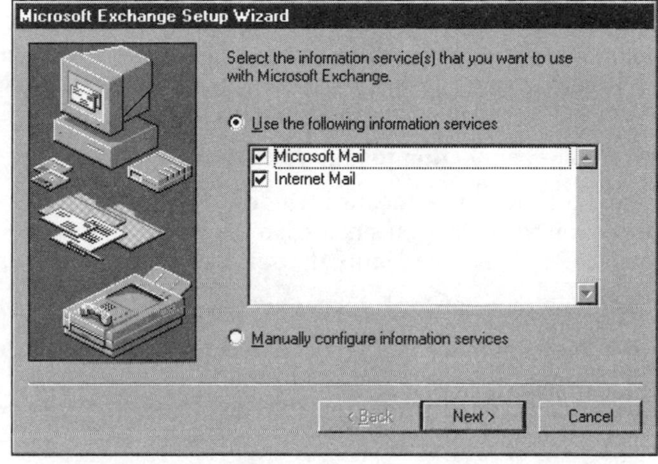

Figure 16-3: The Setup Wizard displays available services — in this case, Internet Mail and Microsoft Mail.

2. **Enter your Microsoft Mail postoffice location.**

   If you're on a network that has Microsoft Mail, you need to supply the path to the postoffice. Don't have any idea what a path is? Ask your Network Administrator what to type in to get to the postoffice.

3. **Select your MS Mail name from the list.**

   For an ongoing MS Mail system, you should see a list of names — select your name. If you don't see your name, ask your Network Administrator to add you to the list.

4. **Supply your Mailbox (if necessary) and your password.**

   After Setup Wizard finds your name and Mailbox, type your Microsoft Mail password into the text box, as shown in Figure 16-4.

Figure 16-4: Enter your MS Mail password in the text box.

5. **Select Internet Mail connection.**

   If you connect to an Internet provider using a modem and a phone line (which is known as a *dial-up connection*), select Modem. If you connect to the Internet through an adapter on your network, select Network.

6. **Enter a Phone connection for Internet Mail.**

   For a dial-up connection, the next window asks for the name of the computer you're dialing. This name isn't anything official, just a name you make up and give to identify the service.

7. **Enter a Phone number for Internet access.**

   Enter the phone number that you use to establish a dial-up connection to your Internet provider. (You can probably get the number from your Network Administrator, if you don't already know it.) The next window informs you of your success at creating a connection.

   This newly made connection is placed in your Dial-Up Networking folder where you can later double-click on it to go get your mail.

8. **Enter a Mail server name or IP address.**

   No matter how you make your Internet mail connection, you need to provide the name or Internet address of the computer that receives your Internet mail (see Figure 16-5). Your Internet service provider supplies this information and if you don't know what it is, ask the Network Administrator.

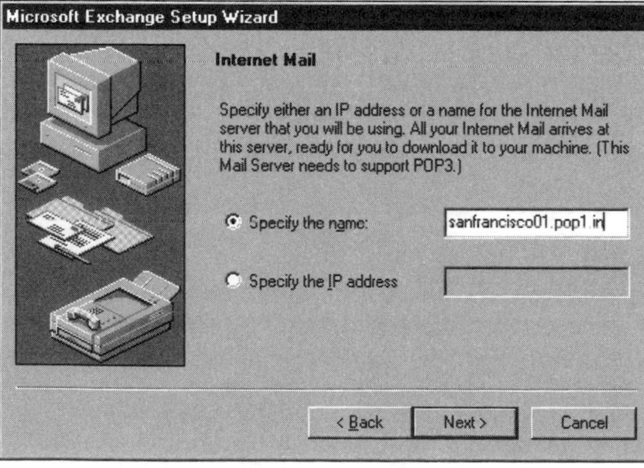

Figure 16-5: Enter the Internet address for your mail server.

9. **Check Selective or Automatic mail transfer.**

   How much Internet mail do you get? How often do you want to read it? How much does it cost to call your Internet connection? Ponder these questions when deciding between Selective or Automatic mail transfer.

   Use Selective mail transfer if you want to use Remote Preview. With Remote Preview you fetch your mail when you want, and you can look at the messages' subject lines so you don't have to get mail you don't want.

   Use Automatic mail transfer if you want the system to automatically establish the connection and transfer all your mail whenever you open Windows Messaging.

10. **Enter e-mail address and full name.**

    Enter your Internet e-mail address in the format `name@domain` in the box labeled Internet e-mail address and your full name (as you want it to appear on your e-mail) in the box labeled Your full name.

11. **Enter Mailbox name and password.**

    Your mailbox name is provided by your Internet service provider. This name is how the mail server identifies your mail location and it's not the same as your e-mail address or the Microsoft Mail mailbox.

12. **Enter a path to your Personal Address Book.**

    The system creates a location for your address book, where you can enter your frequently used e-mail addresses. Just accept the one the system makes for you.

13. **Enter a path to your personal folder file.**

    Your personal folder file is the storage spot for incoming and outgoing messages. Windows Messaging can create multiple personal folder files (as well as address books) if you have need for more than one. Accept this one, too.

14. **Decide if you want Windows Messaging in the Startup group.**

    If Windows Messaging is in the Startup Group, it starts itself whenever you log on to the computer, which is handy in a minor sort of way. After all, you can start Windows Messaging any time by double-clicking on the Inbox icon. But it's up to you.

Now you're ready to use Windows Messaging and send some e-mail to your dear old mom, who runs the network at a famous institute of higher learning, Whatsamatta U.

Doing the Mail Thing

For sending and receiving mail, Outlook Express and Windows Messaging are very similar. The following sections describe how to use both of them — though you use one or the other, not both.

Addressing messages in Outlook Express

To add an address to your Address Book, follow these steps:

1. **Double-click the Outlook Express icon on the Desktop.**
2. **Choose the Tools menu and then select Address Book.**
3. **From the File menu, select New Contact.**

   The Properties box opens as shown in Figure 16-6.

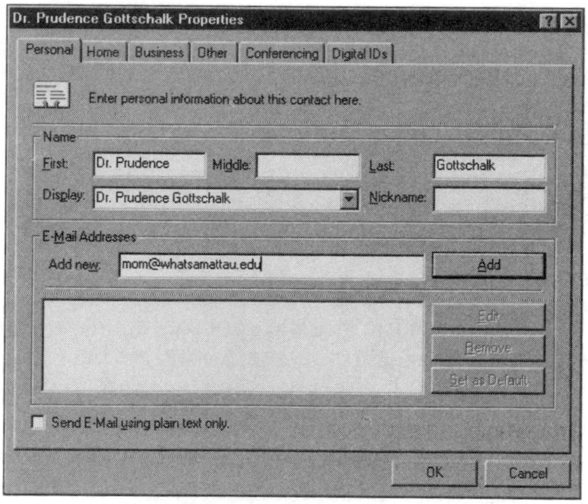

Figure 16-6: Adding a name and address to the Outlook Express Address Book.

4. **Click the Personal tab and fill in the name and e-mail address. Click on OK.**

   You can click any of the other tabs and fill in information about this person's address, phone numbers, favorite cheese — anything you want to keep track of.

5. **Add other names and addresses to the address book by repeating Steps 3 and 4 or close the Address Book by clicking the button with the X in the upper-right-hand corner.**

Addressing messages in Windows Messaging

To add an address to your Personal Address Book, follow these steps:

1. **From the Desktop, double-click on the Inbox icon.**
2. **Choose the Tools menu and then select Address Book.**
3. **From the File menu, select New Entry.**

   This action opens the New Entry dialog box as shown in Figure 16-7. The entry types depend on what mail services are installed — Internet mail, Microsoft Mail, CompuServe mail, or others.

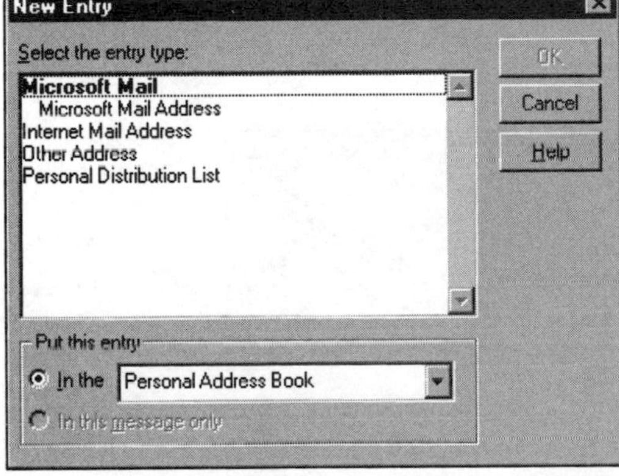

Figure 16-7: Select the entry type from the list by clicking on the one you want.

4. **Select Internet Mail Address and click on OK.**

   This action opens the dialog box shown in Figure 16-8.

5. **Type in Mom's name and e-mail address.**

- Now, whenever you select New Message from the Compose menu, you can click on the To button. This action takes you to your Personal Address Book where you can select a recipient or add a new one.
- By default, the message addresses are kept in a file called mailbox.pab in the Windows Messaging directory.
- The bad news is that if Mom has more than one e-mail address, you have to make a separate entry for each one — otherwise, when you click on the To button to send a new message, you see two entries for Mom, with no sign of which address is which. To get around this limitation, plan ahead: When you add a new name to your Address Book, include a notation to help you later (as shown in Figure 16-9).

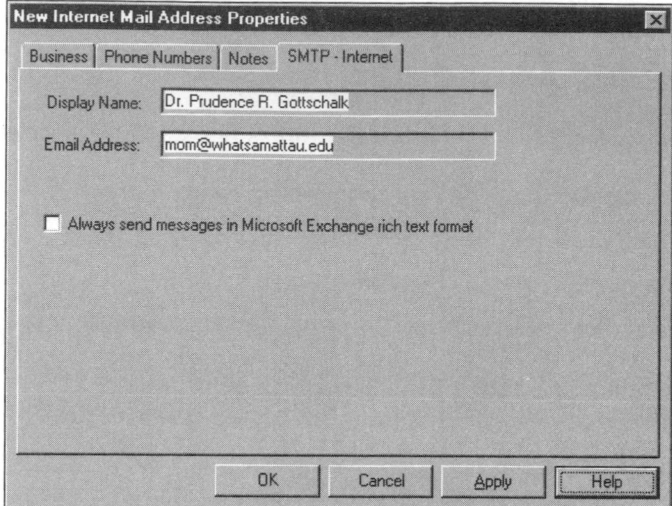

Figure 16-8: Putting Mom in the address book.

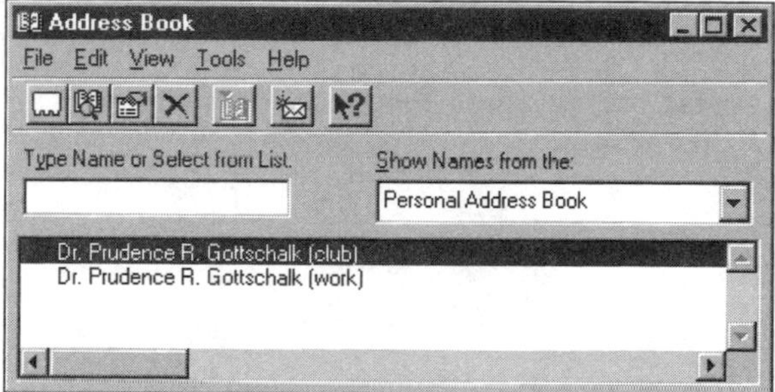

Figure 16-9: Add a notation to names that have more than one e-mail address.

Sending messages in Outlook Express and Windows Messaging

To send a message in either Outlook Express or Windows Messaging, do the following:

1. **Double-click on the Outlook Express or Inbox icon on the Desktop.**
2. **From the Compose menu, select New Message.**
3. **Address and type your message.**

   Figure 16-10 shows mail in Windows Messaging.
4. **Click the File menu, and select Send.**

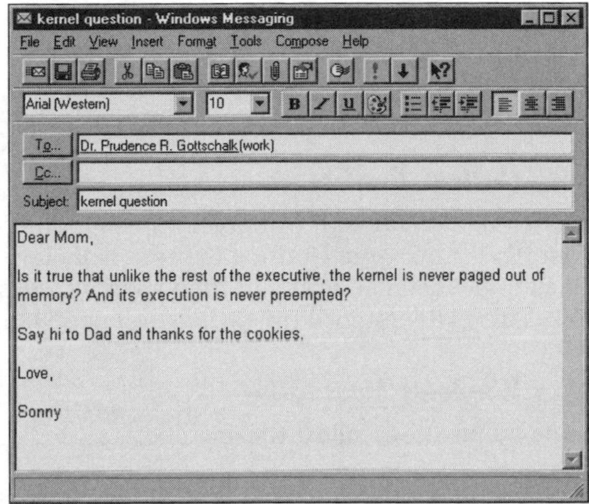

Figure 16-10: When typing a message, whatever is in the subject line becomes the title of the message.

When typing a message, whatever is in the subject line becomes the title of the message.

If you have Remote Mail enabled, open the Tools menu and select Deliver Now (in Windows Messaging) or Send (in Outlook Express) to send mail.

Receiving messages

When you open either Outlook Express or Windows Messaging, the way Internet mail is delivered to you depends on whether your Internet connection is a dial-up connection or a local area network (LAN) connection. Either way, you can go get your mail when you want it, or you can have it done automatically.

With an automatic connection, when you open your mail program it queries your Internet mail server at once and then as often as you specify thereafter. An automatic connection through the network is done almost instantaneously and nothing appears to be happening until the mail pops up in your inbox. If you use a dial-up connection to connect automatically, your mail program opens the phone line, dials your Internet service provider, connects to your mailbox at the Internet service provider, and then puts any messages in your inbox.

Just to confuse matters, incoming mail in both programs is deposited in a folder called an inbox. This is not the same as the Inbox icon on the Desktop. In this chapter, the Inbox icon is always capitalized while the inbox folder is shown in lowercase.

Automatic mail with Outlook Express

Setting up an automatic connection with Outlook Express is tricky on Windows NT. Whether it's set up when Outlook Express is installed or later, dial-up networking has to be installed first and then a whole mess of configuration has to be done. This is definitely a time when you need help.

Automatic mail with Windows Messaging

To set up an automatic connection, follow these steps:

1. **Open Windows Messaging, choose Tools, and select Services.**
2. **Highlight Internet Mail and click on Properties.**
3. **Click on the Connection page, click on the Schedule button, and tell Windows Messaging how often you want it to check for new messages.**
4. **Click on OK four times and you're done.**

Fetching your mail with Windows Messaging

If you use what's called *remote mail preview,* Windows Messaging calls your mail server and then displays a list of your incoming messages. You can then decide which messages you want to read and transfer those messages to your inbox.

To set up remote preview, follow these steps:

1. **Open Windows Messaging, choose Tools, choose Services, highlight Internet Mail, and click on Properties.**
2. **Click on the Connection tab. Put a check mark in the box next to Work off-line and use Remote Mail.**
3. **Click on OK twice.**
4. **Close and then restart Windows Messaging.**

When you want to check for mail, do the following:

1. **Select Remote Mail from the Tools menu.**

2. **From the Tools menu for Remote Mail, select Connect.**

   Your new messages appear.

3. **Highlight the messages you want to transfer to your inbox and select Transfer Mail from the Tools menu.**

Getting your mail with Outlook Express

Getting your incoming mail with Outlook Express couldn't be easier. Double-click the Outlook Express icon on your Desktop and choose the Tools menu and select Send and Receive.

If you connect by having your modem dial the Internet service provider, the Send and Receive option is grayed out (see Figure 16-11), so choose Download All. Windows NT instructs your modem to make the connection, grab all your waiting mail, and deposit it into your inbox.

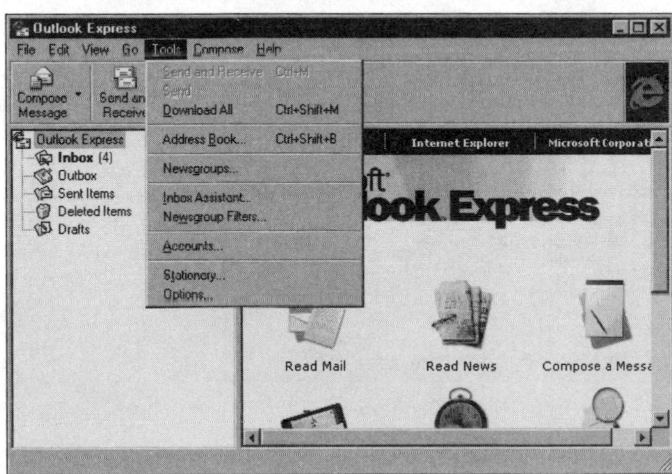

Figure 16-11: The Download All option will cause the modem to dial your Internet service provider and collect your mail.

Reading messages

To read a message in your inbox, just double-click on the message from the list, and the message opens in a window.

If you want to know what any of the buttons mean, just position your pointer over one, and a descriptive box pops open.

If you're used to getting Internet e-mail using other software, you'll notice that Windows Messaging and Outlook Express show only the name of the person sending you the mail with no clue as to where it came from. If you want to see the entire Internet header, open the File menu, select Properties and then click on the Internet tab (or the Details tab in Outlook Express).

Forwarding messages

Sometimes you receive a message that you want to share with someone else. You can forward the message (well, really a copy of the message since the original stays with you) by clicking the Forward button.

This action opens a window that displays original message and gives you the opportunity to add your own comments, as shown in Figure 16-12.

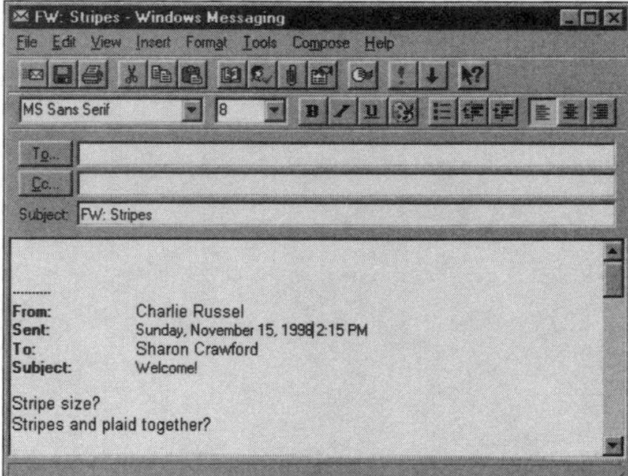

Figure 16-12: Forwarding a message to someone is as easy as can be.

From this screen, you can send your forwarded message directly on its way by specifying the recipient in the To: box and then selecting Send from the File menu. Alternatively, you can specify the recipient and then add your own text to the message by clicking in the text window and typing whatever you have to say. When you're done, send the message as you usually would.

Internet Explorer

The Internet Explorer icon is the little doohickey on the Desktop that looks like a big "e" with a ring around it. Internet Explorer is the Microsoft browser, which you can use to navigate the World Wide Web on the Internet and on what's known as an intranet — Web pages that are published on your own network.

Internet, intranet, what's the deal?

The Internet is a worldwide network of networks, connected by different kinds of high-speed data transmission lines. Your company's network may be connected to the Internet by means of modems or by being one of the networks that make up the Internet. Or, if you're not part of the computer socially elite, you may not be connected to the Internet at all.

An *intranet,* by contrast, is a network that uses Internet technology (specifically Web technology) to share information. Usually when people say intranet, they mean that the "inside" network uses Web pages.

If you have an intranet, you can use Internet Explorer to visit the Web pages on your network. Internet Explorer can also view Web pages on the Internet. If all this sounds potentially confusing — it is. The difference between internal information and external information can become very, very cloudy. This, fortunately, is the problem of the Network Administrator and not yours. However, the administrator's solution may affect how Internet Explorer works for you and how it looks.

The first release of Windows NT 4 included Internet Explorer Version 2.0 — now very old news. To find out what version of Internet Explorer you have, double-click the Internet Explorer icon. Click the Help menu and select About Internet Explorer. If you have any version earlier than 4.0, you should update it. In Version 2.0, open the Go menu and select Internet Explorer Updates. In Version 3.0, click the Favorites menu, then Software Updates, and then Microsoft Internet Explorer. Just follow the instructions on the Web page.

How active do you wanna be?

If you're up-to-date on service packs, you can also have what Microsoft calls an "Active Desktop." What this means is you can make your whole Desktop look like an Internet Web page. If this sounds like something you'd like to do, keep reading. Otherwise, skip this box. To try out Active Desktop, point your mouse at a blank spot on the Desktop and press the right mouse button. Select Active Desktop then slide on over and select View As Web Page. Don't panic when your screen background goes black. That's just Microsoft's way of showing that something dramatic is going on. Click the line at the bottom of the screen that reads "Tell me about Active Desktop" for more information.

To make your Desktop even more Web-like:

- Select the View menu in any window and then click Folder Options. On the General page, click the radio button next to Web style. Click OK.
- Read the Single-click box to decide if you want to change to a Web-like single click. If you click Yes, you notice that when you move the mouse pointer over anything "selectable," the pointer turns into a little cartoon hand. Then a single click of the mouse button opens the object.

Using Internet Explorer

If you've been living in a cave for years and haven't heard of "the Web," you're probably better off. That way you don't have to unlearn all the harder ways of using browsers and can just enjoy using Internet Explorer. So, brush off those cobwebs and step a little closer.

To run Internet Explorer, double-click on the Internet Explorer icon. Figure 16-13 shows the default opening screen — this is the screen that Internet Explorer goes to unless someone has changed the settings. Don't be alarmed if it doesn't look just this way on your computer. Even if the address is the same, Web pages are changed more often than a new baby.

The basic method for using Internet Explorer is to point and click; that is, you point it at a site you'd like to visit, and you're off. To point Internet Explorer at a particular site, click in the Address box and type the Internet

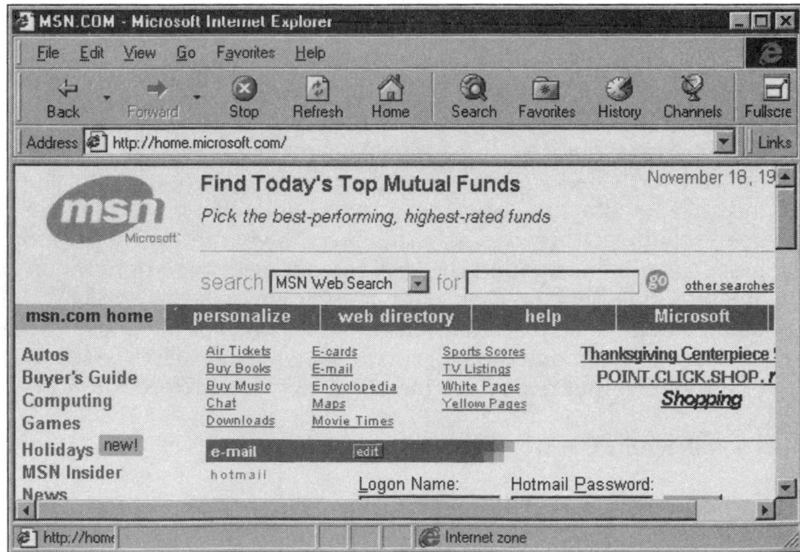

Figure 16-13: The opening screen for a newly installed, networked Internet Explorer.

address (Uniform Resource Locator or *URL*) of the site you want to visit. For example, you can type `www.dummies.com` in the Address box and you end up at the World Wide Web home page for Dummies Press.

If you connect to Web pages on your local network, you need only type in the name of a local Web server.

- To connect to the Internet, you need a connection using a modem on your computer or a connection on your network. Whatever connection you use for Internet mail (earlier in this chapter) is the connection you use for Internet Explorer.

- If you have questions about how to connect to the Internet, your Network Administrator can bail you out.
- After you type in one of these nasty Web addresses, you can open the Internet Explorer Favorites menu and add the site. Thereafter, you need only select the site from the Favorites menu to return.

- If you were at an interesting Web site recently but failed to add it to your Favorites list, you can find the site again by clicking on the arrow next to the Address field to open a drop-down list of your recently visited URLs.

The buttons on the Internet Explorer toolbar are designed to help you navigate quickly and easily. Table 16-1 describes each of the buttons and tells what each button does.

Table 16-1 Button Heaven on Internet Explorer

Button	*Button Name*	*Function*
Back	Back	Returns you to the most recent document you looked at. This button is grayed out if you just started browsing — if you just started browsing, you have no Web pages to go back *to.*
Forward	Forward	Takes you one page forward in the sequence of pages or sites you've already visited. This button is grayed out if you're on the last item on the list of pages and sites you've visited this session.

(continued)

Table 16-1 *(continued)*

Button	***Button Name***	***Function***
Stop	Stop	Halts transmission of a Web page at which you've pointed Internet Explorer. Use this button when transmission slows to a crawl and you'd rather bail out than wait for the page to load completely.
Refresh	Refresh	Refreshes the current page. You may want to click this button if, for example, you have a temporary communications problem with the Web server you're connected to and the page you want to see isn't displayed completely.
Home	Home	Returns you to the start-up home page — the page you saw when you first logged on to the Internet.
Search	Search	Connects to a page full of Internet search engines on the Microsoft Network Home Page. These search programs let you search the Internet for subjects that interest you.
Favorites	Favorites	Opens your list of favorite pages.
History	History	Opens a list of the pages you've visited week-by-week. Click on a week, then a day, and then a site address. Remember as you browse that Internet Explorer keeps track of *every* place you visit and anything Internet Explorer knows, your Network Administrator can find out.

Button	*Button Name*	*Function*
Channels	Channels	Opens a list of preconfigured channels. (For more on Channels, see "Web Viewing channels.")
Fullscreen	Fullscreen	Switches Internet Explorer to a full screen — except for a small tool bar. Click the Fullscreen button a second time to return to a normal view.
Mail	Mail	Starts your mail program. See "Mail in Internet Explorer" section for more info.
Print	Print	Prints the current page.
Links ▸	Links	Click the vertical bar and, while holding the mouse button down, drag to see the built-in Microsoft links. Click a link to open it.

Web Viewing channels

Channels are links to an assortment of Web pages — plus a little more. Click the Channels button on Internet Explorer (or on the Quick Launch portion of the taskbar). This opens Internet Explorer (if it's not already open) with a list of available channels down the left side.

Active Channels are Web sites set up so that you don't have to be connected to the Internet while viewing them. Set them up to download at some specific time you choose and then you can view the pages any time you want. Click on a channel to view it. You see a brief introduction to the channel and a button that says Add Active Channel. Click the button, and you see a box like the one in Figure 16-14. If you want the automatic download, select the last option then click the Customize button.

You can select how much you want to download and when. To modify your subscription later, click the Favorites button and select Manage Subscriptions. Right-click the channel you want to modify and select Properties.

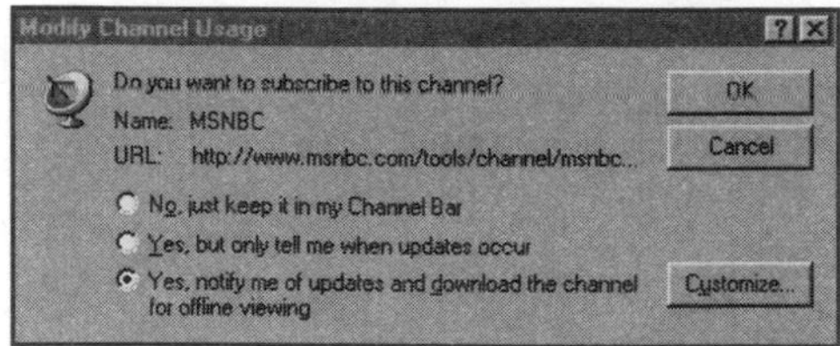

Figure 16-14: Customizing an Internet channel.

- Change the view to full screen, and the channel list slides off the Desktop. To get the channel list back, move your mouse pointer to the left edge of the screen.
- Want channels on your Desktop all the time? Right-click a blank spot on the Desktop and select Active Desktop and then Customize My Desktop. Select the box next to Internet Explorer Channel Bar. Click on OK.

Mail in Internet Explorer

The Mail button in Internet Explorer activates your Outlook Express or Windows Messaging program. The first two items on the Mail menu are ordinary enough. Read Mail opens your mail inbox. New Message opens a window for you to write mail. The next two menu items are special to Internet Explorer. If you're at a Web page that you want to tell someone about, select Send a Link. This opens a mail window with the page's URL already included. Add the address of the person you want to send it to, and the recipient can click the URL and go directly to the page. No need for you to type in a long, long Internet address.

Send Page (see Figure 16-15) lets you send the actual page you're looking at. Again, just provide the address of the recipient.

Using the mouse

Internet Explorer has a multitude of handy features, the best being the use of the right mouse button. Come across a beautiful picture on a Web page? Just right-click on the image, and a menu appears that lets you copy the picture to your Clipboard, save it as a file, or turn the picture into wallpaper for the Desktop.

Other right-click menus let you make a shortcut to a Web page, add the Web page to your Favorites list, or copy a link to the Desktop.

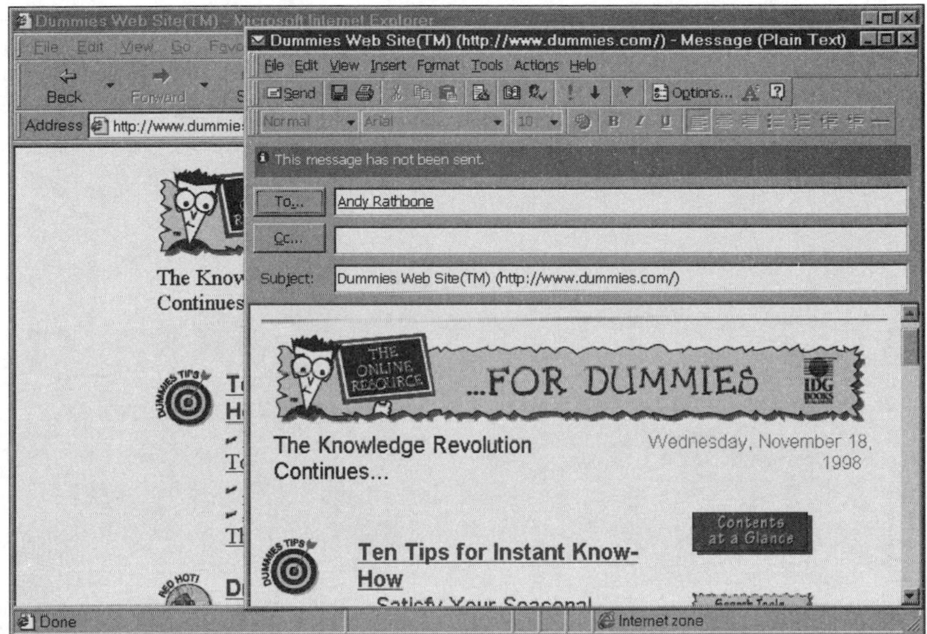

Figure 16-15: Send a stunning Web page to a friend.

To see the underpinnings that make a Web page work, right-click the mouse and select View Source from the menu — you can see all the HTML source code used to build that Web page. If you're learning how to build your own Web pages, you can use this feature to see what the underside of a great Web page looks like.

More cool Internet Explorer stuff

In addition to the features you can find using the mouse, you can find more features from the Internet Explorer menus.

- On the Edit menu, you can cut, copy, paste, or find text on a Web page.
- Text too small? Select the View menu and click Fonts. Choose the next largest size to improve your view.
- Looking at a Web page in Turkish? Select Fonts from the View menu to change the display alphabet.
- To configure Internet Explorer to your own preferences, open the View menu and then select Internet Options.

Some of the tabs in the Internet Options window may not even appear on your system, sparing you the anxiety of not knowing what you can change. In general, however, security options should be determined by the Network Administrator. If you're not on a network, set the Security level for the Internet zone no lower than Medium.

Part IV

Been There, Done That: Quick References for Moving to Windows NT

In this part . . .

Moving from Windows NT 3.51 to Windows NT 4 is like moving into a new house and trying to find the bathroom in the dark. Until you get used to the floor plan, you'll be bumping into things.

After you figure out where things are, that sense of bafflement disappears and you can relax. Of course, some people will always miss their old place with its familiar light switches, windows, and plumbing.

This part of the book is for Windows NT 3.51 owners who've already paid their dues while figuring out Program Manager and File Manager. Here you find ways to make Windows NT 4 work like your old faithful Windows NT 3.51. Or, if you're looking for the quickest way to get the most done, you find it here as well.

Chapter 17

Make Windows NT Work like My Old Version of Windows!

In This Chapter

- Bringing back Program Manager
- Resurrecting File Manager
- Finding Write, Cardfile, Calendar, and Paintbrush

Some of your old favorites from earlier versions of Windows are either gone or not as prominent in Windows NT 4. For example, Windows NT 3.51 and Windows 3.11 both used Program Manager, which Windows NT now shuns. Sure, Windows NT 4 provides replacements that work very well, but some people still enjoy driving their Model Ts.

Luckily for the antique collectors, Windows NT still comes with hidden versions of some of these older programs like Program Manager and File Manager.

This chapter shows you how to pull some of those Windows earlier programs out of the garage.

Where Did My Program Manager Go?

Windows NT dumped Program Manager (used in Windows NT 3.51 and Windows 3.11) in favor of the Start menu, which pops up when you click on the ubiquitous Start button. And after you scratch your head (and play with the Start thing for about 15 minutes), the similarities between the Start menu and Program Manager start to appear.

For example, Program Manager lets you organize your programs in separate Program Group windows. The Windows NT Start menu organizes programs in separate folders branching out from the menu's Programs listing.

But if you prefer the old-style Program Manager for starting programs — or you want to use Program Manager until you grow more accustomed to Windows NT — here's how to rev the ol' program back up:

1. **Click on the Start button and choose Run from the menu.**

   A box pops up, asking you to type the name of a program you'd like to run.

2. **Type** PROGMAN **into the Open box and click on the OK button.**

   The box should look like the one in Figure 17-1. (Make sure that you leave the Run in Separate Memory Space box unchecked.) After you click on the OK button, Program Manager appears, as shown in Figure 17-2.

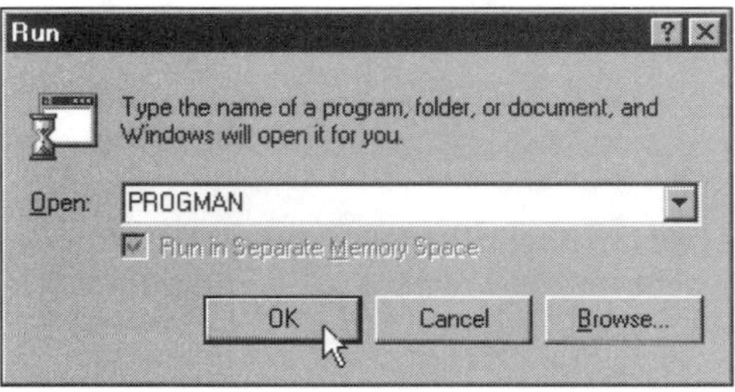

Figure 17-1: Type **PROGMAN** into the Open box to load the old Windows NT 3.51 Program Manager.

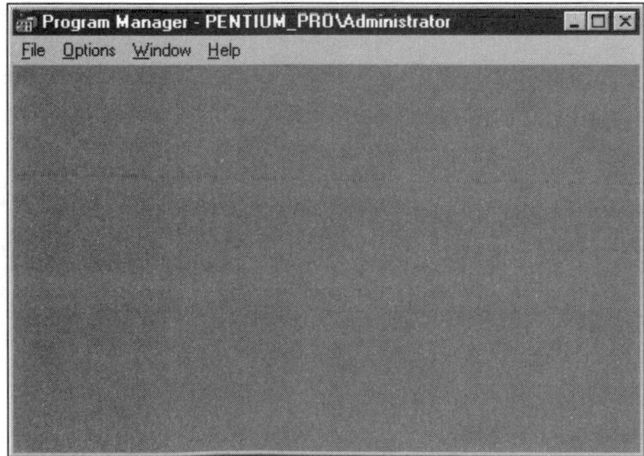

Figure 17-2: The Program Manager in Windows NT 4 can look embarrass-ingly different from the one used in Windows NT 3.51.

Be prepared for a few adjustments, however. First, Program Manager is wearing Windows NT 4 clothing. In fact, it may not have any windows or icons at all, as shown in Figure 17-2. Minimized Program Groups stack themselves along the screen's bottom like cigars in a box, and the Tiling and Cascading features don't work as well as they do in Windows NT 3.51.

- If your Program Manager doesn't have any windows or icons, you have to add them yourself: Open Program Manager's File menu, choose New, click on Personal Program Group, and click on the OK button. Type a description for your new Program Group window into the Description box and click on OK. Voilà! This amazingly painstaking process makes the Program Group take form. You still have to add program icons to the windows, as described next.

- To put a program's icon on Program Manager, just drag the icon there from the My Computer or Explorer program. Windows NT 4 automatically turns the icon into a shortcut — sans the traditional shortcut arrow, however — that can launch the program. (After all, the Windows NT fancy shortcuts are almost the same as the icons in the Windows NT 3.51 Program Manager.)
- Some newly installed programs don't install their icons on Program Manager; they put them on the Start menu instead.
- With the new Program Manager, dragging and dropping icons onto Program Groups, which are minimized along Program Manager's bottom, is harder. The minimized group icons are much closer together than they used to be, so you can't always tell where your dropped icon will fall.

- Closing Program Manager no longer logs you off Windows NT. To log off, you need to click on the Start button, choose Shut Down from the menu, and choose Shut down the computer from the next menu.
- Face it — is Program Manager really worth all this fuss? It's time to move on and start fiddling with My Computer and Explorer, which are covered in Chapter 13.

I Want My File Manager Back!

Nobody really liked the Windows NT 3.51 File Manager, except perhaps the *really* old-timers who struggled with the Windows 3.0 File Manager.

Although File Manager's replacements — the My Computer and Explorer programs included with Windows NT 4 — are slightly easier to use, file management will never compete with a hockey game for entertainment.

If you don't want to learn any new tricks, however, feel free to bypass My Computer and Explorer and return to File Manager — it's included with Windows NT 4. Here's how to bring File Manager to life:

1. **Click on the Start button and choose Run from the menu.**

   A box pops up, asking you to type the name of a program you'd like to run.

2. **Type** WINFILE **into the Open box and click on the OK button.**

   When you click on the OK button, File Manager appears, as shown in Figure 17-3.

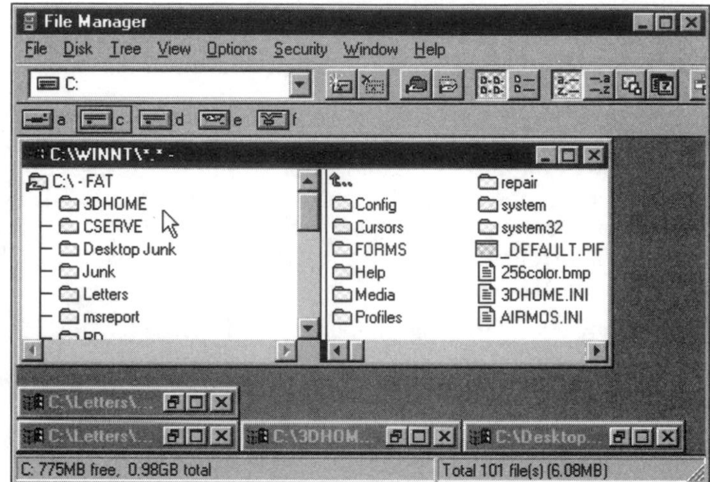

Figure 17-3: Windows NT 4 still includes a File Manager similar to one included with Windows NT 3.51.

This File Manager looks pretty much like the one in earlier versions of Windows. The biggest difference comes when the windows are minimized. Unlike the windows in the earlier version of File Manager, this File Manager's minimized windows look like hot dogs dropped to the window's bottom, as shown in Figure 17-3.

- You can still copy files by dragging them and dropping them into windows inside File Manager. But dropping a file onto a minimized drive is hard because those minimized drives are now hot-dog thin.
- You can't load documents into programs by dragging and dropping them onto the taskbar's list of programs; Windows NT 4 says you can drag and drop files only into open windows.
- Here's another weird one: You can drag files and folders out of File Manager and onto your Desktop. But you can't drag files and folders into your File Manager windows. File Manager is a one-way street pointing toward the Desktop.

- When you rest your mouse pointer over an icon in Windows NT, a box usually pops up and explains the icon's purpose for life. File Manager may be old, but it still has that helpful trick built in.
- You probably won't want to spend much time with File Manager. Instead of spending time figuring out File Manager's limitations, spend that time figuring out how to use My Computer or Explorer. (They're both covered in Chapter 13.)

Where Are Write, Cardfile, Calendar, and Paintbrush?

The Windows NT 3.51 Calendar and Cardfile are gone for good. Windows NT 4 doesn't come with them, and Microsoft figured it didn't need to toss in replacements, either.

If you install Windows NT over Windows NT 3.51, however, your Calendar and Cardfile programs are still on your computer. (Take a peek at the Start menu's Accessories area.)

A new, "improved" version of Paintbrush comes with Windows NT, and you can find it listed in the Start menu's Program area under Accessories. It's now called Paint, and it's described in Chapter 14.

Finally, the Write word processor now calls itself WordPad and can handle much more exciting tasks, like reading and writing Word 6.0 for Windows documents. (It, too, gets its due in Chapter 14.)

Chapter 18

How Can I Do *Anything* in Less than Four Steps?

In This Chapter

- Copying a file to a floppy disk
- Finding the Start button and the Start menu
- Finding a lost file, folder, or program
- Adding programs to the Start menu
- Arranging open windows
- Opening a new compact-disc box
- Changing the screen's wallpaper
- Installing a new program

This is it — quick and easy answers to the Windows NT 4 questions everybody's asking. Feel free to highlight or put sticky notes next to your favorite answers.

How Do I Copy a File to a Floppy Disk (And Vice Versa)?

Want to copy a file from your hard disk to a floppy disk? It's easy! Just do the following:

1. **Double-click on the My Computer icon and open the folder where your file is currently living.**
2. **Using the right mouse button, click on the file's icon and stand back.**

   A menu pops out.
3. **Point at the Send To command.**

   Another menu shoots out.

4. **Finally, click on the name of the floppy disk you'd like to send the file to — drive A or drive B, for example.**

Oh, and don't forget to put a floppy disk into the drive — if you have such a drive. Unfortunately, some networked computers don't come with floppy drives.

This method doesn't work for copying files from floppies to a hard disk; the hard disk doesn't appear on the Send To menu. To move your coveted file to the hard disk, drag the file's icon from the floppy-drive window to the folder on the hard disk. For more information, head to Chapter 13.

How Do I Copy a File to a Different Folder or Drive on a Network (And Vice Versa)?

This one's easy: Just drag the file's icon over to the folder or hard disk. If you can see an icon for a folder or hard disk on your screen, you can drag your file's icon there — and copy the file over there in the process.

Can't remember how to move or copy a file? Then drag the icon from place to place while holding down your right mouse button. Release the button when the icon is in place and choose either Move Here or Copy Here from the convenient menu that pops up.

How Do I Make a Copy of a Floppy Disk?

No floppy drive on your computer? You'll have to track down somebody who has one, or track down your network's administrator. Then follow these steps:

1. **Put your floppy disk in your disk drive.**
2. **With your right mouse button, click on the icon for that floppy drive.**
3. **Choose Copy Disk from the menu that appears.**
4. **Follow the instructions on-screen.**

The Copy Disk command is handy for making backup copies of your favorite programs.

How Do I Find the Start Button and Start Menu?

Normally, you find the Start button lurking on the end of the *taskbar* — a long, ribbonlike string that covers an edge of the screen. Can't even find the taskbar? Then press Ctrl+Esc. That key combination almost always brings up the Start menu — the menu that pops up when you click on the Start button.

How Do I Start a Program?

Click on the taskbar's Start button and point your mouse at the word Programs on the pop-up menu. When you point at the various folders that pop up, the folders open, revealing more options.

Spot the program you're after? Click on its name, and Windows NT 4 brings the program to life. If you don't spot the program, head for the "How Do I Find a File, Folder, or Program?" section coming up next.

More taskbar information lurks in Chapter 12.

You can also start programs from My Computer or Explorer: Double-click on a folder to open it; double-click on a program to load it. Double-clicking on a file usually loads the program that created the file as well as opens the file itself.

How Do I Find a File, Folder, or Program?

Need to find a wayward file, folder, or program? No problem! Just follow these steps:

1. **Click on the Start button and then point at the Find command.**
2. **Click on the Files or Folders option.**
3. **Type the name of your program, file, or folder — or at least as much of it as you can remember.**
4. **Click on the Find Now button.**

The Find program lists all files, folders, and programs on drive C that contain the letters you typed. If you spot your program, double-click on it to bring it to life. If you don't spot what you're after, head to Chapter 8 for a more detailed explanation of the Find program.

How Can I Add Files, Folders, and Programs to the Start Menu?

The congenial Windows NT 4 allows several ways to add files, folders, and programs to the Start menu, but here's one of the easiest:

1. **Double-click on the My Computer icon and find the icon for your file, folder, or program.**
2. **Point at the desired icon and, while holding down the mouse button, point at the Start button.**
3. **Let go of the mouse button.**

That's all there is to it. Click on the Start button, and you see your newly added file, folder, or program at the top of the menu.

Hit Chapter 12 for more tips.

How Do I Keep My Icons Neatly Arranged?

When first installed, Windows NT 4 lines up all your icons neatly in their folders. But if you start changing a folder's size or moving icons around, they quickly lose their orderly arrangement and start overlapping.

The solution follows:

1. **Click on a blank part of the folder with your right mouse button.**
2. **Point at Arrange Icons on the menu.**
3. **Click on Auto Arrange.**

   Now, Windows NT 4 automatically keeps your icons arranged in neat rows.

The downside? Lazy Windows NT 4 makes you repeat this command on *every* window or folder you want to keep automatically arranged. Sigh.

How Do I Organize Open Windows So That They're All Visible?

Too many overlapping windows scattered across your screen? Then use one of the Tile commands so that Windows NT 4 gives each window an equal amount of space on your desktop.

1. **Using the right mouse button, click on a blank part of the taskbar.**

   Clicking near the clock usually works well.

2. **Choose Tile Windows Horizontally or Tile Windows Vertically.**

   Tile Windows Vertically lines up the windows in columns; Tile Windows Horizontally lines them up in rows. Try whichever scheme looks best. Or turn to Chapter 7 for more information.

How Can I Stop Having So Many Open Windows?

If you're opening folders inside of folders inside of folders, soon you have a zillion open windows all bumping rudely into one another. If you want to reuse windows instead of wastefully opening each folder in its own window, do the following:

1. **Click the View menu on any open window and select Folder Options.**
2. **Click the button next to Custom and then click the Settings button.**
3. **In the Browse folders section click the button next to Open each folder in the same window; then click OK, and then Close.**

How Can I Make All My Windows Look the Same?

If you want all your windows to display their contents as large icons or one of the other choices on the View menu, you can set things up to achieve complete uniformity. Just follow these steps:

1. **Select the View menu on any folder and pick the view you want all your folders to have: Large Icons, Small Icons, List, or Details.**
2. **Click the View menu again and select Folder Options.**
3. **Select the View tab and click the button labeled Like Current Folder.**

   A confirmation box opens. If you are sure that this is the step you want to do, click Yes.
4. **Click the Close button at the bottom of the page.**

Although the confirmation box says that the new settings will be available as you open new folders, you may have to restart your system to make everything display correctly.

How Can I Make All My Windows Look Different — and Stay That Way?

Sometimes you find that after you set your windows up *just so,* Windows NT gets forgetful, and you find your careful setup gone from some windows. To remind Windows NT that you know what you want, do the following:

1. **Click the View menu on any open window and select Folder Options.**
2. **Click the View tab and scroll down the Advanced Settings box until you find a box labeled Remember each folder's view setting.**

   Make sure that a check mark appears in the box.
3. **Click OK.**

Now each window will stay the way you put it.

How Do I Set the Time and Date?

To change the computer's time and date, double-click on the taskbar's clock, usually found at the bottom-right corner of the screen. A calendar and clock pop up, allowing you to change the date, time, and even the time zone. Hit Chapter 11 for the full scoop.

How Do I Open a New, Plastic-Wrapped Compact-Disc Box?

Use your teeth, being careful not to scratch your gums. Sometimes a thumbnail works well, or even a letter opener. It's a miracle of technology, but the plastic wrap is often tougher than the plastic case itself.

How Do I Change My Screen's Wallpaper?

To change the background design of your screen, do the following:

1. **Using the right mouse button, click on a blank area of your desktop.**

   A menu pops up out of nowhere.

2. **Next, choose Properties from the pop-up menu.**
3. **See the list of names in the second column, under the word Wallpaper?**

   Click on one of the names for a quick preview.

More wallpaper instructions are hanging around in Chapter 10.

Wallpaper files can be *tiled* across the screen to cover up everything or *centered* in the middle of the screen to hang like a painting. (That's what those Tile and Center commands do — the ones you see in the menu that appears when you click on the taskbar with your right mouse button.)

How Do I Change the Name of a File or Folder?

To change the name of a file or folder, follow these steps:

1. **Click on the icon of the file or folder you'd like to rename.**

   That click highlights the icon, making it change color.

2. **Wait a second or two and then click directly on the file or folder's current name.**

3. **Start typing the new name.**

   The new name automatically replaces the old name.

4. **Press Enter when you're through.**

Windows NT 4 won't let you change every icon's name, however. For example, you're stuck with the names *Recycle Bin* and *3 1/2 Floppy (A:)*, along with a few others.

How Much Room Do I Have on My Hard Disk?

To check out how much room is available at the inn, do the following:

1. **Double-click on the My Computer icon.**
2. **Click on your hard disk's icon with your right mouse button.**
3. **Choose Properties from the menu.**

   A box appears, listing your hard disk's size (and showing you a pretty graph, too).

To keep a wary eye on the amount of room left on a hard disk, open My Computer, open the View menu, and choose Status Bar. My Computer starts displaying the currently selected disk's capacity and amount of free space along the bottom of the window.

How Do I Install a New Program?

Here's the easy way, if everything works the way it's supposed to:

1. **Double-click on the My Computer icon and double-click on the Control Panel.**
2. **When the Control Panel hits the screen, double-click on the Add/Remove Programs icon.**
3. **When the next window pops up, click on the Install button and follow the on-screen instructions.**

Flip to Chapter 11 for more-detailed instructions.

If you're on a big network, however, the Network Administrator probably won't let you install Descent II for lunch-hour, six-person free-for-alls. (Even if you can sneak it aboard, the joysticks will give you all away anyway.)

Part V
Getting Help

"I DON'T KNOW– SOME PARTS OF THE NETWORK SEEM JUST FINE, AND OTHER PARTS SEEM TO BE COMPLETELY OUT OF CONTROL."

In this part . . .

Windows NT can do hundreds of tasks in dozens of ways. That means that approximately one million things can fail at any given time.

Some problems are easy to fix. For example, a misplaced click on the taskbar makes all your programs disappear. Yet one more click in the right place puts them all back.

Other problems are far more complex, requiring teams of computer surgeons to diagnose, remedy, and bill accordingly.

This part lets you separate the big problems from the little ones. You'll know whether you can fix it yourself with a few clicks and a kick. If your situation is worse, you'll know when it's time to call in the surgeons.

Chapter 19

Fixing Windows That Don't Work

In This Chapter

- Getting your mouse to work right
- Escaping from Menu Land
- Installing a driver for a new computer gizmo
- Installing other parts of Windows NT 4
- Clicking on the wrong button
- Thawing a "frozen" computer
- Dealing with DOS programs that don't look right in a window
- Handling a printer that's not working correctly

Sometimes you just have a sense that something's wrong: The computer makes quiet grumbling noises, or Windows NT 4 starts running more slowly than Congress. Other times, something's obviously wrong: Pressing any key just gives you a beeping noise, menus keep shooting at you, or Windows NT 4 greets you with a cheery error message when you first turn it on.

Many of the biggest-looking problems are solved by the smallest-looking solutions. Hopefully, this chapter points you to the right one.

My Mouse Doesn't Work Right

Sometimes, the mouse doesn't work at all; other times, the mouse pointer hops across the screen like a flea. Here are a few things to look for:

- If no mouse arrow appears on the screen when you start Windows NT, make sure that the mouse's tail is plugged snugly into the computer's rump. Then log off and log back on to Windows NT.

- If the mouse arrow is on-screen but won't move, Windows NT may be mistaking your brand of mouse for a different brand. Press Ctrl+Esc to open the Start menu, and use the arrow keys to choose Control Panel (it's hiding under the Settings area). Use the arrow keys to select the Mouse icon, and press Enter. When the Mouse menu appears, press Ctrl+Tab until you highlight the General tab. Press Alt+C to see the list of available mouse breeds, and choose the one that applies to your mouse.

  If none of this stuff works, take your hand off the mouse and raise it in the air to flag down your Network Administrator.

- If the mouse pointer jumps around, there may be a conflict on its interrupt. You may have to pull out the mouse manual and see how to change the mouse's *interrupt setting* to fix this one. Or, better yet, leave this one to the Network Administrator. It can get ugly.
- A mouse pointer can jump around on-screen if the mouse is dirty. To clean it, first turn the mouse upside down and clean off any visible dirt stuck to the bottom. Then remove the retaining ring (turn the little device holding the mouse ball in place — many mice have an arrow showing which way the device moves — until the mouse ball pops out). Wipe off any crud and blow any dust out of the hole. Pull any stray hairs off the little rollers and stick the ball back inside the mouse. If you wear wool sweaters or have cats, you may have to clean the ball every month or so.
- If the mouse was working fine and now the buttons seem to be reversed, you probably hit the left-handed button configuration setting in the Control Panel. Double-click on the Control Panel's Mouse icon and make sure that the configuration is set up correctly, whether you're right- or left-handed.

My Menus Act Weird

If your keystrokes don't appear in your work but instead make a bunch of menus shoot out from the top of the window, you're stuck in Menu Land. Somehow, you've pressed and released Alt, an innocent-looking key that's easy to hit accidentally.

When you press and release Alt, Windows NT turns its attention away from your work and toward the menus along the top of the window.

To get back to work, press and release Alt one more time. Alternatively, press Esc. One or the other is your ticket out of Menu Land.

I'm Supposed to Install a New Driver

When you buy a new toy for the computer, the toy should come with a piece of software called a *driver.* A driver is a sort of translator that tells Windows NT how to boss around the new toy. If you buy a new keyboard, sound card, compact disc player, printer, mouse, monitor, or almost any other computer toy, you need to install its driver in Windows NT. Unfortunately, this installation is often a painful process, so it's covered at the tail end of Chapter 11.

- Companies constantly update their drivers, fixing problems or making them better. If the computer device is misbehaving, a newer driver may calm it down. You can find new drivers from the producing company's World Wide Web page, or by calling the company's technical support lines and asking them to mail you their newest driver.
- A few computer toys won't work with Windows NT 4. Just about anything you buy new will work fine — though it never hurts to ask at the store. However, that modem or mouse you inherit from your brother-in-law will probably need a new driver and — if it's old enough — it may not work at all. And forget about using anything touted as an "USB" device. Those don't work with Windows NT.

His Version of Windows NT 4 Has More Programs than Mine!

Windows NT 4 installs itself differently on different types of computers. As it copies itself over to a hard disk from a compact disc or network, it brings different files with it. When installed on a laptop, for example, Windows NT 4 probably brings along programs that help a laptop transfer files to a bigger computer.

Computers with smaller hard disks probably get the minimum files that Windows NT 4 needs to run. Chapter 3 describes some of the programs and accessories Windows NT 4 comes with; here's how to copy them to your computer if Windows NT 4 left them off the first time:

1. **Double-click on the Control Panel's Add/Remove Programs icon.**

   You can find the Control Panel by opening the Start menu and clicking on Settings.

2. **Click on the Windows NT Setup tab (it's the tab on the right).**

   A box appears, showing the various components of Windows NT 4 as well as the amount of space they need to nestle onto your computer's hard disk.

3. **Click in the little box by the program or accessory you'd like to add.**

   A check mark appears in the box of each item you select. To select part of a category — a portion of the accessories, for example — click on the category's name and click on the Details button. Windows NT 4 lists the items available in that category so you can click only on the ones you want. If you click on the Details button, click on the OK button to continue back at the main categories list.

4. **Click on the OK button and insert your installation disks or CD when asked.**

   Windows NT 4 copies the necessary files from your installation disks onto your hard disk. You can remove a Windows NT 4 accessory by *removing* the check mark from the box next to the accessory's name.

Your Network Administrator has pretty complete control over what information goes on and off a computer. Don't be too surprised if you can't wrest away any more pieces of Windows NT 4 onto your computer.

I Clicked on the Wrong Button (But I Haven't Lifted My Finger Yet)

Clicking the mouse takes two steps: a push and a release. If you start to click on the wrong button on-screen and haven't lifted your finger yet, slowly slide the mouse pointer off the button on-screen. *Then* take your finger off the mouse.

The screen button pops back up, and Windows NT 4 pretends nothing happened. Thankfully.

My Computer Has Frozen Up Solid

Every once in a while, Windows NT just drops the ball and wanders off somewhere. You're left looking at a computer that just looks back. Panicked clicks don't do anything. Pressing every key on the keyboard doesn't do anything — or worse yet, the computer starts to beep at every key press.

When nothing on-screen moves except the mouse pointer, the computer has frozen up solid. Try the following approaches, in the following order, to correct the problem:

Approach 1: Press Esc twice.

That approach usually doesn't work, but give it a shot anyway.

Approach 2: Press Ctrl, Alt, and Delete all at the same time.

The official-looking Windows NT Security box pushes its big shoulders onto the screen, listing six official-looking buttons. Click on the button named Task Manager. A window appears, listing the currently running programs. Click on the name of the program that's causing the mess — you'll often see the word "misbehaving" or something to that effect listed after the program's name — and click on the End Task button. You lose any unsaved work in your program, of course, but you should be used to that.

Want to kill a recalcitrant DOS program? Windows NT usually gives you three options before killing the program: (1) Click on the Cancel button and ignore the situation. (2) Click on the End Task button to yank that particular program off the screen. (3) Give the program five more seconds to finish up what it's doing and leave the screen by itself.

Approach 3: Press Ctrl, Alt, and Delete all at the same time and choose Shut Down.

If none of these methods fixes the problem, try pressing Ctrl+Alt+Delete again and clicking the Shut Down button instead of the Task Manager button.

If you somehow stumbled onto the Ctrl+Alt+Delete combination by accident, press Esc at the unresponsive-application message to return to Windows NT.

Don't push the computer's Reset button and don't turn the computer off and on again, no matter how tempted you may be. Instead, flag down the Network Administrator — who will probably turn the computer off and on again anyway but then it'll be his fault if something gets munged.

My DOS Program Looks Weird in a Window

DOS programs are *supposed* to look weird when running in a window. Windows NT 4 forces the computer to contort into different graphics lifestyles. Most DOS programs look different when displayed in these new graphics modes.

You do have a few alternatives, however:

- Click on the DOS program window to highlight it; then hold Alt and press Enter. Windows NT 4 steps to the background, letting the DOS program have the whole screen. *Then* the DOS program looks normal. Press Alt+Enter to put it back in the window. Or hold Alt and press Esc to return to Windows NT, with the DOS program as an icon listed on the taskbar. (Exit the DOS program normally to return automatically to Windows NT.)
- Play with the DOS program's fonts as described in Chapter 15.
- Buy the Windows or Windows NT 4 version of the DOS program.

The Printer Isn't Working Right

If the printer isn't working right, start with the simplest solution: Make sure that the printer is plugged into the wall and turned on (which may involve a trip down the hall if you're using a networked printer). Surprisingly, this step fixes about half the problems you may ever have with printers. Next, make sure that the printer cable is snugly nestled in the ports on both the printer and the computer that it's attached to — assuming the printer cable is attached to any computer at all. If the printer cable is not attached to a specific computer, it should still have a cable that attaches it to a network hub. Make sure that both ends of that cable are firmly attached. Then check to make sure that the printer has enough paper — and that the paper isn't jammed in the mechanism.

The Windows NT Help program is surprisingly helpful with this one: Open the Start menu, and click on Help. When the Help window appears, double-click on the word Troubleshooting from the Contents page, and click on the line that says If you have trouble printing. Windows NT 4 leads you through a program designed to figure out why the printer's goofing off.

If you still can't get the darned thing to work, you need to call in the Network Administrator. Don't be in too much of a hurry, though. If the network printer has gone down, the disgruntled administrator has probably already heard from several dozen people before you.

Chapter 20

The Terror of the ERROR! ERROR! ERROR!

In This Chapter

- A:\ is not accessible. The device is not ready
- Disk drive is full
- The file or folder that this shortcut refers to cannot be found
- This filename is not valid
- No viewer is capable of reading WordPad document files

Most people don't have any trouble understanding error messages. A car's pleasant beeping tone means that you left your keys in the ignition. A terrible scratching sound from the stereo means that the cat has jumped on that aging turntable.

Things are different with Windows NT 4, however. Its error messages could've been written by a Senate subcommittee, if only they weren't so brief. When Windows NT tosses an error message your way, it usually gives you just a single sentence and rarely describes what you did to cause the error. And even worse, Windows NT hardly ever says how to make the error go away for good.

Here are some of the words you find in the most common error messages that Windows NT 4 throws in your face. This chapter explains what Windows NT 4 is trying to say, why it's saying it, and just what the heck it expects you to do about it.

Not enough memory

Meaning: Windows NT 4 is running out of the room that it needs to operate.

Probable cause: You're trying to make Windows NT work harder than your computer can handle.

Solutions: To fix the problem, first try shutting down some of the programs you currently have running. Do you really need all those programs open?

Or let Windows NT help itself out of the jam: Open the Start menu and choose Help; then double-click on the little book icon that says Troubleshooting. Next, double-click on the question mark icon that says `If you run out of memory`. A window appears, as shown in Figure 20-1.

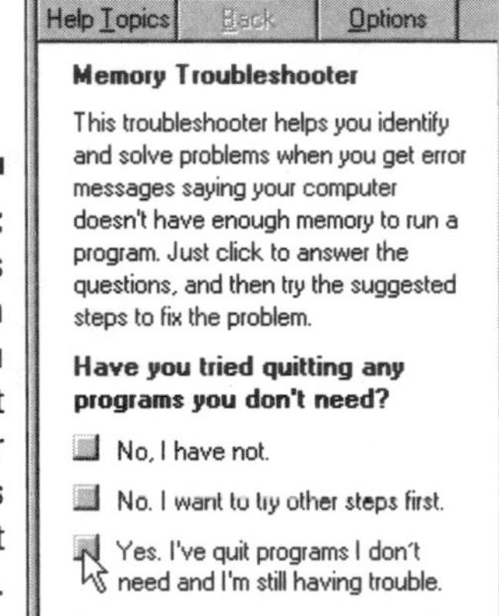

Figure 20-1: Windows NT can help you figure out why your computer is running out of memory.

Follow the instructions in the Help program, and Windows NT can often figure out why your computer's memory is in such short supply.

- Don't forget to simply empty your Recycle Bin as a quick and easy solution. Windows NT doesn't really delete files when you tell it to; it just tosses the files into the Recycle Bin so you can fish them out later if you need them. So to free up disk space for more important things, empty your Recycle Bin: Click on the Recycle Bin icon with your right mouse button and choose Empty Recycle Bin from the menu.
- Whenever you cut or copy a large amount of information to the Clipboard, that information stays there, taking up memory — even after you paste it into another application. To clear out the Clipboard after a large paste operation, copy a single word to the Clipboard. Doing so replaces the earlier, memory-hogging chunk, freeing some memory for other programs.

A:\ is not accessible. The device is not ready

Meaning: Windows NT can't find a floppy disk in drive A.

Probable cause: No floppy disk is in there.

Solution: Slide a disk inside and wish all errors were this easy to fix.

The disk in the destination drive is full

Meaning: Windows NT 4 has run out of room on a floppy disk or on the hard disk to store something.

Probable cause: Windows NT 4 tried saving something to a disk but ran out of space.

Solution: Clear more room on that disk before saving your work. Delete any junk files on the hard disk. BAK (backup) files and TMP (temporary) files often qualify as junk files that you can safely delete, but only if their dates show them to be old and forgotten. Also, delete any old programs you don't use anymore, like those games you snuck onto the computer for playing during lunch hour.

Also, if you're trying to copy something to the hard disk, be sure to empty the Recycle Bin first: Click on the Recycle Bin icon with your right mouse button and choose Empty Recycle Bin from the menu.

The item that this shortcut refers to has been changed or moved. The nearest match, based on size, date, and type, is another item. Do you want this shortcut to point to this item?

Meaning: Windows NT 4 can't find the file or program that's supposed to be attached to a shortcut icon.

Probable cause: Somebody or something has moved or deleted a file or program after a shortcut was attached to it.

Solution: Try using the Windows NT 4 Find program, described in Chapter 8. If the Find program can't find the file or program, double-click on the Recycle Bin to see whether the item is lurking in there and can be dragged onto the Desktop.

A filename cannot contain any of the following characters: \/:*?"<>|

Meaning: Windows NT 4 refuses to accept your choice of filename.

Probable cause: You tried to name a file by using one or more of the forbidden characters.

Solution: Turn to the section about renaming a file in Chapter 12 and make sure that you're not naming a file something you shouldn't. Chances are that you slipped in a question mark or slash.

There is no viewer capable of viewing WordPad Document files

Meaning: Windows NT 4 can't show you what's in that file by using Quick View.

Probable cause: You're probably trying to view a word processor file by using Quick View — that little peek-inside-a-file tool — and that file probably ends in the hidden letters DOC. When Windows NT 4 sees the hidden letters DOC, it thinks it's about to see a WordPad file and gets confused by another word processor's format.

Solution: Quick View simply can't view this file, unfortunately. To see inside the file, you have to load it into its own word processor.

The following trick doesn't always work, but it may: Try dragging and dropping the mysterious file into an open Notepad window. Sometimes, Notepad can display a file's contents. If the words run off the end of the screen, open Notepad's Edit menu and choose Word Wrap. After you finish viewing the file — if you can see it at all — be sure to exit Notepad *without* saving the file. Doing so preserves the file in its natural state.

Deleting this file will make it impossible to run this program and may make it impossible for you to edit some documents

Meaning: You're trying to delete a file containing a program.

Probable cause: You're clearing off some hard disk space to make room for incoming programs.

Solution: First, be very careful — grab a network administrator by the pocket protector if you're not sure what you're doing. Then make sure that you know what program you're deleting before you delete that file. Then don't delete the file unless you're sure that you no longer need that program. Finally, make sure that you have the program's box and installation disks sitting on the shelf so you can reinstall the program if you decide you need it after all.

You must type a filename

Meaning: Windows NT 4 insists that you type a filename into the box beneath a file's icon.

Probable cause: You chose (accidentally or otherwise) the Rename command from a menu or clicked on an icon's title in *just the right* way. Then you deleted the file's previous name, leaving just a blank box.

Solution: Type a new filename consisting of mostly numbers and letters, and you'll be fine. Or if you're frantically trying to get out of this weird situation and don't give a darn about changing filenames, press Esc, and the Rename box dissipates.

Cannot copy file: Access is denied. Make sure the disk is not full or write-protected and that the file is not currently in use

Meaning: You're trying to copy a file to a place that Windows NT doesn't allow.

Probable cause: You're trying to copy a file to a place that can't hold new files — a compact disc, for example, or a write-protected floppy disk. (Those items are covered in Chapter 2.)

Solution: Don't try to copy files to compact discs. This process works only with super-expensive CD-ROM drives, and the Network Administrators usually hog those for themselves. For tips on un-write-protecting a floppy disk, hit Chapter 2.

Access denied

Meaning: You can't get there from here.

Probable cause: You don't have permission to use the file or folder you just selected.

Solution: If you're trying to grab a file or folder on your network — and you're supposed to be able to grab it — the situation is probably just a permission mix-up that your administrator can fix in no time at all.

But if you can't reach a site on the Internet, your network may not be allowing it. In that case, the Access Denied message will probably mention something about a "proxy server" or "firewall." That means your network's administrator isn't allowing access. You can appeal that decision, but be prepared to explain why getting to the Wrestlemania Web site is necessary to your job.

Error opening printer

Meaning: The network can't find the printer you want.

Probable cause: The printer is out of service for some reason.

Solution: Try another printer. If you don't have another printer, walk over and see whether the one you want is plugged in. If the printer looks okay, then you need to find the network administrator.

The Other Computer Did Not Respond

Meaning: No one answered your Chat call.

Probable cause: Either you typed in a computer name that doesn't exist or the other computer isn't active on the network.

Solution: Check the name of the computer. Wait and try again. Go down the hall and *talk* to the person you're calling.

The System Could Not Log You On

Meaning: You can't log onto this machine.

Probable cause: Most likely scenario is that you made a mistake typing in your password, but there can be (sigh) other causes.

Solution: Re-enter your password — slowly this time. Remember, passwords are case-sensitive. To a computer, *bozo* is not the same as *Bozo.* Check to be sure that your username is correct. If you still can't get in after repeated tries, it's time to get help from the administrator.

The Disk Is in Use or Locked by Another Process

Meaning: Something else is using this disk, so you can't use it.

Probable cause: You're trying to format a floppy while Windows Explorer is displaying the floppy's contents.

Solution: Double-click on the C drive so *its* contents display in Explorer's right pane instead of the floppy drive's contents. Then right-click on the floppy drive and choose Format.

Chapter 21

Helpful Handouts from the Windows NT Help Program

In This Chapter

- Finding helpful hints quickly
- Using the Windows NT Help program
- Finding help for a particular problem
- Moving around in the help system
- Making a Find index
- Marking Help sections for later reference

Just about everybody's written a bizarre computer command like Alt+F4 onto a stick-on note and slapped it on the side of the monitor.

Windows NT comes with its *own* set of stick-on notes built right in. You can pop them up on-screen and leave them there for easy access. In a way, they're *virtually* real stick-on notes because they can never escape from inside the computer. Actually, it's probably better that way: You'll never find a "How to Change Wallpaper" stick-on note on the bottom of your shoe one evening.

This chapter covers the Windows NT built-in help system. When you raise your hand in just the right way, Windows NT walks over and offers you some help.

The Quickest Way to Find Answers

Don't bother plowing through this whole chapter if you don't need to: Here are the quickest ways to make Windows NT dish out helpful information when you're stumped.

Press F1

When you're confused in Windows NT, press the F1 key. That key *always* stands for "Help!" Most of the time, Windows NT checks to see what program you're using and fetches some helpful information about that particular program or your current situation. In fact, pressing F1 usually brings up a huge Help program, described later in this chapter.

Click the right mouse button on the confusing part

Windows NT tosses a lot of forms in your face. When a particular form, setting, box, or menu item has your creativity stifled, click on it with your right (the opposite of left) mouse button. A What's This? box appears, as shown in Figure 21-1, letting you know that Windows NT can offer help about that particular area. Click inside the What's This? box, and Windows NT tosses extra information onto the screen, explaining the confusing area you clicked on.

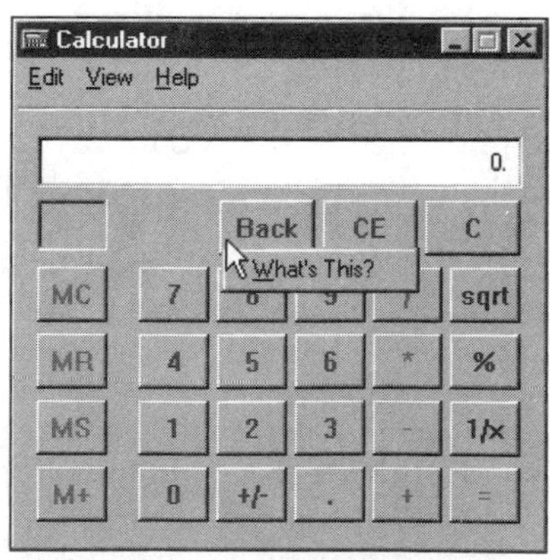

Figure 21-1: Click on confusing areas with your right mouse button; if a What's This? box appears, click on the box to see more information about the confusing area.

Hover the mouse pointer over the confusing icon

Face it: Icons can be confusing, especially when they're arranged in endless little rows like pastries in a bakery shop. In Windows NT's WordPad, for example, which icon helps you find text — the icon of the magnifying glass or the one of the binoculars?

To find out quickly, just let your mouse pointer hover over the confusing icon. In a moment or two, a little box pops up from nowhere, listing the icon's name — and often a short reason for the icon's existence.

This trick doesn't work with all icons, but it works with plenty of 'em, so make it your first line of defense.

Click on the little question mark

Look in the program's upper-right corner. Do you spot a little question mark lurking up there? Then click on it. Your pointer turns into a question mark.

Now, here's the helpful part: Click your newly shaped pointer on any confusing area of the program: boxes, windows, buttons, and icons. A helpful explanation appears, describing what those things are supposed to do. Click on that little question mark again to turn off the feature.

You don't find that helpful question mark everywhere, but keep an eye out for one when a program's obtuseness is starting to get on your nerves.

Choose Help from the main menu

If pressing F1 doesn't get you anywhere, look for the word Help in the menu bar along the top of the confusing program. Click on Help, and a menu drops down, usually listing two words: Help Topics and About. Click on Help Topics to make the Windows NT Help program leap to the screen.

Clicking on About merely brings a version number to the screen, which can be dangerously irritating when you're looking for something a little more helpful.

Click on the leaping arrows

Sometimes the Windows NT Help program scores big: It tells you *exactly* how to solve your particular problem. Unfortunately, however, the Help program says you need to load a *different* program to solve your problem. Don't get grumpy, though: Look for a little "leaping arrow," like the one shown in Figure 21-2.

Click on the little leaping arrow, and Windows NT automatically takes you to that other program you need to use. Yep, it's refreshingly helpful.

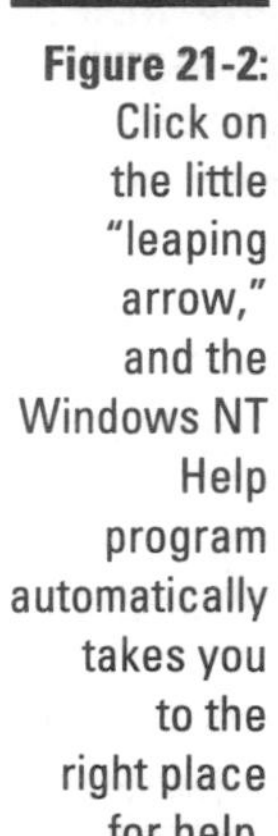

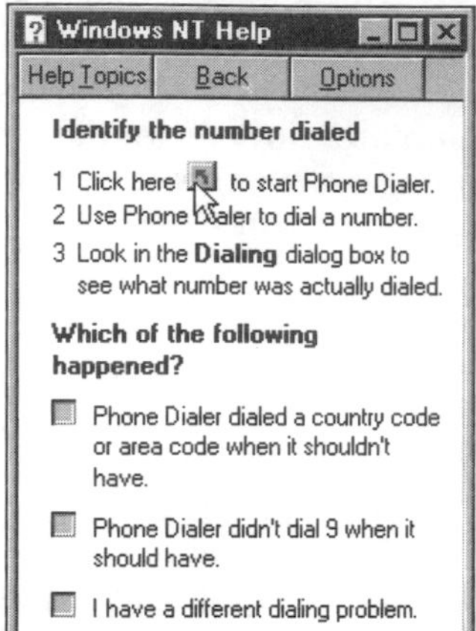

Figure 21-2: Click on the little "leaping arrow," and the Windows NT Help program automatically takes you to the right place for help.

Pestering Windows NT's Built-in Help Program

Almost every Windows NT-based program has the word Help in its top menu bar. Click on Help, and the Windows NT built-in computer guru rushes to your aid. For example, click on Help in Paint, and you see the menu shown in Figure 21-3.

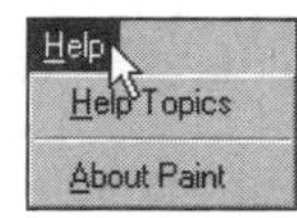

Figure 21-3: Click on the word Help when you mean "Help!"

To pick the computer guru's brain, click on Help Topics, and Windows NT pops up the box shown in Figure 21-4. This box is the table of contents for all the help information that Windows NT can offer on the Paint program.

See any subject covering what you're confused about? Then double-click on it. For example, if erasing has you stumped, double-click on the word *Erasing;* the Help program then shows what additional help it can offer, as shown in Figure 21-5.

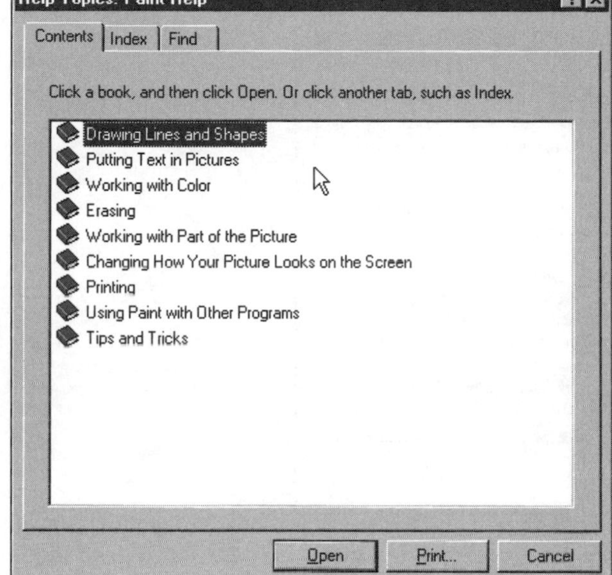

Figure 21-4: Help Topics lists a quick table of contents full of helpful subjects.

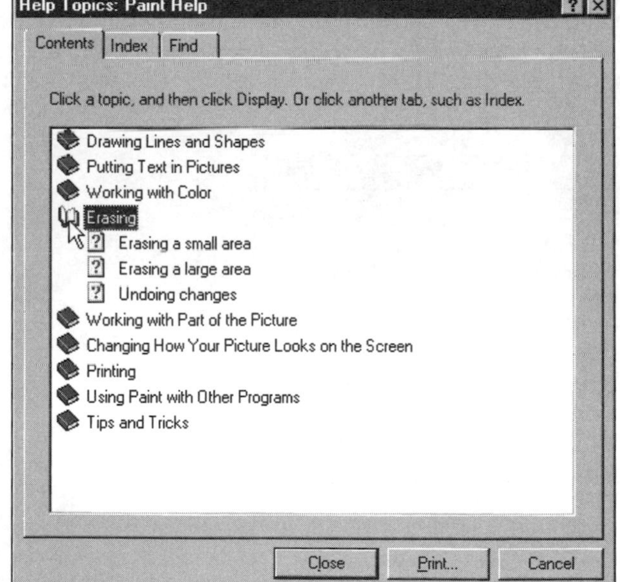

Figure 21-5: Double-click on a topic to see more specific help areas.

Want to see more information on erasing small areas? Double-click on that listed subject, and a new window pops up, as shown in Figure 21-6, bringing even more detailed information to the screen.

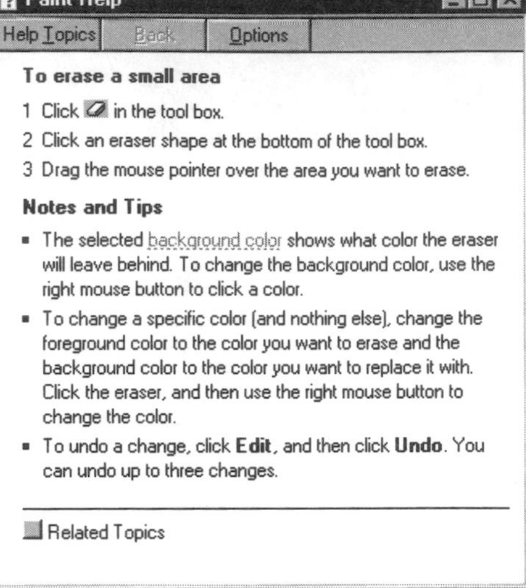

Figure 21-6: By clicking your way from general subjects to more specific areas, you can find the help you need.

Windows NT can offer help with any underlined topic. As the mouse pointer nears an underlined topic, the pointer turns into a little hand. When the hand points at the phrase that has you stumped, click the mouse button. For example, click on the words background color in the Paint Help box, and Windows NT displays more help on what background colors are supposed to mean, as shown in Figure 21-7.

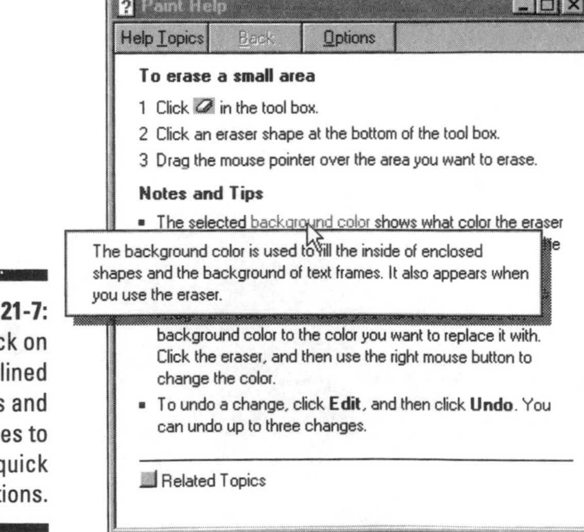

Figure 21-7: Click on underlined words and phrases to see quick definitions.

The Windows NT help system is sometimes a lot of work, forcing you to wade through increasingly detailed menus to find specific information. Still, it can be much faster than paging through the chunky Windows NT manual. And unlike other computer nerds, it doesn't have any Oreo gunk stuck between its teeth.

- The quickest way to find help in any Windows NT-based program is always to press F1. Windows NT automatically jumps to the table of contents page for the help information it has for the current program.
- Windows NT packs a lot of information into its help boxes; some of the words usually scroll off the bottom of the window. To see them, click on the scroll bar (described in Chapter 6) or press PgDn.
- Sometimes you click on the wrong topic, and Windows NT brings up something really dumb. Click on the Help Topics button at the top of the window, and Windows NT scoots back to the contents page. From there, click on a different topic to move in a different direction.
- Underlined phrases and words appear throughout the Windows NT help system. Whenever you click on something that's underlined, Windows NT brings up a definition or jumps to a spot that has information about that subject. Click on the Help Topics button to return to where you jumped from.
- If you're impressed with a particularly helpful page, send it to the printer: Click on Options and choose Print Topic from the menu. Windows NT shoots that page to the printer so you can keep it handy until you lose it.

  Actually, to keep from losing that helpful page, read about sticking an electronic bookmark on that page later in this chapter.
- If you find a particularly helpful reference in the help system, shrink the Help program's window to an icon on the taskbar: Click on the button with the tiny bar, near the window's upper-right corner. Then you can just double-click on the taskbar's Help icon to see that page again.
- To grab a help message and stick it in your own work, highlight the text with your mouse, open the Options menu, and choose Copy. Windows then lets you highlight the helpful words you want to copy to the Clipboard. We dunno why anybody would *want* to do this, but you *can* do it, just the same.

Sticking Electronic Stick-On Notes on Help Pages

Windows NT lets you add your *own* notes to its helpful system of stick-on notes. If you make a stunning revelation and want to remember it for later, these steps let you add a "paper clip" and attach your own notes to a particularly helpful topic:

1. **Click on the word Options at the top of the page.**

   The Options menu appears.

2. **Click on the Annotate option.**

   The Annotate box appears.

3. **Start typing your own notes into the big box.**

   You can type as much as you want. Use the cursor-control keys to move around and the Delete or Backspace key to edit mistakes.

4. **Click on the Save button after you finish entering your note.**

   Windows paper clips your words to the current help page; a tiny picture of a paper clip appears to remind you of your additions.

Whenever you see that help page again, click on the paper clip next to the name of the topic, and your words reappear, as shown in Figure 21-8.

If you ever want to delete your paper-clipped note, click on the paper clip and click on the note's Delete button. Your note disappears.

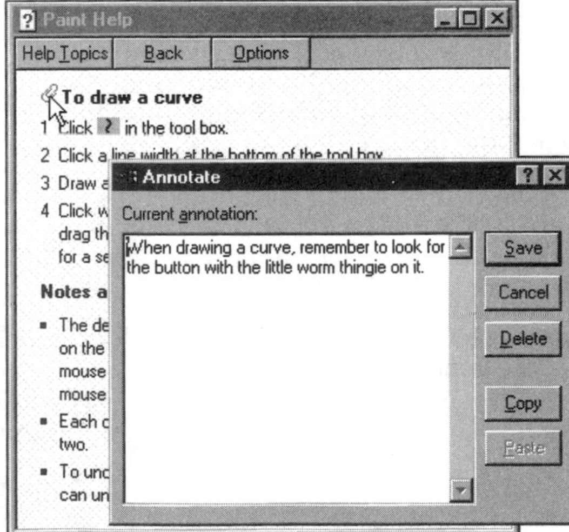

Figure 21-8: Click on the little paper clip to see the reminders you added earlier.

Solving General Problem Areas

If you don't see your problem listed in the particular table of contents page you've accessed, you can find help another way (although it takes a little more time and effort). Click on the Index tab at the top of any help window;

the box shown in Figure 21-9 leaps to the screen. Type a few words describing your problem. As you type, Windows NT shows any matches in the box below.

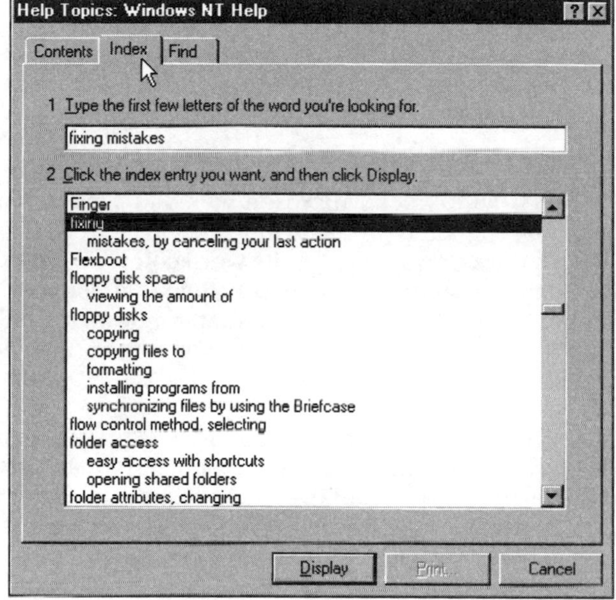

Figure 21-9: Windows NT lets you perform more detailed searches in the Index.

If Windows NT matches what you type with an appropriate topic, click on the topic that looks the most pertinent and then click on the Display button. Windows NT jumps to the page of information that best describes that particular subject.

A quicker way to find help is to click on the scroll bar or press PgUp and PgDn to see what subjects Windows NT is willing to explain. If you see a subject that even remotely resembles what's confusing you, double-click on it. Windows NT brings up that page of help information.

From there, you can jump around by clicking on underlined words and phrases. Sooner or later, you'll stumble onto the right page of information. When you do, give that page a *bookmark,* as described in "Trying to Find the Same Page Again," later in this chapter.

- Windows NT searches alphabetically and, unfortunately, isn't very smart. So if you're looking for help on margins, for example, don't type **adding margins** or **changing margins**. Instead, type **margins** so that Windows NT jumps to the words beginning with M.
- If you have trouble finding help for your specific problem, use the Find command, described in the next section. Instead of forcing you to type

the right words in the right order, the Find command roots through every word in the Help file and brings back every match.

Finding Help on Specific Problems

When you're looking for help on a specific problem, being a casual pointer and clicker is sometimes hard. You want help *now!*

For people who want to make sure that they've wrung every ounce of help from the Windows NT help system, Microsoft included a special Find index: You can tell the Help program to make an index of every word it mentions in its help libraries. That way, you can type the word **color**, for example, and know you'll see every paragraph in the Help system that contains the word *color.* You won't have that nagging suspicion that Windows NT didn't give you help because you didn't type **color monitor** or some other sneaky computer gibberish.

Why doesn't Windows NT come with the Find index already set up and ready to go? Because the Find index eats up a lot of hard disk space. If you can afford the space, however, create the Find index by following these steps:

1. **From within any program, press F1 to bring up its Help program; then click on the Find tab.**

   The Find tab is along the top of the window, toward the right side.

2. **Choose either Express or Custom and then click on the Next button.**

   The Express option adds more help files to the index but uses up much more space. The Custom option lets you choose which help files to add to the index. The Express option is more foolproof, so go for that one if your computer isn't strapped for hard disk space.

3. **Click on Finish.**

   Twiddle your thumbs for a minute or so while Windows NT indexes every word, from *a* to *zone.* You only have to create the index once, thankfully, and then it is yours for the wringing.

- After you create an index, clicking on the Find tab brings you straight to the search area. Type the word you're looking for, and if that word is mentioned in the Help program, Windows NT brings up the nugget of helpful information.
- You have to create an index for each Windows NT-based program you use. This process — although sometimes inconvenient — keeps Windows NT from grabbing huge chunks of hard disk real estate merely to create indexes of programs you never use.

Trying to Find the Same Page Again

The Windows NT help system is better than ever, and finding help for a particular trouble is relatively painless. But how do you return to that page a few minutes — or even a few days — later?

When you find that perfect page, look for the word Bookmark listed along the top. If you spot a button marked Bookmark, you're in luck: Click on Bookmark on the menu bar, choose Define from the menu, and click on the OK button.

Now when you access the help system days or even years later, you can click on the Bookmark menu item. A menu tumbles down, listing the pages that you've bookmarked. Click on the name of the page you're after, and Windows NT hops to that screen. Quick and easy.

The problem? Very few of the Help programs included with Windows NT come with the Bookmark system. Bookmarks seem to be a remnant of older versions of Windows.

Part VI
The Part of Tens

"MY GOD, YOU'VE DONE IT! MILLIONS OF MICROSCOPIC SLINKY TOYS MOVING ACROSS CIRCUITS AT THE SPEED OF LIGHT FORMING THE FIRST SLINKY OPERATING SYSTEM!"

In this part . . .

Everybody likes to read Top Tens in magazines — especially in the grocery store checkout aisle when you're stuck behind someone who's just pulled a rubber band off a thick stack of double coupons and the checker can't find the right validation stamp.

Unlike the reading material at the grocery store, the chapters in this part of the book don't list ten new aerobic bounces or ten ways to stop your kids from making explosives with kitchen cleansers. Instead, you find lists of ways to make Windows NT be more efficient — or at least not as hostile. You find a few tips, tricks, and explanations of eccentric acronyms like *DLL*.

Some lists have more than ten items; others have fewer. But who's counting, besides the guy wading through all those double coupons?

Chapter 22

Ten New Windows NT 4 Features for Windows NT 3.51 Users to Check Out

In This Chapter

- Using the right (not just the left) mouse button
- Peeking inside files with Quick View
- Using long file names
- Using the Recycle Bin
- Highlighting icons with a "lasso"
- Jumping to the right place in Help
- Making a shortcut

Like a new car model, Windows NT 4 adds several improvements over the old Windows NT 3.51 version. Some of the changes are cosmetic, like the fancy new lime-green, 3-D mouse pointers. Other changes are more useful, like the way you can peek inside files without having to load a program.

Consider this chapter a pamphlet explaining some of the best new features Windows NT 4 has to offer over its replacement, Windows NT 3.51.

Check Out the Right Mouse Button

Although mice have come with at least two buttons for the past decade, Windows NT 3.51 never took advantage of the mouse button on the right. The index finger did all the work, clicking and double-clicking on the left button, while the middle finger rested, unused, on the right mouse button.

Windows NT 4 puts your middle finger to work by making the right button just as powerful as the left. The buttons don't do the same thing, though, so here's the rundown:

- Click *once* on something with your *left* mouse button to select it — to highlight an icon, for example.
- *Double-click* on something with your *left* mouse button to not only select it, but to kick start it into action — to load a program, for example, or to open a folder.
- Click *once* on something with your *right* mouse button to bring up a menu that lists the things you can do with that item — adjust its settings, for example, or copy it someplace.

Figure 22-1 shows the menu that pops up after you use your right mouse button to click on a file in the My Computer window.

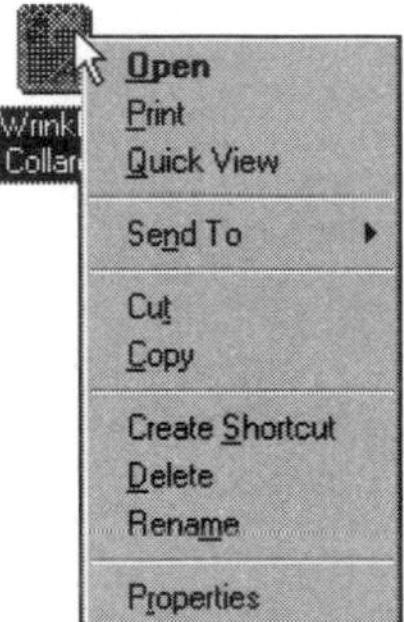

Figure 22-1: Click on a file's icon with your right mouse button, and a menu appears listing things you can do with the file.

If you're unsure of how to work with something on your Desktop, click on it once with your right mouse button. Often, a menu pops up displaying a list of options for you to select from.

Getting Rid of the Double-click

Everyone who uses Windows is used to the venerable convention of single-clicking an item to select it and double-clicking to open it. Everyone who uses the World Wide Web is used to the convention of pointing at an object to select it and clicking once to open it.

With the interface changes added to Windows NT 4, you can adopt the point-to-select, click-once-to-open convention — and you don't have to use the Active Desktop (see Chapter 16) to do it. Just follow these steps:

1. **Click the View menu in any window and select Folder Options.**
2. **In the Windows Desktop Update section, select the Custom option and then click Settings.**

   The Custom Settings page opens as shown in Figure 22-2.

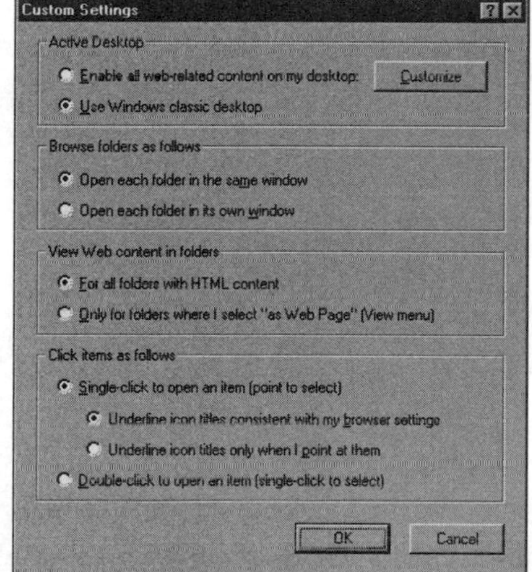

Figure 22-2: Use this page to set your click options.

3. **In the Click items section, select the Single-click option.**

   You can also decide whether you want your icons to be underlined all the time (so they look like things on a Web page) or only underlined when you point to them.
4. **Click on OK when you finish.**

Peering Inside Files without Opening Them

If faced with a plethora of files, how can you tell which one you need? For example, all the icons for files created by the Paint drawing program look the same. How can you check to see whether the file named Sea Food is that lobster picture you are searching for?

You could load the Sea Food file into Paint, but the Windows NT 4 Quick View feature provides a speedier way. Click on the file with your right mouse button, and click on Quick View from the menu that pops up.

A new window (similar to the one in Figure 22-3) quickly appears, showing you the file's contents.

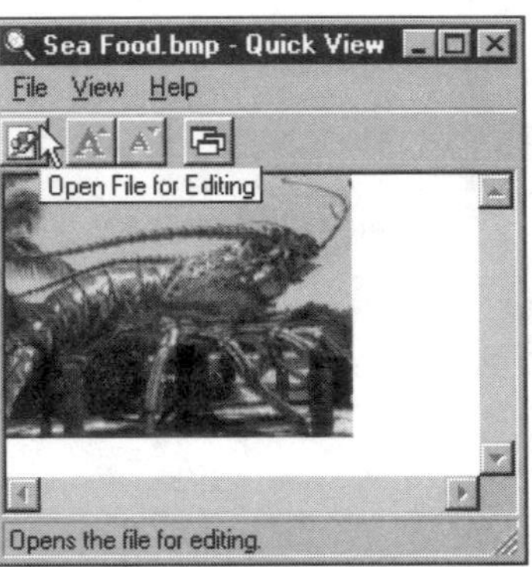

Figure 22-3: Click on a file's icon with the right mouse button, choose Quick View, and a window appears, showing the file's contents.

- Want to open the file for editing? Click on the little Paint icon in the upper-left corner. Windows NT loads Paint, along with your file. The icon for the program responsible for creating the file is always in the upper-left corner.
- If the file on the screen isn't the one you're searching for, feel free to drag another file's icon into Quick View's open window. Windows NT rapidly displays the contents of that file, too.
- Here's the bad news: The Quick View command only works on certain varieties of files. Only the most popular formats are displayed. You can "quick view" your WordPerfect and Microsoft Word files, for example, but you won't be able to peek inside any files made by WordStar or XyWrite.
- You can find more information about Quick View in Chapter 8.

Filenames Can be L-o-o-o-o-o-o-n-g-e-r now

Microsoft said it wouldn't happen in our lifetimes, but Windows NT 4 lets people name their files with descriptions longer than eight characters. Windows NT 4 even lets you use more than one word to name your files, and you can separate the words with a space!

Then again, Windows NT 3.51, Windows 95, and Windows 98 allow longer filenames, too. So what's the big deal? Well, if you're moving up to Windows NT 4 from DOS or Windows 3.1, you'll be so impressed by the feature that it's worth a second mention.

Figure 22-4 shows a few filenames approved by Windows NT 4. As long as you keep the names under 255 characters, you're pretty much okay. (More detailed information on filenames is discussed in Chapter 12.)

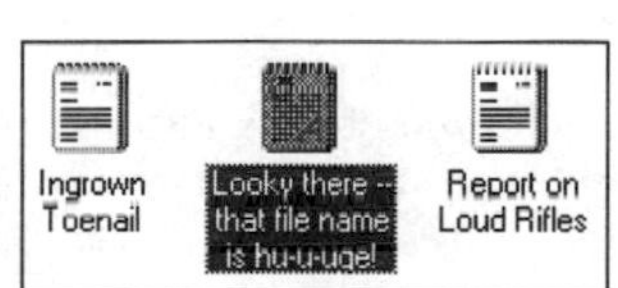

Figure 22-4: Unlike some earlier versions of Windows, Windows NT allows for long filenames containing more than one word.

Plucking Deleted Files from the Recycle Bin

Earlier versions of Windows let you safely retrieve accidentally deleted files, so the concept of the Windows NT 4 Recycle Bin isn't new. The new part is how much easier the Bin makes salvaging deleted files.

Whenever you delete a file, the sneaky Windows NT 4 doesn't *really* delete it. It just hides the file in the Recycle Bin — that little trash can sitting on the Desktop. When you get that sinking feeling that you *shouldn't* have deleted that report on Coelacanth Tailfins, double-click on the Recycle Bin, and you can find your report inside, undamaged.

The Recycle Bin doesn't hold onto deleted files forever, though. It waits until you fill up 10 percent of your hard disk's storage capacity. For example, if you have a 500MB hard disk, the Recycle Bin always holds onto 50MB of your most recently deleted files. After you fill up that 10 percent, Recycle Bin starts shredding the oldest files, and you can't retrieve them.

That 10 percent figure is adjustable, and if you want to change it, hit Chapter 12.

Moving from Windows 95 or Windows 98? The Recycle Bin in Windows NT 4 works the same as it does in Windows 95 and Windows 98, so you have nothing new to figure out.

Grabbing Groups of Icons with a Lasso

This feature doesn't really seem like much, but you'll probably find yourself using it more than you think.

Windows has always allowed several ways to select files and icons. For example, hold down the Ctrl key and click on all the icons you want: Windows highlights each icon you click.

Or, when selecting items in a list, you can click on the first item, hold down the Shift key, and click on the last item in a list. Whoosh! Windows instantly highlights the first item, the last item, and every item in between.

Windows NT 4 can still highlight icons those ways, but it added something new and easier. To select files or folders that are next to each other, you can drag a *lasso* around them. Point just above the first icon you want to grab and, while holding down the mouse button, point just below the last icon you want to grab. Windows NT 4 draws a rectangle around the icons, as shown in Figure 22-5.

The lasso can only be rectangular, so all the files and folders must be next to each other. But you can always lasso the big chunk, and then hold down the Ctrl key to select the stragglers who are away from the main pack.

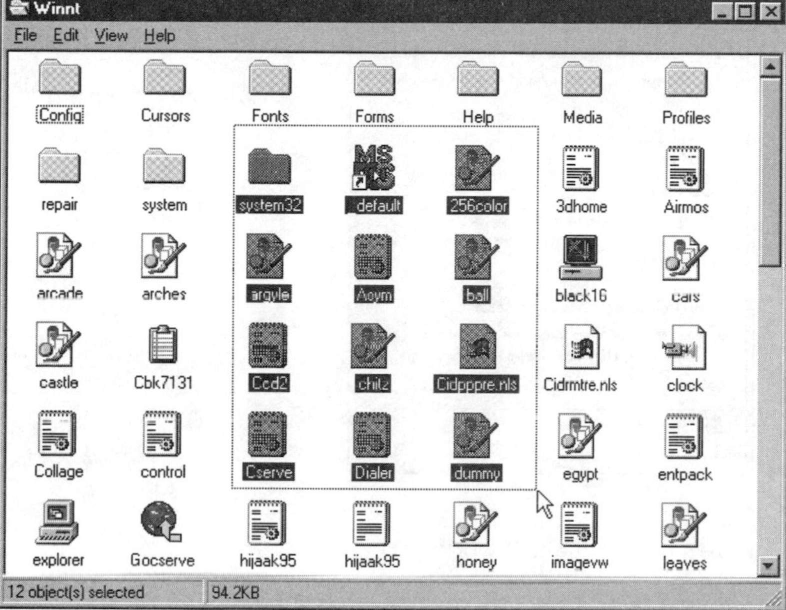

Figure 22-5: Windows NT can drag a rectangle around adjacent files and folders to select them easily.

Hopping to the Right Place in Help

Windows has always come with a helpful Help program. However, the best Windows could do was tell you what part of Windows you needed to use to solve your problem.

Windows NT 4 goes one more step: It not only tells you where to go, it takes you there. Want to know how to put better wallpaper on your Windows Desktop, for example? Type **wallpaper** into the Help program, and Windows NT 4 explains that you need to use the Display Properties area. But the Help program also includes a little button; click on the button, shown in Figure 22-6, and the increasingly polite Windows NT 4 automatically whisks you away to the Display area.

Making a Shortcut

After a while, you find yourself constantly using the same bits and pieces of Windows NT 4. You always use the Pickled Herring Corporate Earnings folder, for example, or the Smoked Fish Packaging Design program.

Sure, you can always plow through your My Computer or Explorer programs until you find the appropriate icons, but an almost magical way exists to speed up the process: a shortcut.

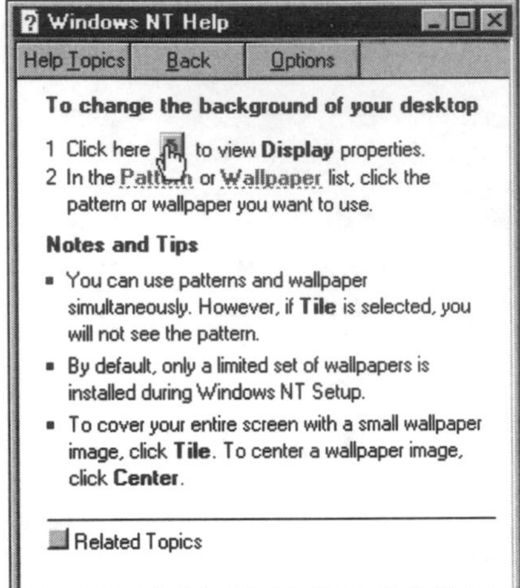

Figure 22-6: Click on the little buttons in the Help program, and Windows NT 4 often takes you directly to the program that can solve your problem.

Here's how to make it work:

1. **Navigate your way through My Computer or Explorer until you find the icon for the folder, program, or file you use most often.**

   Chapter 13 explains the details.

2. **While holding down your right mouse button, drag the icon out of the My Computer or Explorer program and onto your Desktop.**
3. **Release your right mouse button.**
4. **Choose Create Shortcut(s) Here from the menu that pops up.**

A little icon appears on your Desktop that serves as a "shortcut" to the real icon. If the shortcut came from a program, for example, double-click on the shortcut to start the program. Is the icon from a folder? Anything you drop into that icon is routed to that folder. Or, if the icon is from a file, you can double-click the shortcut to access the file.

Be as creative as you like: You can create several shortcuts leading to the same folder, file, or program, for example, making it easy to keep an icon for your Special Stuff folder in all your favorite areas.

The more you play around with shortcuts, the more useful they become.

Chapter 23

Ten Windows NT 4 Shortfalls (And How to Fix Them)

In This Chapter

- Bypassing the menus
- Keeping track of multiple windows
- Keeping the taskbar on-screen
- Fixing the Print Screen key
- Finding all the programs listed on the box
- Understanding why DOS programs run too slowly
- Lining up windows on the screen
- Updating a floppy disk's contents in the Explorer or My Computer program
- Saving a file to a network drive

"Windows NT would be great if only . . . [insert your pet peeve here]." If you find yourself thinking (or saying) this frequently, this chapter is for you. This chapter not only lists the most aggravating things about Windows NT but also explains how to fix them.

Mouse Menus Take Too Long to Wade Through

Windows NT has a zillion menus that you can work through with the mouse, but you don't have to use them. If you want, you can use the keyboard to quickly select everything that you can click on in a menu.

Look closely at the words on the menu bar, along the top of each window.

Somewhere in almost every word, you can spot a single underlined letter. Press and release the Alt key and then press that underlined letter. Try pressing the F in File, for example. Presto! The File menu leaps into place. Then look for underlined letters on the newly displayed File menu. For example, now press S for Save. Presto again! Windows NT saves the current file, without a single mouse click.

To save a file in nearly any Windows NT-based program, press and release Alt, press F, and then press S. It's that simple (after you memorize the combination, that is).

You find these underlined letters everywhere in Windows NT. In fact, you see underlined letters in this book as well. They're the keys you can use to avoid rooting through all the menus with a mouse.

Note: Check out the Cheat Sheet at the front of this book for a list of the most commonly used key combinations.

When maneuvering through the options listed in the Start menu, you only need to click once: Just click on the Start button to bring the Start menu to life. All the other menus contained in the Start menu pop up automatically as the mouse pointer hovers over them. When you spot the program or choice you're after, click on it, and the Start menu loads that program or choice.

- To move from box to box while filling out a form, press the Tab key. Each press of the key takes you to a new part of the form to fill out. Ecstasy!
- For some commands, you hold Alt while pressing a function key. For example, to close any Windows NT-based program, hold down Alt and press F4 (Alt+F4).
- If you accidentally press Alt and are stuck in Menu Land, press Alt again. Alternatively, press Esc and bark loudly until Windows NT lets you out.

I Can't Keep Track of All Those Windows!

You don't *have* to keep track of all those windows — Windows NT does that for you with the taskbar. The taskbar, covered in Chapter 12, lives alongside one edge of your monitor and lists every currently running program by name. Click on the name of the program you want, and that program's window hops to the top of the pile.

Even better, shrink all the open windows into icons except for the window you're currently working on. Then click your right mouse button on the taskbar and click on one of the Tile commands to line everything up neatly on-screen.

In Chapter 8, you find more soldiers to enlist in the battle against misplaced windows, files, and programs.

I Keep Hitting Extra Keystrokes!

If you're a fumble-fingered typist and have trouble with accidental or repeated keystrokes, don't feel like the Lone Ranger. This is so common that Windows NT has a built-in answer. Just follow these steps:

1. **Click your Start button, choose Settings, and click on Control Panel.**

   The Control Panel window opens.

2. **Double-click the Accessibility Options icon.**
3. **On the Keyboard page, click the Use Filter keys box and then click the Settings button to define how you want the keyboard to work.**

While the Accessibility Options are designed for people with disabilities, they can be helpful to anyone. Browse around the Accessibility Properties pages for settings that can enhance your computing *abilities*.

I Can't Find the Darned Taskbar!

The taskbar is a handy Windows NT program that's always running — if you can just find it. Unfortunately, it sometimes vanishes from the screen. Here are a few ways to bring it back:

- Try holding down the Ctrl key and pressing Esc. Sometimes this key combination makes the taskbar appear, but sometimes it only brings up the Start menu.
- Try pointing at the very edges of your screen, stopping for a second or two at each of the four sides. If you point at the correct side, some specially configured taskbars will stop goofing around and come back to the screen.

- If you can see only a slim edge of the taskbar — the rest of it hangs off the edge of the screen, for example — point at the edge you *can* see. When the mouse pointer turns into a two-headed arrow, hold down your mouse button and move the mouse toward the screen's center to drag the taskbar back into view.

In Windows NT 3.51, double-clicking on the Desktop brought up the Task List, which listed all the currently running programs. Double-clicking on the Desktop in Windows NT 3.51 just makes two clicking noises in rapid succession. (The taskbar doesn't appear.)

- If your taskbar disappears whenever you're not specifically pointing at it, turn off its Auto hide feature: Click your right mouse button on a blank part of the taskbar and choose Properties from the pop-up menu. When the Taskbar Options menu appears, click in the Auto hide box until the little check mark disappears. (Or add the check mark to turn *on* the Auto hide feature.)
- While you're in the Taskbar Options menu, described in the preceding bullet, make sure that the Always on top box is checked. That way, the taskbar always rides visibly on the Desktop, making it much easier to spot.

My Print Screen Key Doesn't Work

Like all the other versions of Windows, Windows NT takes over the Print Screen key (labeled *PrtSc, PrtScr,* or something even more supernatural on some keyboards). Instead of sending the stuff on-screen to the printer, the Print Screen key sends it to the Windows NT Clipboard, where it can be pasted into other windows.

- Some keyboards on older computers make you hold Shift while pressing Print Screen.
- If you hold Alt while pressing Print Screen, Windows NT sends the current *window* to the Clipboard — not the entire screen.
- If you *really* want a printout of the screen, hold Shift and press Print Screen to send a picture of the screen to the Clipboard. Paste the contents of the Clipboard into Paint and print from there. (Paint is covered in Chapter 14.)

Windows NT Doesn't Come with All the Programs Listed on the Box

In an attempt to make friends with everybody, Windows NT comes with gobs of programs — more than anybody would ever want. So to keep from making enemies with everybody, Windows NT doesn't fill up your hard disk with every possible program.

For example, Windows NT comes with sounds that make your computer sound like a robot or squawking bird. But it doesn't always install those sounds automatically, nor does it tell you about them. If you want to add those sounds, you have to go back and do it by hand.

Double-click on the Add/Remove Programs icon in the Control Panel (found in the Start button's Settings area) and then click on the Windows NT Setup tab along the top. Windows NT lists the programs it can install and offers to install them for you — a process described in Chapter 13.

(And if you want the robot sounds, double-click on the word Multimedia from the list and make sure that the Robotz Sound Scheme is installed. Then you can activate the Robotz sounds from the Control Panel's Sounds icon.)

My DOS Programs Run Too Slowly (Or Not at All) under Windows NT

DOS programs almost always run more slowly under Windows NT than if they have the whole computer to themselves. They run the slowest when they're in a window. And some DOS programs don't run at all.

Running DOS programs in a full screen speeds them up a little, as does beefing up the computer: adding more memory, or upgrading to a faster Pentium or Pentium Pro computer. More DOS goodies fill Chapter 15.

Lining Up Two Windows on the Screen Is Too Hard

With all its cut-and-paste stuff, Windows NT makes grabbing information from one program and slapping it into another easy. The drag-and-drop methods let you grab names of files from one folder and drag them into another folder to copy them there.

The hard part is lining up the two folders' windows on the screen, side by side. That's where you need to call in the taskbar:

1. **Put the two folders' windows anywhere on the screen.**
2. **Turn all the other open windows into icons (to minimize a window, click on the button with the little line in the window's top-right corner).**
3. **Click your right mouse button on a blank area of the taskbar and click on one of the two Tile commands listed on the menu.**

   The two windows line up on the screen perfectly.

The My Computer and Explorer Programs Show the Wrong Stuff on My Floppy Disk

The My Computer and Explorer programs sometimes get confused and don't always list the files currently sitting on a disk drive. To prod the programs into taking a second look, open the View menu and choose the Refresh command. Or press the F5 key — whichever method is easier to remember.

My Program Won't Save a File to a Network Drive

Many older programs know only about the hard disks (also known as hard drives) on your computer. Like most human beings, they're completely ignorant about networks — and they don't want to go out of their way to learn about them, either. So to save files to a *network drive* (basically, a hard disk on another computer on the network), *you* need to go out of your way. You need to *map* that drive to your computer by following these steps:

1. **Double-click on Network Neighborhood.**

   The Network Neighborhood window appears, showing you the list of other computers on the network.

2. **Double-click on the name of the computer containing your desired hard disk.**

If you want to save some files to a hard disk on Jane's computer, for example, you have to double-click on the name of Jane's computer from the list. (You may need to ask Jane what her computer is named.)

3. **Click your right mouse button on the hard disk you want to use.**

   Found Jane's computer's name? Then click on the folder for her hard disk. If you want to use her C drive, for example, right-click on the folder named C.

4. **When the menu appears, choose Map Network Drive.**

   A window appears, showing you the drive letter that Jane's networked hard disk will use on your system. Here's the weird part, though: The drive letter for the hard disk on Jane's computer will be different from the drive letter for that same hard disk on your own computer. For example, you may select Jane's C drive, but your computer may turn that C drive into its own F drive. Don't worry about it, though. Just save your files to your newly created F drive, and network magic routes them to Jane's C drive.

Chapter 24

Ten (Or More) Ugly Acronyms

In This Chapter

- Ten (plus 17,165) acronyms in alphabetical order
- Helpful pronunciation tips so you won't just mumble them quietly
- What they mean to computer nerds

Computer geeks have a certain fascination for long, complicated strings of words. They've reduced these syllables into short grunts called *acronyms*.

This chapter lists, in alphabetical order, what the nerds are saying, what their grunts stand for, and what those grunts are supposed to mean.

ACL

What it stands for: Access Control List

Pronunciation: Ay-see-ell

What they're talking about: Being such a paranoid operating system, Windows NT uses Access Control Lists to keep track of who's allowed to play with certain things on the computer. In fact, the Network Administrator can even peek at the ACLs to see who's been trying to play with things she wasn't supposed to. Normal users don't have to bother with ACLs.

ASCII

What it stands for: American Standard Code for Information Interchange

Pronunciation: ASK-ee

What they're talking about: A standard for saving information — usually words and numbers — so that most other programs can read it. A Windows NT Notepad file, for example, saves text files in ASCII format.

BIOS

What it stands for: Basic Input/Output System

Pronunciation: BUY-ohss

What they're talking about: Information stored inside a computer that tells programs how the computer is designed. For example, if a program wants data to go to the printer, the program politely tells the BIOS, which subsequently sends the data to the printer. Windows NT sometimes bypasses the BIOS and sends information directly to the computer's parts. This procedure is often faster but can sometimes confuse the rest of the computer.

BMP

What it stands for: Bitmap

Pronunciation: Bitmap

What they're talking about: The format all versions of Windows use for storing graphics files. Paint can read and write BMP files.

DLL

What it stands for: Dynamic Link Library

Pronunciation: Dee-ell-ell

What they're talking about: A file containing information for a program. You can find bunches of files ending with DLL on the hard disk drive. Don't think that they're trash and delete them, or you'll have some wide-eyed programs wandering around the system, searching for their DLLs.

DRV

What it stands for: Driver

Pronunciation: DRY-ver

What they're talking about: Drivers contain brand-specific information about a computer's parts: printers, mice, monitors, and other goodies. You see files ending in DRV scattered throughout the hard disk drive. Don't delete them, or Windows NT won't be capable of talking to your computer's parts.

FAT

What it stands for: File Allocation Table

Pronunciation: Fat

What they're talking about: Windows NT can settle itself down on your hard disk drive in two basic ways. For years, DOS and Windows have been using the FAT method of storing information. The FAT records where files are stored, keeps track of where they're hiding, and locates them when a program needs to use them. To stay compatible, Windows NT can use the FAT method, too. But it can also use NTFS. In fact, most companies use NTFS because it's more efficient than FAT and can be made secure.

GIF

What it stands for: Graphics Interchange Format

Pronunciation: Giff as in "gift"

What they're talking about: In the early years of computing, people wanted a way to store pretty pictures files on their computers. But since people used a wide variety of computers back then — Atari, Commodore, IBM, and Macintosh — they needed a single standard for graphics. So, somebody came up with the GIF format. It's still used widely today on the Internet, although some people say the format's wearing thin. (GIF can store only 256 colors. The newer formats can store millions of colors. Shiver.)

GUI

What it stands for: Graphical User Interface

Pronunciation: Gooey

What they're talking about: Any interface (what's on the screen) based on graphics rather than text. All versions of Windows are GUI. DOS is not. It's text-based.

HAL

What it stands for: Hardware Abstraction Layer

Pronunciation: Hal

What they're talking about: Little known fact: That robot in *2001: A Space Odyssey* actually ran under Windows NT.

(Okay, he didn't. But who *really* cares that HAL stands for the base layer of Windows NT that controls the type of computer hardware on which it's currently running?)

IBM

What it stands for: International Business Machines

Pronunciation: Eye-bee-em

What they're talking about: A huge computer company that designed the first PC, similar to the ones almost everybody uses today. Now, IBM's playing catch-up because all the other companies copied and improved upon its original design. Windows NT runs on an IBM-compatible computer, as well as a few other types of computers.

INI

What it stands for: Initialization

Pronunciation: IN-ee (as opposed to an OUT-ee)

What they're talking about: A file containing customized instructions for a program. Many Windows NT programs look for their own INI file to make sure that they're working according to their user's whims.

Don't mess with the INI files unless you have a specific reason to do so. Changing them around can seriously affect how programs run in Windows NT.

Note: Windows NT now stores most of its customizing information in a more-organized area called a *Registry*.

IRQ

What it stands for: Interrupt Request Line

Pronunciation: Eye-are-cue

What they're talking about: The method that computer parts use to get the attention of the computer's main processor. For example, every time you move the mouse, the mouse sends a signal down its IRQ to the computer's processor, which stops what it's doing and displays the mouse's new position on the screen. Each device needs its own IRQ; if two computer toys try to share one IRQ, both work in a wacky way.

ISDN

What it stands for: Integrated Services Digital Network

Pronunciation: Eye-ess-dee-en

What they're talking about: An international standard for communicating over digital telephone lines, ISDN requires special metal wires and supports data transfer rates of 64 Kbps (64,000 bits per second). Most ISDN lines offered by telephone companies give you two lines at once, called *B channels*. You can use one line for voice and the other for data, or you can use both lines for data to give you data rates of 128 Kbps, much faster than most modems.

LAN

What it stands for: Local Area Network

Pronunciation: Lan

What they're talking about: A bunch of computers linked together in a relatively close geographical setting — in one building, for instance. See WAN, which is covered a bit later in this chapter.

NT

What it stands for: New Technology

Pronunciation: En-tea

What they're talking about: Windows *NT* stands for "New Technology," although Microsoft's been hacking around with the idea for more than a decade.

NTFS

What it stands for: New Technology File System

Pronunciation: En-tea-eff-ess

What they're talking about: A newer, more efficient way of storing files on disks. NTFS is preferred by most Windows NT administrators because it is less subject to data loss than FAT (discussed earlier in this chapter) and has advanced security features.

PCMCIA

What it stands for: Personal Computer Memory Card Industry Association

Pronunciation: Pee-see-em-see-eye-ay

What they're talking about: The group that thought up little credit-card-sized things that slide into laptops to give them extra memory, modems, and other fancy features. Realizing the error of their long-winded ways, the Personal Computer Memory Card Industry Association finally changed the card's name to plain ol' "PC Card" in 1995. (An icon in Control Panel, described in Chapter 11, handles PC Cards.)

PCX

What it stands for: Nothing

Pronunciation: Pee-see-ex

What they're talking about: Some person thought of a way to store graphics in computer files. He picked the letters PCX out of the blue. Today, PCX is one of the most widespread graphics standards. The Windows NT 4 Paint program can read PCX files, but it can't save files in the PCX format. Instead, Paint can handle only the Microsoft graphics file format, known as *bitmap* or BMP files.

PIF

What it stands for: Program Information File

Pronunciation: Piff (rhymes with *sniff*)

What they're talking about: A file containing instructions that Windows NT needs to nurse along troublesome DOS programs. The PIF contains information about the DOS that program's memory needs, along with other data that helps DOS programs live pleasantly with Windows NT. (See Chapter 15 for more dope on DOS.)

RAM

What it stands for: Random Access Memory

Pronunciation: Ram (rhymes with *cram*)

What they're talking about: The memory that Windows NT reads and writes to when making stuff happen on the screen. When the power's turned off, RAM erases itself.

RAS

What it stands for: Remote Access Service

Pronunciation: Razz (as in Razz-a-ma-tazz)

What they're talking about: A way to dial up your network through the telephone lines and use a computer while away from the office.

RISC

What it stands for: Reduced Instruction Set Computer

Pronunciation: Risk

What they're talking about: A breed of computers with special chips built to cut the processing clutter and speed up the action. Windows NT runs on some of these RISC computers, including the MIPS 4000, Digital Alpha, and Sun SPARC workstation.

ROM

What it stands for: Read-Only Memory

Pronunciation: Rahm (rhymes with *bomb*)

What they're talking about: Memory that can't be written to — only read from. For example, a computer's BIOS is stored in ROM. Computerized microwave ovens and other fun consumer electronic goodies sometimes store their instructions on ROM chips as well. The latest technology, called Flash ROM, *can* be written to more than once, but only with special programs.

SCSI

What it stands for: Small Computer Systems Interface

Pronunciation: Scuzzy

What they're talking about: Long the standard for connecting hardware to Macintosh computers, SCSI is increasingly being used in PCs. The SCSI standard can be divided into SCSI (SCSI1) and SCSI2 (SCSI wide and SCSI wide and fast). SCSI2 is the most recent version and allows scanners, hard disk drives, CD-ROM players, tape drives, and many other devices to connect.

TCP/IP

What it stands for: Transmission Control Protocol/Internet Protocol

How it's pronounced: Tee-cee-pee-eye-pee

What they're talking about: First, a *protocol* is a set of rules for communication something. TCP/IP is the set of protocols that all the computers on the Internet use to communicate with one another. In addition, Windows NT comes with built-in TCP/IP that your network undoubtedly uses — though one or two other protocols may also be used internally.

UPS

What it stands for: Uninterruptible Power Supply

Pronunciation: You-pea-ess

What they're talking about: When the electrical power disappears, so do your computer's files — at least the ones that haven't been saved, that is. So, some computers are attached to Uninterruptible Power Supplies. The UPS has rechargeable batteries that kick in and let you calmly save your work when the power dies. (You'll find an icon for configuring the UPS in the Control Panel, although it's mainly there for Network Administrators.)

WAN

What it stands for: Wide Area Network

Pronunciation: Wan (Like the sound of an angry baby)

What they're talking about: A network consisting of computers spread far apart, usually linked by telephone lines. The Internet, for instance, is a WAN.

Chapter 25

Ten Windows NT Icons and What They Do

Windows NT uses different icons to stand for different types of files. That means it's packed with enough icons to befuddle the most experienced iconographer.

Table 25-1 shows pictures of the most common icons you come across in the Windows NT Explorer and My Computer programs and what the icons are supposed to represent.

Most of them represent *data files* — files created by programs — but we've tossed in a few icons that stand for hardware at the beginning to help you get your bearings.

Table 25-1 Icons in Explorer and My Computer Windows

What It Looks Like	*What It Stands For*
3½ Floppy (A:)	3 1/2-inch floppy drive
	5 1/4-inch floppy drive
(C:)	Hard disk
(C:)	Shared hard disk that's accessible on a network (Any icon with that little hand has been shared and can be used by other people on the network.)

(continued)

Table 25-1 *(continued)*

What It Looks Like	*What It Stands For*
	Mapped drive: A folder or drive on another computer that gets a drive letter so your own computer can treat it like one of its own drives
(D:)	CD-ROM drive
	Folder: A computerized storage area for files
	DOS-based program
	Word-processor file created by WordPad
	Batch file: A collection of DOS commands for the computer to run automatically
321	Movie (usually stored in the Microsoft Audio Video Interleave — AVI — format)
	Sound: A recorded sound saved as a WAV file
	Music: A MIDI file containing specially formatted instructions that tell synthesizers or sound cards what sounds to create
System	System file: A technical file for Windows NT to use
Font	Old-style fonts that are stored in a certain size
Fonts	Newer, TrueType fonts that can be easily shrunk or enlarged

What It Looks Like	*What It Stands For*
Help	Help file: contains instructions stored in a special format for the Windows NT Help program
	A text file containing technical information, usually special settings for a program
	Text; usually created by Notepad
	A text file created by Write, a word processor included with older versions of Windows (Write files can be read and saved with the Windows NT WordPad program, described in Chapter 14)
	Bitmap file: graphics usually created by Windows NT Paint or the Windows NT 3.51 Paintbrush program
	GIF: Graphics Interchange Format — frequently used for putting pictures on the Internet
	JPG: Joint Photographic Expert Group, another graphics file format; stores pictures in very small files
	PCX, another graphics file; doesn't stand for anything; unlike in earlier versions of Windows, the current Windows NT Paint program can't save files in the PCX format, but it can read them; TIF (Tagged Image File Format) files look the same
	Scrap: A piece of a document that's been dragged from one program and left on the Desktop for further action (works with WordPad)
	A file that Windows NT doesn't think it recognizes

- To open one of these files and start working with its contents, double-click on it. If all goes right, Windows NT looks at the file's name, grabs the appropriate program, and brings both the file and the program to the screen.
- Unfortunately, Windows NT judges a book by its cover: It doesn't look *inside* a file to see what information the file contains. Instead, Windows NT merely looks at the file's name, particularly the last three letters of the file's name (the extension). If Windows NT recognizes those three letters, it assumes that it recognizes the file, and it tosses the file to what it *thinks* is the right program.

  The result? Sometimes Windows NT uses a familiar icon to represent a file but, because Windows NT tosses the file to the wrong program when you double-click on the icon, the file refuses to open.

- You'll see a few other icons popping up here and there that don't appear in this chart for several reasons. First, newly installed Windows NT programs often come with their own arsenal of icons. Also, My Computer shows some icons that are listed in the Control Panel, so head for Chapter 11's Control Panel chart for the lowdown on those icons.

- To peek inside a file quickly, without opening any files, click on the file's icon with your right mouse button and choose Quick View from the menu. Windows NT shows you the file's contents.

Glossary

Windows NT comes with its own Glossary program. Open the Start menu, choose Help, click on the Contents tab, double-click on the Glossary icon, and subsequently double-click on the Glossary Entries icon.

Plus, the Windows NT Help program lets you look up words on the fly: If you spot an unfamiliar word in the Help program — and it's underlined — click on the word, and Windows NT defines it for you. (The Help program gets its due in Chapter 21.)

But if Windows NT refuses to give you a helping hand, here's a list of some of the more common Windows NT words you'll encounter.

32-bit: Computers push their information through "pipes." The first IBM PC used eight pipes. The next version, the 286, used 16 pipes. A 386 computer can use 32 pipes, but most programs just shoot their stuff through 16 pipes. For extra speed and power, Windows NT uses all 32 pipes at the same time.

account *or* **user account:** When Windows NT runs on a *network,* it lets groups of people access files and folders. To keep track of who's using what, Windows NT assigns each user an account: a collection of information defining who that person is and what he or she is allowed to access, as well as more frivolous information, like wallpaper preferences. See ***log on/log off.***

active window: The last window you clicked on — the one that's currently highlighted — is considered active. Any keys you press affect this window.

address: Name by which the Internet identifies you. The format is *username@hostname,* where username is your user name, logon name, or account number, and hostname is the name of the computer or Internet provider you use. The host name may be a few words strung together with periods.

administrator: The person or people in charge of making the computers work correctly. Administrators set up networks, set up and delete user accounts, and perform other dreadfully thankless tasks. They're also called Network Administrators, System Administrators, or epithets we're not allowed to put in the book.

Apply: Click on this button, and Windows NT immediately applies and saves any changes you've made from the current list of options.

AUTOEXEC.BAT: A file that old-school MS-DOS computers read when first turned on. The file contains instructions that affect any subsequently running DOS programs — and older Windows-based programs as well. Windows NT no longer needs an AUTOEXEC.BAT file, but it keeps one around in case older programs might need to use it. (It also lets you create customized AUTOEXEC.BAT files for any DOS programs that may need them, but that's getting a little technical.)

background: All the screen area behind the active window. Can also mean a process that is going on someplace other than in the active window.

bitmap: A graphic consisting of bunches of little dots on-screen. The graphic is saved as a bitmap file, which ends with the letters BMP. The Windows NT Paint program can create and edit BMP files.

border: The edges of a window; you can move the border in or out to change the window's size.

case-sensitive: A program that knows the difference between uppercase and lowercase letters. For example, a case-sensitive program considers *Pickle* and *pickle* to be two different things.

click: To push and release a button on the mouse.

client: Some computers mainly grab information and process it; other computers mainly spit out information for the first type of computers to process. The grabbers are the clients, which usually run Windows NT Workstation. The spitters are the servers, which usually run Windows NT Server. See ***server.***

Clipboard: A part of Windows NT that keeps track of information you've cut or copied from a program or file. It stores that information so you can paste it into other programs.

cursor: The little blinking line that shows where the next letter you type will appear.

default: Choosing the default option enables you to avoid making a decision. The *default option* is the one that the computer chooses for you when you give up and just press Enter. Default options are usually highlighted and ready to run.

Desktop: The area on your screen where you move windows and icons around. Most people cover the Desktop with ***wallpaper*** — a pretty picture.

dialog box: A window that opens to ask you boring questions or request input. Windows NT and Windows-based programs in general are knee-deep in dialog boxes.

directory: A distinct location on a hard disk for storing files. Storing related files in a directory makes them easier to find. Windows NT no longer uses the word directory; it prefers the word *folder.* See ***folder.***

document: A file containing information such as text, sound, or graphics. Documents are created or changed from within programs. See ***program.***

domain: The basic unit of an NT client/server network. In its simplest form, the domain consists of a server and a couple of workstations that share a common user database and security policy. Not the same as an Internet domain. See ***domain name.***

domain name: A unique name that identifies an Internet site. A given machine may have more than one domain name, but a given domain name points to only one machine. It's also possible for a domain name to exist but not be connected to an actual machine. This is often done so that a group or business can have an Internet e-mail address without having to establish a real Internet site. In these cases, an Internet service provider's machine must handle the mail on behalf of the listed domain name.

DOS: Short for Disk Operating System. An older operating system for running programs. Windows NT can run programs designed for DOS as well as programs designed for Windows. See ***operating system.***

double-click: Pushing and releasing the left mouse button twice in rapid succession. (Double-clicking the *right* mouse button doesn't do anything special.) See ***click*** and ***drag.***

drag: A four-step mouse process that moves an object across your Desktop. First, point at the object — an icon, a highlighted paragraph, or something similar. Second, press and hold your left mouse button. Third, point the mouse arrow at the location to which you'd like to move that object. Fourth, release the mouse button. The object is "dragged" to its new location.

drop: Step four of the *drag* technique (see ***drag***). Dropping is merely letting go of the mouse button and letting your object fall onto something else, be it a new window, folder, or area on your Desktop.

DRV: A file ending in DRV usually lets Windows talk to computer gizmos such as video cards, sound cards, CD-ROM drives, and other stuff. (DRV is short for *driver.*)

FAT: An acronym for File Allocation Table, the file system type used by DOS and Windows and one of the two file system types recognized by Windows NT.

file: A collection of information in a format designed for computer use.

Firewall: A protective filter for messages and logons. An organization connected directly to the Internet uses a firewall to prevent unauthorized access into their network.

folder: An area for storing files to keep them organized. (Formerly called a *directory.*) Folders can contain other folders, for further organization. See ***subfolder.***

format: The process of preparing a disk to have files written to it. The disk needs to have "electronic shelves" tacked onto it so that Windows NT can store information on it. Formatting a disk wipes it clean of all information. Format also refers to the method programs store information in files. WordPerfect stores text in a different format than Microsoft Word for Windows, for example.

highlighted: A selected item. A different color usually appears over a highlighted object to show that it's been singled out for further action.

icon: The little picture that represents an object — a program, file, or command — making that object's function easier to figure out.

INI: Short for *initialization.* INI usually hangs on the ends of files that contain special system settings. They're for the computer to mess with, not users.

Internet: A global network of computers connected by telephone. Currently, people use Web browsing software to connect to the World Wide Web, where they find information ranging from Duracell battery advertisements to up-to-the-minute charts listing the latest locations of earthquakes. Windows NT comes with Internet Explorer software for connecting to the Internet's World Wide Web. (See Chapter 16.)

intranet: A network using the same "language" as the World Wide Web but restricted for use inside a company. Employees may use Internet Explorer to read a corporate newsletter, for example. See ***network.***

IRC (Internet Relay Chat): A system that enables Internet users to talk with each other in real time over the Internet.

log on/log off: By typing a password into a computer, you (the user) can access your user account and start working on Windows NT. Then by logging off, you can temporarily shut down your user account. The point? Logging on and off a computer with a password keeps a system more secure — nobody can use another person's user account to do something sneaky. See ***account*** or ***user account.***

maximize: The act of making a window fill the entire screen. You can maximize a window by double-clicking on its title bar — that long strip across its very top. Or you can click on its Maximize button — that button with the big square inside, located near the window's upper-right corner. See ***minimize.***

memory: The stuff computers use to store on-the-fly calculations while running. The more memory that's stuffed inside your computer, the better it runs. (Windows NT needs at *least* 16MB of memory.) See Chapter 2 for more memory madness.

minimize: The act of shrinking a window down to a tiny icon to temporarily get it out of the way. To minimize a window, click on the Minimize button — that button with the little horizontal bar on it, located near the window's upper-right corner. See ***maximize.***

multitasking: Running several different programs simultaneously.

network: Connecting computers with cables so that people can share information without getting up. Also used to refer to the collection of computers that are linked together.

Newsgroup: On the Internet, a distributed bulletin-board system about a particular topic. Usenet News (also known as Netnews) is a system that distributes thousands of newsgroups to all parts of the Internet.

NTFS (New Technology File System): The preferred file system for Windows NT. Supports long filenames, a variety of permissions for sharing files and a transaction log that allows NT to finish any incomplete file-related tasks if the operating system is interrupted.

operating system: Software that controls how a computer does its most basic stuff: storing files, talking to printers, and performing other gut-level operations. DOS and Windows NT are both operating systems.

password: The secret code you type into a computer while logging on to access your user account (provided you can remember your username). See ***username*** and ***account*** *or* ***user account.***

path: A sentence of computerese that tells a computer the precise name and location of a file.

program: Something that lets you work on the computer: Spreadsheets, word processors, and games are *programs*. See ***document.***

protocol: A set of rules that determines how computers talk to each other. Computers on a network have to all agree on the protocol they're using, or communication breaks down completely. See ***network.***

RAM: Random-Access Memory. See ***memory.***

scrap: When you highlight some text or graphics from a program, drag the chunk to the Desktop, and drop it, you create an official Windows NT *scrap* — a file containing a copy of that information. The scrap can be saved or dragged into other programs. See ***drag.***

server: The backbone of a network. A comparatively large computer set up to deliver large amounts of information to other computers on the network. See ***client, Windows NT Workstation,*** and ***Windows NT Server.***

Shortcut: A Windows NT icon that serves as a push-button for doing something — loading a file, starting a program, or playing a sound, for example. A shortcut icon has a little arrow in its bottom corner so you can tell it apart from the icon that *really* stands for the file or program.

shortcut button: A button in a Help menu that takes you directly to an area that can solve your problem.

shortcut key: As opposed to a Shortcut (see ***Shortcut***), a shortcut key is an underlined letter in a program's menu that lets you work with the keyboard instead of the mouse. For example, if you see the word Help on a menu bar, the underlined H means you can get help by pressing Alt+H.

Shut Down: The process of telling Windows NT to save all its settings and files so that you can turn off your computer. You must choose the Shut Down option, found on the Start menu, before turning off your computer.

Start button: See ***Start menu.***

Start menu: A menu of options that appears when you click on the Start button (located on the taskbar). From the Start menu, you can load programs and files, change settings, find programs, find help, and shut down your computer so you can turn it off.

subfolder: A folder within a folder, used to further organize files. (Also called a *subdirectory.*) For example, a Junkfood folder may contain subfolders for Chips, Peanuts, and Pretzels. (A Celery subfolder would be empty.) See ***folder.***

taskbar: The bar in Windows NT that lists all currently running programs and open folders. The Start button lives on one end of the taskbar.

TCP/IP (Transmission Control Protocol/Internet Protocol): The ***protocol*** that networks use to communicate with each other on the Internet.

URL (Uniform Resource Locator): The standard way to give the address of any resource on the Internet that is part of the World Wide Web. This is an example of a URL: `http://www.dummies.com/index.htm`. The most common way to use a URL is to type it into a Web browser program such as Microsoft Internet Explorer.

username: The name you type into a computer while logging on to access your user account. (Then you type your password and hope you remembered both correctly.) See ***password*** and ***account*** or ***user account.***

VGA: A popular standard for displaying information on monitors in certain colors and resolutions. VGA has been replaced by SVGA — Super VGA — that can display even more colors and even finer resolution.

virtual: A trendy word to describe computer simulations. Commonly used to describe things that *look* real but aren't really there. For example, when Windows NT uses *virtual memory,* it's using part of the hard disk for memory, not the actual memory chips.

wallpaper: Graphics spread across the background of your computer screen. The Windows NT Control Panel lets you choose among different wallpaper files.

window: An on-screen box that contains information for you to look at or work with. Programs run in *windows* on your screen.

Windows NT Server: Windows NT comes in two versions. This is the server version. See ***client, server,*** and ***Windows NT Workstation.***

Windows NT Workstation: Windows NT 4 comes in two versions. This is the client version, although it works fine for networking about ten computers. See ***client, server,*** and ***Windows NT Server.***

Index

• Symbols •

• A •

• B •

• C •

• D •

• E •

• F •

• G •

• H •

• I •

• J •

• K •

• L •

• M •

• N •

• O •

• T •

• U •

• V •

• W •

• Y •

• Z •

Notes

Discover Dummies™ Online!

The *Dummies* Web Site is your fun and friendly online resource for the latest information about *...For Dummies®* books on all your favorite topics. From cars to computers, wine to Windows, and investing to the Internet, we've got a shelf full of *...For Dummies* books waiting for you!

Ten Fun and Useful Things You Can Do at www.dummies.com

1. Register this book and win!
2. Find and buy the *...For Dummies* books you want online.
3. Get ten great *Dummies Tips™* every week.
4. Chat with your favorite *...For Dummies* authors.
5. Subscribe free to *The Dummies Dispatch™* newsletter.
6. Enter our sweepstakes and win cool stuff.
7. Send a free cartoon postcard to a friend.
8. Download free software.
9. Sample a book before you buy.
10. Talk to us. Make comments, ask questions, and get answers!

Jump online to these ten fun and useful things at **http://www.dummies.com/10useful**

For other technology titles from IDG Books Worldwide, go to **www.idgbooks.com**

Not online yet? It's easy to get started with *The Internet For Dummies®*, 5th Edition, or *Dummies 101®: The Internet For Windows® 98*, available at local retailers everywhere.

Find other *...For Dummies* books on these topics:
Business • Careers • Databases • Food & Beverages • Games • Gardening • Graphics • Hardware
Health & Fitness • Internet and the World Wide Web • Networking • Office Suites
Operating Systems • Personal Finance • Pets • Programming • Recreation • Sports
Spreadsheets • Teacher Resources • Test Prep • Word Processing

IDG BOOKS WORLDWIDE BOOK REGISTRATION

We want to hear from you!

Visit **http://my2cents.dummies.com** to register this book and tell us how you liked it!

- Get entered in our monthly prize giveaway.
- Give us feedback about this book — tell us what you like best, what you like least, or maybe what you'd like to ask the author and us to change!
- Let us know any other *...For Dummies*® topics that interest you.

Your feedback helps us determine what books to publish, tells us what coverage to add as we revise our books, and lets us know whether we're meeting your needs as a *...For Dummies* reader. You're our most valuable resource, and what you have to say is important to us!

Not on the Web yet? It's easy to get started with *Dummies 101*®*: The Internet For Windows*® *98* or *The Internet For Dummies*®, 5th Edition, at local retailers everywhere.

Or let us know what you think by sending us a letter at the following address:

...For Dummies Book Registration
Dummies Press
7260 Shadeland Station, Suite 100
Indianapolis, IN 46256-3945
Fax 317-596-5498

BESTSELLING BOOK SERIES FROM IDG